Wilmette Public Library
1242 Wilmette Avenue
Wilmette, Il 60091
847-256-5025

GEORGE WASHINGTON
A LIFE IN BOOKS

PREFACE

After I parked my bicycle and pitched my tent at a roadside campground in the Blue Mountains of New South Wales, a man with a grizzled moustache stepped from a camper parked nearby. He asked me inside for tea and bickies, as Australians call cookies. Never one to refuse another's hospitality, I accepted. As we sat ourselves at the tea table inside his motor home, he introduced me to his wife, and I introduced myself. They could tell by my accent that I was from America. He told me they had motored around Australia countless times but had never traveled overseas. Both admitted they knew little about the United States. Practically the only American they could recall by name was George Washington, so they asked me to tell them more about him.

This incident occurred during a five-month solo bicycle tour of Australia, my last great adventure before starting graduate school at the University of Delaware. In other words, it occurred before I began studying colonial American literature with the world's leading expert in the field, before I became fascinated with the history of books, before I decided to devote my professional career to the subject of early American intellectual life. Asked to provide an impromptu biography of George Washington, I struggled for something to say. Not having studied the history of the American Revolution since—gulp!—the eighth grade, I was hard-pressed to fill in the facts for my kindly Australian hosts.

Gathering my thoughts, meagre as they were, I mentioned the time Washington crossed the Delaware. An iconic moment in American history, the episode was familiar to me mainly because Mom and Dad had bought me a scale model of the event based on the renowned painting by Emanuel Gottlieb Leutze. I can still smell the enamel and glue I used to reconstruct that singular moment in American history. I nearly exhausted my supply of Fiery Red to paint the lining of Washington's cape as it flapped and fluttered in the wind on that raw and gusty Christmas night in 1776.

Next I told them about the brutal winter of 1777–78, the winter Washington and his men spent at Valley Forge, a place I encountered firsthand during a car camping vacation that took our family on a tour of numerous battlefields and historic sites. The stone farmhouse at Valley Forge where Washington made his headquarters stands out in my mind. Having previously heard stories about hardship and privation and frost-bite and starvation among the Revolutionary soldiers at Valley Forge that winter, I found the farmhouse a little too cozy. At the time I wondered why Washington was not sleeping in a tent like his troops. Later I was relieved to learn that Washington did sleep in a tent with his men when the Continental Army first came to Valley Forge. Though he enjoyed the finer things in life, Washington had the sensitivity and the sympathy to understand when it was time for him to make personal sacrifices and suffer the hardships others had to suffer.

Long before our family vacation, Mom had urged us children to save our allowances so we could afford a few special souvenirs. At the Valley Forge gift shop, I purchased a small bust of Washington, which went on my bookshelf after we got home. That boyhood souvenir sits on my desk today. After telling this Australian couple about how Washington crossed the Delaware one winter and spent the next at Valley Forge, my mind went blank. I visualized that tiny bust of Washington back home, but it was mute. After briefly mentioning Washington's presidency, I just plain ran out of facts.

Stalling for time, I took another bite of bickie. After chewing that digestive biscuit once or twice, or maybe thrice, I suddenly remembered the dollar bill in my wallet, the only folding money I had not converted to Australian dollars. I took out the bill and used the engraved portrait of George Washington on its obverse as an emergency visual aid. I spoke of Washington's meticulous dress and his concomitant sense of deco-rum, his clenched lips and firm resolve, his calm eyes and penetrating gaze. If this good-natured Australian couple noticed that I had stopped providing them with facts about George Washington and started inter-preting his portrait, they did not complain. They seemed genuinely pleased with what I told them. By the time I finished, the sun had almost disappeared below the horizon, and Washington's face appeared hazy in the dusk. Leaving their camper to return to my tent, now barely vis-ible in the gloaming, I felt embarrassed that I could not say more about the man known as the Father of His Country—the father of my country.

The present work, therefore, represents my second attempt to tell the story of George Washington's life. This new version is much different from the one I told around the tea table in that camper in the Blue Mountains; it is also much different from the numerous other book-length Washington biographies that have appeared at an astonishing rate over the past few decades. They, too, tell the familiar Washington stories—crossing the Delaware, wintering at Valley Forge, serving as president. In other words, they relate his active life as a soldier and a statesman. *George Washington: A Life in Books*, on the other hand, tells the story of his intellectual life, examining the man through the books he owned, read, and wrote.

A hundred years ago Ezra Pound criticized American history textbooks for ignoring Washington's intellect; Pound's critique still applies. More often than not Washington has been seen as a shelf-filler, someone who decorated his home with books but seldom read them fully or deeply. Here's an alternate theory: though George Washington never assembled a great library in the manner of, say, Benjamin Franklin or Thomas Jefferson, he did amass an impressive and diverse collection of books that he read closely and carefully and that significantly influenced his thought and action.

No one has ever written an intellectual biography of George Washington. Learning about my task, one historian sought to discourage me, asserting that the documentary materials simply do not exist to tell such a story. Unlike so many of the other Founding Fathers, he argued, Washington left little record of his intellectual life. Benjamin Franklin wrote a famous autobiography, among many other occasional pamphlets, essays, and letters, all of which dramatize his lifelong interest in reading and writing. Thomas Jefferson's voluminous correspondence and his massive library provide access to his mind. And John Adams recorded his agreements and disagreements with authors in the margins of his books. Though Washington's surviving comments about books and reading are not nearly as extensive as those of other Founding Fathers, he did leave many different types of evidence that, in the aggregate, can help to reconstruct his life of the mind. The evidence takes many different forms.

Surviving books. Though Washington's library was widely dispersed during the nineteenth century, many of his books do survive. The Boston Athenaeum holds the single largest collection of books formerly in his possession. Additional books survive at Mount Vernon. Other libraries—the Firestone Library at Princeton University, the Houghton Library at Harvard University, the Library Company of Philadelphia, the Library of Congress, the Lilly Library at Indiana University, the Morgan Library, the New York Public Library, the Virginia Historical Society—all hold books from Washington's library in their collections, most of which I have examined.

Marginalia. With the notable exception of his copy of James Monroe's *View of the Conduct of the Executive of the United States*, Washington's surviving books contain little marginalia, but he did write in his books occasionally. Most of the time he did so to correct typographical errors, but sometimes his marginal notes reveal how he read. Occasionally his notes in one book indicate other books he read. The fact that Washington wrote in his books has gone largely unnoticed, because uncovering these notes requires work that some find tedious. One must examine the surviving books meticulously, turning over one page after another in search of the slightest pencil marks showing that Washington did read the volumes that bear his bookplate.

Library catalogues. Much evidence survives to identify books from Washington's library that do not survive. Mainly it comes in the form of library catalogues. Washington himself compiled two such catalogues, which not only list what books he had at Mount Vernon but also demonstrate his level of bibliographical expertise. Lund Washington, his cousin and plantation manager, compiled a list of books at Mount Vernon toward the end of the Revolutionary War. Washington's library was inventoried with his estate after his death. When many of his books went up for sale in the nineteenth century, the booksellers described them in considerable detail. All these various catalogues provide much additional information about Washington's books.

Published writings. The story of the books in Washington's life includes not only those he owned and read; it also includes those he wrote and published. Washington was a reluctant author, but sometimes his professional responsibilities compelled him to publish what he wrote. Occasionally editors, both friends and enemies, took charge and edited Washington's writings, especially his letters, for publication. Several chapters in the present work concern books Washington authored that were published during his lifetime.

Correspondence. As a writer, Washington was at his best when he was writing letters. Like any good letter writer, he shaped his tone and persona to suit individual readers. Though he seldom discussed his reading with his correspondents, sometimes he did provide bookish advice, especially when it came to recommending what military manuals to read or what agricultural manuals were useful. Washington's correspondence, which fills dozens of volumes in the standard edition of his papers, contains numerous references that shed light on his books and reading. His literary allusions are often subtle, and many of them have gone unnoticed previously.

Diaries. Washington kept a diary through much of his life, but his individual diary entries are frustratingly brief. He says where he was and what he did, but seldom does he reveal the inner man. He rarely mentions what he read or what he was thinking. Every once in a while, he does provide a tantalizing clue indicating the importance of one particular book or another. In chapter 7, for instance, I reconstruct the story of how Washington used a book of farriery in his library to try and save the life of a favorite horse that had broken its leg.

Extracts, abstracts, and notes. Washington filled many blank quires of paper with notes he took while reading. Some of these notes come from practical manuals. Others come from books of history and travel. Several of these notebooks survive at the Library of Congress. Amounting to a total of nearly nine hundred pages, Washington's manuscript notes supply a wealth of information about his reading process. Other notebooks survive in fragmented form. The owner of one such notebook disbound it and distributed its individual holograph leaves to friends. Now only three leaves from the original notebook survive.

The image of George Washington as a man of letters is much different from the accepted image of George Washington as a man of action. Like any new interpretation, this new view may take some getting used to, so I ask the reader's patience and indulgence. The story of Washington's intellectual life can be quite exciting. So pour yourself a cup of tea, put some bickies on a plate, settle into your favorite reading chair, and enjoy this new take on Washington's life.

Kevin J. Hayes
Toledo, Ohio

ACKNOWLEDGMENTS

Shortly after I started writing *George Washington: A Life in Books*, I received the Washington College Fellowship in Early American History, which allowed me to spend a month at the Boston Athenaeum, where I could take a good, long look at the single largest collection of books from Washington's library that have survived together. I would like to thank C. V. Starr Center for presenting me the fellowship and the staff of the Athenaeum for all their help. Perhaps no single book in the Athenaeum collection was more useful to me than Washington's copy of Daniel Defoe's *Tour through Great Britain*, which allowed me to write "How George Washington Read Daniel Defoe," a paper I presented at the First Biennial Meeting of the Defoe Society in Tulsa, Oklahoma. I am grateful to conference organizer Robert Mayer for giving me the opportunity to present my findings, the first fruits of my research into Washington's library.

It is my personal habit to work on three or four books simultaneously. While still working on *George Washington: A Life in Books,* I received a fellowship to research *Thomas Jefferson in His Own Time* at the Robert H. Smith International Center for Jefferson Studies at Monticello. This, the best place for researching Thomas Jefferson, also proved to be an excellent place to continue my Washington research. While it did not have any books from Washington's library, it did provide a fine general collection that let me flesh out the story of Washington's intellectual life and provide many background details. The hardworking staff and convivial atmosphere made it a delightful place to work. During my time in Virginia that summer I also took the opportunity to visit Mount Vernon and examine additional books from George Washington's library. I would like to thank Joan Stahl and Michele Lee for all their help. Mount Vernon invited me back to present "George Washington's Field Library" as part of

George Washington Goes to War: The George Washington Symposium, which was held the first week of November 2015. This symposium proved to be one of the best I have ever attended. The papers presented and the conversations that took place between sessions let me test out many ideas and develop them further.

Other libraries—the Firestone Library at Princeton University, the Library Company of Philadelphia, the Lilly Library at Indiana University, the Virginia Historical Society—all of which contain books formerly in the possession of George Washington—also gave me access to their collections and helped me understand how Washington read and learned.

At Oxford University Press, I would like to thank Shannon McLachlan for initially encouraging me to begin this project, Brendan O'Neill for supporting it during the lengthy review process, and Sarah Pirovitz for seeing it through the press. I also thank my wife, Myung-Sook, for her love and support throughout this project. Finally, I thank my parents for all those history-based family vacations we took a long time ago. This book is dedicated to them.

GEORGE WASHINGTON
A LIFE IN BOOKS

CHAPTER I

Meditations and Contemplations

Reading and conversation may furnish us with many ideas of men
and things, yet it is our own meditation, and the labour of our
own thoughts, that must form our judgement.

Isaac Watts, *The Improvement of the Mind*

George Washington understood the power of books early in life. He
started forming a personal library as a boy and added to it all his life.
He treasured the books he owned, later commissioning an engraved armorial bookplate to paste into their covers. He often signed the title pages
of his books, his autographs providing additional marks of ownership.
The changes Washington's autograph underwent as he matured help
date several early acquisitions. According to the handwriting style of their
title-page inscriptions, some of the books that survive from Washington's
library date from his adolescence. Other books he acquired in his late
teens, when he deliberately changed his handwriting style. In adulthood
Washington's signature became fairly consistent, so it is more difficult to
date subsequent acquisitions based solely on handwriting style. But the
books Washington obtained in his youth provide a rich, yet largely untapped, resource for understanding his life, his mind, and his spirit.

Washington's earliest known autograph survives on the title page of
*The Sufficiency of a Standing Revelation in General, and of the Scripture
Revelation in Particular*, a set of sermons the Reverend Dr. Offspring
Blackall presented as the Boyle lectures in 1700. Washington's signature
in this volume dates from around 1741, the year he turned nine.[1] Though
Washington was a precocious child as well as a pious one, Blackall's

Sufficiency of a Standing Revelation does seem like a strange book for him to be reading as a boy. By no means was it standard reading for Anglicans in the eighteenth century.[2] What was Washington doing with it?

Before answering that question, some quick background detail about this book's oddly named author: Offspring Blackall came to prominence during a dispute with the Irish deist John Toland, whose appeal to reason in matters of faith attracted the vanguard of the Enlightenment and whose critique of arbitrary power foreshadowed the political thought of the American Revolution. Men of the cloth were less enthused with Toland's forward-thinking ideas. When he challenged some ancient Christian writings and thus implicitly questioned the Gospel, Blackall attacked. Toland counterattacked. Blackall emerged from the fray with a reputation for defending religion based on divine revelation, or, more simply, revealed religion.

Blackall accepted an invitation to deliver the Boyle lectures in 1700. Though Robert Boyle had made a name for himself with his scientific experiments (think Boyle's law), he was a profoundly devout man. As people questioned religious dogma in the face of modern scientific discovery, deism, which acknowledged the existence of God but followed no particular religion, posed a danger to Christianity. Sensing a threat, Boyle endowed a series of lectures to safeguard religious belief from scientific empiricism. His lecturers sought evidence to substantiate the tenets of Christianity.

The Boyle lecturers did not convince everyone. Benjamin Franklin, for one, encountered some of their lectures when he was fifteen. Having begun to doubt divine revelation, Franklin avidly read the lectures. He had hoped they would quash his skepticism, but they had the opposite effect. Franklin famously explained: "The Arguments of the Deists which were quoted to be refuted, appeared to me much Stronger than the Refutations. In short I soon became a thorough Deist."[3]

Franklin did not say which lecturers he had read, but it is plausible that he read Blackall, who argued that the physical universe and the Holy Scriptures together provided sufficient evidence to affirm Christian belief. By the time Washington turned fifteen, the age Franklin was when he read the Boyle lectures, he could read, understand, and make up his own mind about what Blackall had to say. But what was a nine-year-old Virginia boy doing with a book filled with these heady ideas?

Before he appreciated Blackall's argument fully, Washington could put the book to other uses. Books have many purposes that transcend their texts. Autographing the title page of *The Sufficiency of a Standing Revelation*, Washington took possession of this volume, branding it as his own.

Previously Washington's Blackall had been owned by Samuel Bowman and Robert Wickliff, both of whom had signed their names in it multiple times. Readers leave lasting traces of themselves in their books. Though little else is known of Bowman and Wickliff, their autographs in this surviving volume have saved them from total obscurity. On the verso of the title page, Wickliff wrote his name, supplied some brief biographical detail, and dated his acquisition: 1740.[4] The information reveals that Wickliff was around twelve when he took possession of *The Sufficiency of a Standing Revelation*. Blackall's religious work contains little more to appeal to a twelve-year-old than a nine-year-old. Yet books in general were valuable things in eighteenth-century Virginia. Perhaps Wickliff built up the book in young Washington's eyes to gain an advantage in a trade.

Regardless how he obtained it, Washington took good care of Blackall's book. Like many other Virginians who came of age in the middle third of the eighteenth century, Washington had great respect for the books in his possession—with good reason. In colonial America a personal library was a hallmark of the proper gentleman. It allowed him to display his wealth, his cultural prestige, and his intellectual prowess, to show guests in a subtle and sophisticated way who he was and what he thought.

Washington's copy of Blackall, bound in handsome yet unassuming tooled sheep, marks the earliest known beginnings of what would become his eighteenth-century gentleman's library. The survival of this volume demonstrates its importance to Washington. While giving away some other books from his personal collection, he kept his copy of *The Sufficiency of a Standing Revelation* all his life.

Published in 1717, the year after Blackall's death, the edition of *The Sufficiency of a Standing Revelation* Washington owned was poorly printed. The typographical errors in his copy are corrected by hand. Though it may be impossible to attribute these corrections to Washington definitively, they are consistent with typos he corrected in other books he owned. Washington's typographical corrections provide evidence of his meticulous nature and his penchant for accuracy. Discussing how to understand truth and use reason, Blackall's flawed text mentions "a right understand of the truths already delivered and a right Use of Reason in making Inferences." Recognizing the word "understand" as a misprint for "understanding," the keen-eyed reader placed an asterisk after "understand" and wrote in the corresponding margin: "ing."[5]

In terms of handwriting style, these three letters are inconsistent with the same combination of letters in Washington's adolescent signature, but they are consistent with the "i-n-g" in his teenage signature. Read in light of the handwritten corrections in other books he owned in his youth, the

THE
SUFFICIENCY

Saml OF A *Bowall*

Standing REVELATION *in* General,

And of the *Bowman*

Scriptur REVELATION *in Particular.*

BOTH *Washington*

As to the Matter of *it,* and

As to the Proof of *it;*

George AND *Washington*

That NEW REVELATIONS

Cannot Reasonably be Desired, *and*

Would Probably be Unsuccessful.

In Eight SERMONS,

Preach'd in the

CATHEDRAL-CHURCH of St. *Paul, London;*
At the LECTURE Founded by the Honourable
ROBERT BOYLE Esq; in the Year 1700.

By *OFSPRING,* Late Lord Bishop of EXETER.

LONDON: Printed for *Jer.* Batley at the Dove, *and T. Warner*
at the *Black-Boy* in Pater Noster-Row, 1717.

J. D.

Title page from George Washington's copy of Offspring Blackall, *The Sufficiency of a Standing Revelation* (1717). Boston Athenaeum.

correction in Blackall suggests that Washington read *The Sufficiency of a Standing Revelation* in his late teens. In other words, Washington realized the work was too much for him when he was a boy, but, unlike Robert Wickliff, he did not unload it. Even if he could not fully appreciate the book's text when he inscribed its title page in his boyhood, he apparently looked forward to the day he would. Understanding Blackall took on the quality of an intellectual goal, something to strive for and achieve.

Blackall was one of many devotional authors Washington knew about in his youth. Several of the religious books in his library bear his youthful signature.[6] His youthful attention to devotional literature is not unusual. Many boys and girls raised in the Anglican Church during the eighteenth century started reading religious books around the time of their first Communion. Though Washington read much else during his formative years from magazine verse to mathematical textbooks to stories of travel and adventure, devotional literature shaped the man he would become. Like many other religious books in his library, *The Sufficiency of a Standing Revelation* emphasizes meditation as a devotional practice. Blackall tells his readers: "What I would desire of you is; that you would frequently think of those things which you profess to believe, that you would meditate much and often thereupon, that you would seriously consider the meaning thereof."[7]

The meditative practice defined and delineated by Blackall and other religious authors strongly influenced Washington's thought process. Their influence did not happen instantly. When Washington began his military career, a dangerous impetuosity guided his battlefield decisions. But slowly he came to understand how religious meditation could apply to realms outside religion. As military commander, legislator, and president, Washington would establish a reputation for long, slow, judicious reasoning. The decision-making process he demonstrated as an adult hearkens back to the books he read in boyhood.

Born February 22, 1732, according to the modern (New Style) calendar (which would not be officially adopted until 1752), George was the oldest son of Augustine and Mary Ball Washington. The two had wed on March 6, 1731. Mary was Augustine's second wife. Jane, his first wife, had died in 1729, leaving three children: Lawrence, Augustine (who went by "Austin"), and Jane. Augustine Washington sent both Lawrence and Austin to the Appleby School for their education.

One of the finest schools in the north of England, Appleby offered students an excellent classical education. For generations, Washington boys had been educated at Appleby. Lawrence began attending in 1729, Austin three years later. Both became pupils of Richard Yates, whose tenure at Appleby would span six decades. By all accounts, the two brothers came away from Appleby well educated and well mannered. Both contributed to the library fund Yates had established for Appleby, which would help make its school library one of the finest in Britain.[8]

Lawrence returned to Virginia when he was around twenty and George was around six. Lawrence would prove a powerful influence on his half-brother. The first of Mary's children, George was born at the family home in Virginia near Pope's Creek, a tributary of the Potomac River in Westmoreland County. Five more children would follow, four surviving into adulthood. John Augustine, or "Jack," born in 1736, would be George's favorite sibling. George remembered Jack as "the intimate companion of my youth and the most affectionate friend of my ripened age."[9]

In 1735 Augustine Washington moved his growing family to a plot of land on Little Hunting Creek overlooking the Potomac. Lawrence would name this property Mount Vernon after Admiral Edward Vernon, who led the British expedition against Cartagena, the Spanish colonial port on the northern tip of South America in what is now Colombia, during the War of Jenkins's Ear. (This Anglo-Spanish war is named for Robert Jenkins, an officer in the British merchant naval service whose maiming rallied the English in the face of Spanish bravado.) An officer during the Cartagena expedition, Lawrence had participated as one of the leaders of a daring nighttime amphibious assault. Once ashore, his troops attacked the battery, spiked the cannon, and repulsed the Spanish troops defending the coast.[10]

Admiral Vernon, who planned the assault, thoroughly impressed Lawrence Washington, who was proud to name his home after him. Leaving Lawrence at Mount Vernon in 1738, Augustine Washington relocated to a property on the Rappahannock River opposite Fredericksburg, the county seat. Their home became known as Ferry Farm after the conveyance the Washington family operated across the river.

Augustine Washington was an educated man. He, too, had attended Appleby School. Evidence of his reading is spotty. Only a few books from his personal library survive. One is a copy of the second edition of Henry Crouch's *Complete View of the British Customs*—the standard work on the subject, which people consulted as an official guide. Into his copy of Crouch's *Customs*, he wrote:

> Augustine Washington
> his Book bought the 4th of
> May 1737
> of the Bookseller under
> the Royal Exchange. Cost
> 7/Shillings[11]

This flyleaf inscription reflects the transatlantic voyage Augustine Washington made the year his son George turned five. Motivated partly by business interests and partly by the desire to see how his older boys were doing at Appleby, Augustine accomplished this double goal before returning to Virginia.[12] Crouch's *Customs* became a part of his permanent library at Ferry Farm. Its inscription reveals the personal attitude George's father took toward his library. He understood the importance of recording where and when he bought a new book. Inscribed with such details, a book becomes a physical artifact anchoring its owner to time and place.

Augustine's inscription is fairly idiosyncratic. Rarely do eighteenth-century ownership inscriptions contain such precise detail. With it, Augustine turned the book's front flyleaf into a kind of receipt. His inscription also helped guard against theft, though it lacks the menacing playfulness of such traditional anti-theft flyleaf rhymes as

> Steal not this book
> For fear of life
> For the owner carries
> A butcher-knife.[13]

Augustine inscribed his name on two other pages in Crouch's *Customs*. Though these multiple autographs anticipate his son's double autograph in Blackall's *Sufficiency of a Standing Revelation*, George's ownership inscriptions are nowhere near as specific as his father's inscription in Crouch's *Customs*. Rarely would George inscribe a book's title page with the year he bought it or the price he paid for it.

Since so few volumes from Augustine Washington's library survive, his estate inventory offers the best indication of his literary tastes. Altogether, he owned a library of around a hundred volumes. The size of his collection compares with those of many contemporary Virginia planters. The inventory lists sixty-four titles separately and groups the remainder in a single line: "Sundry old English and Latin books." The library was predominantly belletristic in nature. Augustine owned *The Spectator*, the preeminent English periodical essay series written by Joseph Addison, Richard Steele, and a handful of other contributors. He also had a copy of Alexander Pope's translation of Homer's *Iliad* and a six-volume set of Shakespeare.[14]

Augustine's religious collection was comparatively small. Besides a Bible and a Book of Common Prayer, the only other religious works listed are an abridged version of Gilbert Burnet's history of the Church of England and eight volumes of the Reverend Dr. Samuel Clarke's ten-volume *Sermons*. Clarke's sermons may represent Augustine Washington's attitudes toward religion more fully than anything else. They develop the forward-thinking ideas Clarke had set forth in his Boyle lectures regarding the distinctions between natural and revealed religion. He thought that natural religion could be derived from reason. Clarke's ideas unwittingly supported the deistic argument that revealed religion was superfluous.[15]

It seems improbable that George Washington read these sermons in his adolescence, but his father could have distilled their contents for him as George approached his first Communion. The controversy over revealed religion that Clarke fomented provides another possible clue to help understand what young Washington was doing with a copy of Blackall: he was growing curious about what revealed religion meant.

The second week of April 1743, George, now eleven, was away from Ferry Farm visiting some nearby cousins when he learned that his father had been struck with a sudden illness. He rushed home as fast as he could, but he was too late. Before George returned home, Augustine Washington died on April 12, 1743.[16] His death changed the direction of George's life significantly. Augustine Washington had intended to send him to Appleby, as well, but now George's future was uncertain.[17]

Augustine's will made no provisions for George's education. After her husband's death, Mary Washington decided against sending her oldest son to Appleby. Perhaps she thought the family could not afford it.[18] Or perhaps she was afraid to expose George to smallpox, which adversely afflicted colonials, who had little resistance to the disease. Maria Byrd, another Virginia widow, faced the same decision around the same time as Mary Washington. After the death of her husband, William Byrd II, she considered sending their son, William Byrd III, to England to complete his education. She even began planning the trip but ultimately decided against it. As she wrote a friend, "I thought again he woud certainly get the Small-Pox, which is most terrible fatal to those who are born in America, and that I shoud be accesory to his Death."[19] In George Washington's case the simplest explanation is the best: Mary Washington wanted to keep her oldest son close to her.

George inherited Ferry Farm, where his mother and her younger children remained for several years. As George passed from early adolescence into his late teens, he began spending more and more time with his older brother Lawrence at Mount Vernon. Regardless, his mother's influence on him remained profound. To use George Washington's own touching metaphor, she was the one who took him by the hand and led him from childhood.[20]

History has treated Mary Washington unevenly. Nineteenth-century biographer James Kirke Paulding, who interviewed people who had known her, practically canonized Mary Washington. In Paulding's words, she was "high-spirited, yet of great simplicity of manners, uncommon strength of mind, and decision of character."[21] Given that he dedicated his biography to all the mothers of the United States, Paulding could hardly say anything against Washington's mother. His portrayal of Mary Washington as a saint is fairly typical of the hagiographic George Washington biographies that appeared during the nineteenth century.

Recent biographers have been more critical, using derogatory terms like "harridan," "harpy," and "termagant" to characterize George Washington's mother.[22] No definitive evidence exists to pin down her character with any precision. The truth, no doubt, falls somewhere between saint and harpy. Those who are most critical of Mary Washington's personal behavior have extended their criticism to her intellect. One recent biographer says that she was illiterate.[23] Much evidence exists to challenge this assertion.

A grandson remembered her reading to him on Sunday evenings when he was a child. The boy would follow along as his grandmother read aloud from the family Bible. Listening to her, he "gazed with childish wonder and admiration at the rude representations of saints and angels, and the joys of the redeemed, and shuddered at the sight of the skeleton death and devils with horns and hoofs, holding in their claws pitchforks of fire." This grandson's experience sheds light on that of his Uncle George. The method that Mary Washington used to teach her grandchildren the Holy Scriptures she developed while teaching her own children.[24]

Books containing evidence of Mary Washington's ownership reflect her piety and her personality. They also share a continuity with the devotional books in her son George's library. John Scott's *Christian Life*, an Anglican devotional manual she obtained four years before she married Augustine, stresses the importance of meditation for bringing people closer to God.[25] Scott did not explain how the process of meditation worked, but another devotional author, the Reverend James Hervey, did. Mary Washington's copy of the two-volume edition of Hervey's *Meditations and Contemplations* reflects her attention to the work. She autographed it in four places, once on the back of each frontispiece and twice on the title page of the first volume.[26]

Hervey's *Meditations and Contemplations* was a renowned work that could be found throughout Virginia from the Chesapeake to the Blue Ridge. Planters and lawyers, burgesses and councilors, schoolteachers and parents: almost everyone, it seems, had Hervey in their homes. The number of copies does not fully indicate how widely read Hervey's *Meditations* was in colonial Virginia. People were so enthusiastic about its author's heartfelt sentiments that they shared their copies of *Meditations* with others. Mary Washington, presumably, shared hers with her son George.[27]

Meditations and Contemplations revitalized private devotional practice, giving readers examples of everyday subjects that could be used as the basis for personal devotion.[28] Hervey's meditations among the tombs conveyed the kind of melancholy that appealed to poetic souls. Explaining how to use a flower garden for personal reflection, Hervey said that the mind retains religious impressions more firmly "when the instructive Lessons are found, not on the Leaves of some formidable Folio, but stand legible on the fine Sarcenet of a Narcissus; when they savour not of the Lamp and Recluse, but come breathing from the fragrant Bosom of a Jonquil."[29] According to Hervey, people should practice their devotions outdoors. Mary Washington took his advice. Instead of always staying inside to practice her personal devotions, she often ventured outdoors to a secluded spot near Ferry Farm, a rocky ledge she used as a place for meditation.[30]

Hervey was not working in a vacuum, of course. His idea to use nature as a starting point for Christian devotion perpetuates the thought of earlier writers. Religious authors in the seventeenth century had emphasized the importance of what they called "closet devotions." The phrase does not literally refer to a closet but to a secluded place indoors for personal devotions. Typically, devout Christians would use the Holy Scriptures or some other religious text as a point of departure for their spiritual meditations. After reading a selected passage, they would ponder its meaning before ending their meditations in prayer.[31]

From the late seventeenth century, the potential subjects for meditation gradually expanded beyond the realm of the written word. In *Occasional Reflections upon Several Subjects*, Robert Boyle suggested that everyday objects could form the basis for spiritual reflection: "There is scarce any thing that Nature has made, or that men do or suffer, though the Theme seem never so low, and slight, whence the devout Reflector cannot take an occasion of an aspiring Meditation."[32] Practically anything, Boyle implied, could function as a starting point for spiritual meditation. Jonathan Swift's "Meditation on a Broomstick" parodies the devotional tradition Boyle advocated. So does Benjamin Franklin's irreverent "Meditation on a Quart Mugg."[33]

To his credit, Boyle emphasized the use of natural objects for spiritual meditation, a method others subsequently developed. The approach pervades the work of Samuel Clarke and his fellow Boyle lecturers, who believed people could witness God's handiwork in nature. The most important literary precedent for Hervey's *Meditations* is John Ray's *Wisdom of God Manifested in the Works of Creation*, a book Hervey had read in college.[34] George Washington read the book when he was college-aged or perhaps younger. According to the handwriting style of his title-page autograph, he acquired his copy of Ray's *Wisdom of God* when he was in his teens.

Best known as a scientist, John Ray applied his knowledge of the natural world to demonstrate not only the evidence of God but also the evidence of God's goodness and wisdom. Part devotional manual and part natural history, *The Wisdom of God* presents a natural theology arguing that all aspects of nature—botany, geology, zoology—reveal the shaping hand of a benevolent deity. To the delight of the devout, Ray's account of nature jibes with orthodox interpretations of Holy Scripture.[35] Since God created nature, Ray argued, people have the responsibility to contemplate it. We owe it to God to study creation. The study of natural history amounts to another form of devotion. If those with the ability, leisure, and opportunity to study nature refuse to do so, they detract from God's glory.[36]

Whereas Ray's work appealed to discriminating readers, Hervey had a much broader appeal. Looking back from the nineteenth century, British magazinist John Foster noted the powerful impact of Hervey's *Meditations*, observing that no book contributed more to help people "draw materials of devotional thought from the scenery of nature."[37] Hervey helped take private devotions from the closet into the open air, giving Christian readers like the Washingtons an opportunity to commune with nature and bring themselves closer to God.

Mary Washington also owned Eliza Haywood's *Female Spectator*, a four-volume set of periodical essays devoted to women's issues that could be found throughout colonial America.[38] While providing numerous anecdotes to emphasize traditional feminine virtues—charity, chastity, modesty—Haywood also sought to expand the woman's sphere, emphasizing the importance of books for self-improvement.[39] In one of her finest passages, she offers a paean to the educational and imaginative power of books:

What clods of earth should we have been but for reading!—how ignorant of every thing but the spot we tread upon!—books are the channel through which all useful arts and sciences are conveyed.—By the help of books we sit at ease, and travel to the most distant parts; behold the customs and manners of all the different nations in the habitable globe, nay take a view of heaven itself, and traverse all the wonders of the skies.—By books we learn to sustain calamity with patience, and bear prosperity with moderation.—By books we are enabled to compare past ages with the present; to discover what in our fore fathers was worthy imitation, and what should be avoided; to improve upon their virtues, and take warning by their errors.—It is books which dispel that gloomy melancholy our climate but too much inclines us to, and in its room diffuses an enlivening chearfulness.—In fine, we are indebted to books for every thing that can profit or delight us.[40]

Since Mary Washington could not have acquired either Hervey's *Meditations and Contemplations* or *The Female Spectator* until George was in his late teens, these works did not significantly influence her instruction of him. Still, they suggest Mary's fondness for reading. Parents who read turn their children into readers. The example of Eliza Haywood illustrates this idea. George's library, like his mother's, reflects a curiosity about the writings of Eliza Haywood. The catalogue he compiled in 1764, the year he turned thirty-two, lists Haywood's *Epistles for the Ladies*.[41]

That same library catalogue possesses a wealth of additional information about Washington's devotional reading. Since it retains the shelf organization of his Mount Vernon library, it shows what books he grouped together. Near his copy of Blackall's *Sufficiency of a Standing Revelation* he kept Matthew Hale's *Contemplations Moral and Divine*, which, according to family tradition, Mary Washington read to her children as a basis for lessons in piety and wisdom. She later presented her personal copy to George, which remained a part of his library the rest of his life.[42]

In terms of its influence on her son, Hale's *Contemplations* was the most important volume on Mary Washington's bookshelf. Unlike so many other books from his library, George Washington's copy of Hale's *Contemplations* remained at Mount Vernon well into the nineteenth century. His family honored the work for its instructive value; succeeding generations called the book "a counsellor of past days."[43]

Comprised of short essays its author wrote as devotional exercises and first published in the late seventeenth century, Hale's *Contemplations* appealed to Christian readers regardless of denomination.[44] James Kirke Paulding, who borrowed Washington's copy of the book when he was writing his biography, thought it reflected his piety. Paulding found Hale's *Contemplations* "filled with lessons of virtue and wisdom, clothed in the simple language of sincerity and truth, and adorned in its hoary dignity, like some ancient temple, with rich vines, bearing clusters of flowers, and beautiful even in its decay."[45]

Another book from her personal library that Mary Washington passed along to George was Thomas Comber's *Short Discourses upon the Whole Common-Prayer*, a handsome volume bound in tooled and paneled calf with gilt edges. The book originally belonged to her husband, who inscribed his name on the front flyleaf, the title page, and the first page of the dedicatory epistle. The flyleaf inscription reads:

> August[e] Washington
> his Book 1727

As this inscription's date shows, Augustine acquired the work during his first marriage. Apparently, his second wife had a greater interest in literature than his first. Directly beneath the flyleaf inscription that identifies the book as his, she wrote "and Mary Washington."

A few years after her husband's death, his widow presented the volume to their son George, whose inscriptions suggest that mother and son shared possession of the book for a time. When he was about thirteen, George autographed it using large cursive letters adorned with several flourishes. Beneath his own name, he signed his mother's. On the back flyleaves, George inscribed his father's name several times. The ornate inscriptions show George taking possession of the volume. "This is my book," he seems to say. "I can do with it whatever I please." But these inscriptions also show him acknowledging his father's former ownership.

William H. Bogart examined this copy of Comber many years ago, finding that it revealed much about George Washington's attitude toward his father. Bogart made the point that Washington's inscription revealed "the deference and filial respect of his young years."[46] Washington's surviving papers are silent when it comes to the subject of how he felt toward his father. These boyish inscriptions suggest that George experienced a great sense of loss after his father's death. Shelved in the library at Mount Vernon, George Washington's copy of Comber's *Short Discourses* became a symbol of his absent father.

Like Hale's *Contemplations*, Comber's *Short Discourses* contributed to Washington's devotional meditation. Comber was best known for *A Companion to the Temple and the Closet*, an elaborate commentary on the Book of Common Prayer. He published *Short Discourses* as a more manageable approach to the same subject, the liturgy of the Church of England, but it, too, is a fairly substantial volume. *Short Discourses* explains the Book of Common Prayer and celebrates its greatness.

Besides detailing the sacramental uses of the Anglican prayer book, Comber explains how the Book of Common Prayer could be used in private, personal devotions. Comber's writing style, though somewhat peculiar, was clear and largely devoid of ornament.[47] George Washington got the message. Like other devotional manuals on his bookshelf, *Short Discourses* emphasizes the personal and spiritual value of meditation. Comber intended *Short Discourses* "to furnish the Devout Sons of the Church with Profitable Meditations."[48]

The books Washington added to his personal library in his teens reinforced what he had learned in adolescence. *Seneca's Morals* has been widely acknowledged for shaping how Washington understood the relationship between virtue and happiness. It articulated a stoic philosophy, emphasizing courage, emotional restraint, sacrifice, and tenacity.[49] Previous commentators have identified Seneca as one of the few classical authors Washington read, but *Seneca's Morals* influenced him partly because it echoed ideas he had previously encountered among Christian authors.

In the dedicatory epistle of the edition Washington owned, translator Roger L'Estrange stressed the continuity between Seneca's ethics and Christian belief, comparing *Seneca's Morals* to the Holy Gospel and calling its author "a good honest Christian-Pagan" who could serve as "a Moderator among Pagan-Christians."[50] Seneca gave his readers much food for thought. Herman Melville would call *Seneca's Morals* "a round-of-beef where all hands may come and cut again." Speaking about Seneca elsewhere, Melville observes, "That a mere man, and a heathen, in that most heathenish time, should give utterance to such heavenly wisdom, seems more wonderful than that an inspired prophet should reveal it."[51]

As in many Christian devotional manuals, the word "contemplation" is central to Seneca's text. In chapter 8, "The Due Contemplation of Divine Providence Is the Certain Cure of All Misfortunes," Seneca argues that by contemplating nature people can attune themselves to the ways of God. Other Virginia readers recognized an affinity between Seneca's moral philosophy and Christian belief. Colonel William Fleming, an officer who served in the Virginia Regiment under Washington during the Seven Years' War, shelved his copy of *Seneca's Morals* with Hervey's *Meditations* and Ray's *Wisdom of God*.[52]

Seneca also offered a prescription for reading, which he closely linked to meditation. He advocated reading intensively, not extensively. In other words, it would be better to read a few books over and over again than to read one book after another without thoroughly digesting their contents. As you read, Seneca recommended, choose certain passages as a basis for meditation. Only by thinking can you truly understand what you read.

Through the process of meditation, an author's ideas "become our own, and supply us with Strength, and Virtue."[53]

A remarkable continuity runs through the books Washington encountered in his youth. Blackall, Comber, Hale, Hervey, Ray, Seneca: all these authors stressed the importance of meditation. Other books from Washington's library offer additional examples. In *Causes of the Decay of Christian Piety*, Richard Allestree, another English divine whose writings crossed denominational boundaries, used an organic metaphor to stress the value of meditation: "When that spiritual seed lies loose and scatter'd upon the surface, and is not by deep and serious meditation harrowed, as it were, into the ground, it offers itself a ready prey to the devourer."[54] Upon learning a particular technique, Washington had an uncanny ability to adjust and apply it in different situations. His meditative practice is no exception. As a boy, he learned to meditate as a way of practicing his piety; as an adult he learned how to use his meditation to suit different circumstances.

When faced with conflict during wartime, controversy during his time as a legislator in the House of Burgesses and the Continental Congress, or contradictory views during his presidency, Washington applied his meditative powers to devise solutions to the difficulties he faced. After a battle had been won or a controversy resolved, he meditated further to help understand the meaning of his accomplishments. The most poignant example of his meditative practice comes from a diary entry he wrote the evening that the delegates to the Constitutional Convention finally approved the US Constitution. After serving as president of the Constitutional Convention, Washington returned to his lodgings in Philadelphia, where he could "meditate on the momentous work which had been executed."[55] For George Washington, personal experiences became texts to be used for meditation, a process and practice that shaped his decisions on the battlefield and in the political arena.

CHAPTER 2

Every Boy His Own Teacher

If not to some peculiar end design'd,
Study's the specious trifling of the mind;
Or is at best a secondary aim,
A chase for sport alone, and not for game.
Edward Young, "Love of Fame"

Cubbyholes are magical spaces. Store something in a cubbyhole, and it just might transform itself into something else. Well, that object doesn't really change, but the times change, and so does the person who stored it there, either of which amounts to the same thing. Above the topmost bookshelves in his permanent library at Mount Vernon, George Washington had dozens of built-in cubbyholes, or pigeonholes, as they were called in his day, that is, before that word became a verb and took on pejorative connotations. In those dark compartments he stored many personal papers, some dating back to his adolescence. The manuscripts that Washington saved since his school days in the 1740s became something very different by the end of his life. They transformed themselves into a blueprint of his mind.

This set of miscellaneous manuscripts contains essential documents for reconstructing George Washington's school days. Beyond the exercises that form the lion's share of these early manuscripts, details of Washington's education are sparse. In an unfinished biography, his aide-de-camp, personal secretary, friend, and confidante David Humphreys says that a "domestic tutor" took charge of Washington's education.[1]

Humphreys's precise language offers a good idea of the kind of teacher Washington had as a boy. Typically, affluent families alone could afford domestic tutors for their children. As the job title suggests, the domestic tutor was a live-in teacher who accepted room and board, along with a modest salary. Washington's tutor taught grammar, logic, rhetoric, geometry and higher mathematics, geography, history, and additional "studies which are not improperly termed 'the humanities.'"[2] The name of Washington's domestic tutor has escaped history. Considering the eclectic nature of the surviving school exercises, his editors suggest that Washington had several teachers.[3]

Further evidence shows that at one point in his education Washington did attend school with other boys. Friend and fellow patriot George Mason mentioned to him a man named David Piper, whom he described as "my Neighbour and Your old School-fellow." Like Washington, Piper would turn to surveying once he left school, becoming surveyor of roads for Fairfax County. He was also something of a bad boy. Piper was repeatedly brought to court on various civil and criminal matters. Together Washington and Piper could have attended school at the Lower Church of Washington Parish, Westmoreland County, where Mattox Creek enters the Potomac River, but there is no saying for sure.[4] The story of Washington's education is shrouded in mystery.

His school exercises indicate what he studied inside the classroom and out. They show him mastering many different subjects, learning what he would need to make his way through colonial Virginia whether that way took him down a deer track or up Duke of Gloucester Street. Some of the exercises are dated, revealing that this set of school papers as a whole ranges from 1743 to 1748, that is, from the year Washington turned eleven to the year he turned sixteen. Other evidence demonstrates that he continued his studies beyond the latest exercises in the manuscript collection. Altogether the exercises and the books Washington read during his school days reveal his early literary interests, his fascination with mathematics, and the genesis of his career as a surveyor.

Washington became curious about poetry in his youth, as two manuscript poems that survive with the school exercises reveal. When he first read these poems, he transcribed them to create personal copies he could reread whenever he wished. His copies reveal Washington's ambition to excel in penmanship, and their texts shed light on his state of mind at the end of adolescence.[5]

One is titled "On Christmas Day." Given its subject, the poem's imagery is predictable. It is filled with happy shepherds and hymn-singing angels watching over the newborn savior. The speaker of the poem is female; she ends by reminding herself to remember Christmas always. The bottom corner of the page containing Washington's transcription is torn, so the last two lines of verse are damaged. His source supplies the missing words:

> Oh never let my Soul this Day forget,
> But pay in graitfull praise her Annual Debt
> To him, whom 'tis my Trust, I shall [adore]
> When Time, and Sin, and Deat[h, shall be no more!]

The picture of young Washington that emerges from his copy of this poem is that of a boy confident in his religious beliefs but pleased to have another confirm them. This Christmas poem is akin to a Christmas present, something to treasure for itself and for what it symbolizes.

Washington recorded neither his source nor the poet's name, but "On Christmas Day" comes from the February 1743 issue of the *Gentleman's Magazine*. The published poem is signed "Orinthia"—the pseudonym for Elizabeth Teft, a Lincolnshire poet.[6] The transcription also reveals Washington's fastidiousness. In the *Gentleman's Magazine*, editor and publisher Edward Cave capitalized each line of the poem but avoided capitalizing other nouns. Copying the poem for himself, Washington capitalized the nouns Cave had left uncapitalized, giving the written text a more traditional look.

"True Happiness," the other poem that survives among the manuscripts from Washington's school days, also appeared in the *Gentleman's Magazine*, though in a much earlier issue, that of February 1734.[7] Taken together, the two poems create a vivid picture of Washington's boyhood reading process. After enjoying "On Christmas Day" in a recent issue of the *Gentleman's Magazine*, he wished to read more verse and searched whatever back issues were available. The magazines listed in his father's estate inventory cannot be identified precisely, but they were most likely bound volumes of the *Gentleman's Magazine*, one of the few English periodicals available at the time.[8] Each issue of the *Gentleman's Magazine* contains a poetry column. After he encountered "On Christmas Day," it seems, Washington read a number of back issues until he found another poem he liked, which he transcribed onto the opposite side of the leaf containing "On Christmas Day."

Washington was one of many colonial American readers who enjoyed the *Gentleman's Magazine*. When Edward Cave began editing and publishing this periodical in January 1731, he gave birth to a new form of publication, which, in turn, gave rise to new forms of writing. The start of the *Gentleman's Magazine* marks the start of the modern magazine. It was so successful that sometimes Cave had to reprint back issues to meet demand.[9] Unlike modern magazines, it was not something to read one month and throw away the next but something to treasure, to keep for future reference.[10] Thomas Jefferson shelved bound volumes of this and other magazines with his encyclopedias, seeing them as similar kinds of works.[11] Like sets of encyclopedias, multivolume collections of magazines could serve as repositories of miscellaneous information. A long-running magazine amounted to a modern encyclopedia. Other Virginians treasured their back issues of the *Gentleman's Magazine*.[12] Washington's adolescent use of the *Gentleman's Magazine* is consistent with the way his fellow Virginians used it.

The *Gentleman's Magazine* appealed to readers throughout colonial America. Using the editorial pseudonym Sylvanus Urban, Edward Cave started the magazine as a digest of London newspapers for country readers but quickly expanded its scope, seeking original contributions and cultivating a circle of reader-correspondents willing to submit their work, especially their poetry, for publication.[13] The poetry section that closes each issue provided a forum for Elizabeth Teft and other aspiring poets throughout the English-speaking world.[14]

Different types of literature—political writings, reports of military campaigns, scientific essays—filled the pages of the *Gentleman's Magazine* during Washington's youth. The February 1743 issue is fairly typical. Besides "On Christmas Day" and several other poems, it contains recent parliamentary proceedings, a list of English nobility, an essay about an ongoing economic controversy, an article discussing the wool industry, observations on a passing comet, a slave narrative, political essays, extracts from recent pamphlets, a record of current events, and a list of recent literature.

Publishing maps to accompany the military reports—an innovative technique—*Gentleman's Magazine* let readers imagine the campaigns that the articles described. Perhaps these pages gave Washington his first inkling of military strategy. The miscellaneous essays helped popularize other fields of study, bringing the sciences to general readers in both Great Britain and America.[15] In his library at Mount Vernon, Washington had at least three volumes and several odd numbers of the *Gentleman's Magazine*, the first of many magazines he would collect.[16]

"True Happiness," to get back to the poem, offers a recipe for an ideal life that many local readers found appealing. In the coming years, numerous poems in the *Virginia Gazette* would echo its sentiments.[17] "True Happiness" stresses the value of a prosperous rural existence—a "good

Estate on healthy Soil"—where friends and family would gather "round a warm Fire" and enjoy "a pleasant Joke." The poet's list of necessities for happiness continues as it emphasizes marital bliss, physical fitness, mental equanimity, friendship, conviviality, simple fare, and drink in moderation, in other words:

> A quiet Wife, a quiet Soul,
> A Mind as well as Body whole;
> Prudent Simplicity, constant Friends,
> A Diet which no Art commends;
> A merry Night, without much drinking,
> A happy Thought, without much thinking.

The poem struck a chord with contemporary readers, who appreciated its detailed prescription for happiness. Those who disagreed with some of its finer points knew the text could be modified to suit. For example, Tom Killegrew, the pseudonymous editor of *The Merry Quack Doctor*, a collection of jests, jokes, puns, quibbles, and waggeries, reprinted another version of "True Happiness."[18] The textual differences between the *Gentleman's Magazine* version and Tom Killegrew's text suggest somewhat different ideas of happiness. The "pleasant joke" of the original, a symbol of fun in moderation, gives way to "buckish"—lascivious—jokes in Killegrew's racier version.

As an adolescent and later as an adult, Washington found the even-handed happiness espoused by the anonymous contributor to the *Gentleman's Magazine* more amenable than Killegrew's ribald version. The appeal of "True Happiness" for George Washington also reflects his father's influence. Augustine Washington, who died around the time George most likely encountered this poem, personally exemplified the ideal life it articulates.[19] If Augustine's son George looked forward to a quiet life "without much thinking," however, he was destined for disappointment.

The most renowned document that survives among the school exercises is George Washington's "Rules of Civility and Decent Behaviour in Company and Conversation," a set of 110 rules designed to guide social conduct. Like the two poems, "Rules" is not Washington's composition. These rules stem back to a mid-seventeenth-century conduct book, Francis Hawkins's *Youths Behaviour; or, Decency in Conversation amongst Men*, which itself stems back to a sixteenth-century French work.[20]

Though often discussed, Washington's "Rules" have inspired little curiosity regarding their precise origins.[21] After *Youths Behaviour* appeared,

Hawkins's rules were copied and recopied numerous times. William Winstanley recopied them for inclusion in *New Help to Discourse*, a steady-selling folkbook that constituted an agricultural handbook, conduct manual, and jest book all rolled into one. Including Hawkins's rules, Winstanley instructed readers how to behave in social situations. The rest of *New Help to Discourse* offered numerous topics of conversation. Altogether the contents of Winstanley's book told readers what to say and how to say it. It was one of many books published in the late seventeenth and early eighteenth century designed as conversational aids.[22]

First published in 1669, *New Help to Discourse* went through several reprintings in the coming decades. The work contains extracts from many different sources. As Winstanley admitted in a prefatory poem, he "undertook / To draw from Others Works the following Book." Numerous English editions of *New Help to Discourse* reached the American colonies in the late seventeenth and early eighteenth century. In 1722 Benjamin Franklin's brother James reprinted the book in Boston.[23]

Washington's "Rules of Civility" may stem from Hawkins, but its text comes much closer to Winstanley's. Compare the initial rule in each, first Hawkins, then Winstanley, then Washington:

> Every Action done in the view of the world, ought to be accompanied with some signe of reverence, which one beareth to all who are present.[24]

> Every Action done in the World ought to be done with some Sign of Respect to those that are present.[25]

> Every Action done in Company, ought to be with Some Sign of Respect, to those that are Present.[26]

Either Washington derived "Rules" from Winstanley's *New Help to Discourse* or he got them from an intermediate source. Perhaps his domestic tutor had a set of rules in manuscript to share with students. Such rules of conduct were frequently transmitted from print to manuscript and then from one manuscript to another. Through this process of copying and recopying, numerous changes, some deliberate, others inadvertent, would enter a text.

Many of Washington's rules concern speaking in company. Rule 47, for instance, affirms his preference for pleasant jokes over buckish ones: "Mock not nor Jest at anything of Importance. Break no Jest[s] that are Sharp Biting and if you Deliver any thing witty and Pleasant abstain from Laughing thereat yourself." Rule 58 says, "Let your Conversation be without Malice or Envy." According to rule 62, people should make their words suit the general tenor of a conversation: "Speak not of doleful Things in a Time of Mirth or at the Table." Rule 72: "Speak not in an unknown Tongue in Company but in your own Language and that as those of Quality do and not as the Vulgar." Rule 89: "Speak not Evil of the absent for it is unjust."[27] Other rules concern what to wear, how to stand, how to sit, when to gesture, when not to gesture, how and when to tip your hat, how to behave toward friends, how to behave toward strangers, how to act at the dinner table, and how to blow your nose, cough, sigh, sneeze, spit, and yawn.

Following both Hawkins and Winstanley, Washington also included a rule about reading in the company of others, rule 18:

> Read no Letters, Books, or Papers in Company but when there is a Necessity for the doing of it you must ask leave: come not near the Books or Writings of Another so as to read them unless desired or give your opinion of them unask'd also look not nigh when another is writing a Letter.[28]

Reading aloud in company was a popular diversion in Washington's day. It not only provided a form of entertainment, it also served as a way to introduce controversial new ideas to a gathering of people. Though Washington was not against reading for either entertainment or edification, he apparently believed that a group of people should agree on what to read. As rule 80 has it, "Be not Tedious in Discourse or in reading unless you find the Company pleased therewith."[29]

For the most part, though, reading was a solo activity. According to rule 18, it should stay that way. Reading to yourself in the presence of others is rude. Only read in company when absolutely necessary, and even then ask the others for permission. Reading over someone's shoulder is in poor taste, too. Don't do it. By all accounts, Washington studied these rules closely and sought to obey them all his life. They helped make him the model of a proper gentleman.

The school exercises say little about Washington's linguistic studies. According to "Rules of Civility," correct social behavior does not require a knowledge of foreign languages. Washington himself admitted that he could not read French—but it wasn't for want of trying. Years later he would add to his library at Mount Vernon a copy of Louis Chambaud's French-English dictionary, a methodical work that corrected numerous errors of previous dictionaries.[30]

Washington's library also suggests a general curiosity about Latin. He owned the Latin New Testament edited by Théodore de Bèze, Calvin's friend and successor at Geneva, and Joseph Davidson's Latin/English edition of Ovid's *Metamorphoses*. In a contemporary biographical sketch, John Bell of Maryland said Washington had received "a slight tincture of the Latin language." No other evidence suggests that he studied either Latin or Greek.[31] Later Washington expressed regret about his spotty linguistic knowledge. Toward the end of his life he urged his adopted grandson and namesake, George Washington Parke Custis, to make an effort to retain his knowledge of Latin grammar and composition all his life.[32]

Though Washington never studied Latin formally, he did know a few Latin phrases, including the one that forms the motto for his coat of arms: "Exitus acta probat." Though usually translated "The event justifies the deeds," the motto could be rendered into English differently. Eighteenth-century lexicographer Robert Ainsworth translated it more simply: "All is well that endeth well."[33] Colonel William Ball, Washington's grandfather, also used a Latin motto on his coat of arms: "Coelumque tueri." These words are shorthand for a lengthier passage from Ovid's *Metamorphoses* describing how God created man, which Joseph Davidson translated as follows: "He gave to Man a lofty Countenance, commanded him to lift his Face to Heaven, and behold with erected Eyes the Stars."[34]

It's easy to imagine George Washington dipping into his copy of Ovid to locate the source of his grandfather's motto, a passage inspiring us to look toward the sky and gaze into the heavens. Even if Washington could read little Latin beyond these few key phrases, he could have read the English text of Ovid's *Metamorphoses*, which offered much pleasure reading. Ovid synthesized the ancient mythic tradition and reshaped it into an exciting and readable form. Davidson's English version retains the spirit of the original. A modern translator of Ovid's has compared some episodes from *Metamorphoses* to hardboiled crime fiction, observing that Ovid "has a sadistic streak in him—the fighting of Perseus, the battles of the Centaurs, the rape of Philomela, are as violent and ugly, while they go on, as anything in Mickey Spillane."[35]

Other evidence verifies that Washington closed the gaps in his education by reading English translations of the ancient classics. He read Roger L'Estrange's English version of Aesop's *Fables*. The work stuck with him. Washington's writings contain more than one reference to Aesop. On a nightly basis during the Revolutionary War, he had to devise paroles—passwords for the inspectors of the guard—and corresponding countersigns. He typically used place names, but sometimes he used names of authors for either parole or countersign. One night the parole was "Ethiopia," and the countersign was "Esop."[36] This verbal combination suggests Washington's familiarity with the legendary life of Aesop, who supposedly came from

Ethiopia. Washington also remembered specific fables, including the one about the fox and the grapes, which he recalled years later.[37]

Once upon a time, as Aesop tells the story, a fox stood beneath a grapevine with a succulent bunch of grapes suspended just out of reach. The fox leapt upwards hundreds of times but to no avail. Gradually tiring, the fox realized it was impossible to get those grapes. "Hang 'em," said the fox, making light of his disappointment. "They are as sour as Crabs." After each fable, L'Estrange provided additional analysis, explaining in this instance: "'Tis Matter of Skill and Address, when a Man cannot honestly compass what he would be at, to appear easy and indifferent upon all Repulses and Disappointments."[38] Washington took the advice to heart.

Though he lacked a reading knowledge of other languages, Washington reinforced his mastery of English with *The Royal English Grammar*, a steady seller compiled by James Greenwood, surmaster of St Paul's School in London, who provided eighteenth-century students with an excellent guide to the subject. As one poetical schoolmaster remarked:

> And, if true English you would write,
> By Grammar Rules you must indite;
> And, if those Rules you fain would know,
> On Greenwood's *Grammar* Pains bestow.[39]

Washington owned the third edition of Greenwood, which was published in 1747, the year he turned fifteen.[40] His surviving copy reveals its use: the corners of the pages are heavily worn from frequent bethumbings. Washington's teenaged study of Greenwood shows the limits of his linguistic knowledge. Fifteen was fairly late for studying English grammar. Better-educated Virginia students mastered Latin and had Greek well in hand by that age. Greenwood designed his work specifically for students who had never learned Latin.

Greenwood's *Grammar* goes well with Washington's "Rules of Civility." Whereas the rules stressed the importance of speaking properly, Greenwood extended that idea to the realm of the written word to emphasize the social value of writing properly. In essence Greenwood made English composition a matter of proper social conduct. Extracts from his preface could easily be slotted into Washington's "Rules of Civility." Consider the following comment:

> For tho' it is possible that a Young Gentleman or Lady may be enabled
> to speak well upon some Subjects, and entertain a Visiter with Discourse
> agreeable enough; yet I do not well see how they should write any thing

with a tolerable Correctness, unless they have some Taste of Grammar, or express themselves clearly, or deliver their Thoughts by Letter or otherwise, so as not to lay themselves open to the Censure of their Friends, for their blameable Spelling or false Syntax.[41]

Washington learned his lesson well: his teenage correspondence bears out Greenwood's point. In an undated letter written in his late teens, Washington calls the personal letter "the greatest mark of friendship and esteem you can show to an absent Friend."[42]

The chapter on syntax may be the most important one in Greenwood's book. It calls syntax the end of grammar and demonstrates the importance of joining words together properly, that is, making them both stylistically and rhetorically effective. Like Greenwood's other chapters, it is structured as a series of questions and answers. Greenwood not only taught syntactical rules, he also supplied the exceptions to them. Answering a question about whether an adjective should always come before the noun it modifies, Greenwood said yes, but then explained that in some cases it could come afterwards. In poetry, adjectives were frequently placed after nouns for "the more harmonious sounding of the Verse." Greenwood illustrated the exception with a memorable phrase from Milton: "Human face divine."[43]

Greenwood's advice and examples helped Washington hone his writing skills. The final section of the book, "A Praxis on the Grammar," provides a series of sample texts and discusses each word in every sample, noting all the parts of speech. The section is divided into three subsections. The second discusses the Lord's Prayer, the third the Apostles' Creed. But the initial subsection begins with a series of simple sentences. The very first one is a delight: "Good Boys love good Books."[44]

The attention Washington paid to Greenwood's *Grammar* when he was in his teens indicates a strong desire for self-improvement on his part, an impulse he shared with many other young men in colonial America. He was not the only one to get his grammar from Greenwood.[45] Benjamin Franklin expressed his debt to Greenwood's *Grammar*, which he remembered reading in his teens—"while I was intent on improving my Language." Actually, Franklin misremembered. The work he read in his teens was Charles Gildon's *Grammar*, not Greenwood's.[46] But the reason Franklin gave for reading grammar also applies to Washington, who obviously studied Greenwood to improve his writing skills.

One work both Franklin and Washington read as part of their education was John Seller's *Practical Navigation*, another textbook that could be found throughout colonial America.[47] In his autobiography Franklin says he read Seller's *Practical Navigation* for the geometry it contained but admits he never progressed very far in his study of the subject.[48] Seller's handbook contains much else besides geometry. In essence it taught contemporary students all the mathematics necessary for the practice of navigation. Seller's editor John Colson compared the book to a lighthouse that mariners used to guide themselves safely over the seas.[49]

Seller himself recognized the significance of his subject. In the opening paragraph to *Practical Navigation*, he defined it in grandiose, albeit endearing, terms, calling navigation "the Beauty and Bulwark of England, the Wall and Wealth of Britain, and the Bridge that joins it to the Universe."[50] George Washington studied *Practical Navigation* for its mathematics, but he learned some basic geography as well, copying Seller's geographical definitions verbatim into his school exercises. Following Seller, Washington defined a continent as "a great quantity of Land, not divided nor separated by the Sea, wherein are many Kingdoms and Principalities; as Europe, Asia, and Africa are one Continent, and America is another." Washington's division of continents differs from modern taxonomies, but, as geographers now understand, the continental divisions of the world reflect cultural, intellectual, and social developments more than geographical fact.[51]

Practical Navigation was not the only textbook on the subject Washington read. His copy of Archibald Patoun's *Compleat Treatise of Practical Navigation* at Mount Vernon contains annotations in his hand showing that Washington read the book so closely he recognized a mistake in one of Patoun's examples. Patoun described in detail how to determine the sun's declination at Saint Lucia on April 6 with reference to the tables for the declination of the sun. Carefully studying the example, Washington checked the tables himself and noticed an error. In the margin adjacent to the example Washington noted that Patoun had mistakenly calculated the declination for May 6, not April 6.

Washington also started reading history in his youth, as his copy of Thomas Prince's *Chronological History of New-England in the Form of Annals* indicates. The authenticity of Washington's autograph on the title page of this surviving volume has come under question.[52] The uncertainty is understandable. Few Boston imprints made it to colonial Virginia. Before the first printing press was established in Williamsburg in 1730, most books sold and read in Virginia came from London. Even after the establishment of the local printing industry, Virginians still imported much of their reading material from London. But this copy of Prince's *Chronological History* somehow found its way to colonial Virginia. Another Washington autograph, which appears partway through the volume and which has so far gone unnoticed, verifies his ownership.[53]

Gauging by the initial title-page autograph, Washington acquired this volume when he was in his late adolescence or early teens. Prince's *Chronological History* provides a good touchstone for understanding how the New England Puritans saw themselves in relation to the history of the world. Prince did not start his chronology in 1620, when the Pilgrims landed, or in 1614, when Captain John Smith coined the name "New England," or in 1492, when Columbus reached the New World. He started with Creation. In other words, the Puritans saw the founding of New England as part of God's grand design, which extended as far back as Creation.

The first section of Prince's *Chronological History* goes to 1603, after which its author begins a new section with a second title page: "The New-England Chronology." Washington signed this title page, too, but, according to the style of his handwriting, he did so when he was in his late teens. Like his copy of Offspring Blackall's *Sufficiency of a Standing Revelation*, Washington's copy of Prince's *Chronological History* suggests that he acquired the book in his boyhood, had difficulties with it and set it aside, but returned to it when he was older and read it all.

The school exercises suggest other books Washington read in his youth. On the bottom half of the leaf containing "True Happiness," for instance, he copied a recipe, "To Keep Ink from Freezing or Moulding," which involved putting a few drops of brandy into the ink. He did not name his source, but similar recipes occur in contemporary self-help books, including William Mather's *Young Man's Companion; or, Arithmetick Made Easy* and George Fisher's *The Instructor; or, Young Man's Best Companion*. Washington's text varies slightly from the versions in both works.

During the Civil War, Union troops in Virginia turned up a copy of Mather's *Young Man's Companion* with a dated autograph on its title page: "George Washington 1742." Calling it "one of the most interesting books in the world," a nineteenth-century newspaper reporter overstated its importance but nevertheless reflected the ongoing curiosity about the books Washington read as a boy.[54] Washington's editors have since questioned the authenticity of the dated signature.[55] The possibility that Washington borrowed his recipe for freeze-proof ink from Mather's *Young Man's Companion* suggests that the signature could be genuine and justifies another glance at this practical manual.

Though subtitled "Arithmetic Made Easy," Mather's textbook contains more than mathematics. It presents an eclectic mix of useful information, explaining how to write English, create basic legal forms, understand world geography, maintain a garden, manage fruit trees, and prepare useful medicines. In short, this *Young Man's Companion* was a vade mecum designed to help readers educate themselves in all the fundamental skills necessary to lead a useful, healthful, bountiful life. It offered a book-length prescription for true happiness.

So did *The Instructor*, or, as it was better known, *Fisher's Companion*. As Fisher explains in the preface, his work could serve as "the first Step of forming the young Man's Mind for Business."[56] It helped eighteenth-century readers learn the basics of business without the help of a master. It taught accounting, arithmetic, bookkeeping, practical geometry, and business writing. Furthermore, *Fisher's Companion* provided much additional miscellaneous information: household hints concerning how to candy apricots, pickle cucumbers, preserve currants, and make cider; gardening tips; basic medical information; and an introduction to farriery explaining how to choose, groom, diagnose, and treat horses. Its contents may seem quite basic, but the diversity and practicality of its information made the work useful for more educated readers, too. David Black, a contemporaneous Virginia physician, had a copy of *Fisher's Companion* in his library in Prince George County. So did colonial North Carolina physician John Eustace.[57]

All this talk about books may give the impression that Washington was a bookish lad who spent most days reading, so a slight correction is necessary. A traditional story from his youth that circulated in the family provides a more balanced portrait, depicting him as both a reader and an athlete. One day many local teenage boys participated in a series of wrestling matches. As they competed, Washington sat beneath a nearby tree reading a book. After easily defeating all the others, the strongest boy called for a final competitor, someone who could give him a greater challenge. He taunted Washington, calling him a coward for refusing to wrestle. Washington calmly closed his book, walked into the ring, and, in a fierce but momentary struggle, wrestled the boy to the ground and emerged victorious.

The story sounds fanciful, but a surviving description of Washington's physical stature in his youth provides some corroboration. Buckner Stith, a childhood friend, described Washington as "a sound looking, modest, large boned young Man."[58] Having heard the wrestling story told and retold, G. W. P. Custis felt free to embellish it further. His version includes a comment the loser supposedly made after the match: "In Washington's lionlike grasp I became powerless, and was hurled to the ground with a force that seemed to jar the very marrow in my bones." The other boys cheered for Washington, who, instead of celebrating his victory, returned to the shady spot beneath the tree, picked up his book, and continued reading.[59]

As he matured, Washington's reading became less desultory and more purposeful. Perhaps no single work holds a greater place in his school exercises than William Leybourn's *Complete Surveyor*. When it first appeared in the mid-seventeenth century, Leybourn's textbook marked an advance in the history of books as well as the history of surveying. Leybourn's work represents the successful introduction of the geometrical approach to surveying, a subject he treats with vigor and confidence. In addition Leybourn presented his text and illustrations using a modern page layout that makes his information easily accessible.[60]

The Complete Surveyor remained the standard work in the field well into the eighteenth century. Leybourn helped many early American surveyors get their start. Westmoreland County surveyor Thomas Thompson, for one, owned a copy of Leybourn. But those with better educations and more elite social standing found much to admire in Leybourn, too. The wealthy Virginian Robert "King" Carter's son Landon had Leybourn in his well-stocked library.[61]

Landon Carter had an excellent classical education and, given his druthers, would have preferred spending his time reading Livy instead of Leybourn. But being one of Virginia's wealthiest landowners, he knew that information gleaned from a surveying textbook could help him secure and maintain his extensive property. Two decades older than Washington, Carter became a mentor. Their land dealings sometimes brought them together, and both would serve in the Virginia House of Burgesses. When they first met, Carter was quite impressed with Washington and predicted a great future for him.[62] But he also saw room for improvement. Writing to him in 1755, when Washington was twenty-three, Carter advised, "Always in your Leizure hours regard the inward Man."[63] As his letters to Washington show, Carter did not find their educational differences a barrier to communication. Carter's correspondence with Washington is sprinkled with many charming classical allusions.

Washington greatly appreciated the practical value of Leybourn's *Complete Surveyor*. Its use in his school exercises reveals his dedication to surveying, which gave him a practical outlet for his mathematical skill, one that not only provided a livelihood but also put him in close contact with the land, something that was becoming increasingly important to him. Washington's exercise notebook demonstrates his natural talent for surveying. It contains surveying exercises that are so varied and meticulous that, as one editor has observed, they must have been self-assigned problems.[64]

Though the school exercises do not extend beyond 1748, another book from Washington's library shows that he was still studying mathematics after he had begun his surveying career. He autographed the title page of Guillaume François Antoine L'Hospital's *Analytick Treatise of Conick Sections* and dated his acquisition: March 1750. In this work L'Hospital treats that branch of geometry concerning figures formed from plane sections of a cone: hyperbolas, parabolas, ellipses, and circles. A notoriously difficult subject, conic sections was beyond the reach of most contemporary students. L'Hospital's textbook helped. John Clarke, master of the public grammar school at Hull, found L'Hospital's *Conick Sections* the best available book on the subject.[65]

The date Washington acquired his copy of L'Hospital's work may be most revealing. Though the last dated entry in the school exercises is 1748, Washington's study of conic sections in 1750 shows that his attention to educational texts went beyond what the exercises indicate. By 1750, the year he turned eighteen, the ambitious Washington had already started to establish his reputation as a surveyor. A knowledge of conic sections was not essential to his professional responsibilities, but he found the subject intriguing. Quite simply, he was fascinated with mathematics and sought to learn as much as he could out of his own curiosity. For George Washington, study was not something that ended with youth; it was something to continue throughout adulthood.

CHAPTER 3

Exemplars

I bid him look into the lives of men as in a glass, and to take example from other persons.

Terence, *The Brothers*

Beyond his own, no other family exerted a greater influence on George Washington than the Fairfaxes. At the top of the family stood Thomas, sixth Lord Fairfax, baron of Cameron and proprietor of the Northern Neck, a huge swath of Virginia real estate located between the Rappahannock and the Potomac. His lordship inherited the proprietary upon his mother's death in 1719. He remained in England initially, preferring to hire a series of agents to manage the Northern Neck. Their primary duties involved granting vacant lands and assessing annual quit-rents. Robert "King" Carter served as the proprietary agent for a long time, but after his death in 1732, Lord Fairfax needed a new agent. He had trouble finding a capable manager but eventually chose William Fairfax, a cousin living in Massachusetts.

After a hitch in the army, William Fairfax had been devoting himself to public service in the British colonies. He served as chief justice of the Bahamas, but its hot weather drained his energy and made him sickly. He transferred to Massachusetts, where he served as collector of customs at Salem from 1725 until 1734, when his cousin approached him about becoming the Virginia agent. William Fairfax accepted the position and relocated to Virginia. Lord Fairfax exerted his influence to help his cousin become collector of customs for the South Potomac district as well.

Unlike the Bahamas, Virginia agreed with William Fairfax, and he settled into the comfortable life of a colonial Virginia gentleman. He became lieutenant colonel of the county militia, a position entitling him, like so many other Virginia gentlemen, to be styled "Colonel." Broadening his political influence, he was elected to the House of Burgesses and ultimately appointed to the Virginia Council.

Colonel Fairfax built an imposing Georgian mansion in Fairfax County on the south shore of the Potomac River and named it Belvoir. Located near Mount Vernon, it became a frequent destination for young Washington. Belvoir lived up to its name: it was a beautiful home with a beautiful view—a "high and commanding ground," Washington said.[1] Forty years later he recalled his time at Belvoir with nostalgia: "The happiest moments of my life had been spent there," he reflected. Practically every room in the place brought to Washington's mind the "recollection of pleasing scenes."[2]

The extravagance of the mansion's interior matched the grandeur of its exterior. Belvoir's spacious, high-studded rooms were adorned with rich imported furnishings. Mahogany abounded. Colonel Fairfax's beautiful furniture symbolized his wealth and taste, but one element of the decor at Belvoir had greater resonance: a bust of Shakespeare reflected his love of literature.[3]

Belvoir's fine library provided another way for Colonel Fairfax to display his literary tastes to his guests. A library can do much more than decorative sculpture can. Not only does a well-stocked library symbolize its owner's passion for literature, it also provides a way to gratify that passion. Containing geographies, histories, law books, and works on commerce, horticulture, and travel, the library at Belvoir revealed Colonel Fairfax's wide-ranging intellectual interests. The keen-eyed and quick-witted traveler Andrew Burnaby, who met the family during his stay in Virginia, observed that Colonel Fairfax had "a competent knowledge, not only of the classics, but of the modern languages."[4]

The books at Belvoir verify Burnaby's observation. Colonel Fairfax owned an English-Latin dictionary, a Latin-French dictionary, and a Spanish-English dictionary. His collection also included a copy of Giles Jacob's *New Law-Dictionary*, an authoritative legal reference that could be found in the libraries of many colonial American lawyers.[5] A seven-hundred-page folio, Jacob's dictionary was a hefty work. An eighteenth-century British novelist has a character defend himself by wielding a copy of Jacob's dictionary as a cudgel.[6]

Colonel Fairfax also owned a copy of another sturdy reference work, John Harris's *Lexicon Technicum; or, An Universal English Dictionary of*

Arts and Sciences. Though called a dictionary, Harris's work more closely resembles an encyclopedia. One of the first books demonstrating the significance of Newtonian science, Harris's *Lexicon* is considered the earliest English encyclopedia. It formed the prototype for the more famous encyclopedias from across the English Channel that emerged during the Enlightenment.

Harris found illustrations essential to his *Lexicon Technicum* and criticized other lexicographers for omitting them.[7] Though numerous, the illustrations in *Lexicon Technicum* give it a curious appearance. They can be subdivided into two basic types: diagrams of mathematical and mechanical proofs and illustrations of heraldic symbols. Harris implicitly equates the ability to read a geometric proof and the ability to read a coat of arms, reinforcing the traditional connection between knowledge and class.

Impressed with this encyclopedic work, Washington would add a copy of Harris's *Lexicon* to his own library.[8] His copy remained in the Washington family until Willis P. Hazard, a Pennsylvania antiquarian, acquired it at auction in 1876. The volume changed hands several times since, but it has now returned to Mount Vernon. In a letter pasted inside its front cover, Hazard goes to great lengths to demonstrate that the book did indeed come from Washington's library, though it lacks the tell-tale autograph and bookplate. Hazard neglected other evidence of Washington's ownership in the volume. Several entries in the Mount Vernon copy of Harris's *Lexicon* are annotated in Washington's hand.

Though brief, these annotations show Washington's mind at work. The entry for "Lever," for instance, begins: "Lever is the Second *Mechanical Power*; and so considered, is only a *Balance* supported by a *Hypomochlion*." That last word gave Washington pause—but only for a moment. He quickly realized that Harris's *Lexicon* itself contained the answer and turned back several leaves to the H section and looked up the word. In the field of mechanics, Washington learned, a hypomochlion was a prop placed under a lever to give it leverage—in short, a fulcrum. The word "prop" was more commonly used in Harris's time than "fulcrum." After reading the entry for hypomochlion, Washington turned back to the L section and wrote "prop" in the margin adjacent to the entry for lever, clarifying what the word "hypomochlion" meant.

Washington did not stop there. It was not enough for him to learn these basic mechanical terms. He also wanted to understand the mathematics underlying them. He turned to the M section and read "Mechanicks." This article contains an illustration showing the placement of a fulcrum beneath a lever and contrasting the travel of one arm of the lever with the distance traveled by the other. To help himself understand the mathematics,

Washington annotated the diagram, identifying the arcs, or "spaces," inscribed by both arms of the lever.

Some of the books from Colonel Fairfax's collection Washington read at Belvoir. Others he brought to Mount Vernon, where he read them at his leisure. The copy of William Leybourn's *Complete Surveyor* Washington read was Fairfax's copy. He found the book so useful that he hesitated to return it. Cataloguing the Mount Vernon library years later, Washington discovered that he still possessed Fairfax's copy of Leybourn. Other books he borrowed from Belvoir he returned more promptly.[9]

Beyond what he learned from reading individual volumes in Colonel Fairfax's library, Washington saw how a man's books could reflect his personality. The Belvoir library displayed the colonel as a sophisticated and cultured gentleman, someone involved in local politics but aware of the world at large, in touch with the present but cognizant of the past. He was not a lawyer, but he had a good understanding of the law, good enough to serve him in his role as justice on the bench of the General Court of Virginia. He was not a clergyman, but he had a good understanding of divinity. His scientific knowledge was mainly practical: he knew what he needed to cultivate his garden. He had a healthy curiosity about political and economic theory but sometimes enjoyed poetry. In short, the colonel's broad intellectual outlook gave Washington an attitude to emulate.

Given the proximity of Belvoir and Mount Vernon, close ties developed between the Fairfaxes and the Washingtons. Lawrence Washington married Colonel Fairfax's daughter Anne. Two of her brothers, George William and Bryan, became good friends with George Washington. George William Fairfax's wife, Sarah (Sally), also became close friends with George Washington, a little too close, some said. But Colonel Fairfax, more than any other family member, was responsible for giving George Washington the chance to better himself. Washington's friendship with the colonel confirms Burnaby's impression: "Mr. William Fairfax was a gentleman of very fine accomplishments, and general good character. He was a kind husband, an indulgent parent, a faithful friend, a sincere Christian, and was eminently distinguished for his private and public virtues."[10]

Indebted to Colonel Fairfax's friendship, Washington recommended to his brother Jack that he make friends with the family. George's advice reveals his own relationship with the colonel:

I should be glad to hear that you live in perfect Harmony and good fellowship with the family at Belvoir, as it is in their power to be very serviceable upon many occasions to us as young beginners: I woud advise your visiting there often as one Step towards it. The rest, if any more is necessary, your own good sense will sufficiently dictate; for to that Family I am under many obligations particularly to the old Gentleman.[11]

Colonel Fairfax approached his position as land agent for the Northern Neck with the responsibility it demanded, something his predecessor "King" Carter had not always done. As his regal nickname suggests, Carter had a voracious appetite for land, which led him into some irresponsible and unscrupulous practices when it came to managing the proprietary. When his surveyors located good tracts of land, Carter patented them in his name or his children's.[12] Colonel Fairfax carried out his responsibilities as land agent more diligently but ran into problems due to the disputed boundaries of the proprietary.

Lord Fairfax persuaded the Privy Council in London to order a survey that would settle the boundary dispute once and for all. The survey concluded that the lands under his lordship's control amounted to more than five million acres—around twice as much land than previously assumed. Many found this startling conclusion hard to accept; Lord Fairfax spent eight years pressing his case before the Board of Trade and the Privy Council, which finally upheld the survey's conclusions in 1745. Two years later he emigrated to Virginia, moved in with his cousin at Belvoir, and began overseeing the proprietary himself.

Since Lord Fairfax's responsibilities as proprietor involved granting vacant land throughout the Northern Neck, he created a considerable need for surveyors, an ideal situation for George Washington, who first met his lordship at Belvoir. Impressed with this ambitious teen, Fairfax encouraged him to pursue his surveying career. Washington subsequently helped survey and map two properties in the Shenandoah Valley where Lord Fairfax settled: Greenway Court and Leeds Manor.

These names pay homage to his aristocratic heritage. Lord Fairfax named Greenway Court after a small holding in Kent, which the family had used as a retreat.[13] And Leeds Manor echoes the name of the castle where he was born. Washington was impressed. Like his cousin, Lord Fairfax gave Washington an example of a prosperous and cultured country gentleman.

Lord Fairfax first developed a reputation for his taste in literature while a student at Oxford. Living in London after college, he moved in the best literary circles. Andrew Burnaby said he contributed articles to *The Spectator*.[14] Burnaby's statement has never been substantiated, but it does support his lordship's general association with quality literature. Though few surviving documents reveal the extent of Lord Fairfax's writing, much evidence shows the extent of his reading. Taken together, subscription lists, his estate inventory, and known volumes from his library present a vivid picture of his literary world. The subscription lists, for example, hint that he read ancient classics in English translation, biography, devotional literature, essays, history, and natural history.

Before studying Lord Fairfax's love of books any further, a question: Do subscription lists really indicate the literary tastes of their subscribers? Not all the books Lord Fairfax subscribed to are known, but those that are reveal a pattern. The earliest book he subscribed to was *The History of Kent* by the encyclopedist John Harris. When this book appeared in 1719, Fairfax, one of the most prominent citizens in Kent, was almost duty-bound to subscribe to such a local history—regardless whether he intended to read it. Most of the other English books Lord Fairfax subscribed to appeared during the eight-year period he spent in London awaiting the Lords of Trade and the Privy Council to validate his claims regarding the boundaries of the Northern Neck proprietary. With spare time on his hands, he immersed himself in London's literary scene.

When Lord Fairfax subscribed to the Reverend Dr. Leonard Twells's *Twenty-Four Sermons*, which Twells had presented as Boyle lectures in the late 1730s, he requested the more expensive royal-paper edition. His request indicates the pleasure luxurious objects gave him. Royal paper, a type of large-format paper that created stately volumes with wide, creamy margins, provided a way to enhance a book's physical appearance.

Though it is tempting to see the books Lord Fairfax subscribed to as reflections of his literary taste, they clash with inferences drawn from his estate inventory. Those who inventoried estates in the eighteenth century often recorded individual book titles. Whoever inventoried Lord Fairfax's estate followed the practice, listing the titles of the books in his library at the time of his death. The inventory lists none of the London imprints he subscribed to. If his lordship cared so much for his subscription copies, why didn't he keep them?

Lord Fairfax must have left his books in England when he moved to Virginia. Well, that is the most obvious theory. But it does seem strange that a literary man permanently moving to colonial America, a land where books were sometimes hard to come by, would leave his library behind him. Besides, this theory cannot account for the absence of one book Lord Fairfax subscribed to while living in Virginia: Griffith Hughes's *Natural History of Barbados*, a folio adorned with many handsome engravings.[15] In contrast, Colonel Fairfax, who also subscribed to Hughes's

Natural History, kept his copy all his life. Subscription copies may indicate a subscriber's literary tastes, but there were many possible reasons why someone in the eighteenth century might subscribe to a book, not all of which involved reading.

The subscription list in Hughes's *Natural History* reveals the social contexts of literary subscription. Hughes's list of subscribers contains a special section: "Subscribers from Virginia." The rector of Saint Lucy Parish in Barbados, Hughes published the book himself and financed its publication by arranging as many subscriptions as possible. He deliberately sought out the wealthiest and most powerful Virginians to support his venture. As word went round Virginia, subscribing to Hughes's *Natural History of Barbados* became a sign of social prestige. Ultimately thirty-three Virginians subscribed.

When Hughes published the book, he organized the list of British subscribers alphabetically but ranked the Virginia subscribers in order of social class, Lord Fairfax's name coming first. Securing his lordship's commitment, Hughes gave the project an aura of prestige that helped him gather more Virginia subscribers. Far from being a gauge of reading tastes, a list of subscribers was a reflection of social status, something to keep in mind when it comes to analyzing books Washington subscribed to as well.

The list of Virginia subscribers to Hughes's *Natural History of Barbados* not only reads like a who's who in the colony, it also reads like a who's where in the social order. As a member of both the Fairfax family and the Virginia Council, Colonel Fairfax came second, followed by John Robinson, president of the council. Sadly, Robinson passed away before Hughes's book appeared. The Reverend Dr. William Dawson, a member of the council and president of the College of William and Mary, came fourth. The remaining twenty-nine names appear in the following order: colonels, majors, esquires, and misters.

Though the absence of Lord Fairfax's subscription copies from the estate inventory could indicate that he left them in England, the absence of Hughes's *Natural History* suggests an alternate fate for the missing books. So, too, does the absence of another book from Lord Fairfax's library that survived into the twentieth century, a copy of Robert Beverley's *History of Virginia* inscribed by its author.[16]

Here's a new theory: Lord Fairfax magnanimously presented many of his books to Virginia friends and neighbors before his death. When he died in 1781, his library contained 131 volumes, more than most private libraries in Virginia, but far fewer than the best. Roughly speaking, the books in Lord Fairfax's library at his death fall into two categories:

reference works and pleasure reading. Perhaps both can be subsumed into one general category: books he could read repeatedly.

The largest work at Greenway Court was the twenty-volume *Universal History*, which may seem dry as dust by its title but which offered Lord Fairfax and his houseguests much pleasure reading. George Saintsbury found the *Universal History* "full of good matter well put" and said, "One might be very happy with it (the standard test) in the country inn on wet afternoons."[17] Lord Fairfax also owned at least two different collections of Virginia laws and two copies of Philip Miller's *Gardeners Dictionary*, an authoritative work Washington would add to his agricultural collection. In addition Fairfax had several volumes recording the names of government officials throughout Great Britain and its colonies and documenting political activity in the metropolis.

The remainder of Lord Fairfax's library is belletristic in nature. He had Jonathan Swift's works in thirteen volumes, and, if those were not enough, a copy of the Earl of Orrery's *Remarks on the Life and Writings of Dr. Jonathan Swift*—a work suggesting he took an interest in literary criticism, too. Confirming his critical interests, the works of Nicolas Boileau-Despréaux, France's foremost literary critic of the seventeenth century, also graced the shelves of Greenway Court.

Lord Fairfax owned many novels, including some of the century's best. Though his subscriber's copy of Henry Fielding's *Miscellanies* disappeared before his death, he acquired three novels by the same author and one by his sister Sarah Fielding. He also had a copy of Tobias Smollett's *Adventures of Peregrine Pickle*, two novels by Charlotte Lennox, and many anonymous novels. Like the reference books that remained with them until his lordship's death, these novels were works he could read over and over again.

When Washington visited Greenway Court in 1748, Lord Fairfax's library remained fairly modest. He could not have had *Peregrine Pickle*, first published in 1751, but he could have had Henry Fielding's *Joseph Andrews*, first published in 1742. Since so many of the novels at Greenway Court date from the early 1750s, they suggest that within a half dozen years after settling in Virginia, Lord Fairfax was busy constructing a literary world for himself in the Shenandoah.

Lord Fairfax's portrait, painted late in life, confirms this view. He appears with a book in his hand, his right thumb holding his place midway through the volume. His physical position conveys his impatience with the portrait painter. Hurry up and finish painting, he seems to say, so I can get back to my book. Lord Fairfax represented for Washington a man who made literature a vital part of his life.

Washington recorded his 1748 trip to Greenway Court in a pocket notebook, which he continued to use for miscellaneous memoranda upon returning home. Two consecutive notes he made concern his reading. "I read to the Reign of K: John," he wrote first, followed by, "In the Spectators Read to No 143."[18] The earlier note initially seems too vague to identify; the second reflects Washington's characteristic precision. In the edition of *The Spectator* he owned—the 1745 Glasgow edition—essay no. 143 appears partway through the second volume. So Washington read through the first volume and liked the work well enough to start the second. Presumably, he read the other volumes another time or, at least, dipped into them occasionally. Isaac Watts found all eight volumes of *The Spectator* filled with "so many valuable remarks for our conduct in life, that they are not improper to lie in parlours, or summer-houses, or places of usual residence, to entertain our thoughts in any moments of leisure, or vacant hours that occur."[19]

The Spectator contained much to allure Washington. Working together to create this essay series, Joseph Addison and Richard Steele invented a charming persona to comment on current events and observe contemporary behavior. Mr. Spectator is a keen-eyed London observer who describes what he sees with amusement and gently castigates what deserves castigating. Besides being a good observer, he is also a good listener. Well read and well traveled, he retains a thirst for knowledge. He is both self-confident and convivial. The coffeehouse is his office and his club room, the place where he makes friends and tests out ideas.

The first 143 numbers contain some of the best writing in the series. Topics covered include public credit (no. 3), popular superstition (no. 7), and the meaning of wit (no. 35). *Spectator* no. 25 retells the fable of Jupiter and the Countryman. To reward the countryman for his piety, Jupiter promises him whatever he wishes. The countryman wishes to control the weather on his own estate. Jupiter agrees, and the countryman distributes rain, snow, and sunshine around his farms as he sees fit. At the year's end, he discovers his harvest is much smaller than that of his neighbors, so he asks Jupiter to retake control of the weather before he ruins himself. Washington remembered what he read in *The Spectator*. During the Revolutionary War, he would recall this fable as a lesson against depending on Providence to grant the Continental Army's wishes: "Providence has done—and I am perswaded is disposed to do—a great deal for us, but we are not to forget the fable of Jupiter and the Countryman."[20]

Several numbers of *The Spectator* feature Sir Roger de Coverley, who belongs to the same club as Mr. Spectator. Sir Roger usually lives in the country but comes to London sporadically to enjoy the club life and experience what the city has to offer. Pleasant, obliging, easygoing, mirthful, he also possesses a wealth of common sense. Though a fictional character, Sir Roger gave Washington another model of the ideal country gentleman.

Sir Roger does have his weaknesses, however. He is especially sensitive when it comes to matters of the heart, as *Spectator* no. 113 indicates. One day Mr. Spectator and Sir Roger are walking through some woods near the de Coverley estate. Sir Roger grows melancholy as they proceed, admitting that years earlier he used to visit this part of the woods to think about the young widow who had broken his heart. When Sir Roger's thoughts now turn to her, he again becomes obsessed and almost starts raving about the woman he once loved. Mr. Spectator feels helpless as he watches his friend descend into a near-manic state of obsession. To close the essay, Mr. Spectator finds one of Martial's epigrams appropriate:

> Let Rufus weep, rejoice, stand, sit, or walk,
> Still he can nothing but of Naevia talk;
> Let him eat, drink, ask questions, or dispute,
> Still he must speak of Naevia, or be mute.
> He writ his father, ending with this line,
> I am, my lovely Naevia, ever thine.

This essay has often been read as an object lesson in the dangers of falling in love. Washington did not necessarily interpret it as such, or, if he did, he also recognized other ramifications. He interpreted it as a lesson on the dangers of one man's becoming obsessed with an idea and being unable to break his obsession or see another's point of view. Washington would remember Martial's lines from *The Spectator* and apply them many years later.[21]

By *Spectator* no. 122, Sir Roger has recovered his equanimity. He and Mr. Spectator once again find themselves traveling through the countryside near the de Coverley estate. They encounter two men arguing over the right to fish a nearby stream. Given his local leadership and reputation for justice, Sir Roger agrees to mediate their dispute. After hearing both sides, he concludes "with the air of a man who would not give his judgment rashly, that much might be said on both sides."

Returning to his estate at the day's end, Sir Roger and Mr. Spectator stop for refreshments at a local inn. The innkeeper, previously a servant in Sir Roger's household, has honored his former employer by creating a sign in his likeness, the sign of "The Knight's Head." Sir Roger politely explains that the sign is inappropriate, so the innkeeper quickly repaints it, modifying the facial features, adding some whiskers, and rechristening it "The Saracen's Head." To some eyes Sir Roger's face remained discernible beneath the Saracen's. Sir Roger frankly asks Mr. Spectator what he sees as he looks at the sign, his head or the Saracen's? Mr. Spectator hems and haws, but, pressed for an answer, he responds, "Much might be said on both sides."

The phrase that Sir Roger articulates and Mr. Spectator repeats would come to exemplify Washington's approach to conflict: to weigh two opposing sides of an issue and see the positive aspects of both. *Spectator* no. 122 demonstrates the pleasurable utility of such periodical essays. Washington liked *The Spectator* well enough to add another major periodical essay series to his personal library, *The Guardian*. The handwriting style of the ownership inscription in his copy suggests that Washington acquired *The Guardian* when he was around seventeen.[22] Also written by Addison and Steele, *The Guardian* is second only to *The Spectator* in the history of British periodical essays. *The Guardian* explores charity, honor, justice, knowledge, and many other ideas central to contemporary conduct literature.

This particular edition of *The Guardian* has an excellent index, which enhances the usefulness of the work, transforming it into a handy reference. *Guardian* no. 161, for instance, is indexed under the word "honour." The index assigns this essay a title: "A Discourse upon True Honour." *Guardian* no. 161 observes, "The Sense of Honour is of so fine and delicate a Nature, that it is only to be met with in Minds which are naturally Noble, or in such as have been cultivated by great Examples, or a refined Education."[23] Like so much else that Washington read in his late teens, *The Guardian* emphasized the importance of examples for developing worthy personal qualities. Washington took to heart what *The Guardian* had to say. His sense of honor would become a defining personal characteristic.

Since Washington noted precisely where he stopped reading *The Spectator*, the note he made about reading English history seems vague in comparison. Actually, it's not. His note about reading "to the Reign of K: John," may seem to refer to almost any history of England, but it is nearly as specific as Washington's reference to reading *The Spectator*. "The Reign of King John" is the title of a chapter in Richard Baker's *Chronicle of the Kings of England*. Washington did not mention Baker's title in his notebook because he did not need to: it was the most popular history of England in the early eighteenth century.[24]

Baker's *Chronicle* first appeared in 1693 and went through eleven editions to 1733. The work became a fixture in homes across Great Britain and throughout the colonies. Henry Fielding called it "the great Favourite of my Youth."[25] In *The Spectator* Sir Roger de Coverley keeps a copy of Baker's *Chronicle* prominently displayed in his hall window. He reads the work often and draws pertinent observations from it. Virginia gentlemen followed Sir Roger's lead. William Byrd II, for instance, had a copy in his library at Westover and drew many observations from it.[26]

Baker offered Washington much in terms of information, outlook, and example. Opening with a description of the earliest known times in Britain, he imposed a scholarly rigor on his materials, discounting quasi-fictional accounts and excluding "such stuff which may please Children, but not riper Judgments."[27] The story of King Arthur, whose life has been more highly embellished than that of any other English king, Baker told in a single paragraph. He ignored the rich legends surrounding King Arthur's life but honored him for instituting the Knights of the Round Table, which effectively eliminated all questions concerning precedence, teaching "heroical Minds not to stand upon Place, but Merit."[28]

King Alfred, in contrast, receives much more attention. In the face of hardship, Alfred spent his time "learning Policy from Adversity, and gathering Courage from Misery." He had great discipline, dividing the day into three equal periods, one for contemplation, reading, and prayer; another for health and recreation; and the last for affairs of state. Baker praised Alfred for his piety and his learning. Alfred encouraged the development of education to make sure British youth would be "trained to know God, to be men of Understanding, and to live happily."[29]

Starting with William the Conqueror, from whom all subsequent British kings have descended, Baker devoted separate chapters to each. Like Alfred, King William appears as an ideal ruler. After proving himself "a valiant General in War," he became "a provident Governour in Peace." While praising King William, Baker did not hesitate to critique some of his actions. Requiring all legal documents to be written in French "upon a Pretence to dignify the *French* tongue," William really sought "to intrap Men thro' Ignorance of the Language." Law French, as it became known, would remain the language of the British legal system for centuries. In other legal matters, however, King William was exemplary. He was the one, Baker asserted, who "brought in the trial by the Verdict of twelve Men."[30]

It is not hard to see why Washington stopped reading Baker's *Chronicle* where he did. The chapter before "The Reign of King John" relates the life and reign of King Richard I, which reads like a comedy of errors. Soon after ascending to the throne, Richard led thirty thousand men on a crusade to the Holy Land, an enormously expensive endeavor that stretched Britain's finances thin. Taken prisoner in Europe on his return journey, Richard required Britain to pay an exorbitant ransom for his release, virtually exhausting the nation's greatly depleted coffers.

Toward the conclusion of the chapter, Baker incongruously praises King Richard. Explaining why he was known as Richard the Lionheart, Baker calls him valiant, but also stresses his fairness, mercy, piety, and wisdom. Inadvertently, the chapter contrasts King Richard's self-centered actions during his life and his posthumous reputation for courage and wisdom. This disparity appears to have been too much for George Washington to stomach. After reading about Richard the Lionheart, he quit reading Baker's *Chronicle* altogether.

Washington continued enlarging his personal library in his teens. In 1747 he purchased from his kinsman Bailey Washington a fifty-year-old pamphlet: Hippolyte du Chastelet de Luzancy's *Panegyrick to the Memory of His Grace Frederick, Late Duke of Schonberg*.[31] Considered one of the finest military minds of the seventeenth century, the Duke of Schomberg, as his name is typically spelled, gave Washington an example of another leader devoted to his principles. Schomberg established his reputation as a marshal in the French army, but when France revoked the Edict of Nantes, Schomberg left for Berlin, where he became the leader of the Huguenot refugees. When the Prince of Orange made his famous expedition to England in 1688, Schomberg joined him as second in command. He served the remainder of his life as a general in the English army.

The panegyric reminded Washington of his educational deficiencies. "Education makes us truly what we are," de Luzancy observed, calling it the "Foundation of Great Actions." Washington may not have been able to match Schomberg's education, but he could aspire to his physical prowess. De Luzancy continued: "He had a Robust, and Strong Body, capable of the greatest Hardships. He was Naturally Active, a great lover of Exercise, Healthful and Temperate to Admiration. He neither Courted nor Fear'd Danger; ever Himself, ever Fortunate, ever preventing the worst, and Surmounting the greatest Difficulties." These words sound almost like a description of George Washington.[32]

De Luzancy also had great respect for Schomberg's sense of responsibility: "His Duty was his greatest Passion; and the discharge of the Noble Trusts put into his hands, his only pleasure."[33] One additional piece of evidence verifies Washington's ongoing respect for the Duke of Schomberg: he named a slave Schomberg. Though the act of naming a slave scarcely sounds like an honor, it was not uncommon for Virginia slaveholders to name slaves after figures from history they respected. Washington had another slave named Caesar.

The evidence suggests that the teenaged Washington enjoyed reading, but he did not spend all his time at Belvoir with his nose stuck in a book. Far from it; he was quite smitten with a young female member of the Fairfax family, presumably Mary Cary, George William Fairfax's sister-in-law. This "very agreeable Young Lady," Washington told a friend, "in a great Measure cheers my sorrow and dejectedness."[34]

Mary was one of several girls on whom Washington set his heart in his boyhood, a group that also included Frances Alexander and a young woman only known to history as the "Low Land Beauty." It may seem incongruous to picture George Washington as a love-struck teen, but, like young Roger de Coverley's, his heart was apparently quite fragile in his youth. When a pretty girl rebuffed him, Washington turned away from love and looked toward loftier pursuits—until the next pretty girl came along.

Two love poems, or, to be precise, two attempts at love poetry survive among the miscellaneous notes Washington kept in the late 1740s. His editors question whether he wrote them. Though they contain imagery and diction characteristic of much Augustan verse, more and more the poems seem like his compositions. The speaker of the first poem, having surrendered to "Cupid's feather'd Dart," is left bleeding in the face of a pitiless lover. At night he seeks "soft lulling sleep and gentle repose" through which he may "possess those joys denied by Day."[35]

The second poem is an acrostic to Frances Alexander, the first letter of each line formed from her name. Washington made it through the hardest line—"X"—but abandoned the task after one more line, leaving the last four letters of her name without corresponding lines of verse. For the X-line, he referred to the wealthy Persian ruler Xerxes, who was not "free from Cupid's Dart." Perhaps Washington's reuse of the Cupid cliché helped him realize he was not cut out for poetry.

Despite their mediocrity, these poems reveal that Washington recognized poetry as a way of articulating emotion. His reference to Xerxes now seems the most significant aspect of these poems, at least in terms of Washington's personal outlook. Best known for his invasion of Greece, Xerxes and his massive Persian army came up against the three hundred Spartans at Thermopylae. Led by Leonidas, the Spartans resisted Persian advances for three days straight and were only defeated when a traitor led the Persians down a secret path. Technically Xerxes won the battle, but the three hundred Spartans are remembered for their bravery, dedication, and fortitude.

Herodotus's history provides the fullest account of Xerxes's invasion of Greece. Washington reveals his familiarity with the invasion elsewhere in his papers. During the Revolutionary War, he used "Leonidas" as the parole one night and "Thermopylae" another. Washington also named one of his horses Leonidas.[36] Xerxes's defeats actually provide more valuable lessons than his victories. All Xerxes's riches could not defeat a nation with superior knowledge of war and naval expertise. The story of Xerxes's ultimate defeat encouraged Washington to further his own knowledge of war.

Washington's personal contact with the Fairfaxes in his mid to late teens and the books he read at that age influenced him similarly. Much as Lord Fairfax and Colonel Fairfax provided models for him to emulate, the books Washington read provided many exemplary figures on which he could pattern his life. Eliza Haywood suggested that books, especially history books, help us discover which behaviors to emulate and which to avoid. In the character of Sir Roger de Coverley, *The Spectator* provided the model of the British country gentleman. And in the works of Baker, de Luzancy, and Herodotus, Washington could read about different leaders and styles of leadership. The men Washington met and those he read about in his teens would significantly shape the man he would become.

CHAPTER 4

Travel Writing

Learning is acquired by reading books; but the much more necessary learning, the knowledge of the world, is only to be acquired by reading men, and studying all the various editions of them.

Earl of Chesterfield, *Letters to His Son*

During his 1748 surveying trip to the Shenandoah, George Washington kept a journal, which vividly displays his personal outlook at sixteen. A blend of unusual incident and quotidian detail, this, his earliest known journal, reveals Washington's curiosity, literary taste, and love of the land. The content of his journal resembles the travel books in his teenage library. In other words, what Washington wrote reflects what he liked to read.

Previously he had traveled little, but his first trip to the Shenandoah opened his eyes to the vast potential of the American continent. The journal shows him appreciating the land to the west in terms of both agriculture and aesthetics, its bounty and its beauty. One page records with delight a handsome grove of sugar maples; another conveys his perception of the richness and fertility of the soil, its nearly boundless capacity for growing grain, hemp, and tobacco.

Washington's limited backwoods experience led him into some embarrassing greenhorn mistakes. Given a choice between sleeping outdoors on the ground and sleeping indoors in a bed one night, he chose in over out. As his fellow surveyors stayed outside, he entered a rustic cabin, certain he had made the better bargain. Relating the episode in his journal, Washington created an incisive, albeit self-effacing portrait. Once indoors he prepared for bed by removing his clothes in an orderly fashion. Climbing into bed, he discovered that it consisted of a few handfuls of straw loosely matted together. In lieu of bed sheet and quilt, a threadbare blanket supplied the only covers. Worse yet, the blanket was infested, in his words, with "double its Weight of Vermin such as Lice, Fleas, etc."[1] Though vermin-filled beds were a problem in some of colonial America's finest homes, the presence of lice and fleas in this tumbledown cabin reinforces the traditional association between poverty and pests.[2]

That evening Washington endured the creepy-crawly bedding as long as he could, but finally the bugs got the better of him. He stood up, unfolded his clothes, put them on, and went outdoors to spend the rest of the night sleeping on the ground with his companions, whom he undoubtedly found chuckling over his rookie mistake. In the future, Washington promised himself, he would sleep by a fire in the open air before he would ever sleep indoors under such squalid conditions.

During this wilderness experience, Washington grew accustomed to unexpected inconvenience. Coming to supper one day, his fellow surveyors found neither table linen nor silverware, but they seemed undaunted. As Washington told the story, the men hardly minded at all. They simply unsheathed their hunting knives and used them as impromptu eating utensils. Forced to eat without plates another day, they used big chips of wood instead. Washington's account of the incident celebrates the joys of camping.

Their campsite that evening marked the edge of civilization. Though they chose a site in some woods near a wild meadow, the meadow contained a large haystack, which let them feed their horses and soften their camp beds. Once they pitched the tents and built a large fire, they prepared for dinner. It was every man for himself that evening. The men skewered venison steaks with forked sticks, broiled them, and then plated the steaks on some slab-like wood chips.

The fullest entry in Washington's 1748 journal concerns an encounter with a Native American war party. In late March a group of Indians returning from a campaign surprised him and the others—pleasantly surprised them, that is. The Indians greeted the surveyors cordially but could not mask their disappointment with the recent war campaign, having obtained only one scalp, a gruesome fact Washington noted with nonchalance. Loosening up after a few drinks, the Indians agreed to demonstrate a war dance. Washington recorded the event in detail: his journal entry constitutes an important firsthand account of Native American music and dance.[3]

Upon clearing a large circle, the Indians built a bonfire in the middle. They seated themselves around it before one made a grand speech, telling the others how to dance. Once he finished, the best dancer among them jumped up like someone instantly awoken from a deep sleep and darted about the ring in a comical manner. The other dancers followed suit, all performing with vigorous musical accompaniment. One of the musicians pounded a drum made from deerskin stretched tightly across a pot half filled with water. Another rattled a gourd filled with shot and adorned with a piece of a horse's tail. The drummer drummed, the rattler rattled, the dancers danced, and the teenaged Washington watched, enthralled.[4]

As much as the journal entry reveals about Native American customs, it may say more about Washington's personality. Besides registering his fascination with the folkways of others, it shows his recognition that such customs should be recorded for posterity. The journal entry further indicates his meticulousness. Having made up his mind to record the episode, he did so in detail, capturing both sound and image, going as far as to note precisely how the Indians crafted their musical instruments. Teenage journals typically contain maudlin personal reflections. Washington's account of Native American dance shows that recording the remarkable behavior of others was more important than capturing his personal thoughts.

After returning from the Shenandoah, Washington fueled his new-found interest in travel by reading. According to the handwriting style of his ownership inscriptions, he acquired several books of travel in his late teens. Travel literature taught him much about the behavior and customs of people from around the globe.

Daniel Defoe's four-volume *Tour through the Whole Island of Great Britain* was the most substantial work of travel literature in Washington's small but growing library. Defoe originally published his *Tour* in the mid-1720s. Washington owned the 1748 edition, that is, the one revised and expanded by Samuel Richardson, the author of *Pamela*. Each volume in Washington's surviving copy contains brief marginal notes and corrections consistent with those in other books from his library. Most of the marks correct typographical errors. A list of shires in Scotland in the fourth volume, for instance, contains the name "Dumbar." Washington supplied the missing suffix in manuscript, changing the place name to "Dumbarton."[5]

More substantial manuscript annotations occur in the second volume. At one point, Defoe digresses on the British habit of "following Foreigners in most Things, even from the Coxcomb in Dress, up to the Historian," referring, for example, to "the Performance of a late foreign Author, of the Affairs and Transactions of this Country: whereby the Translator, and Undertakers, to usher it out in *English*, got, at least, 10,000*l*. when it had nothing more, but rather much less, to recommend it, than any of our own *English* Histories."[6] Washington underlined the phrase "late foreign Author" and wrote "Rapin" in the margin. He also underlined the word "Translator," whom he identified as "Tindal" in the margin. Washington knew Defoe was talking about Nicholas Tindal's translation of the *History of England* by Paul Rapin de Thoyras.

Rapin's *History of England* does not appear in any of the catalogues of Washington's library, nor is it mentioned in his papers. But he clearly knew the work. Rapin's *History* introduced many colonial American readers to Whig history. Though Washington is seldom recognized for his intellectual pursuits, his knowledge of Rapin's *History* suggests that he, too, read one of the fundamental works that shaped the thought of several Founding Fathers. Benjamin Franklin, for one, appreciated the thoroughness of Rapin's research and recognized the results of his patience: "The Author employed Seventeen Years in composing it, and as he had (by consulting the ancient Records of the Tower) much better Helps than any Historian that went before him, it is esteemed the best History of England yet published."[7]

Having partially read Richard Baker's *Chronicle of the Kings of England*, Washington was unwilling to leave his knowledge of English history there. He read Rapin to deepen his understanding. Rapin emphasizes the Saxon roots of liberal democracy and explains that Saxon kings could neither change the laws nor levy taxes at their will.

Elsewhere in the second volume of his *Tour through Great Britain*, Defoe mentions "the *Man-Devil* Doctrine, too successfully propagated of late Years, *That Private Vices are public Benefits*."[8] Though these phrases were italicized in Defoe's text already, Washington added further emphasis, underlining both "*Man-Devil*" and "*Private Vice are public Benefits*." He also wrote the words "Fable of the Bees" in the margin, acknowledging Defoe's reference to Bernard Mandeville's controversial treatise, *The Fable of the Bees; or, Private Vices, Publick Benefits*. Washington did not necessarily accept the idea that the pursuit of self-interest contributed to social progress and prosperity; few of the Founding Fathers did.[9] But his marginal note reveals his cognizance of Mandeville's argument.

Like Rapin's *History*, Mandeville's famous work is mentioned in neither Washington's library catalogue nor his surviving papers. The documentary evidence simply cannot tell the whole story of his literary life. The book culture of colonial Virginia involved much borrowing and lending. Friends loaned Washington copies of books like Rapin and Mandeville, and he loaned friends books from his personal collection. The story of Washington's reading extends well beyond the walls of his library.

Virginia Woolf called Defoe's *Tour through Great Britain* "the sort of book one can read all day, turning the pages as a sheep eats grass."[10] Washington's marginalia in his copy of Defoe's *Tour* suggests that he enjoyed it similarly, that is, with relaxation and patience. His thorough typographical corrections show that he read the four-volume work page by page, taking the time to read and ponder its text. The book taught him much about Great Britain and demonstrated the power of travel writing in the hands of a master.

In the early eighteenth century it was not unusual for the title of a book about a particular geographic region to begin with the phrase "The History and Present State." In terms of its content, if not its form, Defoe's *Tour* resembles other contemporary works that described the present state of a nation: it minimizes British history to create an up-to-date picture of Great Britain. "Present state" books were more well-respected than travel writings. Robert Beverley, for instance, begins *The History and Present State of Virginia* with a critique of travel writing: "There are no Books (the Legends of Saints always excepted,) so stuff'd with Poetical Stories, as Voyages."[11]

The fact that Defoe titled and structured his work as a book of travels reflects his confidence in the genre. Furthermore, a book of travels gave Defoe more freedom than either a history or a "present state." He did not have to dwell on detail, to count the population, gauge the rainfall, or measure the distance from one place to another. In terms of style Defoe's *Tour* comes closer to an essay or a memoir. The essay-like form gave him the freedom to cultivate a personal voice within his national account.

Defoe omitted from his story much that was old-fashioned or outmoded. He staunchly avoided explaining natural phenomena in religious terms. *Tour through Great Britain* is a thoroughly secular narrative. Instead of characterizing natural occurrences as instances of "remarkable providence," he saw them for what they were. Relating what had happened to the cathedral at Chichester, for instance, he explained how lightning had blasted a huge hole in the spire but left both cathedral and spire standing. The cathedral survived not because of divine providence but because it was "an admirably sound and well-finished Piece of Workmanship."[12] Man, not God, was the creator responsible for the survival of Chichester cathedral.

Tour through Great Britain also critiques the stilted, highly artificial writing style that had influenced earlier topographical literature. Defoe especially disliked ornate poetic diction and pastoral imagery. Emphasizing the natural beauty of Salisbury Plain, he used the kind of language that came naturally. Before describing the Thames, he said he would exclude the fanciful detail poets preferred. Instead he would stress what really made the river glorious: its bridges, docks, fortifications, hospitals, and public buildings.

Defoe wrote *Tour through Great Britain* in clear, crisp engaging prose. He stripped away all artifice from the story of Great Britain because he knew the nation could stand on its own without it. So, too, could its language. Not only does *Tour through Great Britain* champion the British nation, it also celebrates the English language. Defoe preferred words derived from Anglo-Saxon over those from Latin. Describing a coastal landmark in Devonshire known as Hercules's Promontory, he expressed his dislike of this Latinate name, calling it what forthright sailors and plain country people called it: "Hartland Point" or, even better, "Hearty Point."[13] Modern, muscular English, he saw, provided the best way to describe modern, secular England. Defoe's straightforward prose influenced Washington's writing style, as his subsequent travel journals demonstrate.[14]

Tour through Great Britain cherishes British foodways. Describing his visit to Cheddar, Defoe emphasized the excellence of the cheese that takes its name from the village. Traveling through the North Midlands, he stopped for refreshment and enjoyed some Yorkshire ale, which he found nearly perfect.[15] George Washington, too, enjoyed strong British ale and aged English cheese: Defoe's *Tour* reinforced his tastes. With its contrary qualities—its smooth texture and sharp taste—double Gloucester was Washington's favorite kind of cheese. The annual orders he sent to Great Britain before the American Revolution include sizeable quantities of both cheese and ale.

Though devoted to Great Britain, Defoe's *Tour* contains much that appealed to colonial Virginia readers. Volume 4 discusses Scotland, which played a major role in both the history and present state of Virginia. Considering the number of Scots who had emigrated there in search of opportunity, Defoe observed, "*Virginia* may be rather called a *Scots* than an *English* Plantation."[16] He also said that the port of Glasgow was ideally suited for importing from and exporting to Virginia. To Defoe's eye, the Virginia trade had helped make Glasgow the finest city in Great Britain after London. Overall Defoe's discussion of Scotland verifies how essential the story of Virginia was to the history of Great Britain.

In light of the American Revolution Washington's copy of Defoe's *Tour through Great Britain* takes on further significance. Among eighteenth-century readers Defoe's book fostered a great fondness for the British nation. He painted a charming portrait, displaying what made Great Britain great. Defoe's Britain is a delightful place filled with industrious people who exemplify their nation's finest qualities. As a young man, Washington ardently desired to visit England.[17] Rebelling against Defoe's Britain was a difficult thing for him to do. The presence of Defoe's *Tour* in Washington's library shows that when he rebelled against Great Britain, he rebelled against a nation that represented much he loved.

Additional books in his library taught Washington about different parts of the world. *A Compleat History of the Piratical States of Barbary*, which he also acquired in his late teens, combines an English translation of Laugier de Tassy's *Histoire du Royaume d'Alger* with other pertinent matter. The English title identifies the work as a history, but the book is more of a "present state," as its author admits in his preface. When it came to Algiers, he explained, "I have been the more concise, as to the Antiquity and Revolutions of this Kingdom, that I might give a circumstantial Detail of its present State."[18]

Though the title does not identify the book as a travel narrative, this history achieves authority from the fact that its author was an eyewitness to what he describes. The title page characterizes him as a "gentleman who resided there many years in a public character." Reinforcing his reliability, he asserts that travelers can provide a good perspective on the lands they visit. As soon as he makes this assertion, however, he modifies it, clarifying that he meant such business travelers as merchants and traders—those who travel for a reason—not those "giddy Travellers, who are sent abroad from their Father's Fire-side, merely to see fine Things."[19]

The nations of the Barbary Coast had previously received much negative press, but Laugier de Tassy appears notably open-minded toward Algiers and its neighbors. His preface concludes: "I have endeavoured to divest myself of all kind of Prejudice, in order to set the History of these States in a proper Light, that my Readers may form a true Judgment of them, by observing the Virtues and Vices which are blended in their Constitutions."[20] Washington, who made open-mindedness a personal trademark, appreciated the stance Laugier de Tassy took in his *Compleat History*. Perhaps the book helped determine Washington's attitude.

Commodore George Anson's *Voyage Round the World*, another work Washington acquired in his teens, was the most popular book of travel in colonial America.[21] Some contemporary readers associated it with *Robinson Crusoe* and *Gulliver's Travels:* all three captured the imagination of young readers yet gave them works they could return to as adults. The account of Anson's circumnavigation helped fill gaps in the geographical knowledge of its readers. They could follow his changes in latitude and longitude as he and his dwindling squadron circled the earth.

A Compleat *Washington*

HISTORY

OF THE

PIRATICAL STATES

OF

BARBARY,

VIZ.

Algiers, } { **Tripoli,** and
Tunis, } { **Morocco.**

CONTAINING

The Origin, Revolutions, and prefent State of
thefe Kingdoms, their Forces, Revenues, Policy,
and Commerce.

Illuftrated with a PLAN of *ALGIERS*,
and a MAP of *BARBARY*.

By a GENTLEMAN who refided there many Years in
a public Charaĉter.

LONDON:

Printed for R. GRIFFITHS, at the *Dunciad* in *St. Paul's
Church-Yard.* 1750.

Title page from George Washington's copy of *A Compleat History of the
Piratical States of Barbary* (1750). Boston Athenaeum.

The work let young readers practice using their globes as they traced his route. Goethe, for one, read the book as a boy, an experience he fondly recalled in his autobiography and one that many young eighteenth-century readers shared: "Lord Anson's *Voyage round the Globe* combined the dignity of truth with the rich fancies of fable; and, while our thoughts accompanied this excellent seaman, we were conducted over all the world, and endeavored to follow him with our fingers on the globe."[22]

Though typically called *Anson's Voyage*, the work was not written by Commodore Anson, who led the squadron sent on an expedition to the South Seas during the Anglo-Spanish War to attack Spanish vessels and Spain's colonial settlements. According to the book's title page, the Reverend Richard Walter, chaplain to the expedition, compiled the work, but Benjamin Robins, a mathematician and engineer, had a hand in its composition as well.[23]

Despite who wrote what, the preface to *Anson's Voyage* follows the critical dictates of the time, stressing that the book would both delight and instruct its readers. Though *Anson's Voyage* would tell a thrilling tale of adventure, it would also promote navigation, encourage commerce, and advance British national interests. Wherever possible, the narrative corrects misinformation from previous travelers. Most likely, Robins wrote the passages correcting previous nautical errors. And it must have been Robins who stressed the importance of a good geographical education.

Such emphases appealed to Washington. The narrator of *Anson's Voyage* laments "how very imperfect many of our accounts of distant countries are rendered by the relators being unskilled in drawing, and in the general principles of surveying."[24] These remarks confirmed the career path Washington had chosen and reinforced the value of surveying. Not only did it provide a way for a man to earn his living in the Virginia backcountry, it also gave him a skill useful for exploring faraway lands. Washington never used his knowledge of surveying for this second purpose, but it was a comfort to know he could.

The vivid imagery and moving vignettes of *Anson's Voyage* make it stand as one of the masterworks of British travel literature. The narrative of the adventures of Anson's crew paints a picture that combines astonishing beauty with darkly ominous detail, as the trying experiences the sailors undergo near Cape Horn demonstrate. Once the squadron passes the Le Maire Strait near the southern tip of South America, the men felt relieved, assuming the worst was behind them. They were wrong.

The work's humanity gives *Anson's Voyage* a touching aspect that quickens the blood and raises gooseflesh. It frequently mentions the number of men lost through danger and disease. Scurvy claimed more victims that any other single cause. Two-thirds of the way through the story, the narrator relates that only seventy-one men remained capable of duty, a chilling statistic: "This, inconsiderable as it may appear, was the whole force we could collect, in our present enfeebled condition, from the united crews of the *Centurion*, the *Gloucester*, and the *Tryal*, which, when we departed from *England*, consisted all together of near a thousand hands."[25]

Deaths from accident were much rarer than those by disease, but the narrative makes the accidental deaths more palpable. During shore leave, a falling tree killed one sailor. A sea lion killed another. A third died from drowning. The story of the drowning victim is heart-wrenching. Working to keep the ship safe during a hellacious storm, this seaman was washed overboard. Those who could see him in the water below were helpless to save him: "We perceived that notwithstanding the prodigious agitation of the waves, he swam very strong, and it was with the utmost concern that we found ourselves incapable of assisting him; indeed we were the more grieved at his unhappy fate, as we lost sight of him struggling in the waves, and conceived from the manner in which he swam, that he might continue sensible, for a considerable time longer, of the horror attending his irretrievable situation."[26]

Despite the tremendous loss of life, what becomes evident throughout *Anson's Voyage* is the endurance of the survivors, men who never give up in the face of death, who rise to the occasion to do what their commander orders, to do whatever must be done to keep the ships afloat and sustain their war against the Spanish regardless of hardship and despair. *Anson's Voyage* stirred the emotions of many eighteenth-century readers, George Washington included.

Laurence Echard's *Gazetteer's or News-Man's Interpreter* and Patrick Gordon's *Geography Anatomiz'd*, two other works Washington acquired in his late teens, reinforced his interest in geography. Echard designed his book for all readers who "frequent *Coffee-Houses*, and other places for News."[27] The emergence of the newspaper as a medium of communication created the need for geographical knowledge. It did no good for a newspaper contributor to tell readers what was happening in other parts of the world if they did not know where those other parts were.

A small-format book printed with two columns per page, Echard's work made a convenient pocket reference. But it was not without drawbacks. In the all-too-brief entry for Virginia, the 1751 edition of Echard's *Gazetteer* identifies Jamestown as the chief city in the colony. When it came to Virginia geography, Echard was several decades out of date. But misinformation can become information in retrospect. Echard's *Gazetteer* reveals how spotty British knowledge of the American colonies was in the mid-eighteenth century.

Gordon's *Geography Anatomiz'd*, the standard school textbook in the field, could be found throughout the American colonies. Washington owned the nineteenth edition, printed in 1749. His surviving copy is a handsome volume, complete with a rubricated title page and several foldout maps drawn by the London atlas maker John Senex. Clearly, Washington's study of geography continued after his formal schooling had ended.

The most distinctive feature of Gordon's textbook is his set of geographical paradoxes. Gordon presents a list of seemingly anomalous descriptions and asks readers to identify where on earth those strange phenomena occurred. He sought to startle readers as a way of provoking their curiosity and prompting them to learn more about geography by unraveling the paradoxes he presented. Among many others, Gordon's paradoxes include the following: "There is a certain Island in the Baltick Sea, to whose Inhabitants the Body of the *Sun* is clearly visible in the Morning before he ariseth, and likewise in the Evening after he is set."[28] Nowhere in his textbook did Gordon provide an answer key, but he did explain the omission: "We think it not fit to pull off the Vizor, or expose those masked *Truths* to publick View, since to endeavour the unmasking of them may prove a private Diversion, both pleasant and useful to the ingenious Reader."[29]

Of course there may be another reason why Gordon omitted an answer key. Some of these paradoxes are impossible to solve: the places they describe do not exist. They are what one modern reader calls "Borgesian places": lands of legend that remain the province of the imagination.[30] Though these elusive places may only exist beyond the realm of physical geography, they provoked the thought of many students. They may not have extended their geographic knowledge, but they did wonders for their imagination.

A different work helped Washington further his geographical study: Herman Moll's *Atlas Minor*. The foremost cartographer of his day, Moll may be best known to students of English literature for the maps he made for *Robinson Crusoe*. His maps also inspired those in *Gulliver's Travels*.[31] In *Atlas Minor*, Moll included a set of sixty-two maps illustrating every part of the known world, including some detailed maps of North America. Moll's atlas, typically found in only the finest libraries of the day, gave Washington's collection an aura of class and sophistication.

Except for Moll, Washington's teenage set of travel books and geographies was fairly typical of the times. Many readers in the colonial South read the same works, which could be found in libraries throughout the Chesapeake region.[32] Reading these books of travel and geography,

Washington familiarized himself with some of the same books his friends and neighbors read. His growing geographical knowledge gave him a font of ideas he could interject in polite conversation among worldly and well-read friends.

Closely related to books of travel, the novels in Washington's library also fueled his spirit of adventure. Novels were not his favorite kind of reading. Though Lord Fairfax influenced his literary tastes, Washington owned far fewer novels than his lordship. The novels Washington did own closely resemble his books of travel in terms of both plot and organization. Andrew Michael Ramsay structured *Travels of Cyrus*—a heavily didactic novel—as a journey relating its hero's adventures among the magi and the Greeks. *Travels of Cyrus*, in Benjamin Franklin's words, is "full of fine reflections, moral and political."[33] The journey motif made all the instructive material easier for readers to assimilate.

In *The History of Tom Jones*, Henry Fielding sent his picaresque hero on a series of adventures crisscrossing the English countryside. And the eponymous hero of Tobias Smollett's *Adventures of Peregrine Pickle* takes an extended tour of Europe. The travel elements of these novels gave Washington further information about the places their heroes visited, and the episodic plots propelled their adventuresome heroes from one exciting locale to the next.

The travel books, geographies, and novels within young Washington's life are so fascinating that it is tempting to give them too much attention. But they must be read in relation to other aspects of his life. Though he enjoyed reading, he was no bookman. Books were never his first priority: other activities typically took precedence. Books about different lands occupied much less time than his own land did, that is, the land he surveyed and the properties he acquired. From the time he became official surveyor for Culpeper County, Washington accepted as many surveying jobs as he could. He gained sufficient knowledge and earned enough money from surveying to start investing in land himself: a lifelong passion.

From 1749 into 1751, he spent much time at Mount Vernon with his half-brother. Lawrence Washington had a lot to teach George—provided his health held out. He was suffering from consumption. His physician recommended he travel to Barbados, where the renowned Dr. William Hillary practiced medicine. If anyone could save him, Dr. Hillary could. Lawrence asked George to accompany him. Doing so would temporarily halt his career as a surveyor, but George, who was devoted to his brother, agreed to go. Besides helping Lawrence, George would have an opportunity to travel, to enjoy the kinds of experiences he had so far only read about in books.

An important event in George Washington's life, the trip also has ramifications for the history of the Caribbean. Their decision to visit Barbados
marks a crucial shift in the historical perception of the region. People formerly perceived the Caribbean climate as dangerous and disease-ridden.
Going to Barbados, the Washington brothers were among the earliest who
traveled from the American mainland to the Caribbean for health reasons.[34]

George apparently studied for the trip ahead of time, reading Colonel
Fairfax's copy of Griffith Hughes's *Natural History of Barbados*.[35] A beautifully printed and illustrated book, Hughes's *Natural History* contains
several engraved plates. The page design of the volume is also quite handsome. Marginal glosses guide readers through the work, and quotations
from poetry leaven the scientific discourse. *Natural History of Barbados*
is very much a celebration of the genre. Whereas history and biography
often concern people's duplicitous behavior and violent passions, natural
history celebrates health, pleasure, and serenity.[36] In retrospect the literary
aspects of Hughes's *Natural History* may be more notable than the scientific ones. Hughes had an in-depth knowledge of classical literature, but
his scientific expertise seems more superficial.[37] Though Hughes's *Natural
History* is not considered an important contribution to scientific knowledge, George Washington, as the reference to the work in his journal
shows, learned much about Barbados from reading Hughes.

Lawrence and George Washington sailed the last week of September
1751. The voyage was trying: thirty-seven days would pass before they
reached Barbados. The diary Washington kept shows a much greater
sense of purpose than the journal of his trip to the Shenandoah. Though
the manuscript is severely damaged, the surviving parts of Washington's
Barbados journal contain more detail than his earlier one.

He began keeping a diary in narrative form but a few days into the trip
switched to maintaining a log in chart form. Washington's daily chart does
contain some narrative elements, a few with literary pretensions. One entry
characterizes the sea as the "fickle and merciless Ocean."[38] Washington's
words echo a phrase given currency by "Nancy's Complaint," a popular
song that concludes:

> Think not of the merciless Ocean
> My Soul any Terror can have;
> For soon as the Ship makes its motion,
> So soon shall the Sea be my Grave.[39]

George continued his journal once they reached Barbados, switching
from chart back to narrative form. He recorded the people they met, the

places they went, and the things they did. Overall its contents show what he learned from the travel literature he had read.

On Tuesday, November 5, they consulted Dr. Hillary. A distinguished physician who had studied at Leiden under Herman Boerhaave, Hillary gave Lawrence hope for recovery yet recommended he and his brother take a house in the country, advice that reflects Hillary's belief in the environmental concept of disease, that unhealthy air and putrid water cause many illnesses.[40]

They rode beyond Bridgetown city limits that evening to find a house. Constructed of stone consisting of fossilized coral, the house they found had a quaint look to their eyes, but the surrounding scenery offered a sense of grandeur. George wrote that they were "perfectly enraptured" with the beautiful prospect. The cane, the corn, and the fruit trees were all "a delightful green," a color these Virginians were unused to seeing in November.[41] The house had a commanding view of Carlisle Bay, so they could watch the flutter and flash of sails as the boats came and went.

The first two weeks of November were refreshing. One day they enjoyed the greatest bunch of fruit George had ever seen: granadilla, guava, lemon, orange, pomegranate, and sapodilla. George also enjoyed avocado, and pineapple quickly became a favorite, too. He tasted the "forbidden fruit," a rare citrus fruit not dissimilar to grapefruit, which is now nearly extinct.[42] George recorded nothing more about fruit in Barbados, forbidden or otherwise, in his journal, explaining: "There are many delicious Fruits in this but as they are particularly describ'd by the Revd Mr Hughes in the Natural histy of the Island [I] shall say nothing further."[43]

Brief as it is, Washington's comment reveals much about his attitude toward keeping a journal. He understood writing as a communal task: a travel journal situates its author within a community of writers, past and present. Though writing about his own experience, Washington saw no need to repeat what previous authors had written; he only needed to record new information. When his personal experience coincided with that of an author he had read, he did not bother recording it. For Washington, writing and reading were complementary activities. What he read in Hughes's *Natural History of Barbados* affected what he wrote in his journal. As a genre in which he excelled, the travel journal would continue to form an important part of Washington's literary life.

In addition to the natural aspects of Barbados, Washington enjoyed its man-made features. As one of Britain's most valuable colonial possessions, Barbados was well fortified. Washington studied the entrenchments erected to protect against enemy invasions, and he visited Charles Fort on Needham's Point, which guarded the entrance to Carlisle Bay. He described the fortifications in his journal, counting the number of guns and batteries. Charles Fort was the first fort Washington had ever seen.[44]

Washington further enhanced his literary life in Barbados by attending the theatre. On Thursday, November 15, he witnessed a performance of George Lillo's *The London Merchant; or, The History of George Barnwell.* The first play Washington is known to have seen, the Bridgetown performance of *George Barnwell* sparked a fascination with the stage that would last a lifetime. Recording the performance in his diary, Washington wrote, "The character of Barnwell and several others was said to be well perform'd."[45] Notably, Washington recorded the opinion of others instead of making his own critical remarks. Either he thought that it was more important to record the impression of others, or he lacked confidence in his own critical powers.

As the play that triggered Washington's love of the theatre, *George Barnwell* is strangely appropriate. Having premiered in London two decades earlier, *George Barnwell* is a landmark in the history of British drama: it introduced the genre of domestic tragedy. Lillo's play eschewed the long-standing notion that a tragic hero must be an aristocratic figure. Dramatizing the life of a merchant, Lillo essentially democratized tragedy. Despite its tragic ending, *George Barnwell* celebrates the world of commerce and the men who made their way in it.

Two days after attending the theater, George Washington was afflicted, or, in his words, "strongly attacked," with smallpox. The disease left him pockmarked, yet it also immunized him. No longer would he need to worry about contracting the disease. He could walk among the sick the rest of his life and not worry that smallpox would strike him down. What Tobias Smollett said about Godfrey, the brave young soldier in *Peregrine Pickle*, equally applies to Washington: "The scars of the small pox, of which he bore a good number, added a peculiar manliness to the air of his countenance."[46]

Though George recovered from smallpox by mid-December, Lawrence's condition had improved little, if at all, since their arrival. Lawrence would leave Barbados for Bermuda; George would return to Virginia. On Sunday, December 22, George boarded the *Industry*, which weighed anchor and left Carlisle Bay that morning. The downtime aboard ship let him catch up his journal. He wrote about the people, agriculture, government, and commerce of Barbados and described additional curiosities. On Christmas Eve, for instance, he wrote, "A Fresh gale (or what in this part of the World is called a fiery Breeze) hurried us past the Leeward Islands."[47] He enjoyed such quaint local sayings. Though the phrase "fiery breeze" circulated in the vernacular of the West Indies, perhaps no one had recorded it before: Washington made sure to do so.

Toward the end of January 1752, he touched the Virginia shore and continued to Williamsburg, where he delivered some papers to Governor Dinwiddie. Nearing sixty and quite fat, Robert Dinwiddie looked as imposing as he was. A native of Scotland, he had attended the University of Glasgow, where he received an excellent education, as anyone might guess by his library at the Governor's Palace. Washington was starting to realize that a man's library could tell others who he was.

Dinwiddie's library indicated his curiosity about many different fields of study: ecclesiastical history, ethics, history, poetry, religion, and science.[48] After graduating from college, Dinwiddie had followed the path of many of his countrymen and entered the transatlantic mercantile trade. The British colonies intrigued him to such an extent that he settled in Bermuda, where he became one of the island's leading citizens.

Appointed surveyor general of the royal customs for the Southern District of North America in 1738, Dinwiddie oversaw the Bahamas, Jamaica, and the mainland colonies from Pennsylvania southwards. The position entitled him to a seat on the Virginia Council, which he attended sporadically. In 1751 he became lieutenant governor of Virginia. Traditionally, the lieutenant governor served as the working governor of Virginia. He was the one who settled in the colony and assumed the day-to-day administrative tasks while the royal governor remained in England, doing little save collecting a fat salary.

After meeting Governor Dinwiddie, Washington returned to Mount Vernon to resume his surveying career. As it turned out, Lawrence's trip to Bermuda did nothing to improve his health. His consumption only grew worse. There seemed to be nothing he could do about it. In June he returned to Virginia, where his condition deteriorated rapidly. On July 25, 1752, Lawrence Washington passed away. With his death, George not only lost a brother, he lost a friend, a mentor, and a father figure.

CHAPTER 5

The Journal of Major George Washington

O Winter, ruler of the inverted year!
William Cowper, "The Winter Evening"

Lawrence Washington's death left vacant the office of adjutant of the Virginia militia, a position that involved overseeing and inspecting militia companies throughout the colony. Though George Washington had received much military knowledge from his brother, so far he had no formal military training or any battlefield experience. What he lacked in terms of firsthand contact he made up for in first-class ambition. Eager to establish a military career of his own, he actively sought his brother's old office.

Colonial authorities could see that Virginia had grown too populous for one man to oversee all its militia companies. Instead of appointing a single officer to fill the vacancy, they split the office of adjutant into four positions, each supervising a different part of the colony. In February 1753 Governor Dinwiddie appointed George Washington adjutant of the Southern District of Virginia with the rank of major. The governor later reassigned him to the position he preferred, one much closer to home: adjutant of the Northern Neck.

The position as adjutant opened up further opportunities for George Washington, just as he had hoped. In the early 1750s, French activity in the Ohio valley became increasingly aggressive, and, in the words of one observer, "Governor Dinwiddie thought it high Time to come to an

Éclaircissement."[1] In other words, Dinwiddie decided that the British and French should reach some kind of mutual understanding about the frontier. Consequently, he wrote a letter to the French commandant. Writing the letter was the easy part; putting it into the hands of the commandant hundreds of miles from Williamsburg would be more difficult.

Washington volunteered for the mission. Leaving Williamsburg the last day of October 1753, he braved cold, wet, miserable conditions through the American wilderness over the next two and a half months but successfully delivered the message to the French commandant of the Ohio valley and safely returned to Williamsburg, reaching the city on January 16, 1754.

Aware the governor would expect a detailed account of his mission, Washington had kept a journal throughout his backwoods experience. Though he was only twenty-one, his journal demonstrates remarkable maturity—and considerable literary skill. It marks a significant advance over his earlier travel journals. His sense of responsibility partly accounts for the improvement: he understood the profound significance of this mission and the value of recording it in precise detail. His sense of audience contributes to its literary quality. Washington knew he would be presenting the journal to a well-educated and well-read British governor with excellent taste. Perhaps members of the governor's council would also read his manuscript journal, and maybe some of the Lords of Trade back in Britain. Washington's increasingly broad travel reading had helped refine his prose style. It is difficult to read the clean, crisp prose of his journal and not think of Defoe's *Tour through Great Britain*.

Upon returning to Williamsburg, Washington delivered his manuscript journal to Governor Dinwiddie. Recognizing it as an insightful account of the relations between the English and French in America and a valuable source of information about the American frontier, the governor rushed the journal into print. Washington had little time— perhaps only a few days—to prepare the manuscript for publication. His prefatory remarks explain that he had "no Leisure to consult of a new and proper Form to offer it in, or to correct or amend the Diction of the old."[2]

He was being modest. Before his revisions the narrative was fairly well polished. His last-minute changes quicken its pace, soften a few hasty judgments, and enhance the excitement. The work appeared under a straightforward title: *The Journal of Major George Washington*. Suddenly Washington found himself a published author. *The Journal of Major George Washington* is the first of several works Washington wrote and published in his lifetime. Though he never had authorial ambitions,

Washington understood that, with his increasing fame, what he wrote would need to be published. He accepted the role of author reluctantly, but he accepted it nonetheless.

The Journal of Major George Washington captured the public imagination. Newspapers up and down the East Coast republished it serially. The *Maryland Gazette*, for one, reprinted it in March 1754. American editors and British publishers recognized the work as a crucial document in the emerging conflict between Great Britain and France. The *Boston Gazette* reprinted the journal from the *Maryland Gazette*. The following headnote prefaces the first installment in the *Boston Gazette:* "The Storm arising in the West, being the present Topic of Conversation, we think we cannot oblige our Readers, at this Juncture, with any Thing more entertaining than *Major Washington's* Journal to *Ohio*, who was sent last Fall, by the Governour of *Virginia*, to the Commandant of the *French* Forces there."[3] Thomas Jeffreys, a London printer, engraver, and mapmaker who kept a weather eye out for geographical books published in America, also reprinted *The Journal of Major George Washington*, complete with a map of the Ohio valley.[4]

Enjoying Washington's journal, one eighteenth-century reader commented, "The manliness of his style—correctness in detail—and solidity of judgment—render it a very interesting performance."[5] Literary historian Richard Beale Davis has praised its vivid description, use of dialogue, and briskly paced narrative.[6] Though few others have considered the work's literary qualities, *The Journal of Major George Washington* deserves recognition as a major contribution to the history of colonial American travel writing.

Revising his journal for publication, Washington had the opportunity to relive the experience and shape it for a wider audience, a readership beyond a small circle of colonial administrators. The narrative's first paragraph is headed October 31, 1753, the day Governor Dinwiddie commissioned him and the day Washington left Williamsburg. The next day he reached Fredericksburg, where he hired as his interpreter Jacob Van Braam, a Dutch-born French teacher a few years older than him. Together these two young men traveled to Alexandria, where they acquired some necessary supplies. They continued to Winchester, obtaining horses and additional baggage for their wilderness trek. Washington encapsulated all these activities within the opening paragraph of *The Journal of Major George Washington*. Before that paragraph ends, two weeks have passed, and the two men have reached Wills Creek (now, Cumberland, Maryland).

On Wednesday, November 14, the day they arrived at Wills Creek, Washington hired Christopher Gist to lead them to Logstown. A surveyor, explorer, and Indian scout, Gist, now approaching fifty, may have been more familiar with the Ohio valley than any other American colonist alive. On behalf of the Ohio Company, he had already explored the valley as far west as the mouth of the Scioto River. Washington's journal contains little information about Gist or, for that matter, any of the men who joined the expedition. The absence of personal detail suggests he did not have time to elaborate.

Washington was capable of incisive character sketches, as a letter he wrote a few years later verifies. This letter provides the single best pen portrait of Gist available: "He has had extensive dealings with the Indians, is in great esteem among them; well acquainted with their manners and customs—is indefatigable and patient: Most excellent qualities indeed, where Indians are concerned! And, for his capacity, honesty and Zeal, I dare venture to engage."[7] Such description may be unnecessary to the journal. Washington did not need to develop the personal characteristics of Gist or the other backwoodsmen he hired at Wills Creek. He let their actions speak for them.

Christopher Gist also kept a diary of their mission. Gist's diary does not contradict Washington's, but it does differ in terms of emphasis. Gist stressed certain episodes in his diary, Washington others. Each provides information the other omits. Not only does Gist's account help tell a fuller story, it also reveals the gaps in Washington's journal. Essentially Gist's account shows what Washington omitted and inadvertently reveals Washington's literary skill. Read in light of Gist's diary, *The Journal of Major George Washington* demonstrates how its author used his writing ability to present readers with a carefully crafted version of himself.

Despite the miserable weather, they left Wills Creek the day after arriving. It took them another week to reach their next crucial destination. Washington did not use the journal as a forum for complaint. Rather, he simply related the adverse conditions as a matter of fact: "The excessive Rains and vast Quantity of Snow which had fallen prevented our reaching Mr. *Frazer's*, an Indian Trader, at the Mouth of *Turtle-Creek*, on *Monongehela*, 'til *Thursday*."[8]

By "Mr. *Frazer's*" Washington meant the Indian trading post John Fraser had established on the Monongahela River at the mouth of Turtle Creek. Earlier that year the French had forced Fraser from his other trading post, the one at Venango, which they commandeered as their local headquarters. Upon seeing the Monongahela, Washington realized they would have to unburden their horses and swim them across. The kind-hearted Fraser agreed to loan them a canoe to transport their baggage ten miles to the forks of the Ohio River. Two men went in the canoe while Washington led the others on horseback across the freezing cold river.

Reaching the Ohio before the canoe, Washington had the opportunity to take a good look around. He could see that this location was well situated for a fort. The journal beautifully captures his experience. The pace of the narrative slackens as its author describes a moment of calm and contemplation. An experienced surveyor and nascent military strategist, he pauses to ponder the land's commercial and military value. At this point the journal presents a vivid self-portrait of its author, which has the quality of a tableau.[9] Three months shy of his twenty-second birthday, Washington gazes westward into the wilderness and imagines what the continent will become.

Visiting the location where the Ohio Company intended to erect a fort (near present-day Pittsburgh), Washington found it comparatively inadequate in both economic and strategic terms. The knowledge of military strategy he brought to bear as he analyzed both locations is extraordinary. Though he had gained some military knowledge in conversation with Lawrence, his brother's influence seems inadequate to explain Washington's deep perspective of the situation. To be sure, he had an intuitive grasp of military strategy, but intuition alone cannot explain the understanding he displayed on this, his first military mission. In the coming years Washington would keep abreast of the latest military literature, but before this mission he had read few, if any, recent books on the subject. Where did his military knowledge come from?

By the time he had begun this journey, he was familiar with one or two military classics. A letter from William Fairfax asserts that Washington owned a copy of Julius Caesar's *Commentaries*. The figure of speech Caesar used just before crossing the Rubicon—"The die is cast"—would become a favorite with Washington. Suetonius's *History of the Twelve Caesars*, a work Fairfax had in his library at Belvoir, is the source of the saying.[10] Fairfax was reasonably confident that Washington also owned a copy of Quintus Curtius's *History of the Wars of Alexander the Great*, though he could not say for sure.[11] Why did Fairfax assume Washington owned a copy of Quintus Curtius? Apparently, young Washington could hardly stop talking about the exploits of both Julius Caesar and Alexander the Great. Other evidence confirms his knowledge of these two great military commanders. Redecorating Mount Vernon a few years later, he ordered busts of Alexander the Great and Julius Caesar to adorn his home. Washington also obtained several decorative prints illustrating Alexander's victories in battle.[12]

Quintus Curtius's *History of the Wars of Alexander the Great* could have taught Washington much about what makes a great leader. Relating the life of Alexander, Curtius faced a challenge. The climax—the death of Alexander's greatest enemy, the Persian king Darius—occurs less than halfway through the story. The remainder of Alexander's conquests as he proceeded east to India were not as difficult or dramatic as his fight against Darius's troops. What sustains the narrative is the force of Alexander's personality. Relating his exploits, Curtius shows the personal qualities a great leader requires: camaraderie, clemency, decisiveness, flexibility, a mind that enjoys wrestling with problems, practicality, resolution in the face of danger, self-control, a sense of efficiency, and a strong will. Despite his appreciation of Alexander's leadership qualities, Curtius's *History of Alexander* is not hagiography. Curtius identifies Alexander's faults as well as his virtues. During lulls between battles, Alexander would give in to his vices and fall into dissipation. And his temper sometimes got the better of him.

Written as a narrative, not a practical manual, Caesar's *Commentaries* nonetheless could be read as a military guide. It provides more useful detail about strategy than Curtius's *History of Alexander*. Caesar's story of his military exploits in Gaul emphasizes the importance of engineering: building bridges, constructing fortifications, erecting siege towers, making roads. Yet Caesar was a pragmatist. Good roads are important, but an army should only build them when they have the time. In the heat of combat, speed, stealth, and surprise are vital elements of success. Efficient communication is also essential. Furthermore, a commander needs to understand the mindset of his men. Sufficient provisions are necessary not only for assuring the welfare of the troops but also for securing their loyalty. Courage is important; discipline is more important. Soldiers should not let courage outstrip discipline. A commander must take several steps to understand the enemy: analyze its tactics, scrutinize its fortifications, and survey its territory. Flexibility is key. He must be willing to adjust his strategy to adapt to the enemy, the terrain, and the weather. As Washington scouted locations for a possible fort to defend against the French, he apparently did so by keeping the thought of Julius Caesar's Gallic exploits in mind.

Besides giving him much practical military information, Caesar's *Commentaries* also gave Washington another model for writing. John Seelye observes that *The Journal of George Washington* and the accounts of other diplomatic and military missions Washington undertook are "neat and spare, as in Caesar's *Commentaries* taking their life from events, not style."[13]

Near the site where the Ohio Company planned to erect its fort lived Shingas. "King of the *Delawares*," as Washington called him. To be precise, Shingas was a principal chief of the Unalechtigo tribe of the Delaware. Washington saw him as a useful ally and invited Shingas to accompany him to Logstown, one of the main Indian trading villages in the Ohio valley. Shingas agreed. They reached Logstown late Saturday afternoon, November 24. Or, as Washington phrased it in a more vivid yet no less accurate way: "We arrived between Sun-setting and Dark, the 25th Day after I left *Williamsburg*."[14]

Washington quickly learned from John Davison, an Indian trader and interpreter working out of Logstown, that Tanacharison, the Seneca chief better known as Half King, was at his hunting cabin on Little Beaver Creek. Washington really needed to speak with him, but in his absence, he spoke with Monacatoocha, the Oneida chief who acted as second in command at Logstown. Through Davison, Washington informed Monacatoocha of his mission to present a message to the French commandant and urged him to send for Half King. Aware of the importance of hospitality in Native American culture and wanting very much to foster their friendship, Washington invited Monacatoocha and other local leaders to his tent that evening.

Waiting for Half King the next day, Washington took advantage of the extra time to collect useful military information about the land and the strength of the French forces. Once Half King finally arrived, Washington, speaking through Davison, invited him to his tent for a private conference. Relating this episode, Washington's journal reflects the seriousness and significance of their meeting. Half King was an influential figure who would play a crucial role in Washington's wilderness adventure.

In September Half King had led a group of Indians to the French fort at Presque Isle to warn the French commandant, Pierre Paul de la Malgue, sieur de Marin, against French expansion into the Ohio valley. (The title "sieur" could mean gentleman or lord of the manor, but its usage was less rigid than the English terms "sir" or "lord.") Washington wished to know how the journey went and how Marin had received him.

Recording Half King's response in his journal, Washington applied some fairly sophisticated narrative techniques. He used indirect discourse to report how Half King described the route to the French fort: "He told me, that the nearest and levellest Way was now impassable, by Reason of many large mirey Savannas; that we must be obliged to go by *Venango*, and should not get to the near Fort under five or six Nights Sleep, good Travelling."[15]

Reporting how Marin received Half King, Washington continued using indirect discourse. Partway through the account he switched to direct discourse to quote Half King's speech to Marin. Washington's use of direct discourse lends immediacy to the conference between Marin and Half King, giving it the quality of a flashback. The italic typeface of the published journal reinforces the shift in voice and time.

After supplying what appears to be a word-for-word transcription, Washington qualified it, stating, "This he said was the Substance of what he spoke to the General, who made this Reply."[16] Marin's speech to Half King follows. Presenting the speech in direct discourse, Washington brings the experience alive and effectively shows Marin's self-centered nature. The accuracy of Marin's speech is suspect, however. After all, it had gone through several interpretive filters before it reached the pages of Washington's journal. Washington was quoting translator John Davison quoting Half King quoting Marin, who likely delivered his original speech through a translator as well.

Marin's speech makes him seem snobbish and superior, even haughty. He takes a deprecatory attitude toward the Native Americans, addressing Half King as "My Child" and likening Indians to insects: "I am not afraid of Flies, or Musquitos, for *Indians* are such as those." In this speech Marin exaggerates the strength of the French forces and, in so doing, insults Half King's intelligence, saying he had as many troops as grains of sand on the beach. The most unusual part of Marin's speech, as Washington recorded it, is the part containing an inserted parenthetical adverb: "It is my Land, and I will have it, let who will stand-up for, or say-against, it. I'll buy and sell with the English (mockingly). If People will be rul'd by me, they may expect Kindness, but not else."[17] How did Half King express Marin's mocking tone? Though presenting a version of the speech, the journal provides no additional clues about its telling.

Washington had several reasons for recording the speeches of Half King and Marin in direct discourse. His penchant for precision is one. The same quality that made him an expert surveyor compelled him to record his experiences as precisely as possible. Washington's transcription of these speeches also indicates the seriousness he brought to his mission. He understood that diplomatic exchanges could have vast repercussions. Failed communications could lead to war. A record of these speeches offered evidence of French and Indian attitudes toward one another.

Literary reasons also motivated Washington to incorporate these speeches in his journal. Indian treaties, which typically incorporated numerous speeches, had already emerged as a popular form of literary entertainment in early American culture. The treaties between colonists and Native Americans reflected, as Lawrence Wroth put it, "the passion, the greed, and the love of life of hard-living men brought into close relationship without parallel conditions in the history of either race to guide its conduct."[18] Contemporary readers, Washington included, found these diplomatic encounters fascinating.

In his personal library Washington had a copy of *The Treaty Held with the Indians of the Six Nations, at Lancaster, in Pennsylvania, June, 1744.* This particular treaty had considerable literary and cultural appeal. Benjamin Franklin reprinted two hundred copies of it for resale in Great Britain. Another American reader sent a copy to a friend on the Isle of Man, which, he told him, would provide "some insight into the Genius of those people we brutishly call savages."[19] There's no telling precisely when Washington acquired his copy, but most likely he knew it before he undertook this mission. He clearly understood the rhetorical conventions of Native American diplomacy.

By including Marin's speech in his narrative, Washington also established a point of comparison with his own speech to Half King and the other Indians, whom he addressed in council on Monday, November 26. Washington recorded his own speech in direct discourse, too. It begins: "Brothers, I have called you together in Council, by Order of your Brother the Governor of *Virginia.*"[20]

In the journal both Marin and Washington express their relationship with the Indians as a figurative kinship. Whereas Marin uses the word "Child" to address Half King, Washington uses "Brothers" to address the members of Half King's council. Calling Half King his child, Marin indicates his sense of superiority. Washington, alternatively, demonstrates camaraderie and equality.

When it came to the practice of diplomacy in colonial America, one of the biggest obstacles to negotiation involved the concept of time. The Native American attitude toward time was much more relaxed. Conversely, colonial Americans were more anxious to get things done as quickly as possible. Washington was no exception. His eagerness to finish his business partly stemmed from personal inclination, but it also reflected both his sense of duty and his practical nature. He was an army officer following orders, orders stipulating that he deliver his message to the French commandant with all possible dispatch. In addition he knew that as winter approached, he risked dangerous weather every day he delayed.

During their negotiations Half King engaged in some classic stall tactics. Initially Washington could not mask his impatience. The journal captures the tension arising from their disparate attitudes toward time.

Ultimately Washington relented, explaining that "it was impossible to get-off without affronting them in the most egregious Manner."[21] His behavior hints that he had learned much more from his "Rules of Civility" than the rules themselves. He also learned an outlook that let him generate new rules of behavior when the standard ones no longer applied. As Half King's delaying tactics continued, Washington adjusted his behavior accordingly: "I consented to stay, as I believed an Offence offered at this Crisis, might be attended with greater ill Consequence, than another Day's Delay."[22]

On Friday, November 30, Washington and his men, accompanied by Half King, an old Iroquois chief named White Thunder, and a young Seneca warrior known simply as "The Hunter," set off for Venango, which they reached the following Tuesday, December 4. John Fraser's old trading post was now flying French colors and serving as a regional French headquarters. Here Washington met Philippe Thomas de Joincaire, sieur de Chabert, who served as the chief Indian interpreter for the French. Wanting to deal with Captain Joincaire on his own terms, Washington kept him and Half King separate as long as he could. Upon meeting Joincaire, Washington did not even mention he was traveling with Half King.

Joincaire informed Washington that he had command of the Ohio, but also that Washington would have to deal with his superior officer. Unbeknownst to Washington, sieur de Marin, who had been Joincaire's superior, had died at Fort Le Boeuf on October 29. Jacques Le Gardeur, sieur de Saint-Pierre, had succeeded Marin as commandant of the French forces in the Ohio country, and he was stationed at Fort Le Boeuf.

This disheartening piece of news meant that Washington still had several more days of cold, wet, weary travel ahead of him. For the time being he tried to make the most of his encounter with Joincaire. He accepted the captain's invitation to join him and his men for dinner. Washington's account brings their decadence and dinner conversation alive: "The Wine, as they dosed themselves pretty plentifully with it, soon banished the Restraint which at first appeared in their Conversation; and gave a Licence to their Tongues to reveal their Sentiments more freely."[23]

Recording their conversation, Washington used indirect discourse but nevertheless caught the tone and tenor of what the French said, down to the expletive they used. He wrote:

> They told me, That it was their absolute Design to take Possession of the *Ohio*, and by G——they would do it: For that altho' they were sensible the English could raise two Men for their one; yet they knew, their Motions were too slow and dilatory to prevent any Undertaking of theirs.[24]

Washington learned that the French understood the shortcomings of British military strategy, something he stored in his memory for later use. The more the French drank, the more Washington learned. He discovered how many men they had at each fort south of Lake Ontario, where all four of the French forts were located, and how they were provisioned. He also learned how long it took for additional troops and supplies to travel from Montreal.

Washington hoped to leave Wednesday morning, December 5, but excessive rain prevented his departure. The delay let Joincaire learn that Washington was traveling with Half King. Eager to win over this Seneca chief, Joincaire became chummy with him. Expecting favors from the French, Half King now refused to leave Venango. Thursday night Washington left John Davison with Half King to help him get going on Friday morning, but it took the combined efforts of Davison and Gist to roust Half King and his men. Though the rain had let up, travel remained daunting. All the recent rain and snow made the rivers downright treacherous.

The journal provides little detail about the next stage of their trip, but Gist recorded the conditions more fully. On Friday, they found Sugar Creek high and swift. They cut down some trees to create a makeshift bridge to transport their gear but had to swim their horses across. Washington and Gist took the lead and crossed with their boots on. By Friday night they had traveled only five miles past Venango.

They made twenty-five miles on Saturday, but the strenuous effort took its toll: one horse could travel no further, and the others would perish without considerable time for recuperation. On Sunday the ninth, they reached the big crossing and started constructing a raft, but the river was too fast and too deep. An alternate route took them through mire and swamp.[25] They had another river to cross the next day. Happily, The Hunter killed a bear, and its succulent meat helped fortify the men.

Gist's diary supplies much information about the challenging terrain they crossed and the hardships they encountered. Instead of relating the treacherous conditions himself, Washington used his journal to describe the land's enormous agricultural potential: "We passed over much good Land since we left *Venango*, and through several extensive and very rich Meadows; one of which I believe was near four Miles in Length, and considerably wide in some Places."[26] More than anything, Washington's journal sounds like colonial promotion literature as it boasts about the richness of the land.

They did not reach Fort Le Boeuf until after sunset on Tuesday, December 11. Early the next morning Washington met Le Gardeur de

Saint-Pierre, the new French commandant, who had only arrived himself about a week earlier. Washington wrote a brief personal description: "He is an elderly Gentleman, and has much the Air of a Soldier."[27] Though nowhere else in the journal does Washington supply such character descriptions, he does so here for one simple reason: no one in Virginia had any experience with Le Gardeur de Saint-Pierre. Washington provided a quick verbal sketch of the French commandant to let his readers picture him. Upon his arrival Washington presented his commission to the commandant as well as the letter from Governor Dinwiddie.

Before they could consider the documents, the French had to translate them. As their translators worked, their officers left Washington alone: a strategic error. With no one looking over his shoulder, he took the opportunity to measure Fort Le Boeuf, study its construction, pace off the distance between the fort and the water, and count the number of dwellings, outbuildings, and canoes. Before the French reached a decision about Washington's commission, he had fully assessed the strengths and weaknesses of Fort Le Boeuf.

Two days passed without a French decision but with many inches of new snow. Washington grew wary about the return trip. Getting weaker by the day, the horses would not last much longer. He sent three men and all the horses back to Venango; he would follow in a canoe. Increasing his anxiety, the French continued to gain the Indians' favor, bribing Half King and the others in an effort to dissuade them from returning with him.

On Friday night, he received word from the French in the form of a letter addressed to Governor Dinwiddie. This formal document, though lengthy, came down to one key sentence: "As to the summons you send me to retire, I do not think myself obliged to obey it."[28] As far as the French were concerned, they had come to the Ohio valley to stay. Le Gardeur de Saint-Pierre's letter reinforced the urgency of Washington's mission. Having now received official word regarding their intentions, Washington grew anxious to return to Williamsburg with all due haste.

He prepared for his departure on Saturday the fifteenth. Le Gardeur de Saint-Pierre seemed helpful, but Washington recognized his duplicity. According to the journal, "The Commandant ordered a plentiful Store of Liquor, Provision, etc. to be put on Board our Canoe; and appeared to be extremely complaisant, though he was exerting every Artifice which he could invent to set our own Indians at Variance with us, to prevent their going 'till after our Departure."[29]

Washington softened this statement when he revised his journal for publication. In his original version, instead of "exerting every Artifice which he could invent," Le Gardeur de Saint-Pierre was "plotting every

Scheme that the Devil and Man cou'd invent, to set our Indians at Variance with us."[30] Omitting the proverbial expression as he revised the manuscript, Washington removed the comparison between the devil and the French commandant and made the account more literal, if less colorful.

He stayed until the next morning, December 16. The French were still plotting to keep the Indians there, but Half King relented, agreeing to leave with Washington. Half King, White Thunder, and The Hunter went in one canoe, Washington and Gist in another. The French manned three canoes to accompany them. Washington summarized the trip to Venango briefly: "We had a tedious and very fatiguing Passage down the Creek. Several Times we had like to have staved against Rocks; and many Times were obliged all Hands to get out, and remain in the Water Half an Hour or more, getting over the Shoals. At one Place the Ice had lodged and made it impassable by Water; therefore we were obliged to carry our Canoe across a neck of Land a Quarter of a Mile over."[31]

Gist's account of this segment of the trip is much more detailed. He noted, for instance, that one canoe overturned, destroying the cargo and powder and shot of the French. Another day a second canoe overturned. Gist wrote, "We had the pleasure of seeing the French overset, and the brandy and wine floating in the creek."[32] Washington said nothing about either the French canoe accident or their loss of liquor. Unlike Gist, he took no pleasure in the misfortune of others, or, if he did, he did not say so in either the manuscript journal or the published one.

At Venango, which they reached on Saturday the twenty-second, they met the rest of their men waiting with the horses. Having suffered an injury, White Thunder told Washington he would stay at Venango. Half King decided to stay with him. Washington disliked leaving them both with Joincaire, but he could do little to alter the situation. He cautioned Half King against Captain Joincaire's schemes. The Hunter, ever trustworthy, agreed to continue with Washington. Though the figure of the Noble Savage would not emerge in American literature for decades, The Hunter, in Washington's hands, becomes a crucial prototype.

The horses were in such bad shape Washington ordered most of the men to put packs on their backs and walk. He created a vivid self-portrait for the journal, explaining that he himself donned "an *Indian* Walking Dress" and walked together with the others for three days.[33] The going was slow, and the cold and snow made their travel more treacherous. Anxious to deliver his message, Washington hurried ahead with Gist, leaving Van Braam in charge of horses and baggage.

Gist expressed some uncertainty about Washington's decision, worrying that this young gentleman was unused to hiking such long distances.

Gist's diary conveys his concern; Washington's journal contains no such uncertainty. Instead the journal shows Washington going about his duties without hesitation: "I took my necessary Papers; pulled-off my Cloaths; and tied myself up in a Match Coat. Then with Gun in Hand and Pack at my Back, in which were my Papers and Provisions, I set-out with Mr. *Gist*, fitted in the same Manner, on *Wednesday* the 26th."[34]

Depicting himself adorned in a matchcoat, Washington develops his self-portrait further. Though it derives from an Algonquin root word, the term "matchcoat" referred to European-made units of woolen cloth about two yards long, which were traded to the Indians, who wore them as loosely wrapped cloaks. Among the Indians in the mid-eighteenth century, it was fashionable to wear matchcoats with woven belts, one of the few items of Native American manufacture that still formed part of Indian dress.[35] Washington apparently belted his matchcoat and, in so doing, reinforced his physical resemblance to an Indian in the journal. Adorned in a matchcoat, Washington himself wears the mantle of the Noble Savage.

On Thursday the twenty-seventh, Washington and Gist entered a Delaware village with the ominous name of Murdering Town. Relating the events of that day, Washington told the story briefly in the journal; Gist wrote it up in great detail, complete with dialogue. After passing through Murdering Town, they met an Indian, who called out to them, pretending friendship and offering to carry Washington's pack. The three continued together for eight or ten miles. The Indian also offered to carry his gun; Washington politely refused. Both Gist and Washington began to mistrust the man, whose behavior seemed increasingly erratic. Crossing a meadow, he got ahead of them in the woods, turned, leveled his musket, and fired.

Having missed them both, he rushed behind a big white oak to reload. Before he could do so, they caught up with him. Gist was ready to shoot the man dead then and there, but Washington refused. During the Revolutionary War, Washington would establish a reputation for clemency among prisoners of war. Whereas the British army often gave no quarter, Washington refused to kill his captives and instead treated them humanely. The episode with the Murdering Town Indian shows that Washington's mercy in battle manifested itself long before the Revolutionary War.

"As you will not have him killed," Gist privately said to Washington, "we must get him away, and then we must travel all night." Gist devised a clever scheme, pretending that they thought the Indian had fired solely to communicate his position to them.

"I suppose you were lost, and fired your gun," Gist said to him. The Indian readily agreed with Gist's seemingly innocent conclusion and assumed he still had their confidence. He assured them that his cabin was just a little further. "Well," Gist continued, "you go home; and as we are much tired, we will follow your track in the morning; and here is a cake of bread for you, and you must give us meat in the morning."[36]

Gist silently tracked him for a long way before doubling back to rejoin Washington, who had made a small fire to guide Gist back through the darkness. After setting their compass by firelight, they resumed their trek, reaching the head of Piney Creek before daybreak. They continued hiking until dark the next day, when it was finally safe enough to sleep.

On Saturday the twenty-ninth, they reached the Allegheny River. Since the rivers they had crossed recently had been frozen, they expected the Allegheny would be, too, but it was only frozen partway across. The ice that had formed along the riverbanks increased the danger by constricting the river's flow and accelerating its current. To make the crossing more treacherous, ice from upriver had broken into blocks, which floated rapidly downstream. Whereas Washington had treated their run-in with the Murdering Town Indian briefly, he told the story of how they crossed the Allegheny in much greater detail. He clearly recognized the setting's dramatic potential.

Developing this episode for the journal, George Washington deserves credit for introducing the motif of the tension-filled wintertime river crossing to American literature. Harriet Beecher Stowe would effectively utilize this same motif when she had Eliza cross the Ohio River by stepping over big chunks of ice in *Uncle Tom's Cabin*, an episode the stage performances of the work seldom failed to dramatize. D. W. Griffith would reuse the motif, having Lillian Gish cross a rapid river filled with hunks of ice in *Way Down East*. Like Stowe and Griffith after him, Washington understood how a swiftly flowing, ice-filled river could create dramatic tension. Here's his version:

> There was no way for getting over but on a Raft: which we set about, with but one poor hatchet, and finished just after Sun-setting. This was a whole Day's Work: we next got it launched, and went on Board of it: Then set off. But before we were Half Way over, we were jammed in the ice in such a Manner, that we expected every Moment our Raft to sink, and ourselves to perish. I put out my setting-Pole to try to stop the Raft, that the Ice might pass by; when the Rapidity of the Stream threw it with such Violence against the Pole, that it jerked me out into ten Feet of Water; but I fortunately saved myself by catching hold of one of

the Raft-Logs. Notwithstanding all our Efforts we could not get the Raft to either Shore, but were obliged, as we were near an Island, to quit our Raft and make to it.[37]

Stranded on the island in the middle of the river, Washington and Gist went to bed with the knowledge that they would have to cross that dangerous river the next day—or die trying. But, almost magically, a cold front moved in as they slept, dropping the temperature and freezing the rest of the river. They woke up and simply walked across.

As they leave the wilderness on the way back to Williamsburg at the end of the journal, Washington gives readers one final image, a great one: "We met seventeen Horses loaded with Materials and Stores for a Fort at the Forks of Ohio, and the Day after some Families going out to settle."[38] Washington's image beautifully captures a crucial moment in American history. As he and Gist—the soldier and the trailblazer—return from the wilderness, they encounter pioneers venturing west to settle the land.

CHAPTER 6

A Memorial Containing a Summary View of Facts

Ay me! what perils do environ
The man that meddles with cold iron!
Samuel Butler, *Hudibras*

"La Belle Rivière": so the French used to call the Ohio River. And in the mid-eighteenth century they longed to make this beautiful river and the rich, fertile land it circumscribed a part of French North America. William Smith, the eighteenth-century historian of New York, assessed the situation as he pondered the beginnings of the Seven Years' War in his *Review of the Military Operations in North America*: "The French, jealous of the growth of the English colonies, were now meditating all possible arts to distress them, and extend the limits of their own frontier."[1]

Reports of French incursions into the Ohio valley filtered back to Williamsburg by 1754, riling Governor Dinwiddie so much he started recruiting troops to send west to defend British territory against the French and their Native American allies. The governor gave Joshua Fry, best known for the classes in mathematics and natural philosophy he taught at the College of William and Mary, command of the Virginia forces. Though this professor-turned-colonel had little military experience, Fry did have a superb knowledge of the land. Three years earlier he had collaborated with Peter Jefferson—Thomas's father—to create the most accurate and detailed map of Virginia to that time. Dinwiddie appointed George Washington to serve as Fry's lieutenant colonel.

Before spring Governor Dinwiddie learned that French troops were on the move and progressing more quickly than expected. He ordered Washington to assemble the men he had enlisted so far, pack the provisions he had gathered, and head westward. Fry would follow later, according to the governor's plan. For the time being Washington would lead the campaign. He and his men left the last day of March 1754. With all the recent rain the creeks and streams and rivers spilled over their banks, forming dangerous obstacles for cross-country travel. The roads and trails were thick with clayey mud that stuck to every boot, hoof, and wagon wheel that passed. The movement of Washington's men was less a march than a slog. He recorded their slow pace in the notebook he brought along to chronicle the campaign.

Two months later, on May 28, his forces engaged a French and Indian party led by Joseph Coulon de Villiers, sieur de Jumonville. The British and French exchanged gunfire. This, Washington's first firefight, thrilled him to the core. As he famously said in a postscript to a letter he wrote his brother Jack three days later: "I can with truth assure you, I heard Bullets whistle and believe me there was something charming in the sound."[2]

Jack shared the letter with friends, who enjoyed it so well they made copies of it. One person who got hold of a copy indiscreetly sent it to the London Magazine, which published the entire letter in its August issue, making George Washington a published author again. In its printed form his letter found a wide readership in England. Even King George II read the London Magazine. Upon reading Washington's comment about the charming sound bullets made, the king remarked, "He would not say so, if he had been used to hear many."[3] Fifteen minutes after it had begun, the skirmish was over. The Virginians had won, and Jumonville was dead.

Washington's decision to engage the enemy might have been too sudden and too rash. Afterward the French claimed their troops had been on a mission to deliver a peaceful warning. From the British perspective Washington's action against the French threat was justified. According to one contemporary observer, Jumonville "was slain in fair Battle in open Opposition to the English, when he attempted to take their Convoy."[4] Jumonville's death had profound implications: it proved to be the spark that kindled the Seven Years' War. Commenting on the death of Jumonville a few years later, Voltaire quipped, "So complicated are the political interests of the present times, that a shot fired in America shall be the signal for setting all Europe together by the ears."[5]

The skirmish with Jumonville did not stop Washington's campaign. At Great Meadows his men built a fort he christened Fort Necessity. Planning a second fort, he chose an ideal location on Red Stone Creek.

Before his troops could erect it he learned that a much larger party of French and Indians under the command of Louis Coulon de Villiers—Jumonville's brother—was heading toward Fort Necessity hell-bent on revenge. Around twelve hundred men strong, the French and Indian party sought dark justice for Jumonville's death. Washington and his men left Red Stone Creek and returned to Fort Necessity, where they joined forces with James Mackay's Independent Company of regulars.

The presence of British regulars created some tension with the Virginia troops. From the colonial perspective the regulars were paid too much for doing too little. Despite the animosity between British and colonial troops, Washington respected their leader—"a brave and worthy officer," he called Mackay.[6] Colonel Fry never did reach Fort Necessity. Having fallen badly from his horse, he perished the last day of May. George Washington, at twenty-two, found himself commander of the Virginia army.

Despite his youth Washington had a dominating presence. Six feet tall and nearly two hundred pounds, he cut a figure most men admired. When he was astride his horse, few could command greater respect. An accomplished equestrian, Washington inspired awe wherever he rode, even among such expert riders as Thomas Jefferson and the Marquis de Chastellux. Jefferson called him "the best horseman of his age, and the most graceful figure that could be seen on horseback." Chastellux used similar language. Washington was "a very excellent and bold horseman, leaping the highest fences, and going extremely quick, without standing upon his stirrups, bearing on the bridle, or letting his horse run wild."[7]

The Battle of Great Meadows did not allow Washington to demonstrate his equestrian skills. Instead he and his men were pinned down inside the poorly designed Fort Necessity. The battle began as the French attacked the fort on July 3, 1754. Fierce fighting continued all day. By nightfall Washington sadly realized the French had the Anglo-American forces greatly outmanned and outgunned. He prudently decided to surrender. William Smith, who considered him "a young gentleman of great bravery and distinguished merit," explained: "Col. Washington, observing the great superiority of the enemy, who now began to hem him in on all quarters, found himself under an absolute necessity of submitting to the disagreeable terms that were offered him."[8] Smith's choice of words was inadvertent. At least one hopes he was not punning on the name of the fort when he mentioned the grim necessity of submission.

Washington and Mackay signed articles of capitulation, but, unbeknownst to them, a devilish detail concerning Washington's campaign had been altered in translation. Coulon de Villiers tricked him into signing a document admitting he had deliberately assassinated sieur de

Jumonville. John Huske called these articles of capitulation "the most in-famous a *British* Subject ever put his Hand to."[9] A Boston merchant living in London, Huske scarcely masked the disdain he felt toward the Virginia native in command. Such regional bias would dog Washington through-out his military and political career.

From the time he and his men had left Alexandria until a week before the French attack, Washington had diligently maintained a journal, which somehow ended up in the hands of the French. Perhaps they forcibly took it from him. Perhaps they confiscated it with other official British papers. Or perhaps Washington accidentally left it behind when he evacuated Fort Necessity. Regardless how they obtained it, the French understood its propaganda value: they could use his journal to justify their aggression against the British on the American frontier. Only a few French officers scrutinized Washington's journal at first, but it gradually found its way into print and caught the attention of the French and English reading public.

French military commanders also recognized that Washington's jour-nal contained useful information about their Anglo-American enemy. They sent the manuscript to Montreal, where translators prepared at least two different French versions of the journal, and scriveners made multi-ple copies to distribute to other colonial officials.[10] Baron de Longueuil, lieutenant governor of Montreal, received one. Marquis Duquesne, the governor of New France, received another.

After reading it closely, Duquesne sent an abridged version to his sub-ordinate, the sieur de Contrecoeur, commander at Fort Duquesne. In a lengthy cover letter dated the second week of September 1754, Governor Duquesne lambasted Washington: "You will see that he is the most im-pertinent of men, but that he is as clever as he is crafty with credulous savages. Besides, he lies a great deal in order to justify the assassination of Sieur de Jumonville, which has recoiled upon him, and which he was stupid enough to admit in his capitulation!"[11]

The crotchety Duquesne could hardly suppress a sneer as he thought about Washington, who represented what he viewed as characteristic British duplicity. Duquesne also had some snide remarks for the Iroquois, calling them hypocrites for first promising to help the Virginians and then abandoning them when they needed help the most. As the short-sighted Duquesne read Washington's journal, he could hardly imagine the French would have difficulty conquering Anglo-American forces. To him the journal read like a chronicle of dissension: the colonial American troops seemed ill-prepared, ill-equipped, and ill-suited to wage war on the French. Duquesne indulged his fancy in the cover letter to Contrecoeur. He imagined reading the journal in Washington's presence at the moment of his surrender: "There is nothing more unworthy, and lower, or even blacker than the opinions and the way of thinking of this Washington! It would have been a pleasure to read his outrageous journal to him right under his nose."[12]

In the coming months Duquesne apparently read Washington's journal over and over again. It became something of an obsession for him, even affecting how he interpreted the changing seasons. In a letter to Contrecoeur the following March, for example, Duquesne characterized the time of year as "the season when Mr. Washington had the most troubles and hardships because of the floods."[13] Though he scoffed at the leader of the Virginia troops, Duquesne was obviously moved by Washington's words.

After returning home from his defeat at Fort Necessity, Washington looked forward to getting back to the battlefield and advancing his military career as war between Great Britain and France escalated. His status as a colonial subject hindered his progress. Having served as both lieutenant colonel and commander of the Virginia forces, he learned the British government now barred colonial officers from holding a rank higher than captain, regardless of their previous service. Washington resigned his commission—to the dismay of General Edward Braddock, commander in chief of the British forces in America. Braddock recognized Washington's military capabilities and asked him to serve as his aide. Washington accepted the position but stubbornly refused to take a reduction in rank or a cut in pay. Instead, he arranged to serve as a volunteer with neither rank nor pay.

In the spring of 1755 Braddock led an expedition to gain control of the forks of the Ohio River. As he and his men neared Fort Duquesne in early July, Washington warned the general that the French fought differently in America than they did in Europe and urged him to attack Indian-style. Though Braddock had recruited Washington as his aide, he was strangely reluctant to take his advice.

Dr. Alexander Hamilton—the witty Annapolis physician, not to be confused with Washington's future secretary of the treasury—interviewed some of the officers who had accompanied the expedition. Dr. Hamilton described Braddock's behavior as "austere and Supercilious," his temper "haughty and Imperious." Braddock, Hamilton continued, "was only barely civil from the teeth outwards to Major George Washington one of his Aids de Camps, a Youth of an undaunted and brave Spirit, whose deserts are beyond my expression."[14] Washington had held the rank of colonel at Fort Necessity, but he now held no rank. That Hamilton called him a major indicates how firmly *The Journal of Major George Washington* had established his soldierly reputation.

Braddock planned to fight in rigid formation, the way the British had fought and won in the past. His outspoken aide offered to lead the provincial troops separately, so they could, in Washington's words, "engage the enemy in their own way."[15] Braddock met the offer with scorn and, on July 9, 1755, promptly led the British and colonial troops to slaughter. The bloodshed was at least partly caused by Braddock's refusal to accept Washington's advice. Retelling the history of the Seven Years' War soon after a peace had been reached, Oliver Goldsmith attributed the tragedy to Braddock's refusal to employ "irregulars on the flanks of his army" or "to scour the country through which he was to march."[16]

During the Battle of the Monongahela, as the conflict became known, the French forces and their Indian allies ambushed the British, killing hundreds of men, including many officers. Braddock himself was mortally wounded, as Dr. James Craik sadly realized while attending the general in his final moments. Craik, having already served under Washington at Fort Necessity, was becoming a good friend. Their friendship would last a lifetime.[17] Washington escaped injury at the Battle of the Monongahela, though he had two horses shot from beneath him, and though, in Dr. Hamilton's words, his "upper Coat was almost shot to tatters with musket balls."[18] Washington guided the surviving troops to safety.

On July 17 Washington, Craik, and the other survivors reached Fort Cumberland, Maryland, where Washington heard a rumor about his own death. Worried the rumor might reach home before him, he wrote his brother Jack, taking a light-hearted tone to let him know he was alright: "As I have heard since my arrival at this place, a circumstantial account of my death and dying Speech, I take this early opportunity of contradicting the first, and of assuring you that I have not, as yet, composed the latter."[19]

Washington's letter to his brother follows a tradition of American humor established by Captain John Smith. From the founding of the Jamestown colony a century and a half earlier, dark humor had been an early American coping strategy, a defense mechanism useful for enduring otherwise unendurable horror.[20] Washington's sense of humor helped him cope with the tremendous bloodshed and loss of life he encountered at the Battle of the Monongahela.

By no means could his sense of humor efface the horror from his memory. Three decades later, he could still see the carnage in his mind's eye. In an unguarded moment, Washington vividly recalled:

The shocking Scenes which presented themselves in this Nights March are not to be described—The dead—the dying—the groans—lamentation—and crys along the Road of the wounded for help (for those under the latter descriptions endeavoured from the first commencement of the action—or rather confusion to escape to the 2d division) were enough to pierce a heart of adamant. The gloom and horror of which was not a little encreased by the impervious darkness occasioned by the close shade of thick woods which in places rendered it impossible for the two guides which attended to know when they were in, or out of the track but by groping on the ground with their hands.[21]

The exquisite lyricism of this text, regardless of its horrific imagery, suggests that Washington had mulled over the episode time and time again, refining his memory, trying to come to terms with what had happened. Beginning with the trope of the indescribable, he nonetheless attempts to describe what had happened. A catalogue of gut-wrenching images and sounds follow. Linked together with a series of dashes, they have a stutter-step quality. The horrors occur in succession yet without being coherently connected. Using the deliberate correction ("action—or rather confusion"), Washington conveyed his ongoing uncertainty about the situation. Years after the event he was still grappling with how to express the bloody loss of life. His figurative language elevates his description to a kind of poetry, albeit a dark and disturbing kind. He ends with an absurdist image worthy of Samuel Beckett, depicting the guides mired in such obscurity they must grope their way through the darkness with their hands outstretched before them.

Soon after the tragic event, Washington parceled out praise and blame. In a letter to Governor Dinwiddie, he expressed his appreciation of the British officers who "in general behaved with incomparable bravery." He had greater praise for the Virginia troops, who, he famously said, "behaved like Men, and died like Soldiers." Unlike Dr. Hamilton and other contemporary commentators, Washington did not critique General Braddock. But he did come down hard on the British regulars, who "broke and run as Sheep before Hounds, leaving the Artillery, Ammunition, Provisions, Baggage and in short everything a prey to the Enemy." Seeking to rally the British troops in order to regain the ground they had lost and recover the equipment, Washington and his supporters had, he wrote, "as little success as if we had attempted to have stopped the wild Bears of the Mountains or rivulets with our feet, for they would break by in spite of every effort that could be made to prevent it."[22]

Washington's role in the battle earned him the praise of his contemporaries. The Reverend Samuel Davies, for one, called him a "heroic youth." Alluding to Washington's perilous escape from the battle, Davies prophesized, "I cannot but hope Providence has hitherto preserved in so signal a manner for some important service to his country."[23]

With Braddock's death Governor William Shirley of Massachusetts became commander in chief of the British forces in America, and he shifted the focus of the war to Canada, a decision that left the Virginia frontier open to attack. The House of Burgesses passed legislation creating a conscript army of up to two thousand troops and appointed Washington colonel of the Virginia Regiment and commander in chief of all Virginia forces. Despite Washington's burgeoning military expertise, his troops could do little to stop the Indian raids along the frontier.

Adding to his frustration Washington encountered further difficulties regarding the relative rank of British and colonial officers. As commander of the Virginia forces, he depended on Fort Cumberland as a strategic outpost, but a British captain there claimed to outrank Colonel Washington, arguing that an officer's commission in the regular British army trumped an officer's commission in the colonial army, regardless of rank. The governor of Maryland supported the captain. Washington protested. So did Governor Dinwiddie. The matter was referred to Governor Shirley.

When correspondence proved fruitless, Washington took drastic measures. He rode from Virginia to Boston on horseback in February 1756 to plead his case. The journey brought him through Philadelphia and New York on his way to Boston—places he had never visited before—and gave him a broad perspective on colonial America, a perspective that would serve him well in the coming years. Shirley invalidated the captain's commission and made Colonel Washington the ranking officer in Maryland.

Shirley's actions fixed the problem in Washington's case but did not solve the ongoing conflict between the relative rankings of British and colonial officers. For the rest of 1756 through the following year, Washington served as commander of the Virginia and Maryland troops on the frontier. He continued to hone his military skills and develop his administrative abilities.

As the French waged war against the British in the North American wilderness, French propagandists did their part to justify the conflict in print, Jacob Nicolas Moreau taking the lead role in this regard. As a political propagandist, Moreau had only recently come to the fore. From his perspective, current political and religious challenges to the French monarchy threatened both public authority and social order. Moreau took it upon himself to defend absolute royal power in the face of these threats.

A pamphlet he had published in 1755 defending royal authority as the basis of political and social order attracted the attention of the French crown. Consequently Moreau became a paid propagandist for the Ministry of Foreign Affairs. He was assigned the task of pleading the case of France against England in the Seven Years' War. Moreau's defense of French monarchical authority both during and after the war earned him the title of royal historiographer.[24]

When a manuscript copy of Washington's journal reached Moreau's hands, he chose to include it in *Mémoire Contenant le Précis des Faits avec Leurs Pieces Justificatives* (1756), a work issued by the French government as propaganda to explain the reasons for the rupture between France and Great Britain and to urge support for the war. According to one recent historian, Moreau's version of Washington's journal constituted "an unofficial codicil to France's formal declaration of war, a testimony to the justice of France's cause."[25]

Initially released in quarto as an official government document, Moreau's *Mémoire* was republished in less expensive, smaller format editions for the French reading public. Reprinted at The Hague later that year, it was disseminated across Europe. Washington unwittingly found himself a published author again. Given the way Moreau treated his journal, its publication cannot be considered a distinction.

Since Washington's original diary does not survive, the French translations are the only known versions of it. Allowing for a number of deliberate omissions and for what naturally gets lost in translation, Washington's editors agree that the fullest known translation roughly coincides with what Washington wrote.[26] The greatest damage Moreau did to Washington's journal was not in translation but annotation. Moreau read it much as Duquesne had, and his footnotes reflect his derogatory attitude. Overall Moreau used his annotations to undermine what Washington had written, twisting his words to make them say whatever Moreau wished them to say.

Quoting one letter signed "Contocarious," Moreau asserted that Washington used this Indian name to endear himself to the people he intended to delude.[27] Moreau made this assertion without knowing what Contocarious meant or how Washington gained the name. Actually, the name was not necessarily flattering. As Washington later told David Humphreys, Half King had given him the name during his diplomatic mission to Fort Le Boeuf in 1753. It means "Town Eater." Half King did not necessarily sense any town-gobbling predilections in George Washington; he had given him the name because it was the Indian name of his great-grandfather, John Washington.[28] In the Native American oral tradition, the Washington family remained well known, and its genealogy was preserved as part of the communal memory.[29] Known as Contocarious among the North American Indians, George Washington had little choice when it came to signing documents intended for a Native American audience. He signed his letter this way simply to identify, not endear, himself to the Indians.

Elsewhere in his journal Washington had explained that Governor Shirley would send six hundred troops "to harass the French in Canada." Though Shirley's action represented a strategic decision to shift the war from the backcountry of Pennsylvania and Virginia to Canada, Moreau interpreted it as a general indication of the bellicose nature of the British, expressing himself in feigned amazement in another footnote: "Behold the English always attacking."[30] At a place in the text where Washington cited Half King as the authority for the warlike intentions of Jumonville's party, Moreau placed a note questioning the statement's authority. Washington had clearly attributed his information to Half King; Moreau's annotation denies the authority of the Native American voice.[31]

Copies of Moreau's *Mémoire* reached the American strand toward the end of 1756. One was found on board a French vessel captured by a British privateer and brought to Saint Kitts. A gentleman from there brought it to New York. Soon afterward British privateers seized another French vessel, on which they found several more copies of Moreau's *Mémoire*. Philadelphia publisher James Chattin and New York publishers Hugh Gaine and the firm of James Parker and William Weyman agreed to sponsor a translation, which they would jointly publish by subscription. Issuing a broadside dated January 29, 1757, announcing the translation and soliciting subscribers, Chattin advertised his edition before the New York publishers advertised theirs.[32] His expedience created some tension between them.

Describing the volume's contents in his proposal, Chattin let potential subscribers know that it would contain what he called "The Journal of Major Washington." Calling him a major in his proposal, Chattin reinforces the impact of Washington's earlier work, *The Journal of Major George Washington*. Washington's exploits on the frontier had already helped create a name for him beyond the borders of Virginia. As Christopher Gist told him around that time, "Your Name is more talked of in Pennsylvania than any Other person of the Army."[33]

The month after Chattin published his broadside advertisement soliciting subscribers for the book, Washington came to Philadelphia. His purpose was pragmatic: he sought an audience with John Campbell, fourth earl of Loudon, the new commander in chief of the British forces in North America. The precise date of Washington's arrival is unknown, but his accounts show that on February 24, 1757, he subscribed to Chattin's Philadelphia edition of Moreau's *Mémoire*.[34]

Lord Loudon was notorious for keeping people waiting. Benjamin Franklin would tell a story about coming to see Loudon one day and meeting a messenger who was waiting on his lordship. When Franklin returned to see Loudon two weeks later, he met the same messenger again and welcomed him upon his return. The man replied, *"Return'd? No, I am not gone yet!"*[35]

Loudon would not reach Philadelphia until nearly three weeks after Washington, who consequently had plenty of extra time on his hands. The French edition of Moreau's *Mémoire* made Washington uneasy. Aware it contained information about his conduct, he grew anxious to read it, so anxious he could not wait until the English edition appeared. He felt helpless not knowing what was in the book. Washington obtained a copy of the French text and hired a translator to render into English both his journal and the French account of the battle at Fort Necessity. The translator completed his task the third week of March, when Washington paid him.[36]

Having learned about the forthcoming translation of Moreau's *Mémoire*, an unknown correspondent wrote to ask Washington's opinion of the volume. Washington responded with some comments on the text of what was supposedly his journal:

> In regard to the journal, I can only observe in general, that I kept no regular one during that expedition; rough minutes of occurrences I certainly took, and find them as certainly and strangely metamorphosed; some parts left out, which I remember were entered, and many things added that never were thought of; the names of men and things egregiously miscalled; and the whole of what I saw Englished is very incorrect and nonsensical.

With confidence in the Philadelphian he had hired to translate the text of his journal back into English, Washington held the French translator and editor accountable for the errors introduced to his text.[37]

His comments about the journal represent Washington's first known critical remarks on his own writing. Referring to his journal as "rough minutes of occurrences," he was being modest. So far his writing skills had improved with every journal he had kept. Regardless of his modesty, Washington took great pride in his writing and hated to see it mangled. He had an excellent memory and recalled some things he had written in his journal that the French had omitted. These omissions clashed with his penchant for precision. Washington disliked seeing all the details he had so carefully recorded so carelessly ignored.

Chattin stayed ahead of Gaine throughout the book's production. By the first week of June, Chattin had issued a handsomely printed octavo edition of the work. It proved to be one of his most distinguished imprints. He later fell on hard times and left the printing business.[38] When Chattin's edition appeared, Gaine had yet to finish printing the New York edition. To make his belated edition more marketable, Gaine undercut Chattin's price, advertising that the forthcoming book would be considerably cheaper than the Philadelphia edition.[39] Early American consumers were often willing to forego first editions for cheaper ones issued later. The firm of Parker and Weyman did not print its own edition, but instead issued sheets from Gaine's edition with a different title page. All three share the same title: *A Memorial Containing a Summary View of Facts, with Their Authorities: In Answer to the Observations Sent by the English Ministry to the Courts of Europe.*

Washington's journal was also republished in England and Ireland. A London edition of Moreau's *Mémoire* appeared in late 1757. Copies of the American translation may have reached England before the British edition appeared, but London publisher William Bizet independently commissioned an English translation, which he issued as *The Conduct of the Late Ministry; or, A Memorial; Containing a Summary of Facts with Their Vouchers, in Answer to the Observations, Sent by the English Ministry, to the Courts of Europe.* Washington's journal also appeared as an appendix to the Dublin edition of William Smith's *Review of the Military Operations in North America.*

British readers received *The Conduct of the Late Ministry* with indignation. While admitting the French had a right to publish whatever they wished to publish, they saw no reason why French propaganda should be imposed upon English readers. The *Monthly Review* wondered: "What business have we to strengthen their efforts, and extend the circulation of their sophistry, by the additional aid of our own language?" With a sigh of relief, the reviewer concluded that the work would not make any English readers sympathetic to the French cause and dismissed the volume with a few brief comments.[40]

The *Critical Review* devoted more space to *The Conduct of the Late Ministry*, but its conclusions were much the same as those of the *Monthly Review*. According to the *Critical Review*, the documents that constituted the book simply did not prove what its French compiler wanted them to prove. The reviewer saw through Moreau's obfuscatory annotations. Since the documents themselves did not say what Moreau wanted, he annotated

them to suit the purpose of propaganda. The *Critical Review* concluded
with the hope that an enterprising British author would refute the book.[41]

No book-length refutation came forth, but the publishing history of
George Washington's journal does not stop with the first issue of the
London edition of Moreau's *Mémoire*, which was reissued two years later
under a more captivating title: *The Mystery Reveal'd; or, Truth Brought
to Light*. According to its complete title, which is so long that it threatens
to nudge its outermost letters off the edges of the title page, the work presented extraordinary facts relating to the conduct of the late ministry,
supported by authentic papers and memoirs that "neither confidence can
out-brave, nor cunning invalidate." As if the provocative subtitle were
insufficient, the title page also contained a menacing Latin motto: "*Monstrum
horrendum!*" These words come from Virgil's description of Polyphemus
in the *Aeneid:* "A monster dreadful, misshapen, huge, whose sight was
destroyed." The Latin phrase was often used as shorthand to express the
dreadful, hideous nature of any monstrous thing.[42]

The book's sensational title is representative of the typical output of its
publisher, who also issued such cheap, bawdy novels as *The Reform'd
Coquet* and *Adventures of a Rake*. In short, *The Mystery Reveal'd* was just
another cheap book issued to generate some quick cash for its publisher.
The *Monthly Review* was not fooled by this meretricious product, commenting: "Here we, too, have a mystery to reveal, and a truth to bring
to light; for this pamphlet is itself an errant imposition on the Public.
Monstrum horrendum is the motto to this pretended revelation; and *monstrum horrendum* say we, when we reflect on the *ars meretriciae* of these
literary midwives: the present publication being no other than a vamp'd-
up title-page to an old pamphlet first published in 1757."[43] The words
George Washington wrote on a wilderness trail had found their way to
Grub Street.

CHAPTER 7

Home and Garden

Friends, books, a garden, and perhaps his pen,
Delightful industry enjoyed at home,
And Nature in her cultivated trim
Dressed to his taste, inviting him abroad—
Can he want occupation, who has these?
                    William Cowper, "The Task"

Martha Dandridge Custis, a twenty-six-year-old widow, had more going for her than the young women George Washington had known in his youth. Meeting her when he was twenty-five, George saw Martha as a woman of substance, someone who took him seriously and whom he could take seriously. A short woman with chubby cheeks, Martha was physically unremarkable, but she had a comportment that beguiled her suitor. Perhaps Abigail Adams described Martha's demeanor best: "Her manners are modest and unassuming, dignified and feminine, not a tincture of hauteur about her."[1] That Martha Custis was quite possibly Virginia's wealthiest widow under thirty did not diminish her appeal. George courted her through the spring of 1758, when he returned to military service.

Not until this year was the thorny issue of military rank among British and colonial officers resolved. Finally, colonial officers would be treated with parity—or so it seemed. Satisfied with the outcome of this controversy, Washington resumed command of the Virginia Regiment, serving under General John Forbes, along with seven thousand British regulars. A veteran of the War of the Austrian Succession, Forbes faced a new

J. Rogers, after a painting by John Woolaston, *Mrs. George Washington*, steel engraving. Frontispiece to Rufus Wilmot Griswold, *The Republican Court; or, American Society in the Days of Washington* (1854; New York: Appleton, 1867). Kevin J. Hayes Collection, Toledo, Ohio.

challenge once assigned the arduous task of capturing Fort Duquesne. Determined to avoid Braddock's errors, he approached his assignment methodically.

General Forbes tolerated Washington's colonial troops but had little respect for them. "An extream bad Collection of broken Innkeepers, Horse Jockeys, and Indian traders," he called them, "a gathering from the scum of the worst of people."[2] Though a great student of the art of war, Forbes was not overly pedantic. Unlike Braddock, he recognized the importance of adapting his military strategy and techniques to suit local conditions. "In this country," he admitted, we "must comply and learn the Art of Warr, from Ennemy Indians or anything else who have seen the Country and Warr carried on in itt."[3]

Forbes and Washington clashed when it came to choosing a route to Fort Duquesne. Whereas Washington felt they should follow Braddock's original route, Forbes decided to cut a fresh road through western Pennsylvania. In this instance Washington seems motivated less by military strategy than by commercial impulses. He knew that whichever road the army cut through the wilderness would affect western expansion. The route Forbes chose would benefit Pennsylvania, not Virginia.

Problems with supplies and manpower delayed the trip for months, and Forbes's meticulousness compelled them to proceed at a snail's pace. The French saw the British forces as a juggernaut, albeit a very slow one. By the time British and colonial troops neared Fort Duquesne in late November, the French had burned down the fort and decamped. Washington's last campaign during the Seven Years' War thus ended in anticlimax.

Once he returned home from the war, George and Martha were married. On January 6, 1759, presumably at her estate on the Pamunkey River, they tied the knot. That April George brought to Mount Vernon Martha and her two children, John Parke Custis, then four years old, and his two-year-old sister, Martha Parke Custis—Jacky and Patsy, as they were known in the family. Washington assumed responsibility for his two stepchildren and raised them as his own. In addition he undertook the burdensome task of administering Jacky's large and complex estate.

Settling into the life of a gentleman farmer, Washington worked hard to make Mount Vernon and its outlying plantations a success. His marriage provided the impetus to decorate the house and develop the farm. The month after bringing Martha to Mount Vernon, he placed a sizeable order with the London firm of Robert Cary and Company. Cary had been handling the Custis family affairs in London, so Washington saw no reason to discontinue the business relationship. The firm received regular consignments of tobacco from the Custis plantations and supplied whatever manufactured goods the family needed. Washington also let Cary handle much of his own business affairs in London.[4]

The first order he placed with the firm included a bedstead decorated with fashionable blue curtains plus matching window curtains, coverlet, and upholstery. Decorating their bedroom, Washington sought to impress his bride. He wanted to have everything just right, "to make the whole furniture of this Room uniformly handsome and genteel." This initial order also included several other items to enhance their home and elevate their lifestyle: carpeting, china, glassware, ivory-handled cutlery, and, of course, books.[5]

The specific books Washington ordered reflect his desire to broaden his agricultural knowledge. So far he had been doing what all the big Virginia planters did: dedicating his time and land to tobacco, a demanding crop. It was hard on the soil and hard on the enslaved men and women who tended it. The books Washington ordered after his marriage described alternate crops and alternative approaches to farming. They reflect his desire to diversify his plantations.[6]

Washington ordered the "newest, and most approvd Treatise of Agriculture" and *A New System of Agriculture*, or "a Speedy way to grow Rich," as he paraphrased its subtitle.[7] These orders reveal his eagerness to learn the latest agricultural methods, which would help his plantations turn a handsome profit without relying on tobacco. He also requested a gardening handbook and the latest edition of a standard work on farriery.

Cary filled the order as best he could. Typically he subdivided Washington's requests, distributing parts of each order to whichever suppliers who were best qualified to fulfill them. He passed book requests to John Clarke, a prominent London bookseller, who obtained three of the works: the second edition of *A New System of Agriculture*, Batty Langley's *New Principles of Gardening*, and William Gibson's *New Treatise on the Diseases of Horses*. This last work was more difficult to procure. Clarke, who may have been exaggerating, said only one copy of Gibson's *New Treatise* could be had in all of London, but he procured it for Washington.[8] All three titles stress the novelty of the works. Though the ones by Langley and Gibson were already several years old, the fact that the word "new" appeared in their titles made them seem cutting edge.

The author of *A New System of Agriculture; or, A Plain, Easy, and Demonstrative Method of Growing Rich* identifies himself solely as a "Country Gentleman." His true identity has escaped history. Agriculture, strange to say, was a hot topic in the 1750s; enterprising London publishers could turn a handsome profit issuing books on the subject. Many farming handbooks sprouted not from the soil of the English countryside but from cracks in the pavement of Grub Street. In retrospect this so-called country gentleman seems more like a cleverly crafted persona, a rhetorical strategy to validate its author's agricultural ideas. The book does contain some useful advice, but harebrained schemes with little practical value eventually take over the text. Critiquing the author's ideas, a contemporary reviewer quipped, "His *three capital schemes* are as *romantic* as ever entered the head of a writer on *rural* oeconomy."[9] The level-headed Washington, one suspects, found the author's get-rich-quick schemes disappointing.

A New System of Agriculture resembled many other contemporary works of husbandry: heavy on theory and light on practice. Whereas this and other contemporary agricultural works reflect increasingly scientific methods, the theorists risked losing touch with the soil. Other agricultural writers promoted their works by emphasizing practical foundations. In Maryland Charles Carroll of Carrollton—a signer of the Declaration of Independence—had an excellent agricultural library. Recommending one agricultural book to Washington, Carroll assured him that its author's knowledge of the subject was based not in theory but in experience.[10]

William Fairfax, who knew Langley's work, may have recommended him to Washington.[11] After receiving his copy of Langley's *New Principles of Gardening*, Washington inscribed the title page. He recorded its cost in the left-hand corner and wrote his name and the year in the right: "Geo. Washington. 1760." A major contribution to the history of landscape gardening, Langley's *New Principles* would profoundly influence the garden Washington designed for Mount Vernon. Langley's gardening vocabulary became his.

Washington also accepted Langley's aesthetic, that the curved line was the line of beauty. The preference for curved over straight lines in garden design became so prevalent in the second half of the eighteenth century that some found it a source of humor. In *The Clandestine Marriage*, one of the era's leading stage comedies, a social climber named Sterling hopes to marry his daughter to a baronet. Sterling boasts to him that his garden contains no distasteful straight lines but instead is "all taste—zigzag— crinkum-crankum—in and out—right and left—to and again—twisting and turning like a worm."[12]

New Principles of Gardening, a veritable diatribe against regularity, reads like a manifesto. Langley said that nothing was "more *shocking* than a *stiff regular Garden;* where after we have seen one quarter thereof, the very same is repeated in all the remaining Parts, so that we are tired, instead of being further entertain'd with something new as expected."[13]

New Principles of Gardening contains many plans for irregular gardens, but Langley's theoretical outlook surpassed his practical designs. While clamoring for irregularity, Langley presented designs that seem comparatively formal and artificial.[14]

Though *New Principles of Gardening* reflects the fashions of the 1720s, Langley's advice often transcends the times. Here's one lasting idea: "There is nothing more agreeable in a Garden than good *Shade*, and without it *a Garden is nothing*." Here's another: "Those great *Beauties of Nature*, HILLS and VALLEYS, were always levelled at very great Expences to complete their Regularity, or otherwise I may justly say, the total ruin of the *Gardens*."[15] Langley's emphasis on keeping the terrain as natural as possible appealed to prosperous Virginians who sought pleasure gardens of their own.

Washington found the garden plans attractive yet impractical, being too complex for use at Mount Vernon. He radically simplified Langley's ideas to apply them to his situation. Washington kept the concept that a garden should be a large park surrounding all four sides of a house and that it should contains a variety of elements.[16] He already had one of Langley's most fundamental requirements for a great garden: a beautiful and extensive view. The expanse of the Potomac provided a magnificent view, "the most beautiful view in the world," according to one eighteenth-century visitor.[17] Washington carefully landscaped the slope from the house down to the river to frame the view, not obscure it.[18]

Books belonging to the Custis household came to Mount Vernon upon Martha's marriage to George. There's little evidence to indicate which works belonged on Martha's bookshelf—with two notable exceptions. When she had married Daniel Custis in 1749, Martha took possession of a family manuscript dating back to the seventeenth century. A two-part work, the manuscript consists of "A Booke of Cookery" and "A Booke of Sweetmeats." Whereas the second part is devoted to sweets, the first is devoted to savory dishes. It contained recipes for stuffed leg of veal, roast leg of mutton, Oxford sausages, capon poached after the Flanders fashion, porridge of old peas, and many kinds of savory pies: chicken pie, pigeon pie, veal and bacon pie, and even humble pie (humbles, or umbles, are the organ meats of a deer). Martha would continue to use this manuscript recipe book throughout her marriage to George and ultimately pass it down to her granddaughter. "A Booke of Cookery" serves as a reminder of the ongoing importance of manuscript culture in eighteenth-century America. Many different English cookbooks were published during the century, but there is no evidence that Martha Washington added any to the library at Mount Vernon. Her manuscript cookbook was so detailed and so thorough that others were unnecessary.[19]

Martha also had a manuscript music book that she kept during her first marriage and continued to use throughout her second. It contained the airs of Handel; minuets and gavottes of Jean-Baptiste Lully, a seventeenth-century French composer; and such popular songs as "Lovely Nancy," "The Wedding Day," and "Oh Dear, What Can the Matter Be," all in Martha's handwriting. Her interest in Handel is part of the times. All connoisseurs of music, John Quincy Adams observed, are "extravagantly fond of Handel." Her appreciation for the baroque stylings of Lully is more unusual, but not unheard of. Regardless, it is fun to imagine George and Martha Washington dancing a gavotte through the halls of Mount Vernon.[20]

Books from her first husband that came to Mount Vernon also included one of Gervase Markham's numerous works on farriery, most likely *Markham's Master-piece*.[21] Wanting something more up to date, Washington ordered the latest edition of William Gibson's *New Treatise on the Diseases of Horses*.[22] The foremost British authority on the care of horses, Gibson wrote several works on farriery, but *New Treatise* is his masterwork. Washington's eye for horseflesh has been taken as a natural gift, but he understood that books could expand his knowledge.

Less than two months after Gibson's *New Treatise* reached Mount Vernon, Washington had the opportunity to put the book to use. An unusual storm brought damaging winds and excessive rain late one Thursday evening in February 1760. By Friday morning, the storm abated enough to let him spend much of the day outdoors erecting a fence around his peach orchard. Friday afternoon he went to Belvoir to invite Lord Fairfax to dinner. Returning to Mount Vernon that night, Washington discovered that the right foreleg of Jolly, one of his best wagon horses, was, in his words, mashed to pieces. A heavy tree limb had fallen on Jolly during the storm the previous night, badly breaking its leg.[23]

Gibson's *New Treatise* was useless on this occasion. Since Gibson saw a horse's broken leg as a death sentence, he had nothing to say about how to set one. Desperate to save Jolly, Washington reverted to Markham, who supplied more amenable advice: "The old Traditions in Horse leachcraft affirm, that all Fractures above the Knee are incurable; and so despairing, they cease to make Practice. But they are much deceived; for neither the Fracture above the Knee, nor the Fracture below the Knee is more incurable in a Horse than in a Man, if the Farrier can tell how to keep the Horse from struggling, or tormenting the Member grieved."[24]

Markham provides detailed instructions, which Washington followed as closely as he could. First sling up the horse with a strong double canvas and then raise it so that its hooves just barely touch the ground. For a broken foreleg, elevate the front of the horse, so that it can place its weight on its hind legs. Once the horse is slung, reset the bone and then wrap it in a cloth of unwashed wool newly pulled from a sheep's back, binding it fast to the leg with a smooth linen roller soaked in oil and vinegar. Splint it with three broad, smooth, strong splints, binding them fast at each end with a thong, keeping the horse's leg very straight.

According to Markham, the horse would have to stay in its sling and the splints would have to stay on its leg for forty days: a hard prescription. Two days later, Washington discovered that Jolly had fallen from its sling, struggled considerably, and reinjured the leg. Sadly, he now had no choice and ordered Jolly to be shot to death.

Though neither Gibson nor Markham could help him save Jolly, Washington did not dismiss the written word as a way of learning more about practical methods of caring for his horses. Within the next few years, in fact, he acquired *The Complete Horseman; or, Perfect Farrier*, a work by Jacques Labessie de Solleysel, a self-taught horseman and veterinarian who taught the art of horsemanship to French nobility. The leading authority on the subject in France, Solleysel broke new ground in the diagnosis and treatment of equine diseases. His *Complete Horseman* gave Washington additional information to supplement Gibson and Markham.

Besides telling how to cure sick horses, Solleysel discussed the art of riding, describing a horse's natural movements, the rider's proper position, the use of the spur, and the way to execute the movements of dressage.[25] Though Washington's horsemanship continually impressed others, his riding skill was not merely a matter of natural ability. The presence of Solleysel in his library indicates that Washington studied how to ride more effectively—and more elegantly.

Unsure what Washington had meant when he requested the "newest, and most approvd Treatise of Agriculture," Clarke narrowed the possible works that fit the description down to two and sent both: Francis Home's *Principles of Agriculture and Vegetation* and Edward Lisle's two-volume *Observations in Husbandry*. Washington had not intended either, but once they arrived he added both to his growing library.

According to Dr. Alexander Hunter, Home's *Principles* was "a work well deserving the attention of every philosophical farmer."[26] Home was one of the earliest experimenters to apply chemistry to agriculture, thus putting agriculture on a sound, scientific basis. His rigorous methodology

Currier and Ives, *Genl. George Washington: The Father of His Country* (New York, ca. 1856), lithograph. Library of Congress, Prints and Photographs Division, Washington, DC (reproduction number: LC-USZC2-2427).

is clear throughout the work. He potted plants in soil treated with different chemicals, measured the results, and compared their efficacy. Washington would develop a reputation for his agricultural experiments at Mount Vernon; they were partly inspired by this book he received accidentally. He would continue studying how chemicals affected plant growth, later acquiring an innovative treatise outlining the connection between agriculture and chemistry.[27]

Edward Lisle's *Observations in Husbandry*, while making no pretense of being a complete guide to its subject, gave readers a huge amount of agricultural information. Despite its haphazard quality, the book contains a vast amount of practical detail and a number of agricultural observations.[28] Lisle deserves credit for collecting traditional wisdom that had circulated orally among British farmers for generations, which new farmers could now put to good use.

Before receiving either Home's *Principles* or Lisle's *Observations*, Washington wrote Cary a follow-up letter clarifying what he meant by the newest and most approved agricultural treatise: one that was "done by various hands—but chiefly collected from the Papers of Mr Hale."[29] A few more letters of clarification crossed the Atlantic before Washington received what he wanted: *The Compleat Body of Husbandry*. According to its title page, this work was based on papers assembled by someone named Thomas Hale, about whom nothing else is known. Hale may be a fictional persona invented by the actual compiler, possibly the miscellaneous writer John Hill.[30]

The work found other readers in early America. In Maryland Charles Carroll—not Charles Carroll of Carrollton but his distant cousin, who is generally known as Charles Carroll, Barrister—had a copy at Mount Clare, his home on the outskirts of Baltimore. Carroll's correspondence shows him using the work for reference. On one occasion he copied from *The Compleat Body of Husbandry* a long list of seeds—beetroot, broccoli, celery, and many other vegetables—which he ordered directly from London.[31]

Like Edward Lisle, the compiler of *The Compleat Body of Husbandry*—Hale or Hill or whoever—understood the value of tried-and-true farming methods. Washington saw similarities between the two authors and shelved their works together at Mount Vernon.[32] *The Compleat Body of Husbandry* reinforces the practice-over-theory argument. Too often, its author claims, farms have been ruined by inexperienced farmers following the latest methods espoused by inexperienced agricultural authors. Recording traditional methods, on the other hand, was difficult: old timers hesitated to share their ideas with bookish compilers. Happily, the author of *The Compleat Body of Husbandry* found several farmers willing to share their practical ideas. Enhancing these old methods with newer approaches, the work supplied valuable advice for young farmers. George Washington belonged to its ideal readership.

In June 1764 Washington purchased from the *Virginia Gazette* office in Williamsburg an agricultural book by his boyhood friend Buckner Stith.

The daybooks of the *Gazette* office list the title as "Treatise on Tobacco." Its real title is unknown, because no copies of it survive. Apparently, the work presented a general overview of tobacco culture in Virginia.[33] It is unfortunate that it has been lost: the one surviving letter Stith wrote to Washington shows he had a delightful writing style and a passion for tobacco, its cultivation and its use. In the letter he says that smoking three bowls can induce a pleasant inebriation, a heady feeling of nostalgia and excitement.[34]

The year Stith published his pamphlet, other writers warned readers about the dangers of tobacco. In *Cautions Against the Immoderate Use of Snuff Founded on the Known Qualities of the Tobacco Plant*, John Hill advocated total abstinence from tobacco, recommending the British government ban its use altogether. Some readers thought Hill protested too much. Reviewing the pamphlet, Sir Tanfield Leman, a London physician, said Hill was "arraigning a *fashionable* custom, with as much acrimony as an antiquated Prude would rail against the frailty of the flesh." Seizing upon one of Hill's more frivolous arguments, that snuff could lead to excessive belching, Sir Tanfield wondered: "Supposing this wicked powder of Tobacco should travel from the stomach downward to the intestines, and cause certain commotions *deorsum*, might not the consequential explosions, *a posteriori*, give equal, if not greater offence to delicacy than the unmannerly eructations *a superiori?*"[35]

In retrospect Hill's discussion of tobacco's harmful effects is astonishingly modern. He was the first to identify a relationship between snuff and nasal cancer.[36] There is no evidence that Washington read Hill's *Cautions*, but his decision to shift agricultural production at Mount Vernon from tobacco to other crops, though economically motivated, could have been influenced by health concerns. By 1764 Washington had already started growing wheat as a cash crop. Over the next five years he expanded his wheat production twentyfold. He also began producing other cash crops—hemp, flax, oats—slowly phasing out the cultivation of tobacco at Mount Vernon.[37]

Among Washington's surviving papers is a set of notes transcribing or summarizing many passages from Jethro Tull's *Horse-Hoeing Husbandry*, the agricultural manual that laid the groundwork for the so-called "new husbandry," which departed from traditional methods of agriculture by incorporating the latest technological developments. Washington's notes from Jethro Tull reinforce the shift in agricultural production his farm at Mount Vernon was undergoing. He transcribed Tull's discussions of wheat and hemp at considerable length.

Washington took additional notes from Jethro Tull elsewhere. His 1760 diary contains a lengthy paraphrase from Tull regarding the cultivation of alfalfa. His editors have identified the copy Washington used as the 1751 edition of *Horse-Hoeing Husbandry*, but this title is not listed in his 1764 library catalogue, nor does a copy of it survive among his other books. Its absence from the Mount Vernon library may have something to do with practices of borrowing and loaning books in early America. Did Washington borrow the book from a friend and take notes from it, thus obviating the need for him to purchase a copy for himself? Or did he loan his copy of *Horse-Hoeing Husbandry* to a friend who never returned it?

If the second option is the case, Washington would not be the last person to loan out his copy of Jethro Tull and never get it back. Thomas Jefferson loaned his to Edmund Randolph, who lost the book.[38] It is a testament to the utility of Jethro Tull's *Horse-Hoeing Husbandry* that borrowers hesitated to return the book. By 1786 Washington could no longer do without a copy of Jethro Tull at Mount Vernon and ordered a new edition, neatly bound and lettered.[39]

The almanac was another kind of book on the colonial farmer's bookshelf. Typically published a few months before the start of a new year, almanacs gave farmers essential information to help them decide when to sow and when to reap. Williamsburg booksellers sold Virginia almanacs interleaved with blank pages, which provided users with plenty of white space to record miscellaneous notes throughout the year. Thomas Jefferson bought an interleaved copy of the *Virginia Almanack* every year and filled the blank pages with notes. So did George Washington.

Washington used his interleaved almanacs as diaries. A copy of Joseph Royle's *Virginia Almanack for 1762* is his earliest surviving almanac. His manuscript notes in it capture the day-to-day activities at Mount Vernon that year. On February 9, for example, he recorded, "Began Plowing for Oats." He did not finish plowing for oats—about twenty acres later— until Saturday, March 20. The following Saturday, he finished sowing and harrowing his oats, forty-four bushels altogether. The last Monday in April he began planting corn at all his plantations, a task that would take until the first Tuesday in May.[40]

Other notes concern current building projects at Mount Vernon. Guy, a local bricklayer from a neighboring plantation, came to Mount Vernon in early May. Washington noted, "Guy began the Garden Wall, after having built an Oven in the Kitchen, laid the hearth, and repaird the back."[41] Additional details Washington recorded in the 1762 almanac bring alive other aspects of his daily life. That month he recorded receiving a cask of Leith ale from a tavern keeper in Piscataway: a potent brew. This year he also imported twelve dozen bottles of "fine old Porter."[42]

Though Washington enjoyed imported ale from England and Scotland, eventually he would brew his own at Mount Vernon.

Many of the notes in the 1762 almanac concern livestock, several about breeding. In late May, for example, Washington hired a neighbor's stud horse to service his mares. The horse covered both Young Countess and the black mare; the next day the same horse covered the chestnut mare, but Young Countess and the black mare both refused.[43] In his *New Treatise on the Diseases of Horses* William Gibson demurely avoided discussing how to breed horses. Washington gained his knowledge on that subject locally by word of mouth.

An interleaved almanac provided a convenient place to record daily activities throughout the year, but it remained useful once the year ended, when a note-filled almanac transformed itself from an ephemeris into a lasting reference work. Washington saved his almanacs from one year to the next. As he matured as a farmer, he used earlier almanacs to gauge his subsequent progress. Every year he could compare his current efforts and results with those of previous years.

Washington's diary entries in his almanacs, brief as they are, also illuminate his personality, as John Seelye has recognized. While admitting that Washington "was not an inspired keeper of a diary," Seelye observes that reading his diaries straight through gives the impression of the progress of "an ideal Provincial Squire, who begins with earnest efforts at agrarian improvements and moves toward fox hunting and improving his breed of hound, and in the background as it were we can see an ever widening vista, as Mount Vernon gives way to the Ohio Valley and Williamsburg."[44]

Not all day-to-day notes needed to be saved. From 1759 Washington began carrying an ivory table book to record miscellaneous notes.[45] Fashioned from several oblong strips of ivory attached together at one end so that they could be spread out like a fan, ivory table books had many advantages over interleaved almanacs. They were convenient, durable, reusable, and waterproof. The table book provided a way to take notes on the fly. Furthermore, its leaves could be inscribed, wiped clean, and reinscribed. As Jonathan Swift wrote in his playful poem "Written in a Lady's Ivory Table-Book," all it took to blot a message out was the "power of spittle, and a clout."[46] Washington could inscribe daily notes in his ivory table book, transfer the most important ones to an interleaved almanac, and then erase the table book to use it again.

Throughout his first year of marriage Washington continued to obtain decorative objects for Mount Vernon. The third week of September 1759, he wrote Robert Cary requesting some statuary for his home, including six busts. Washington's choice of historical figures says much about the men he admired. In addition to busts of Alexander the Great and Julius Caesar he ordered those of King Charles XII of Sweden and Frederick II, king of Prussia. He wanted all four the same size—less than fifteen inches tall—because he planned to use them to fill the broken pediments over the doors at Mount Vernon.

Washington also ordered busts of the Duke of Marlborough and Prince Eugene of Savoy for either end of another pediment.[47] Grouping Marlborough and Prince Eugene, Washington revealed his knowledge of their exploits. The two commanders were close friends who served together during the War of the Spanish Succession. Prince Eugene helped Marlborough achieve his glorious victory at Blenheim.

While the agricultural books show Washington settling into the life of a gentleman farmer, the busts he wanted reveal a contrary impulse: they show him longing for the battlefield. All these famous leaders were best known for their military exploits. Contemporaries held them up as models to emulate. To prove that the Virginia Regiment could trounce the more powerful French forces, the Reverend Samuel Davies used both Alexander the Great and King Charles XII of Sweden as examples. In the first number of his "Virginia Centinel" essay series, Davies wrote that Alexander the Great, commanding a force of thirty thousand troops, routed Darius, who had an army of half a million. Furthermore, Davies continued, Charles XII of Sweden, with eight thousand Swedish troops, overwhelmingly defeated a hundred thousand Russian soldiers.[48]

Washington's admiration of these prominent military figures reflects his reading. Like many eighteenth-century Virginians, he enjoyed biographies of great men. Grub Street biographer John Bancks wrote several works that became popular in colonial America.[49] Years later Washington would order John Bancks's *History of the Life and Reign of the Czar Peter the Great*, but he could have read Bancks's biographies of Prince Eugene of Savoy and the Duke of Marlborough by the time he ordered busts of them in 1759.

Frederick II, king of Prussia, the latest figure on the list of famous soldiers Washington wanted to honor at Mount Vernon, was recognized as a great hero because of his victory over the French, with whom Great Britain and its colonies were still fighting. Numerous verse tributes to Frederick had appeared in the American press.[50] In "The Royal Comet," James Sterling, another man of letters in colonial Maryland, honored Frederick the Great as

> The first in the charge, and the last in retreat,
> A statesman and monarch, yet true to his word;
> A soldier, with honour, more bright than his sword.[51]

According to the popular perception of him in North America, Frederick the Great possessed many of the same qualities Washington admired and sought to cultivate himself.

Cary had trouble locating busts of any of these men. He could find none of Charles XII of Sweden, nor could he find busts of the others in the size Washington needed. Cary offered some alternatives, explaining that he could easily obtain busts of Addison, Aristotle, Chaucer, Cicero, Homer, Horace, Jonson, Locke, Milton, Newton, Plato, Pope, Seneca, Spenser, Swift, Dryden, and Virgil.[52] Poets and philosophers? No, Washington replied, he was uninterested in the busts of any of these figures. To adorn his home he wanted men of action, not men of letters. Washington later reconsidered. When the Belvoir estate went up for sale, he purchased William Fairfax's bust of Shakespeare for Mount Vernon.[53]

Washington also ordered statues of two wild animals. He was less choosy about the beasts than the busts. "Furious Wild Beasts of any kind" would do. He imagined these animals "approaching each other and eager to engage." Given the opportunity to decide which beasts would go best, Cary chose two statues patterned on some antique Italian lions, neatly finished and bronzed.[54]

In addition Washington ordered some smaller ornaments for the mantelpiece, again leaving the details to his London agent. Cary outdid himself this time. He selected a group of four prominent figures: Aeneas bearing his father, Anchises, from the flames of Troy upon his shoulder, accompanied by Aeneas's wife, Creusa, and their son Ascanius, all neatly finished and bronzed. The group of figures captures a precise moment in classical legend. After the Greeks took Troy and set it aflame, they permitted Aeneas to remove what he most esteemed. Consequently Aeneas carried his crippled father, Anchises, through the flames and thus saved his life. Aeneas also rescued his son from the fire and brought him to Italy. Creusa accompanied them, but, according to the traditional story, she was accidentally separated from Aeneas.

Placed at Mount Vernon, this group of statues gave the Washington home a rich set of classical associations. Presenting a story about rescue from fire, the Aeneas group served as a good luck charm, symbolically protecting Mount Vernon from conflagration, an ever-present danger for eighteenth-century homeowners. It also reinforced the importance of family, symbolizing the love between father and son, husband and wife. Furthermore, the image of Aeneas carrying Anchises indicates the importance of filial piety. Leaving the ruins of Troy behind him, Aeneas also symbolizes *translatio*, the idea that, as George Berkeley famously put it,

"Westward the Course of Empire makes its Way."[55] Aeneas leaving Troy is one manifestation of this idea; the settling of America is another.

Cary sent two bronze vases ornamented with faces and festoons of grapes and vines and two more groups of statuary to rest on the mantle. One group featured Bacchus, the god of wine. A symbol of merrymaking, Bacchus helped assure a joyful home. The other group featured Flora, the Roman goddess of flowers and gardens, thus guaranteeing beauty and prosperity.

Washington needed more than symbols to assure Mount Vernon's prosperity. He continued expanding his agricultural library over the next few years. *The Practical Husbandman*, which he would add by 1764, consisted of papers selected from the Transactions of the Society of Improvers in the Knowledge of Agriculture in Scotland by its secretary, a successful Scottish farmer named Robert Maxwell. *The Farmer's Compleat Guide*, an anonymous work Washington added to his library around the same time, contains information about managing stock, growing grain, cultivating beans and peas and turnips, raising hemp and hops, and manuring soil. The knowing farmer, Washington later observed, was "one who understands the best course of Crops; how to plough—to sow—to mow—to hedge—to Ditch and above all, Midas like, one who can convert every thing he touches into manure, as the first transmutation towards Gold."[56]

The two most important agricultural works Washington acquired in the 1760s were Philip Miller's *Gardeners Dictionary* and Duhamel du Monceau's *Practical Treatise of Husbandry*. Miller could be found in libraries throughout colonial America; Duhamel was rarer. Only the best agricultural libraries, like that of Charles Carroll, Barrister, had both.[57]

On his travels through North America, Swedish naturalist Pehr Kalm asked people what they considered the best book on the subject of horticulture. They generally agreed that Miller's *Gardeners Dictionary* "was the best of all, and that when one has it, no other book is afterwards required, because there is found in it everything that is in the others, and much more besides, and that both more clearly and better worked out than in any other, although the others often have manifold more words."[58] Washington owned Miller's *Abridgement of the Gardeners Dictionary*. Though less detailed than Miller's original, the abridgment was still a hefty quarto, consisting of over nine hundred closely printed pages.

Many farmers appreciated Miller's information about trees. So did Washington. Instead of limiting himself to English varieties, Miller sought to incorporate much about American species. As an unpublished manuscript at Mount Vernon reveals, Washington compiled lengthy notes on many different species of trees—dogwood, horse chestnut, laurel, locust, magnolia, red bud, sassafras. He kept his copy of Miller's *Gardeners Dictionary* nearby as he wrote, supplementing his notes with additional information from the book.

After reading Miller's article on various types of magnolias, Washington wrote a kinsman traveling to South Carolina, asking him to obtain some magnolia seed. Washington also mentioned Miller to another correspondent, whom he asked to send seed for some pine trees and other evergreens. Washington kept reading Miller's *Gardeners Dictionary*, which continued to impress him. In a follow-up letter, he observed that Miller "seems to understand the culture of Trees equal to any other writer I have met with."[59]

A dated autograph on Washington's copy of Duhamel's *Practical Treatise of Husbandry* enhances its rubricated title page: "G. Washington—1764."[60] The volume also contains brief marginal annotations in Washington's hand on dozens of pages. Duhamel divided his text into four parts. Washington's marginalia are largely restricted to the second part of the book. Since the first part contains no marginalia, one might conclude that Washington skipped that part altogether and went directly to part 2.

Washington's marginalia are not the only evidence to indicate his attention to the work. A set of notes in his hand at the Library of Congress shows that he thoroughly digested part 1. As he read Duhamel, he copied long passages of text into a separate notebook. These manuscript notes caution against making too many generalizations about Washington's reading process based solely on his marginalia. He took notes in different ways at different times for different reasons, even from the same work.

The nature of the individual parts of Duhamel's treatise help explain Washington's notes. Part 1 consists of general information about several aspects of husbandry; part 2 presents the results of numerous agricultural experiments. Washington took notes from part 1 to help him learn and remember Duhamel's ideas. His manuscript notes in part 2 mainly serve to make the book a more useful reference work. Much of his marginalia converts the original measurements to proper English ones. Washington's notes make Duhamel's text easier to reread and Duhamel's experiments easier to replicate.

That the notes largely concern the cultivation of wheat reinforces Washington's ongoing shift from tobacco. Some of his notes in Duhamel's *Husbandry* resemble ones he made in his copy of Harris's *Lexicon Technicum:* they concern units of measurement and ways of measuring different agricultural products. Washington also wrote in parts 3 and 4 of Duhamel's *Husbandry*, but his later annotations mainly correct typographical errors. Correcting some mistaken roman numerals, for example, he deliberately made his handwriting resemble roman type. Brief as they are, these corrections demonstrate that he thoroughly read parts 3 and 4 as well.

Washington's notes reveal his interest in the possible benefits of the use of tillage, as opposed to the sole use of dung. In addition, Duhamel's defense of the Rotherham, or patent, plough convinced Washington to acquire one for himself. When his patent plough finally broke down, Washington returned to Duhamel for further inspiration but ultimately designed a plough of his own.[61] His agricultural activity at Mount Vernon shows that he learned much else from Duhamel's *Husbandry*. Soil preparation, crop rotation, and the value of detailed record-keeping from year to year: Duhamel recommended all these aspects of farming, and Washington followed them. His agricultural innovations made him a leader among Virginia farmers.[62]

He continued to expand his agricultural library throughout his life. One more example must suffice: John Abercrombie's *Hot-House Gardener*. He who "loves a garden loves a greenhouse, too," William Cowper observed.[63] Washington was no exception. Sure enough, he would install a stately greenhouse at Mount Vernon. The structure was partly inspired by the one Charles Carroll installed at Mount Clare. His wife, Margaret, took primary responsibility for the Carroll greenhouse. She prided herself on her oranges and lemons, and the Mount Clare greenhouse developed a reputation beyond the bounds of Maryland. As Washington designed his, he realized that he lacked sufficient knowledge for the task, nor could he find anyone in Virginia who could help. Consequently he wrote Tench Tilghman, Margaret Carroll's cousin, asking him to describe the Mount Clare greenhouse in detail. When Tilghman consulted her, she was happy to answer Washington's numerous queries herself.[64]

It took him a couple of years to finish constructing his Mount Vernon greenhouse and a few years after that before Washington found a gardener with greenhouse expertise. He subsequently wrote directly to Margaret Carroll, accepting her offer to supply him with specimens from her greenhouse. She sent twenty pots of lemon and orange trees and five boxes of other greenhouse plants to Mount Vernon.[65]

Washington's greenhouse is a beautiful sight, inside and out. Impressed with it during his visit to Mount Vernon, the Chevalier d'Yrujo offered to present him a book on the subject. Washington graciously accepted. The book turned out to be Abercrombie's *Hot-House Gardener*, which came with engraved and hand-colored illustrations.[66]

The story of Washington's greenhouse shows him gathering information in several different ways. Initially he tried to learn about greenhouses personally: he asked friends and neighbors what they knew. When he could not find sufficient local expertise, he broadened his horizons and looked to Maryland for help, writing Tench Tilghman first and later directly corresponding with Margaret Carroll. Eventually he did meet a gardener with greenhouse experience, but even with what he learned about greenhouses personally and through his correspondence, Washington welcomed a book on the subject. Personal contact, correspondence, and the printed word: all gave Washington complementary ways of learning about gardens, about greenhouses, about anything.

CHAPTER 8

George Washington, Bibliographer

Pr'ythee lead me in:
There take an inventory of all I have
William Shakespeare, *Henry VIII*

Bibliography is a clean-up task. At least that's what some people think. Once the dust of history settles, the bibliographers rush in to take stock, to list the books that record what had happened. In the world of the colonial Virginia gentleman, however, bibliography was a more active, ongoing pursuit. Twice during his life George Washington exercised his bibliographical skill. His book cataloguing duties came with his responsibilities as administrator of his stepson's estate and as resident and proprietor of Mount Vernon, someone who took pride in the home he was creating for himself, his wife, and her two children. As part of his estate Jacky Custis had inherited a sizeable library, one he was still too young to appreciate. Until he was old enough to have a home of his own, his books would form a handsome feature of Mount Vernon's increasingly sophisticated decor. They would provide the Washington family with the kind of library that graced the finer homes across Virginia.

Most of the books Jacky inherited had been assembled by his grandfather, John Custis of Williamsburg, who was brother-in-law to the greatest bookman in colonial Virginia, William Byrd II. After John Custis's death in 1749, his son Daniel Parke Custis inherited the library. He did little with it before his death in 1757. The lion's share of the collection stayed at the Custis home on Francis Street in Williamsburg, though some books—amounting to perhaps one-sixth of the whole—remained at the Custis plantation in New Kent County.[1]

As administrator of his stepson's estate, George Washington had to decide what to do with Jacky's books, which totaled around three hundred titles in over five hundred volumes. He could either sell them and add the proceeds to the boy's already considerable fortune or keep them to aid his education. The appraisers had not placed much monetary value on the library, so Washington knew the books would fetch little at auction. They possessed much greater intellectual worth than monetary value.[2]

While in Williamsburg in 1759, Washington stopped by Francis Street to inventory his stepson's books. The list he created reveals his abilities as a bibliographer. In the eighteenth century, books were typically shelved according to format: folio, quarto, octavo, duodecimo. William Byrd, who divided his books into general subject areas, subdivided them according to format, placing the largest volumes—the folios—on the bottom shelf. The next largest set of books—the quartos—he put on a shelf above the folios, with the octavos and duodecimos above them. The catalogue of Byrd's library preserves the shelf organization established by its owner.[3]

Washington's catalogue of the Custis library also seems to preserve its shelf organization, at least at first. It begins with a folio section, followed by a quarto section. After the quartos, Washington supplied a third heading consistent with a typical format organization: larger octavos. He provided no further format designations. The rest of the catalogue lists not only larger octavos but also smaller ones and duodecimos. The only other heading is "broken sets."

Under "broken sets," Washington listed the titles of several multivolume works with one or more volumes missing. By the time he catalogued the collection, only four volumes from a six-volume edition of Jonathan Swift's *Miscellanies* survived. Somehow the second and fifth volumes had disappeared. Similarly, just four of the six volumes of Alexander Pope's *Poetical Works* survived, the first and last ones having been misplaced.[4] The "broken sets" category suggests that the Custis collection had been at least partially rearranged. To be sure, these sets were previously shelved by format or author or subject, not by the fact that they were broken. Most likely the appraisers grouped these odd volumes together. Broken sets, after all, have much less value than complete ones.

Some author groupings and subject clusters are discernible. Three volumes of Milton's poetry—*Paradise Lost*, *Paradise Regained*, and *Poems*—are listed together, but Milton's *Defense of the People of England*—a work championing the voice of the people that would influence the political discourse of the American Revolution[5]—appears with other seventeenth-century prose works. Washington turned to one section of the library to read Milton's verse, another to read his prose.

Several medical treatises appear together in Washington's catalogue of the Custis library. Some are historical, such as Dr. Nathaniel Hodges's *Loimologia*, which presents an account of the London plague of 1665 from a contemporary physician who bravely stayed in the city during the outbreak to treat the afflicted. Others are more practical in nature. The collection included four how-to medical handbooks by William Salmon, all shelved consecutively. This grouping suggests a general subject organization with a subdivision for authors.

Salmon had no formal medical training. His writings combined traditional wisdom that circulated in the oral culture with information gleaned from previous medical books. His medicinal recipes were firmly grounded in the long-standing theory of the four humors, the idea that illness stems from an imbalance in the four principle bodily fluids: blood, phlegm, black bile, and yellow bile. Salmon's works were decades out of date by the time Washington took possession of the Custis library, but the master of Mount Vernon had no great curiosity about modern developments in medical science. Unlike Benjamin Franklin, who kept himself apprised of all the latest medical advances and assembled one of the finest medical libraries in eighteenth-century America, Washington's medical knowledge never really progressed beyond the popular medical handbooks of William Salmon.

Though John Custis grouped his medical books together, other works in his library seem organized by language. The deficiencies in Washington's linguistic education prevented him from listing Latin titles separately. He counted them instead, listing sixty-six Latin books of different sizes at one point and fourteen Latin books elsewhere.[6] The fact that Washington listed two sections of Latin books instead of one suggests that the books were grouped that way in the Custis collection. William Byrd had a distinct section of classics in his library; the sixty-six Latin books forms John Custis's main collection of classics.[7]

Evidence of an organizational scheme is sufficient to warrant a theory: John Custis shelved his larger books according to format but devised a hybrid organizational scheme, partly by subject and partly by author, for the rest of his Williamsburg library. After giving the library a sense of order, he grew lackadaisical about maintaining that order. Over time he reshelved his books wherever they fit rather than where they belonged. Though the appraisers may have done some rearranging when it came to the broken sets, otherwise they left the books as they found them, and Washington catalogued the library as he found it.

His main reason for cataloging the Custis library before moving the books was to create a record of what his stepson had inherited, but there seems little doubt about the thrill Washington experienced as he foresaw how this excellent collection of books would look at Mount Vernon. His cataloguing process likely started slowly, an assumption based on the very first title he listed, Mark Catesby's *Natural History of Carolina, Florida and the Bahama Islands*, the earliest illustrated study of American flora and fauna and, indeed, one of the most beautiful books to emerge from the colonial American experience. Who could look at this stately volume and not linger over its numerous hand-colored engravings?

The first plate in Catesby's *Natural History* deserves extended perusal. It depicts a bald eagle as it swoops toward the surface of a river to grab a fish in mid-air, the same fish a forlorn hawk has dropped after being pestered by the eagle. Using this particular plate to open his *Natural History*, Catesby demonstrated the bald eagle's symbolic and iconographic value. Catesby's dramatic imagery would influence the Continental Congress's decision to choose the bald eagle as the defining symbol of the United States.[8] George Washington loved to entertain; sharing volumes of engraved plates was a popular after-dinner diversion in fashionable eighteenth-century homes. The Custis copy of Catesby's beautiful book was one of several books of plates in his library that Washington could share with visitors.[9]

Other folios in the Custis library included Sir Roger L'Estrange's English translation of Aesop's *Fables* and an atlas of England. The edition of Aesop looked familiar to Washington. It should have: it was the same translation he had read as a boy. The book he listed as "English Atlas by Phil Lea" was *The Shires of England and Wales*, a collection of maps published by London globe-maker Philip Lea based on the detailed maps originally created by the father of English cartography, Christopher Saxton.

Washington discovered several renowned books of travel in the Custis collection, including Jean de Thévenot's *Travels into the Levant*. This work could be found in some of the finest homes in colonial Virginia from the Governor's Palace to William Byrd's Westover. Samuel Henley, a professor at the College of William and Mary, also enjoyed the work.[10] *Travels into the Levant* chronicles the adventures of its intrepid author, a seventeenth-century Frenchman who journeyed from Constantinople to Hyderabad.

As a traveler, Thévenot developed a habit of settling in a city for a matter of weeks or months to learn the language and familiarize himself with local customs, knowledge that served him well once he returned to the road. His powers of observation and expression let Thévenot distinguish himself as a travel writer. He wrote with authority tinged by charm, a style that delighted his readers. Thévenot had a keen visual sensibility, creating colorful vignettes that stayed in a reader's mind. Professor Henley especially remembered a scene from Thévenot's *Travels* describing a lavish reception for which two hundred oil lamps had been strung in a line from one tree to another to form a grand illumination welcoming the new pasha of Egypt.[11]

After Washington catalogued the Custis library, he made arrangements to transport it to his home. From the time the Custis books arrived until Washington catalogued the entire Mount Vernon library, he acquired few additional volumes. For the most part the Custis books satisfied his desire for pleasure reading. Having been assembled by Jacky's grandfather, the collection was somewhat outdated, but it did contain several works that remained relevant, including some of the most important contributions to politics and history from the early eighteenth century. After agriculture, history was George Washington's favorite subject.[12]

The Custis collection included the major works of the radical English Whigs of the early eighteenth century, including *The Independent Whig*, a three-volume collection of periodical essays by John Trenchard and Thomas Gordon.[13] These essays speak out against the authority of the church but also address more wide-ranging political concerns. Trenchard and Gordon found the individual conscience the only valid authority in matters of religion or politics.[14] *Cato's Letters*, another multivolume collection of periodical essays by Trenchard and Gordon that formed part of the Custis collection, treats the subject of civil and religious liberty in considerable detail. *Cato's Letters*, which could be found in numerous colonial American libraries, would also influence revolutionary thought.

Adopting the voice of Cato, Trenchard and Gordon chose a mouthpiece that symbolized personal liberty. In ancient Rome Cato had stabbed himself to death in preference to living under Julius Caesar's bondage. Washington could have learned more about the historical Cato from reading Plutarch's *Lives*—another work from the Custis collection he came to know. During the Revolutionary War, he would use the name Plutarch as both parole and countersign on separate occasions. He used the name Cato similarly. Plutarch's *Lives* is the source for Cato's moving statement: "Let us rescue our liberties, or die in their defence."[15]

Joseph Addison had popularized the historical figure with *Cato, A Tragedy*, which was performed numerous times in revolutionary America.

It was George Washington's favorite play. He often saw *Cato* performed: his soldiers even performed it at Valley Forge.[16] Washington's letters frequently echo Addison's sentiments. In the American mind the historical Cato, Addison's tragic hero, and Trenchard and Gordon's spokesman all became amalgamated into one overarching representative hero, who could, and would, be invoked to support the cause of American liberty.[17]

Cato's Letters emphasizes that people rightfully have the power to protest, resist, and, if necessary, rebel against tyrannical leaders. The work also shows that freedom of speech can help guarantee liberty and assure progress. Cato's fifteenth letter contains a vivid statement on the subject of freedom of speech: "Without Freedom of Thought, there can be no such Thing as Wisdom; and no such Thing as publick Liberty, without Freedom of Speech.... This sacred Privilege is so essential to free Government, that the Security of Property; and the Freedom of Speech, always go together."[18] Washington never specifically mentions reading either *The Independent Whig* or *Cato's Letters* in his correspondence, but his political statements echo their sentiments and thus suggest his knowledge of them.[19]

The catalogue of the Mount Vernon library Washington prepared after bringing the Custis books to his home reveals other books he added to his personal collection during the early 1760s. The most substantial work Washington added around this time was another history: Tobias Smollett's *Complete History of England*, an eleven-volume set. Telling the story of Britain from the time of Julius Caesar to the middle of the eighteenth century, Smollett helped Washington connect his knowledge of classical biography with his understanding of English history.

Initially intending to write a history according to Whig principles, Smollett changed his mind and opinions as he researched the subject. Smollett's *Complete History of England* is remarkably free from political bias, synthesizing the writings of several highly opinionated Whig and Tory authors. Washington already knew Smollett from his picaresque novel *The Adventures of Peregrine Pickle*. With his *Complete History of England*, Smollett brought a novelist's capacity for storytelling and character development to historical narrative.[20]

George Washington's catalogue of the Mount Vernon library is undated, but he had to have compiled it after the summer of 1763, when he obtained his copy of Smollett's history.[21] Another work listed in the catalogue—Duhamel's *Husbandry*—helps date the catalogue more precisely. The edition of Duhamel that Washington owned was published in 1762, but the daybooks from the *Virginia Gazette* office indicate that he acquired

Duhamel's *Husbandry* in April 1764.[22] He apparently compiled the library catalogue shortly after acquiring his copy of Duhamel.

Washington also numbered each bookcase: an aspect of the library that reflects his growing sophistication as a bookman. Furthermore, he distinguished his books from his stepson's. As he began the catalogue, he placed initials next to each title to show who owned what. "JC" appears adjacent to some titles, "GW" to others. Partway through the catalogue, Washington abandoned these designations, realizing they were unnecessary. The 1759 catalogue of the Custis library, which he retained, obviated the need for indicating ownership in this new catalogue.

The 1764 catalogue reveals how John Custis's organizational scheme influenced Washington's. In the eighteenth and early nineteenth century, books were often shipped and shelved in the same cases. When William Byrd arranged to have his London library brought to Virginia, he had the books packed in the same cases he had used to shelve them in his London apartment. Similarly, when Benjamin Franklin left Paris for Philadelphia in 1785, he had his library packed in the bookcases from his Paris library, each case forming one shelf of books. And when Thomas Jefferson sold his personal library to Congress, he sold the books along with their cases and shipped them from Monticello to Washington with the books already shelved in precise order. Jefferson's personal system of library organization thus provided the fundamental organization for the Library of Congress.[23]

Read against one another, Washington's two catalogues suggest that the shelf organization at Mount Vernon paralleled Custis's shelf organization: many of the books retained the relative positions at Mount Vernon that they had held at the Custis home on Francis Street. Apparently, Washington also shipped the books as they were shelved.

Once he got the Custis library back to Mount Vernon, he combined it with his own personal library. Since the Custis collection was much larger than his, he integrated the two by reshelving his own books among those of his stepson. Washington thus used Custis's library organization to determine where to shelve his books. In the first bookcase, for instance, Catesby's *Natural History* again comes first, with Philip Lea's English atlas second. Next, Washington shelved his copy of Herman Moll's *Atlas Minor*, recognizing these two atlases belonged together. Similarly, he placed his own copy of Aesop's *Fables* adjacent to his stepson's copy of the same work.

For smaller-format books, Washington did some modest rearranging. He made an effort to shelve collections of voyages together, an indication that these were among the books that interested him most. In the Custis

Library at Mount Vernon (National Photo company, ca. 1909), photographic print. Library of Congress, Prints and Photographs Division, Washington, DC (reproduction number: LC-USZ62-114284).

library Captain William Dampier's *Voyages* and Alexandre Olivier Exquemelin's *History of the Bucaniers of America* had been shelved separately. Washington brought the two together and grouped them with his copy of *Anson's Voyage*, a longtime favorite.

Among the authors represented in the Custis library, Exquemelin and Dampier belong among the likely ones that Washington read. Exquemelin, a seventeenth-century Dutch buccaneer, not only recounted his personal adventures of travel, he also related stories of Dutch, English, French, and Portuguese pirates who plundered Spanish ships and raided Spanish settlements in the Americas. Exquemelin's work has been called the "Handbook of Buccaneering." *Bucaniers of America* held considerable appeal for many Anglo-American readers. As Edwin Wolf has observed, Exquemelin's pirates were essentially British heroes: their prey, after all, had been the Spanish treasure galleons.[24]

Though Dampier also spent much time as a buccaneer, he had wider scientific interests that elevated him above more run-of-the-mill pirates. Through his strenuous efforts at sea, he earned the right to be called an explorer. Dampier's narrative does show Exquemelin's influence. Partly by reading *Bucaniers of America*, Dampier understood the value of taking careful notes and recording traditional stories from the different places he visited. As an author he had a good sense of balance. Dampier understood how description could be used to enhance both the pleasure and the utility of his writing, yet he also knew that too much description could bog down a narrative. He shrewdly recognized when to salt a historical section with personal anecdote. And he had a good sense of audience. He knew his work would be read by merchants, scientists, and statesmen and wrote with all of them in mind.[25]

Dampier's *Voyages* found favor among the best English writers of the eighteenth century. The work influenced some renowned imaginary voyages, including *Robinson Crusoe* and *Gulliver's Travels*, both of which could be found among the Custis books at Mount Vernon. By Washington's adolescence, *Robinson Crusoe* and *Gulliver's Travels* were already standard works read by boys throughout the English-speaking world; almost surely Washington read them in his youth.[26] The Custis library gave him the opportunity to peruse them again.

The second volume of Custis's surviving copy of *Gulliver's Travels* hints that Washington did reread *Gulliver's Travels* after he brought his stepson's books to Mount Vernon. Handsomely printed with generous leading and wide, creamy margins, this edition of *Gulliver's Travels* made for a luxurious reading experience. The edition was not perfect. Page 45 of the second volume contains a misprint. The word "myself" was accidentally printed "mmself." That misprint is carefully corrected by hand in the Custis copy.[27] The neat, scarcely noticeable manuscript correction closely resembles the corrections Washington made to typographical errors on several pages in his copy of Duhamel's *Husbandry*. The manuscript correction to the text is a telltale sign that Washington did read the Custis copy of *Gulliver's Travels*.

Once he moved the Custis books to Mount Vernon and integrated his own library with his stepson's, they formed a fine collection that greatly contributed to the aura of class and sophistication Washington sought to achieve. But the library at Mount Vernon was not just part of the home's luxurious decor. It offered George Washington numerous opportunities for pleasure reading. *Gulliver's Travels* and the histories of pirates were not the only works from the Custis collection that appealed to him. Additional evidence suggests that he also enjoyed other books from the collection.

According to an anecdote that circulated into the twentieth century, a friend stopped by Mount Vernon one day and found its owner reading the poetry of Alexander Pope. Washington's waggish yet anti-Catholic friend feigned surprise and teased him for being "in meditation with the Pope."[28] This traditional story may be apocryphal, but it does reinforce the close relationship between Washington's reading process and his practice of meditation. Though the broken set of Alexander Pope's *Poetical Works* in the Custis collection was missing two volumes, the remaining four left Washington much to enjoy. The second volume, for example, contained Pope's "Essay on Man," a work that brilliantly encapsulates Enlightenment ideas concerning humankind's place in the universe. *Poetical Works* was not the only work by Pope shelved at Mount Vernon. Washington also owned a copy of Pope's translation of Homer's *Odyssey*.[29]

It makes sense that Washington would want to read Pope's poetry. Pope enjoyed enormous prestige in eighteenth-century America, especially in the South. One of Washington's correspondents linked Pope with John Dryden and Jonathan Swift, who together formed the great triumvirate of modern English verse.[30] Pope's heroic couplets provided the model for much early American verse, and quotations from Pope formed an important part of the gentlemanly discourse. Knowledge of Pope's verse was practically de rigueur in mid-eighteenth-century Virginia society.

Already Washington had received at least one lesson on the applicability of Pope's verse. After he had assumed command of the Virginia Regiment during the French and Indian War, he selected a sympathetic young man named John Kirkpatrick as his secretary. When the Reverend Samuel Davies underwent a sudden change of heart toward the Virginia Regiment and attacked it in his "Virginia Centinel" essay series, Kirkpatrick wrote to comfort Washington, identifying envy as the root cause of Davies's hurtful remarks and finding appropriate a quotation from Pope's "Essay on Criticism." Quoting from memory, Kirkpatrick wrote: "Envy, will Merit like a Shade pursue, / And alike a Shadow prove the Substance true."[31] Once he familiarized himself with Pope's verse, Washington himself took to quoting Pope. Writing from Cambridge, Massachusetts, during the Revolutionary War, he elaborated how the American forces took possession of Dorchester Heights and shelled British positions the first week of March 1776. Washington's troops prepared to defend themselves against a counterattack, but the British did not respond. He told his correspondent: "I will not lament or repine at any Act of Providence because I am in a great measure a convert to Mr Popes opinion that whatever is, is right, but I think every thing had the appearance of a successful Issue if we had come to an Ingagement on that day."[32] As he accepts Pope's famous dictum from "Essay on Man," Washington expresses a twinge of regret at the way the situation turned out: he was confident his troops could have successfully repelled the British forces.

Washington's recreational pursuits drew him to another book in the Custis collection: Theophilus Lucas's *Memoirs of the Lives, Intrigues, and Comical Adventures of the Most Famous Gamesters and Celebrated Sharpers*. More a contribution to the literature of roguery than a practical manual, Lucas's *Memoirs* nevertheless appealed to everyone who loved to play cards, and George Washington loved to play cards. He already had two card playing manuals in his own library: *Hoyle's Games* and Richard Seymour's *Compleat Gamester*. In addition to providing rules for card games, Seymour discussed other games, including billiards and chess.

Once the Custis books reached Mount Vernon, Washington reshelved his two gaming books, placing them with Lucas's *Memoirs*. Both biography and cautionary tale, Lucas's work did help honest players recognize card sharks in order to avoid being swindled by them.[33] Seymour's *Compleat Gamester* emphasized a knowledge of cards as an essential social skill, comparing it to the ability to engage in conversation.[34] Lucas provided readers with many intriguing anecdotes that could pepper conversations that took place over the card table.

After cataloguing the Mount Vernon library in 1764, Washington continued to add to it, as his surviving invoices reveal. The fourth week of June 1766, for instance, he ordered a long list of items from Robert Cary, including several books.[35] In light of other items Washington listed, perhaps the books should not be emphasized too much. This same order also contains a request for three dozen packs of "Harry Cards," that is, playing cards decorated with the image of Henry VIII.

Harry cards were one type of playing cards popular in the eighteenth century. Boston bookseller Henry Knox, who would later serve under Washington as a general during the Revolutionary War and eventually become his secretary of war, stocked three types: Harry, Mogul, and Merry Andrew playing cards.[36] Eighteenth-century playing cards were not as durable as the laminated cards of today, but three dozen packs was still a sizeable order for an individual. The size of Washington's order indicates how important card playing was to him. On any given night at Mount Vernon, he could more likely be found seated at his mahogany card table with Mrs. Washington and their friends and neighbors than curled up with a good book.[37]

Washington's financial accounts also reflect his passion for playing cards. He typically bet small sums as he played and meticulously recorded his winnings and losses. Almost never did he record which card games he played. Instead, he simply noted how much he won or lost "at cards."

When he was in his late teens, he did record losing five shillings at loo. Also known as lanterloo, loo was a fast-paced game suitable for any number of players.[38]

The presence of *Hoyle's Games* at Mount Vernon suggests that the card game Washington typically played was whist. Edmund Hoyle first published his *Short Treatise on the Game of Whist* in 1742. It went through numerous editions, which gradually contained the rules for other card games. By the mid-1760s the work had become the foremost authority on the rules of card playing. It gained such authority that the phrase "according to Hoyle" became a proverbial way to emphasize the validity of anything. Through the eighteenth century whist, a precursor to bridge, remained the most respectable four-handed card game. It was played in fashionable circles throughout colonial Virginia.

David Cobb, one of Washington's aides during the Revolutionary War, used to tell a story about playing whist with him. One time Cobb and Washington played as partners against a Virginia clergyman and a physician. The clergyman turned out to be a terrible card player. As he lost one trick after another, his partner lost his temper and started swearing like a sailor. Aghast at the doctor's foul mouth, the pastor put down his cards and refused to play any further. The doctor apologized, promising not to utter another oath in the room. They consequently resumed their game. The clergyman played as poorly as before, but the physician managed to keep his temper in check. They lost one trick after another, until they lost the game and, finally, the rubber. Having kept his anger bottled up throughout the match, once play had ended, the doctor could no longer stand it. He ran to the empty chimney, thrust his head up, and let fly a volley of oaths. Washington laughed and laughed until tears ran down his cheeks.[39]

Washington also enjoyed quadrille, a game similar to whist. His correspondence shows that when he ordered a mahogany card table he also ordered some quadrille counters.[40] If Washington dipped into that broken set of Jonathan Swift's *Miscellanies*, he could have found a poem in the third volume called "A Ballad on Quadrille." This song, which reflects the game's popularity in Swift's day, humorously portrays quadrille as the Devil's game:

> Kings, Queens and Knaves, made up his Pack,
> And four fair Suits he wore;
> His Troops they were with red and black
> All blotch'd and spotted o'er;
> And ev'ry House, go where you will,
> Is haunted by this Imp Quadrille.[41]

Whereas card games provided much entertainment at Mount Vernon in the 1760s, books provided much useful knowledge. The books listed in Washington's June 1766 order were all practical works. Godfrey Smith's *Laboratory; or, School of Arts*, for one, supplied a variety of information concerning the decorative arts. It explained how to draw and paint, offered a primer on landscape gardening, and provided an introduction to architecture. The first volume of Smith's *Laboratory* had appeared in 1738, and it had reappeared in several subsequent editions. By the time Washington requested the work, it had gone out of print. Cary could not locate a copy.

Cary did find a copy of another work Washington wanted: Robert Dossie's *Handmaid to the Arts*. Eighteenth-century readers sensibly criticized how-to manuals if they were overladen with too much theory and not enough practical advice. British critic William Bewley felt that Dossie struck the right balance in his *Handmaid to the Arts*, providing just enough theory to carry out the practice.[42] Dossie supplied useful information about many different artistic techniques: drawing, enameling, gilding, japanning, painting, staining, and varnishing. Besides giving eighteenth-century homeowners much useful advice, Dossie's *Handmaid to the Arts* would influence some of the most important painters in Revolutionary America.[43]

The most substantial work in Washington's June 1766 order is *Museum Rusticum*, a periodical collected in six volumes and containing a selection of papers communicated to the Society for the Encouragement of Arts, Manufactures, and Commerce, a British organization that offered prizes to promote experiments in agriculture and other practical fields of endeavor. Washington asked Cary to send all the volumes published so far and stipulated that further ones be shipped as they appeared. Cary located the six-volume set of *Museum Rusticum* and promptly sent it to Mount Vernon.[44]

Fellow Virginia patriot Richard Henry Lee also hoped to obtain a copy of the work. Consequently he asked his brother Arthur, then in England, to send the multivolume set to him. In his response, the notoriously cantankerous Arthur Lee snarled, "I have not sent you the *Museum Rusticum*, because it is certainly too dear for its usefulness." Washington himself paid one pound, nineteen shillings for the set but found it well worth the price.[45]

Though agriculture predominates, the contributors to *Museum Rusticum* discussed a variety of useful topics. The first volume, for instance, contains articles on methods of brewing brown beer, cultivating cucumbers, gathering and curing hops, increasing milk production, managing bee

George Washington's bookplate, from his copy of Robert Dossie, *The Handmaid to the Arts* (1764). Boston Athenaeum.

boxes, and storing turnips. Other articles treat how to dye wool and how to stain elm to resemble mahogany. One discusses how to manufacture saltpeter, something that would become increasingly important in the run-up to Revolution: saltpeter was an essential ingredient in the manufacture of gunpowder. Some of the articles discuss topics directly pertinent to American farmers. One treats North American viticulture. Another concerns the cultivation of tea, describing experimental tea plantations in South Carolina. A third explains how to cultivate hemp and flax in America, crops Washington would cultivate himself.

Despite its practical bent, *Museum Rusticum* was not a model of great writing. Reviewing the first two volumes, William Kenrick complained about the length and verbosity of the articles.[46] Such prolixity did not faze Washington, who found much information in *Museum Rusticum* he could apply at Mount Vernon. Though he had a standing order with Robert Cary for any future volumes, Washington reiterated his request in 1767, eagerly asking Cary if a seventh volume had been published.[47] It had not. *Museum Rusticum* ended with the sixth volume.

The same time Washington asked about any further volumes of *Museum Rusticum*, he also ordered William Markham's *General Introduction to Trade and Business*, a manual providing detailed instructions about business law, business mathematics, and business writing. Markham designed the work to help readers navigate their way through the increasingly complex world of trade and commerce. Markham almost swaggers as he writes. By following these instructions, he tells his readers, they can master the world of business. In addition, Markham's detailed discussion of penmanship, as one modern reader has observed, manifests Enlightenment ideas about how the mind can control the body.[48] Markham's textbook greatly enhanced the business acumen of contemporary readers. Washington did not devote an inordinate amount of effort to Markham's business methods. The same time he ordered *General Introduction to Trade and Business*, he requested six dozen more packs of Harry cards.

The book orders Washington placed with Robert Cary in the years after bringing the Custis collection to Mount Vernon help reveal how he used his stepson's library. Nearly all the books Washington purchased during the mid-1760s were practical works. He bought almost no biographies, no collections of verse, no histories, no novels, no travels—that is, none of the kinds of books he typically read for pleasure. For a long time, the Custis collection gave Washington all the pleasure reading he needed.

CHAPTER 9

The Education of John Parke Custis

Love goes toward love, as school-boys from their books;
But love from love, toward school with heavy looks.
                    William Shakespeare, *Romeo and Juliet*

Years would pass from the time Jacky Custis came to Mount Vernon until he was old enough to read and appreciate the fine library his grandfather had assembled, but George Washington understood the importance of putting books into his stepson's hands as early as possible. He also understood the importance of teaching his stepdaughter, Patsy, to read. In January 1760, Washington spent one shilling, six pence, on books for the two children. That November, the month Jacky turned six, he spent five more shillings on books for him and his sister.[1] The following year Washington hired a domestic tutor to live at Mount Vernon and guide the studies of both children.

He found an able tutor in Walter Magowan. Magowan's background before he came to Mount Vernon is a mystery. Some say he came from Scotland, but this supposed identity derives from a heated remark the Reverend Jonathan Boucher made in a moment of spite when he called Magowan a "raw Scotchman."[2] A derogatory epithet, the phrase "raw Scotchman" means roughly the same as "country bumpkin." It need not be taken literally. Other evidence suggests that Magowan was born in Ireland and emigrated to Virginia in his youth. He was in his mid-twenties when he came to Mount Vernon to tutor the Custis children.[3] Regretting his own educational deficiencies, Washington sought for his stepson the kind of proper gentleman's education that circumstances had denied him.

At Washington's request, Magowan designed a rigorous program of study for Jacky Custis.

Before Magowan's arrival Washington had introduced the boy to the language of Caesar. Describing Jacky's knowledge of Latin, Washington, with a tinge of hyperbole, wrote, "He began the study of it as soon as he could speak."[4] Eighteenth-century students typically learned the rudiments of Latin before undertaking Greek. Magowan initially planned for Jacky to start learning Greek while quite young. Perhaps Washington exaggerated the boy's early exposure to Latin in an effort to accelerate his education, or perhaps Magowan devised an innovative scheme to teach Latin and Greek simultaneously.

The year Jacky turned eight Magowan asked Washington to order several schoolbooks, including Alexander Dunlop's Greek grammar, Benjamin Hederich's Greek lexicon, and some reading texts in Greek, including an edition of the works of lyric poet Anacreon and the New Testament.[5] The absence of Latin texts from this list reflects Magowan's belief that the Latin library of Jacky's grandfather would be sufficient for his grandson's education. Along with the Greek works Magowan also ordered textbooks in many other subjects: bookkeeping, geography, history, and Roman antiquities.

The order reveals much about Magowan's educational approach. He believed that teaching ancient languages in isolation was insufficient. They should be taught in conjunction with related subjects. Attention to Roman antiquities could supplement the study of Latin. Knowledge of ancient history could enhance the study of both Latin and Greek. Though the classical languages formed the core of the eighteenth-century gentleman's education, Magowan understood the value of teaching practical subjects. Since Custis would inherit a large, complex estate, he would need basic bookkeeping skills. Though well founded, Magowan's educational scheme proved too ambitious for an eight-year-old boy, especially one as indolent and easily distracted as Jacky Custis. The study of Greek would have to wait.

The schoolbooks Washington obtained for his stepson a year and a half later indicate a major shift in Magowan's pedagogical approach. Perhaps a grandfather's books were unsuitable for a grandson's education. Jacky needed more basic textbooks. In 1764, the year his stepson turned ten, Washington purchased from the office of the *Virginia Gazette* copies of James Greenwood's *London Vocabulary* and *The Preceptor*, an all-purpose textbook compiled by London editor and publisher Robert Dodsley. This same year he also ordered Erasmus's *Colloquies*.[6]

James Greenwood—the same Greenwood whose English grammar Washington had studied in his youth—compiled *The London Vocabulary* to introduce students to Latin. According to the title page of this textbook, Greenwood took an approach to teaching Latin that follows Johann Amos Comenius's centuries-old *Orbis Pictus*, the first illustrated reading book printed in Europe. Greenwood's *London Vocabulary* presents a series of chapters treating natural phenomena and physical objects. Illustrations introduce many of the chapters, which consist of explanatory texts presented in English and Latin in parallel columns. The work remained a popular schoolbook through the colonial period, though the title irked some revolutionary parents: the first American edition of *The London Vocabulary* was retitled *The Philadelphia Vocabulary*.

The dialogues that form Erasmus's *Colloquies* had been a cornerstone of Latin education for centuries. New selections gave them a contemporary flair. The edition prepared by English schoolmaster John Clarke appealed to more students in eighteenth-century America than any other. To make the educational process as delightful as possible Clarke deliberately selected Erasmus's most comical dialogues.[7] Erasmus had the power to entertain students as they learned. Using lively repartee and vivid description, his dialogues develop character and incident in a manner that looks forward to the novel.

Two and a half years later Jacky's Latin education had progressed far enough for him to resume his study of Greek. Shortly after his stepson's twelfth birthday, Washington ordered an up-to-date Greek grammar. As Jacky began learning Greek, he continued his Latin education, reading Virgil while working through the Greek grammar and dipping into the Greek Testament.[8]

Magowan remained at Mount Vernon to tutor Jacky and Patsy Custis until the Christmas holidays in 1767, when he would visit England to receive holy orders. Since the entirety of British North America formed part of the diocese of London, colonial candidates for the Anglican ministry had to go to England to be ordained by the bishop of London. While supporting his decision, Washington was upset that Magowan quit teaching the Custis children in December but did not depart until March, leaving them without a teacher for months.[9] Patsy could continue reading at home under her mother's tutelage, but Jacky needed a new teacher with expertise in the classics. Before going to England, Magowan apparently recommended Jonathan Boucher. Besides serving as rector of St. Mary's Parish in Caroline County, Boucher, like many colonial Virginia clergymen, also ran a boarding school to supplement his clerical salary.

In late May Washington wrote Boucher to ask if he would accept Jacky as a student at his school, located about six miles from Fredericksburg. He described his stepson as "a boy of good genius, about fourteen yrs of age, untainted in his Morals, and of innocent Manners." Washington exaggerated Jacky's age: it would be nearly six months before he turned fourteen. Furthermore, he offered to pay Boucher an extra ten or twelve pounds a year to provide special care, telling him Jacky was "a promising boy—the last of his Family—and will possess a very large Fortune."[10] The part about the large fortune piqued Boucher's interest. He knew how to turn a wealthy student to his advantage.

Washington had not necessarily mentioned Jacky's wealth to secure his acceptance to Boucher's school; he mentioned it to stress the danger inherited wealth possesses for immature boys. The letter reveals Washington's anxiety: he told Boucher that he wanted to make Jacky "fit for more useful purposes, than a horse Racer."[11] Washington feared his stepson would end up like so many other sons of wealthy parents—as a wastrel who would run through his fortune while accomplishing little in life. When it came to Jacky Custis, Washington's concerns were well founded.

Jacky arrived at Boucher's boarding school that June with two horses and a slave named Julius. Somehow he carelessly neglected to bring one essential: his Greek grammar. Jacky's neglect augurs the direction his studies would take. Washington accompanied Jacky to school to meet his new teacher. Boucher was an odd-looking fellow. His future wife found him a mass of contradictions:

> In person, inelegant and clumsy, yet not rough and disgusting; of a dark complexion, and with large but not forbidding features. Of a thoughtful yet cheerful aspect; with a penetrating eye, and a turn of countenance that invites confidence and begets affection. Manners—often awkward, yet always interesting; perfectly untaught and unformed, conformable to no rules, yet never unpolite; incapable of making a bow like a gentleman, yet far more incapable of thinking, speaking, or acting in a manner unbecoming a gentleman, never knew a person of so low an origin and breeding with so high and improved a mind; a thorough gentleman as to internals and essentials, tho' often lamentably deficient in outward forms.[12]

Regardless of Boucher's unusual appearance and strange mannerisms, Washington found him satisfactory. Over dinner on Thursday, June 30, 1768, they discussed Jacky's education.

No record of their dinner conversation survives, but the two men reached an agreement regarding the direction Jacky's studies should take. A half dozen years earlier Boucher had drafted a treatise defending the value of a traditional education based on the study of Greek and Latin. His treatise, which circulated in manuscript, prompted James Maury—Thomas Jefferson's teacher—to refute what Boucher said. Maury questioned whether a classical education was essential for American students.[13]

Many other educational theorists of the eighteenth century would broach the issue. In *Proposals Relating to the Education of Youth in Pensilvania* (1749), the document that would lead to the formation of the Philadelphia Academy (University of Pennsylvania), Benjamin Franklin similarly questioned the value of a classical education. Washington insisted his stepson pursue a traditional education based on the classics, the same kind of education his brother Lawrence had received at the Appleby School.

A staunch believer in the value of hard work, Washington also wanted to make sure Jacky's new teacher provided a demanding program of study. Boucher agreed to keep Washington informed of his stepson's progress. Discussing Jacky Custis's educational difficulties, Washington and Boucher would exchange numerous letters in the coming years. Though previously unrecognized as such, their correspondence forms a significant contribution to the history of American education. As the two men grappled with the problem of Jacky Custis, both would question the basic process of education.

Soon after Jacky arrived, Boucher realized the boy needed additional books to continue his study. Upon learning of the fine Custis library at Mount Vernon, Boucher requested two Latin works in particular. His request gave Washington the opportunity to delve into parts of the Custis collection he had not examined since cataloguing the library at Mount Vernon four years earlier. Boucher asked for Cicero's *De Officiis* and Livy's history of Rome.[14]

His need for these particular works reveals much about the state of Jacky's education. Livy was typically taught late in a boy's Latin education, usually after Virgil. Since Custis had been reading Virgil with Magowan, Boucher intended to pick up where his predecessor had left off. As a textbook Cicero's *De Officiis* could do double duty. A classic of moral philosophy as well as a model of Latin prose, *De Officiis* could be used to teach both ethics and composition. Washington searched the Mount Vernon library and found the copy of Cicero's *De Officiis* but could not find Livy. He forwarded Cicero to Boucher, along with the Greek grammar Jacky had forgotten.[15]

Within a month of Jacky Custis's arrival his new teacher had a fair understanding of the boy's limitations. Boucher understood that Jacky, or Jack, as he now preferred, had neither the talent nor the desire to become an accomplished classical scholar. Instead of admitting his inability to teach the boy and thus losing such a wealthy student, Boucher turned his back on the classical education he held dear.

In a progress report to Washington Boucher deemphasized the classical curriculum to stress the value of a well-rounded education, one that aimed to create people who are both wise and good, that sought "not only to cultivate the Understanding, but to expand the Heart, to meliorate the Temper, and *fix the gen'rous Purpose in the glowing Breast*."[16] Boucher often showed off his reading in his letters, using literary references for rhetorical effect. His watchwords here come from the "Spring" section of James Thomson's philosophical poem *The Seasons*. In a celebrated passage, Thomson stresses the joy of teaching:

> Delightful Task! to rear the tender Thought
> To teach the young idea how to shoot,
> To pour the fresh Instruction o'er the Mind,
> To breathe th' enlivening Spirit, and to fix
> The generous Purpose in the glowing Breast.

Before Custis had completed his third month at Boucher's school, he took a break from his studies and returned to Mount Vernon. He lingered there, nursing an illness, staying even longer after his mother fell ill. Martha Washington indulged herself by keeping her son nearby throughout her own illness. The situation reflects the difficulty Washington faced as a stepfather, the difficulty all stepfathers face. He wanted to discipline his stepson when necessary, but he could only go so far without upsetting the boy's mother.

Embarrassed by Jack's lengthy absence from school, Washington wrote a letter to Boucher in October, apologizing for keeping him so long and conveying his stepson's promise to focus on his studies: "He now promises to stick close to his Book, and endeavour by diligent study to recover his lost time—he will have nothing (that we know of) to interrupt him till the intervention of the Christmas Hollidays, when you will please to give him leave to return home."[17]

This letter reveals a pattern of behavior Jack Custis would repeat throughout his time at Boucher's school. He would slack off, promise his stepfather that he would concentrate on his studies, and then slack off again. Washington appears to take his stepson at his word in this October letter, but gradually he would recognize the boy's promises to shape up as empty ones.

Jack returned to Mount Vernon at Christmas and stayed for over a month.[18] A growing family crisis tempered the holiday festivities this year. Jack's sister, Patsy, had shown signs of epilepsy when she was six years old, but in 1768 she suffered her first grand mal seizure. Her seizures subsequently became more frequent. Patsy's epilepsy created constant worry, and she required continual attention. None of the medical books in the Custis library could help: there was no known cure for epilepsy.

A steady stream of doctors with an assortment of medicinal remedies visited Mount Vernon in the coming years. When both medical books and physicians proved ineffective, Washington resorted to a folk remedy, having a local blacksmith fashion an iron ring for Patsy to wear to guard against seizures. According to tradition, iron could work magic, but, needless to say, Patsy's new ring did nothing to cure her illness.[19]

Magowan, now the Reverend Walter Magowan, returned to Virginia in time to celebrate the holidays at Mount Vernon in 1768. This Christmas he brought presents in the form of books: on his departure for England earlier that year Washington had allowed Magowan to spend up to forty pounds sterling to purchase "Sundry Books" for Jack.[20] Shortly after the holidays, Magowan left Virginia for Maryland to become rector of St. James's Parish, Anne Arundel County, the same parish Boucher had been maneuvering to obtain for himself. Boucher was understandably upset upon learning that Magowan had taken the position he wanted. It was Boucher's jealousy on this occasion that led to his derogatory "raw Scotchman" remark. The two men reconciled in the coming years: on at least one occasion they came together at Mount Vernon.[21]

Custis's lengthy absence from school forced Washington to write Boucher another letter of apology. Washington seems less certain about his stepson's dedication to his studies in this January letter than he had in the October one: "After so long a vacation, we hope Jacky will apply close to his Studies, and retrieve the hours he has lost from his Book since your opening School—he promises to do so, and I hope he will."[22]

Having a slave at his beck and call, especially one as eager to please as Julius, Jack could indulge his distractions. Washington and Boucher agreed that Julius had to go. After Washington replaced him with Joe, a more serious and strong-minded servant, his stepson shaped up considerably. By mid-July 1769 Boucher could hope that Jack's laziness was not incurable.

Boucher took advantage of the Custis fortune by overcharging for the maintenance of Jack's horses. Washington readily paid for their upkeep, essentially telling Boucher to spend what he needed without bothering him with such trivialities. Boucher took further advantage, submitting to Washington a list of fifty books that, he claimed, Jack needed for his studies. The list names several standard Latin authors and some rudimentary Greek textbooks, which duplicate ones Jack already owned. Overall the list suggests that Boucher had planned an ambitious program of study for Jack Custis.[23] Some of the listed titles seem less like textbooks for students and more like books Boucher wished to read himself. Regardless, Washington diligently ordered them. After the books arrived at Mount Vernon, they took an inordinate amount of time to reach the school— much to Boucher's consternation.

The most significant work among these new books was the twenty-volume duodecimo edition of Cicero published by Foulis in Glasgow with notes by the abbé d'Olivet. Described by Boucher as a "very neat edition," the Foulis Cicero was handsomely printed in large, legible type. Nothing indicates whether the beautiful typography motivated Jack to broaden his knowledge of Cicero. The set has since been broken up. Its twentieth volume, the only one known to survive, contains no evidence indicating whether he read it.[24]

Boucher devised another way to benefit from the Custis fortune. As a capstone to Jack's education, he planned a grand tour of Europe for the boy—with himself as guide, of course. Pitching the idea to Washington, Boucher said the grand tour would form an excellent part of Jack's education, not only in itself but also to motivate his study beforehand. The promise of the trip, Boucher argued, would stimulate Jack "to pursue his Studies with greater Earnestness, when He recollects how often He must be put to the Blush, if He appears illiterate amongst Men of Letters, into whose Company, in Travelling."[25] In other words, as Jack prepared for the trip, he would finally realize the importance of a good education and pursue his studies with renewed vigor.

The reasoning of Jack's teacher seemed backwards to his stepfather. Though Washington admitted that travel could help to "form the manners, and encrease the knowledge of observant youth," he did not believe that dangling a European vacation carrotwise in front of his stepson would motivate the boy. Instead, Jack should master his studies before ever being promised a lavish journey to Europe. He should not travel through Europe until he was sufficiently instructed in classical knowledge.[26] Washington did not forbid the trip altogether but asked Boucher to sketch out his plan more fully.

Boucher was relieved that Washington did not reject his travel plan outright. Had he insisted Jack complete his classical education before embarking on a grand tour, Boucher knew the trip would never happen. Lately Jack's education was making almost no progress whatsoever. To convince Washington of the advantages travel would have for his stepson, Boucher brought his rhetorical skills to bear.

The detailed letter he wrote on May 21, 1770, to explain the advantages of travel cleverly uses literary allusion, direct discourse, and figurative comparison to make its point. Boucher compared the untraveled person to the "Caribbee Indian" that Joseph-François Lafitau mentions. Offended at being called a savage, Lafitau's Indian exclaims, "I know no Savages but the Europeans, who adopt none of our Customs!" Furthermore Boucher cleverly alluded to Baron Thunder-ten-tronckh, the father of Cunégonde in Voltaire's *Candide*. People who never travel, Boucher argued, have a severely limited perspective. They suppose "like the Baron Thonder ten Tronck, that both his Country and Countrymen, are the finest of all possible Countries and People."[27]

Alluding to a character from *Candide*, Boucher apparently assumed Washington knew the work. He could have. *Candide* was fairly well known in colonial Virginia. Patrick Henry, for one, had a copy in his library. So did Colonel William Fleming.[28] Boucher's letter was persuasive enough that Washington agreed to give the planned journey further thought and sought the advice of several friends in Williamsburg.

Soon after his May 21 letter to Washington, Boucher made arrangements to move to Annapolis, where he would become rector of St. Anne's Church. He also planned to relocate his school to Annapolis and hoped Custis would move to Annapolis to continue his studies. Now fifteen, Jack was more than willing to move. His stepfather viewed the prospect with trepidation. At Boucher's rural school in Caroline County, Jack had comparatively few temptations, but Annapolis was a dangerous place for a wealthy lad with an absence of personal resolve. Despite his stepfather's misgivings, Jack moved to Annapolis in late July.

Within a matter of months Washington noticed a change in the boy, and not for the better. Not only was he not studying, he had dropped all pretense of study. His mind, in his stepfather's words, seemed "a good deal relaxed from Study, and more than ever turnd to Dogs Horses and Guns." In addition, Jack was becoming something of a dandy, developing an obsession for clothes and other fineries. Washington wrote Boucher, urging him to redouble his efforts to keep the boy's education on track: "I must beg the favour of you therefore to keep him close to those useful branches of Learning which he ought now to be acquainted with, and as much as possible, under your own Eye."[29] If Boucher could not assure him of Jack's progress and dedication to study, Washington would remove him from school.

Boucher responded with frankness. He cautioned Washington that Jack, in addition to his laziness, was displaying signs of interest in the opposite sex that seemed inappropriate for a fifteen-year-old. Boucher was apprehensive about Jack's "Love of Ease, and Love of Pleasure—Pleasure of a Kind exceedingly uncommon at his Years." He continued, "I must confess to You I never did in my Life know a Youth so exceedingly indolent, or so surprizingly voluptuous: one would suppose Nature had intended Him for some Asiatic Prince."[30]

By the time another Christmas rolled around, Washington saw that Jack had made almost no progress in his study of Greek. Were he to insist that Jack continue studying ancient languages, Washington now realized, he would be taking time from more practical fields of learning. Sadly, his dream of giving Jack the classical education of a proper gentleman had failed to come true. If he were to abandon Greek, Jack might have the opportunity to learn more practical subjects. Writing to Boucher again, Washington outlined these other subjects. In his letter, he grouped his suggestions in a single paragraph, but they can be separated, numbered, and presented as a set of educational maxims:

1. To be acquainted with the French Tongue, is become a part of polite Education; and to a Man who has any idea of mixing in a large Circle, absolutely necessary.
2. Without Arithmetick, the common affairs of life are not to be managed with success.
3. The study of Geometry, and the Mathematics (with due regard to the branches of it) is equally advantageous.
4. The principles of Philosophy, Moral, Natural, etc. I should think a very desirable knowledge for a Gentleman.[31]

These words show Washington rethinking precisely what a gentleman's education meant. Formerly he had accepted the traditional idea that a gentleman's education meant a classical education. Now he considered the skills a gentleman might need in his day-to-day life.

Washington remained disappointed that Jack had neglected his education during his years with Boucher. The more he thought about the situation, the angrier he got. By mid-1771 he was tired of Jack's laziness and his excuse-making and tired, too, of the positive spin Boucher kept putting on the boy's progress. Jack had been studying with Boucher for three years, yet it scarcely seemed as if the boy had learned anything more than he had already learned from Magowan. Jack's knowledge may have actually regressed. He had started studying Greek with Magowan, but now he seemed incapable of construing the simplest sentence in Greek. Washington was starting to see Jack's time with Boucher as a huge waste.

In terms of classical learning, Boucher had to admit that Jack had learned little since Magowan left Mount Vernon, but, in his own defense, Boucher reiterated the argument that a good education involved much more than learning the classics. Boucher had continued to plan a grand tour for Jack. From Washington's perspective Jack had not learned enough at school to justify a European vacation. After acquiring a knowledge of Latin, students could pick up French rapidly, but Jack, in his stepfather's words, knew "nothing of French, which is absolutely necessary to him as a traveller."[32] His reluctance to learn French is another manifestation of Jack's laziness. Not only did he lack the language skills for European travel, Jack simply had not studied hard enough to justify the trip as a reward. No, Washington said once and for all, there would be no grand tour for Jack Custis.

Regarding Boucher's central point, that there was more to education than merely becoming a scholar, Washington agreed. Though he was willing to admit that students should study practical subjects they could use as adults, he was still unwilling to abandon the idea of a classical education. Gaps in his own education had made Washington sorely aware of his personal limitations. Though lacking a classical education himself, Washington responded to Boucher, formulating one of the briefest, yet most eloquent defenses of traditional learning ever written: "I conceive a knowledge of books is the basis upon which other knowledge is to be built."[33]

Gallivanting around Annapolis to attend afternoon horse races and evening dress balls, Custis found many ways to occupy his time instead of studying. His wealth gave him entrance to the city's finest residences and helped him expand his personal circle of acquaintances. He befriended Charles Willson Peale, a local painter at the start of a career that would eventually make him one of the most distinguished portraitists in early America. Having spent two years in London studying with Benjamin West, Peale had returned home to seek an American clientele. Custis correctly surmised that his stepfather would be interested in having his portrait painted.

Equipped with a letter of introduction from Jonathan Boucher, Peale, accompanied by Jack Custis, arrived at Mount Vernon on May 18, 1772. Washington agreed to have Peale paint his portrait and also arranged for him to paint miniatures of Martha and her children. For his portrait Washington dusted off his old uniform from the Virginia Regiment, which let Peale portray him as a military man.

Peale's portrait does not do Washington justice. Though he had turned forty earlier that year, Washington retained the strength and athleticism of a much younger man, but the picture hardly reveals his fitness. His pose is static, and he looks flabby. The waistcoat cannot cover a sizeable paunch. With his left hand behind his back and his right tucked into the waistcoat, Washington does not look like a man of action. Peale's personal reminiscence of Mount Vernon paints a much different picture. After his visit he would frequently relate an anecdote confirming Washington's great physical strength and depicting him as a much more athletic and dynamic figure.[34]

Near Mount Vernon one day Peale had joined some young men competing against each other by "pitching the bar." During this traditional athletic contest, competitors hurled a heavy iron bar to see who could throw it the furthest. Sir Walter Scott commemorated this rural sport in verse, observing:

> Their arms the brawny yeomen bare,
> To hurl the massive bar in air.

As they played in the neighborhood of Mount Vernon, contestants marked their distances with wooden pegs, the furthest one a goal for other contestants to surpass. As they were playing, Washington suddenly appeared among them, asking one of the competitors to point out the furthest peg. They had all stripped to the waist for the competition, but Washington did not bother to bare his brawny arms. Without taking off his coat, he grabbed the bar and hurled it into the air. It struck the ground far beyond the furthest peg.

"You perceive, young gentlemen, that my arm yet retains some portion of the vigor of my earlier days," Washington said with a smile as wide as the Potomac. As he walked away, he told them, "When you beat my pitch, young gentlemen, I'll try again."

Leaving Mount Vernon, Peale and Custis went different ways. On Washington's recommendation Peale headed to Williamsburg, where he hoped to find other distinguished Virginians willing to sit for their portraits. Custis returned to Maryland—but not to Annapolis. In late 1771 Boucher had left Annapolis to become rector of Queen Anne's Parish in Prince George's County, Maryland, where he re-established his school. Jack had come with Boucher to his new school. So had another student,

Charles Calvert, who was the son of Benedict Calvert of Mount Airy and a direct descendant of the founder of Maryland.

Staying with Boucher, Jack may have promised his stepfather to dedicate himself to study, but this he did not do. Given his voluptuous nature, Jack found other things to do in Prince George's County besides study. Charles Calvert's sister Eleanor, or Nelly, as she was familiarly known, caught Jack Custis's eye. At eighteen he made up his mind to marry her. Washington made up his mind to send the boy to college before a marriage could take place.

But which college? Colonial America now offered several institutions of higher learning. Washington had many factors to consider before he settled on a school for the boy. He wanted the best possible college for his stepson, of course, but location was also a factor. Though George Washington wanted to get Jack away from Nelly Calvert, Martha Washington wanted to keep her son close. Washington decided against William and Mary, not only because of the "Inattention of the Masters" but also because it afforded "no pleasing prospect to a youth who has a good deal to attain, and but a short while to do it in."[35] After asking around, he concluded that the Philadelphia Academy would be best for Jack. Since the Philadelphia Academy deemphasized classical learning in favor of a more practical education, Jack's resistance toward Latin and Greek would not be an obstacle to his advancement.

The first week of January 1773 Washington wrote Boucher, asking if he would write a letter of recommendation for Custis to the Philadelphia Academy.[36] Boucher alternatively suggested King's College (later renamed Columbia). Though disappointed with Boucher's inability to control Jack's behavior and channel the boy's energies toward serious study, Washington still respected his opinion. When Washington learned that Dr. Myles Cooper, the president of King's College, had introduced extensive reforms in terms of both curriculum and discipline, he chose King's College and made preparations to escort his stepson to New York.

Washington planned to leave Mount Vernon for New York on Monday, May 10. Jack left two days earlier to visit Nelly Calvert at Mount Airy, where Washington met up with him. Though he still felt that Jack was too young to marry, Washington could hardly complain about his stepson's fiancée. Nelly's family was one of the oldest and most distinguished in Maryland. Nelly personally distinguished herself in terms of charm, intelligence, sensitivity, and wit. After spending Monday night at Mount Airy, George Washington, Jack Custis, and Jack's servant Joe left for New York.

They reached New York the last week of May. Washington introduced himself and his stepson to Dr. Myles Cooper, and together they arranged to make Jack's time in college as comfortable as possible. Jack's wealth gave him an advantage over less fortunate students, so he became a favorite among the professors. He even dined with his teachers, a privilege denied to other students. In addition Jack's apartment was fairly sumptuous for a college student. Here's how he described it to his mother: "I have a large parlour with two Studies or closets, each large enough to contain a bed, trunk, and couple of chairs, one I sleep in, and the other Joe calls his."[37]

While in New York, Washington took the opportunity to indulge his passion for the theater. On Friday evening, May 28, he attended a performance of *Hamlet*. Washington was exposed to Shakespeare in his adolescence: his father had a copy of Shakespeare's plays in his library. Containing an edition of Shakespeare, the Custis library let him reread Shakespeare whenever he wished. Regardless how well Washington knew his Shakespeare beforehand, the 1773 visit to the playhouse in New York is the first known time he saw a Shakespeare play performed.

Washington's writings reverberate with Shakespearean echoes. In one general order during the Revolutionary War, for example, he encouraged his officers to see themselves as a "band of brothers," using a phrase from *Henry V*:

> We few, we happy few, we band of brothers;
> For he, to-day that sheds his blood with me,
> Shall be my brother.[38]

Washington could cite Shakespeare's comedies as well as his history plays. He typically elevated his language when he wrote to others with a literary bent. In a letter to the poet and songwriter Francis Hopkinson, for example, Washington said he had grown more accustomed to sitting for his portrait. Originally he felt considerable impatience while the painters painted, but now he could "sit like patience on a Monument whilst they are delineating the lines of my face." Washington borrowed his simile from a speech Viola makes to Orsino in *Twelfth Night*:

> she pin'd in thought,
> And with a green and yellow melancholy
> She sate like Patience on a monument,
> Smiling at grief.[39]

Another favorite phrase comes from *The Tempest*. During the Revolutionary War Washington found puzzling how the British troops took possession of American towns without conquering American forces and armament. He informed a correspondent: "They well know, that it is our arms, not defenceless Towns, they have to Subdue, before they can arrive at the haven of their wishes; and that till this end is accomplished, the superstructure they have been endeavouring to raise 'like the baseless fabric of a vision' falls to nothing."[40] He borrowed his simile from a speech Prospero makes in the fourth act of *The Tempest*. Washington would take the opportunity to see *The Tempest* performed in Philadelphia during the Constitutional Convention, after which he again repeated Prospero's words. When a correspondent sent him a political pamphlet criticizing his cabinet, President Washington refuted the author's unsubstantiated accusations, observing that "many of his Charges are as unsupported as the 'baseless fabric of a Vision.'"[41]

With Jack settled at King's College, Washington left New York the last day of May, riding into a warm south wind. He had one more encounter with higher education this trip. After spending the night at Perth Amboy, he headed for Princeton, where he met the president of the college and future signer of the Declaration of Independence, John Witherspoon. As a personal favor, Washington had agreed to pay the tuition of William Ramsay, Jr., the son of his good friend William Ramsay of Alexandria.

Tragedy struck after Washington returned to Mount Vernon. On Saturday, June 19, 1773, Patsy Custis, at seventeen, had another seizure, this time a fatal one. Patsy suffered what is now labeled sudden unexplained death in epilepsy (SUDEP), during which death occurs from a seizure-associated cardiorespiratory arrest and its ensuing complications. The report Washington made to a family friend the following day is heart-wrenching:

> She rose from Dinner about four Oclock, in better health and spirits than she appeard to have been in for some time; soon after which she was siezd with one of her usual Fits, and expired in it, in less than two Minutes without uttering a Word, a groan, or scarce a Sigh.—this Sudden, and unexpected blow, I scarce need add has almost reduced my poor Wife to the lowest ebb of Misery.[42]

Times of great emotion often inspired Washington's writing, but his description of Patsy Custis's death is not just a sentimental flourish. Washington's account of his stepdaughter's death is now recognized as one of the earliest well-documented eyewitness descriptions of SUDEP.[43]

John Witherspoon, wood engraving, From Evert A. Duyckinck and George
L. Duyckinck, *Cyclopaedia of American Literature* (New York: Charles
Scribner, 1856), 1:277. Kevin J. Hayes Collection, Toledo, Ohio.

Nelly Calvert, who happened to be visiting Mount Vernon, also witnessed Patsy Custis's death. Her presence was a great comfort to George and Martha Washington. Nelly's good nature helped soothe their heartache. She almost seemed to step into the void created by Patsy's death. Washington still felt his stepson was too immature to marry, but he could take comfort in the kind and sensitive young woman Jack had chosen to wed.

Saddened by the news of Patsy's death and lonely from his separation from Nelly, Jack Custis endured college life until September, when he left New York for Mount Vernon. He intended to return to King's College, where he hoped to deepen his study of moral philosophy. To that end he asked his stepfather to order several books on the subject. But the appeal of married life was too strong for him to resist. On February 3, 1774, John Parke Custis and Eleanor Calvert were married during a candlelit nighttime ceremony designed to suit the couple's romantic inclinations.

Though George Washington had wanted Jack to finish college first, Martha Washington approved of her son's marriage. As the boy's stepfather, he could only push the issue so far. Martha did think that the wedding came too soon after Patsy's death. Still in mourning for her daughter the first week of February, she thought it would be bad luck to attend her son's wedding ceremony wearing black. She stayed at Mount Vernon while George and Lund Washington—the devoted cousin who would serve as the plantation manager of Mount Vernon for many years—left for Mount Airy to attend the ceremony.

Jonathan Boucher thought the marriage to Nelly would provide the kind of stabilizing influence Jack Custis had been unable to find at school. As he told Washington: "Miss Nelly Calvert has Merit enough to fix Him, if any Woman can: and I do, from the fullness of a warm Heart, most cordially congratulate his Mother and Yourself, as well as Him, on the Happiness of his having made this most pleasing of all Connexions, with this the most amiable young Woman I have almost ever known."[44]

Boucher's time with Jack Custis influenced his educational theory. In one sermon he discussed the subject of a classical education:

> Instead of indiscriminately compelling all our youth, with or without a genius adapted to such studies, to spend the whole period of education in fruitless attempts, "merely (as Milton says) to scrape together a little miserable Greek and Latin," it is much to be wished some discrimination could be made, and that boys hereafter may be taught, not words only, but such things as they are best qualified to learn, and such as are likely to be of most use to them in the part they are hereafter to act in the great drama of life.[45]

Discussing the educational philosophy of the colonial South, Richard Beale Davis attributed Boucher's new attitude to his maturation as a schoolmaster.[46] Boucher's personal experience suggests a more specific cause. The double challenge he faced—educating Jack Custis and justifying the boy's education in letters to George Washington—helped Boucher rethink his pedagogical approach and devise a more pragmatic educational philosophy. Washington may have failed in his efforts to give his stepson a proper gentleman's education, but his correspondence with his stepson's teacher gave him a forum for contributing to the central debate over American education in the eighteenth century.

CHAPTER 10

Revolutionary Pamphlets

Pamphlets, those leaves of the hour, and volumes of a season and even of a week, slight and evanescent things as they appear, and scorned at by opposite parties while each cherishes their own, are in truth the records of the public mind, the secret history of a people.

Isaac D'Israeli, *Amenities of Literature*

In George Washington's cash accounts, the entry for August 6, 1774, contains the following item: "Mr Jefferson's Bill of Rights 3/9."[1] The entry may seem cryptic, but it really isn't. To be precise, Washington spent three shillings, nine pence, to subscribe to a fund that would finance the publication of Thomas Jefferson's *Summary View of the Rights of British America*, a pamphlet the Williamsburg printer Clementina Rind would issue in a matter of days. Washington was one of several Virginia patriots who subscribed to the fund to publish the work. From the summer of 1774 through the following winter, he added numerous other pamphlets to his library that track the revolutionary fervor as war between America and Great Britain loomed.

Thomas Jefferson had not composed his work for publication. Neither had he provided its title, *A Summary View of the Rights of British North America*. He wrote it as a resolution to present before the Virginia Convention, the extralegal gathering in Williamsburg designed to debate what should be done regarding the Crown's increasingly callous and belligerent attitude toward the American colonies. After leaving Monticello for Williamsburg, Jefferson was struck down with a case of dysentery. He returned home but sent copies of his manuscript to Williamsburg, where it caused a considerable stir.[2]

Peyton Randolph, who would be elected chair of the Virginia Convention, received one of the two manuscript copies Jefferson had prepared. It was read aloud one evening at Randolph's Williamsburg home to a large group of people.[3] Edmund Randolph, Peyton's nephew, recalled the applause the work elicited that evening. Peyton Randolph's guests recognized that Jefferson had gone much further than anyone before him had dared. "The young ascended with Mr. Jefferson to the source of those rights," Edmund Randolph recalled, but "the old required time for consideration before they could tread this lofty ground, which, if it had not been abandoned, [it] at least had not been fully occupied throughout America."[4] Despite the work's enthusiastic reception among the Revolutionaries, the Virginia Convention found Jefferson's ideas much too radical to sanction officially.

Though the Virginia Convention failed to approve Jefferson's resolution, his supporters saw they could outmaneuver the convention by putting his words in print and thus giving them a wider currency. George Washington's role in the publication of Jefferson's pamphlet has so far gone unnoticed, but the entry in his cash accounts, brief as it is, reveals his active participation in bringing the pamphlet to print. Dated August 6, the last day of the Virginia Convention and at least two days before *Summary View* was published, the entry reveals that Washington was not merely buying a copy of the pamphlet; he was contributing to the cost of publishing it.

Washington's description of the work—"Mr. Jefferson's Bill of Rights"—suggests that, as of August 6, 1774, the forthcoming pamphlet had yet to gain its final title. The title Washington temporarily gave it not only captures the work's essence, it also reveals his view of the significance of Jefferson's pamphlet to political history.

In modern American culture the phrase "Bill of Rights," of course, refers to the list of rights that form the first ten amendments to the US Constitution. Before the American Bill of Rights, the phrase generally referred to the English Bill of Rights, which Parliament had presented to William and Mary, then the Prince and Princess of Orange, in the late seventeenth century, basing their accession to the English throne on their acknowledgment of these rights. Washington was familiar with the text of the English Bill of Rights: Tobias Smollett had reprinted it in his *Complete History of England*.[5]

Equating Jefferson's work with the English Bill of Rights, Washington revealed how he understood the task the American colonists faced.

Essentially, they had to repeat what the English citizenry had done the previous century, that is, assert their fundamental rights as British subjects. Invoking the English Bill of Rights to describe Jefferson's bold statement of the rights of colonial British subjects in North America, Washington also revealed his cyclical view of history. Whenever a sovereign power infringes upon the rights of its citizenry, the people must rise to reassert their rights.

The active role Washington played in the publication of Jefferson's *Summary View* in August 1774 is consistent with his behavior during earlier times of political conflict. With each controversy of the past, Washington had obtained the most pertinent pamphlets available. During the so-called Parson's Cause, he acquired pamphlets on both sides of the controversy over the Two Penny Act, which sought to curb the salaries of Virginia clergymen during an economic downturn. After the Stamp Act's repeal, Washington obtained a copy of *The Examination of Doctor Benjamin Franklin*, a transcript of Franklin's testimony before the House of Commons regarding the Stamp Act, which was crucial in securing its repeal. With further British incursions on colonial American rights in the late 1760s, Washington obtained John Dickinson's *Letters from a Farmer in Pennsylvania*. On both constitutional and theoretical grounds Dickinson made a strong case for opposing the measures the British imposed on the American colonies.[6]

Jefferson's *Summary View* caps a flurry of revolutionary activity that had taken place since the Boston Tea Party, which had occurred in December 1773. Attending the House of Burgesses in May 1774, the Virginians had learned about the Boston Port Bill and the other "Intolerable Acts"—the punitive measures passed by Parliament in the wake of the Tea Party. Washington had voted for a resolution calling for a day of prayer and fasting to protest the Intolerable Acts and to show Virginia's solidarity with Massachusetts.

Learning about the resolution, Governor Dunmore dissolved the House of Burgesses. "This Dissolution," Washington informed a correspondent, "was as sudden as unexpected for there were other resolves of a much more spirited Nature ready to be offerd to the House which would have been adopted respecting the Boston Port Bill . . . but were withheld till the Important business of the Country could be gone through."[7]

After the governor dissolved the House, Washington went to the Raleigh Tavern with the other burgesses, where they could debate what to do. They agreed to a general congress of representatives from throughout colonial America and arranged the Virginia Convention for August, when they hoped that "some vigorous measures will be effectually adopted to obtain that justice which is denied to our Petitions and Remonstrances."[8] Besides providing a forum for articulating their grievances, the Virginia Convention would also elect delegates to the First Continental Congress.

So far Washington's revolutionary activities had not precluded his intellectual pursuits. On Wednesday, June 15, he went to the Capitol in Williamsburg to attend a meeting of the Virginia Society for the Advancement of Useful Knowledge. Modeled on both the Royal Society of London and the American Philosophical Society, this scientific organization had been established the previous year and had met sporadically since then. Washington had joined in November 1773. He renewed his membership at the June meeting, as did others, including Jefferson. The meeting was well attended, and those members present elected a new slate of officers. John Page of Rosewell was elected president and George Wythe vice president.[9]

Jefferson called the organization the "Society of Arts," a shorthand name emphasizing its role in the development of new technology that could be put to practical use. At the June meeting members voted to grant John Hobday a medal and a monetary award for the model of his newly invented wheat-threshing machine, which the society found ingenious. Also at this meeting they elected several corresponding members of the society, including Benjamin Franklin, John Coakley Lettsom, David Rittenhouse, Benjamin Rush, and John Smibert.[10]

Electing corresponding members from Philadelphia to Boston, the Virginians demonstrated a sense of intercolonial cooperation. Their scientific correspondence thus parallels the current work of revolutionary committees of correspondence throughout the American colonies. Electing Lettsom—a British physician—as well as other British scientists, the Virginians demonstrated that intellectual and scientific pursuits transcended political divisions. Political conflict need not stand in the way of scientific progress.

The same day he attended the meeting of the Society for the Advancement of Useful Knowledge Washington purchased a pamphlet by Samuel Henley: *A Candid Refutation of the Heresy Imputed by Ro. C. Nicholas Esquire to the Reverend S. Henley*. Professor Henley had been one of the founding members of the society and had served as its first secretary. After coming to Virginia, he involved himself in much religious and political controversy. "A savage polemicist who pushed against the bounds of propriety," Henley had engaged in a heated newspaper correspondence with Robert Carter Nicholas over the previous year.[11] This pamphlet sought to refute Nicholas's latest charge, that Henley was a heretic.

A Candid Refutation is an odd mix of erudition and idiosyncrasy. Nicholas had used much hearsay to demonstrate Henley's alleged heresy. He had quoted words that his wife and others—Mary Cary Ambler, Richard Bland, John Page—had supposedly heard Henley say. Some of these statements were taken out of context. Henley was a wag and an instigator. He often tossed off challenging ideas in conversation as a way to shock and provoke others, to get them thinking more deeply. He did not necessarily intend such bold remarks to be taken seriously or to be used against him. *A Candid Refutation* also reflects Henley's scholarly bent. His footnotes are filled with erudite references and quotations, a few in Latin or French. Some footnotes have footnotes of their own. Still, they are not without a sense of fun. Arguing that descriptions of devilish possession should not be taken literally, Henley supplied a footnote recounting Bishop Smalbroke's discussion of devils that enter a herd of swine (Mark 5:12–13). The bishop allotted three and a fraction to each animal in the herd. Smalbroke's division earned him the nickname Bishop Split-Devil.

Washington's surviving copy of Henley's *Candid Refutation* shows that he read the work carefully. After the preface, a list of errata appears under the heading: "Errors which the Reader is requested to correct." Washington followed this instruction, making numerous manuscript corrections to the text throughout his copy of Henley's pamphlet.[12]

A Candid Refutation can be read as both an erudite religious treatise and a contribution to local gossip. The Virginians mentioned in the text were Washington's friends, so he was naturally curious about what Henley had to say about them. Sometimes the erudition was beyond him, but Washington knew several of the books Henley referenced: Addison's *Cato*, Milton's *Paradise Lost*, *The Spectator*, and others. Besides his eloquent defense against Nicholas's slander, what shows most clearly in *A Candid Refutation* is Henley's understanding of the relationship between reason and faith. Henley calls himself a "rational Christian" and argues that Scripture can withstand scrutiny. Subjecting religion to reason, in Henley's view, could only strengthen belief.

In July 1774 Washington had attended meetings in Alexandria, Virginia, with other interested citizens of Fairfax County to debate what should be done about British encroachments on American freedom. Together he and George Mason co-authored the *Fairfax County Resolves*, which called for a boycott of British goods, expressed support for Boston, and agreed to the meeting of a Continental Congress. They presented the Fairfax County Resolves to the public on Monday, July 18, at the county courthouse in Alexandria. The citizens of Fairfax County adopted the resolves and named Washington the head of a committee to take charge of the county's interests.

During the Virginia Convention, Washington was elected one of seven Virginia delegates to the First Continental Congress, scheduled to convene in Philadelphia the following month. In addition the delegates passed an association, that is, a document setting forth their common purpose. Clementina Rind printed it as a half-sheet broadside under the title *An Association, Signed by 89 Members of the Late House of Burgesses*. Washington purchased several copies of this broadside, some to distribute to his neighbors in Fairfax County, others to take with him to Philadelphia. The Virginia Association would serve as a model for the association the First Continental Congress would pass.

Patrick Henry and Edmund Pendleton, two other delegates to the Continental Congress, came to Mount Vernon on Tuesday, August 30, so they could set out for Philadelphia together the next day. Washington had much farm business to take care of beforehand. Isaac Hobday, who was traveling through Virginia to encourage farmers to adopt his brother's wheat-threshing machine, reached Mount Vernon this Tuesday. Having seen a working model at a meeting of the Society for the Advancement of Useful Knowledge, Washington was already convinced of its usefulness. He engaged Isaac Hobday's services to oversee the construction of a new wheat-threshing machine at Mount Vernon.

The last day of August proved to be exceedingly hot, as Washington recorded in his weather log, but Martha gave the trio a good send-off.[13] Pendleton came away from Mount Vernon quite impressed with her. Afterwards he told a friend, "I was much pleased with Mrs. Washington and her spirit. She seemed ready to make any sacrifice, and was very cheerful, though I know she felt very anxious. She talked like a Spartan mother to her son on going to battle."[14]

"I hope you will all stand firm—I know George will," she said. "God be with you, gentlemen!"

Traveling by horseback, the three arrived in Philadelphia on Sunday, September 4, and headed for the City Tavern, or, as it was also known, the New Tavern. Located on Second Street, the City Tavern contained several large club rooms, which made it an ideal gathering place for delegates to the First Continental Congress. Along with the others, Washington returned here on Monday, when all their credentials were read. Together they elected Peyton Randolph president and Charles Thomson secretary. In addition, they chose a place for the Continental Congress to meet. The Carpenters' Guild of Philadelphia kindly offered Carpenters' Hall, a handsome Georgian building on Chestnut Street, as a meeting place. The delegates accepted the offer.

Unlike Patrick Henry, Washington was not a great public speaker, but he did articulate his thoughts in conversation with others. Silas Deane, a delegate from Connecticut, said that Washington "speaks very modestly in a cool but determined style and accent."[15] More of a listener than a speaker, he heard what others had to say and recognized what to do to get things done. As Patrick Henry said, "Colonel Washington, who has no pretensions to eloquence, is a man of more solid judgment and information than any man on the floor."[16]

By the time the First Continental Congress adjourned in late October, it had passed a series of resolutions, which were collected together as an association, to which the delegates affixed their names. *The Association, &c.*, as it was simply titled, was printed in Philadelphia as both a pamphlet and a broadside and reprinted in Boston as a broadside.[17] The pamphlet was easier to tote around, but the broadside was ideal for posting as a public document for all to read.

Upon reading *The Association, &c.*, one Loyalist poet found it ripe for parody. In Revolutionary America, the "versification" was a form of political parody used by both patriots and Loyalists. It basically involved taking a serious piece of prose and rendering it into satirical verse. Since the Stamp Act, numerous political speeches, proclamations, and other official documents had been parodied through versification.[18] That *The Association, &c.* would share the same fate seems almost inevitable. Sure enough, it was soon versified and published. It appeared under the name "Bob Jingle," the pseudonymous satirist who facetiously styled himself "Poet Laureat to the Congress" but whose true identity remains unknown.

Titled *The Association, &c. of the Delegates of the Colonies at the Grand Congress, Held at Philadelphia, Sept. 1, 1774, Versified and Adapted to Music*, this versification consists of three parts: a ballad, a recitativo in heroic couplets, and a chorus in tetrameter couplets. At the end the pamphlet reprints Continental Congress's association, apparently to demonstrate the cleverness of the versification by letting interested readers compare Bob Jingle's verse compare to the original prose. Though written to spoof the congressional association, this pamphlet helped circulate it further. Pundits nowadays worry about the American people receiving political information from parodies of the news. As Bob Jingle's *Association* and the numerous other revolutionary versifications show, Americans have been receiving political news through parody since the nation began.[19]

The fact that George Washington had a copy of Bob Jingle's *Association* in his library indicates his attitude toward such parodies. Curious about the opposition to the Continental Congress, he eagerly read what others thought about its actions. His ownership of the work further reflects both open-mindedness and a sense of humor. Washington had enjoyed reading poetry since boyhood, and he was unafraid to hear what others thought about him and his role as a delegate to the Continental Congress.

The congressional association amounted to an agreement among the American colonists not to import or consume materials from Great Britain, nor to export agricultural products to Great Britain. This non-importation, non-consumption, and non-exportation agreement, to use the language of the association, provided a way to protest the actions of Parliament and redress the grievances of the American people.

Transposing the language of the Continental Congress into ballad stanzas, Bob Jingle intones:

> That these are mighty Grievances,
> Must be by all consent;
> Therefore we will exert our might,
> To get them straight redress'd.
>
> The Method we have hit upon,
> To bring this Scheme to bear,
> Is *Import—Export—Consump-non*,
> And this will do't, we swear.[20]

Bob Jingle uses many of the same words he found in *The Association, &c.*, but the ones he adds change the tone considerably. Having Congress call the agreement a "Method we have hit upon," Bob Jingle detracts from the careful deliberations that occurred in Carpenters' Hall that September and October. He makes it seem as if the delegates had stumbled upon the idea for the agreement purely by chance. Having Congress say, "And this will do't, we swear," Bob Jingle portrays the delegates as immature and uncertain of themselves. Theirs are the words of a schoolboy trying to convince classmates about something he is unsure of himself.

The middle part of Congress's text enumerates a series of measures the Americans would take to assure the success of the association. Number eight, for example, encouraged economy, frugality, and industry and promoted the development of American manufacturing. It discouraged such forms of extravagance and dissipation as cockfighting, gaming, and horse racing. Furthermore, it simplified mourning practices, freeing Americans from having to wear mourning dress and letting them express their sorrow simply: a black crepe armband for men and a black ribbon or necklace for women. Congress also discouraged the practice of giving gloves and scarves at funerals.

Converting this eighth measure into heroic couplets, Bob Jingle presents the following verse paragraph:

> And eighthly, when we are quite rid of our Trade,
> And, stript of our Money, mere Shepherds are made,
> We'll see no Horse-racings, nor e'en a Cock-fight,
> Our only Diversion to eat, sleep, and sh-te,
> And when a Son dies, we will take no more Notice,
> Than, as if one should say, I know nor care who 'tis,
> With a Piece of black Crape, we will sit down content;
> When all our old Cloaths are quite tatter'd and rent;
> The giving of Gloves and of Scarfs we'll decry,
> When we've got none to give, faith, let who will die.[21]

Bob Jingle obviously wonders whether a ban on cockfighting and mourning dress will really help enforce the non-consumption agreement. By themselves the individual components of the eighth measure may seem insignificant, but they show how delegates to the Continental Congress questioned all aspects of their lives and scrutinized long-standing social customs to probe their fundamental significance. When it came to the tradition of mourning dress, for example, they could see how unnecessary it was. Far from an expression of sorrow, it seemed like a tradition that contributed to British coffers. Mourning dress was expensive and had to be ordered from Britain. Americans did not have to wear British mourning dress to convey the loss they felt upon the death of a loved one.

The tetrameter couplet, a vehicle for parody since Samuel Butler wrote *Hudibras* in the seventeenth century, was already a well-established form for humorous satirical verse among early American poets, structuring such masterworks as Ebenezer Cook's *Sotweed Factor* and Robert Bolling's "Neanthe." Bob Jingle suggests that one particularly sly delegate to the Continental Congress—a "crafty *Reynard*"—forced the others to sign the association against both their will and their better judgement.

Bob Jingle's versification may be the most entertaining pamphlet to critique the First Continental Congress, but numerous others appeared as well. Some pamphleteers used the sterner vehicle of prose to articulate their opposition. *Free Thoughts, on the Proceedings of the Continental Congress*, to sample another work from Washington's library, appeared the month after Congress adjourned. The author published the work pseudonymously, identifying himself solely as "A Farmer" on the title page.

Colonial writers, including some who had little to do with farming, commonly used this pseudonym to appeal to their American readers. John Dickinson, a Philadelphia lawyer, assumed the persona of a Pennsylvania farmer to articulate his political views. The "Farmer" pseudonym manifests another eighteenth-century American ideal, namely, the ideal of classical agrarianism, which viewed rural life as a source of virtue, health, and happiness.[22]

At the end of *Free Thoughts* the author provides an additional clue to his actual identity, signing himself, "A. W. Farmer." It did not take long for New York readers to recognize that the "A" was not an initial but an indefinite article and that "W" was short for Westchester. A. W. Farmer was none other than the Reverend Samuel Seabury, rector of Westchester, New York.

A contributor to the *New-York Journal* described how contemporary readers reacted to Seabury's *Free Thoughts*. When the pamphlet was read aloud before a gathering of twenty or thirty people, they condemned it as "one of the most treacherous, malicious, and wicked productions that has yet appeared, from the implacable enemies of the British colonies and nation."[23] This contributor exaggerates, but his words do reflect the animosity Seabury provoked. *Free Thoughts* appeared without a printer's or a publisher's name, but some of its opponents suspected that the Tory publisher James Rivington had printed the work, and they burned copies of *Free Thoughts* on his doorstep.

Maintaining the farmer persona throughout the work, Seabury raised some valid points about the association's enforceability. Congress intended to appoint local enforcement committees to assure compliance with the non-consumption aspect of the agreement. Seabury felt the activities of the committee men would be an invasion of privacy. While his objections to the practicality of the association have some validity, he failed to understand the ideological and philosophical basis of Congress's grievances.

Seabury ignored the basic idea of equality underlying the American cause. He observed: "If I must be enslaved, let it be by a KING at least, and not by a parcel of upstart lawless Committee-men. If I must be devoured, let me be devoured by the jaws of a lion, and not *gnawed* to death by rats and vermin!"[24] In other words, Seabury accepted the longstanding concept of the chain of being, the hierarchy that placed lion above rat, king above man. He refused to acknowledge the radical concept of the American Revolutionaries: that king and committee man are both men, neither one fundamentally better or worse than the other.

After each day in the Continental Congress, Washington maintained a busy social schedule, dining with other delegates as well as prominent Philadelphia merchants, magistrates, and intellectuals. In his diary he recorded whom he dined with and where he went after dinner but provided no additional details. Journals and reminiscences of others sometimes help paint a fuller picture. On Monday, October 17, for example, Washington wrote that he spent the evening at the home of Thomas Mifflin, a Philadelphia merchant who represented Pennsylvania in the Continental Congress. Washington's diary contains no additional information about the evening, but Benjamin Rush described it in his autobiography, *Travels through Life*.

Still in his twenties, Rush had already established himself as one of Philadelphia's leading physicians. Besides being a man of science, he was also a fine writer who understood the value of recording anecdotes for posterity. This evening Mifflin's company included John Adams, Samuel Adams, and Charles Lee, a British army officer who had cast his lot with the American patriots. Impressed with Lee's extensive military experience, Washington was happy to have him on the American side—at least at first.

Rush was initially quite impressed with Washington. After meeting him in 1775, he informed a correspondent: "He has so much martial dignity in his deportment that you would distinguish him to be a general and a soldier from among ten thousand people. There is not a king in Europe that would not look like a valet de chambre by his side."[25] On this particular evening, those gathered at Mifflin's home considered the consequences of the actions taken by the First Continental Congress. As Rush recalled, John Adams said that he did not expect Great Britain to redress the colonial grievances, nor did he foresee the possibility of reconciliation. Rush recorded a toast John Adams uttered on the occasion.[26]

"Cash and Gunpowder to the Yankees!" Adams exclaimed as he lifted his glass.

Though Congress continued to meet until October 26, 1774, some of the Virginia delegates left Philadelphia to reach Williamsburg in time to attend the House of Burgesses, which was scheduled to convene the first Thursday in November. Before they left, Richard Bland, Benjamin Harrison, and Peyton Randolph placed their trust in Washington and authorized him to vote for them.[27] That Washington stayed until Congress adjourned indicates the diligence and seriousness with which he accepted his position as delegate.

The evening Congress adjourned, Wednesday, October 26, the delegates hosted a gathering at the New Tavern to honor those citizens of

Philadelphia who had entertained them while Congress had been in session. Rush also recorded this event for posterity. He observed, "The company was large, and the conversation animated by the most fervid patriotism." The evening was filled with enthusiastic toasts and playful banter. William Livingston of New Jersey, who had a great reputation as a wit, "contributed very much to the pleasure of this evening by his facetious stories and conversation."[28] Rush found most memorable Samuel Ward's prophetic words. A delegate from Rhode Island, Ward believed that not only would the American Revolution provide the basis for government in the New World, it would inspire other nations around the globe.

"May the fire which has been recently kindled upon the altar of liberty in America, enlighten all the nations of the world into a knowledge of their rights," Ward toasted.

When Washington left for Mount Vernon, he asked his friend William Milnor to send him additional political pamphlets as they appeared. Milnor complied and, in November, sent an anonymous pamphlet titled *A Friendly Address to All Reasonable Americans, on the Subject of our Political Confusions*. With this "Vile pamphlet," as he called it, Milnor also sent a refutation: *Strictures on a Pamphlet, Entitled a "Friendly Address to All Reasonable Americans, on the Subject of our Political Confusions."* Anticipating how Washington would react, Milnor wrote, "If you have patience to read the first, I think you will be diverted with the last."[29]

The first work, which came from the pen of the Reverend Dr. Thomas Bradbury Chandler, is not nearly as well written as Seabury's *Free Thoughts*, nor is its argument as cogent. Chandler preys upon his readers' fears, asserting the infallibility of Great Britain and assuming that any challenge to the Mother Country would be crushed. William Hooper, a North Carolina delegate, called this so-called friendly address a "trifling performance" and recognized its author's shameless fearmongering. Hooper complained: "The Author has wrote to the passions—to inflame and mislead weak minds. He has conjured up the Horrors of a Civil War to affright the timid."[30]

Despite Hooper's dislike of *A Friendly Address*, he was upset by what happened to the pamphlet in Philadelphia, where patriots treated it the same way New York patriots had treated Seabury's *Free Thoughts*. Hooper informed a correspondent that through "a mistaken zeal of the people," the *Friendly Address* had been prevented from being sold publicly in Philadelphia. He continued:

Strange Infatuation that while we contend with enthusiastick ardor for the liberty of the press ourselves that we should with such an intolerating spirit deny it to others. It is a strange freedom that is confined to one side of a Question! Doctrines in politicks that will not bear a freedom of discussion carry with them more than a suspicion of being erroneous, and I am confident that the world will not be so easily gulled in these as in the unquestionable mysteries of Church faith. They will take the freedom to think for themselves, and even to condemn what will not upon a fair dispassionate enquiry stand the test of solid reason and sound Criticism.[31]

The best way to treat such a trifling work, Hooper believed, would simply be to ignore it, but it was not ignored. A lengthy rebuttal appeared in the *New-York Journal* by an author who styled himself "Americanus."[32] The finest response came from Charles Lee, the author of *Strictures on A Friendly Address*, the other pamphlet Milnor sent Washington.

Besides being an experienced soldier, Lee was also an accomplished scholar, and he applied both skills in his rebuttal to Chandler's *Friendly Address*. Lee brought many other aspects of his irascible personality to bear: his wit and his vanity, a gift for satire combined with flippancy, confidence in his own personal knowledge, and a deep animosity toward those in power. Contemptuous of both king and Parliament, which had ignored his military talents, Lee had come to America just one year earlier and quickly taken the side of the colonists against British tyranny. Chandler's *Friendly Address* provided an ideal platform for articulating his ideas. Milnor was right: *Strictures* is great fun after the doom and gloom of *A Friendly Address*.

Charles Lee may have met Washington two decades earlier when they served together under General Braddock during his disastrous expedition against Fort Duquesne, but they became good friends when Washington was in Philadelphia for the First Continental Congress. Washington invited Lee to visit Mount Vernon. Lee accepted the invitation, arriving on December 30 and staying until January 4. His stay gave the two much time to talk, and Lee's stories of his military experiences greatly impressed Washington. Besides serving in the French and Indian War, Lee had served under General John Burgoyne in a British expedition to Spain, as aide-de-camp to King Stanislaus of Poland, and as a major general in the Polish army. In addition he had joined the Russian army in Moldavia to fight against the invading Turks.[33]

Washington received a number of other pamphlets in the aftermath of the First Continental Congress, not all of which were political. Or perhaps they were. In times of conflict everything becomes political, even farming. Take the case of *An Essay on the Culture and Management of*

Hemp. Solely by its title, this fifty-two-page pamphlet may seem like an agricultural treatise, but the circumstances of its publication closely resemble those of contemporary political pamphlets.

Prior to its publication *An Essay on Hemp* was read aloud to several members of the Annapolis committee of safety, who, as Charles Carroll of Carrollton informed Washington, were so impressed with the work that they recommended its publication. By the first week of March 1775, it was in press. Before printing was complete, Carroll wrote to Washington, suggesting that the pamphlet would be particularly useful to the American colonies during the present conflict.[34]

With his letter Carroll included some sample pages from *An Essay on Hemp*. He hoped Washington would help distribute the work in Virginia. Aware that a second Virginia Convention was fast approaching, Carroll thought it would provide an ideal opportunity to promote the pamphlet in Virginia. There is no evidence to indicate that Washington served as Virginia agent for this pamphlet, as Carroll hoped, but he did obtain a copy of the complete work, which he added to his agricultural library at Mount Vernon.

In March 1775 delegates to the Virginia Convention from all parts of the colony headed to Richmond and assembled at St. John's Church. Richmond had been chosen over Williamsburg as the gathering place for the convention this year because the local citizens who stood up to the British administration were increasingly unwelcome in the colonial capital. This group of over a hundred men included nearly all of Virginia's foremost leaders.

The convention began on Monday, March 20, when the delegates began discussing the dire situation the American colonists faced. By Thursday the debate had reached a fever pitch. Many Virginians recognized the necessity of war, but some still needed convincing. Washington's friend Patrick Henry rose to the occasion, delivering the most memorable speech of the convention and of his life, the speech that ends with the exclamation: "I know not what course others may take; but as for me, give me liberty, or give me death!"

As part of its proceedings, the Virginia Convention also elected delegates to the Second Continental Congress. Peyton Randolph received the largest number of votes, with Washington second and Henry third. Thomas Jefferson was elected first alternate, in case Peyton Randolph would be unable to fulfill his responsibilities as a delegate, which proved to be the case. Congress was scheduled to convene in May, but before it met, the Massachusetts militia and the British army clashed at Lexington and Concord. The war had begun.

CHAPTER 11

———————

Common Sense and Independence

The birthday of a new world is at hand.

Thomas Paine, *Common Sense*

With an aura of foreboding, the Second Continental Congress convened in Philadelphia on Wednesday, May 10, 1775. The clash between the Massachusetts militia and the British army at Lexington and
Concord had occurred less than a month earlier.

After the British troops retreated to Boston, the Massachusetts militia
posted sentinels across the river on Prospect Hill to oversee the city, thus
beginning the siege of Boston. In Philadelphia the nervous tension among
the congressional delegates was palpable—and understandably so. Five
weeks later the standstill between Massachusetts and British forces would
erupt into the Battle of Bunker Hill, which the British won but only at a
big and bloody cost. Having left Carpenters' Hall, their former meeting
place, the congressional delegates now met at the State House, or, as it
would become known to history, Independence Hall.

In a brilliant display of self-fashioning, Washington came to the
Continental Congress in uniform. Some say he wore the uniform of the
Virginia Regiment; more likely he wore the blue-and-buff uniform of the
new Fairfax Independent Company, which he had been training recently.[1]
Those who saw him in Philadelphia that May could see that Washington
was ready for whatever the Continental Congress might decide.

Fellow congressmen recognized his preparedness for war and gave
him a leading role in military planning. Washington was appointed chair
of a committee to advise New York on its defense. In addition he chaired

one committee to draft plans for a system to supply all the colonies with guns and ammunition and another committee to draft rules and regulations to govern the American troops. Electing him to the chair of these committees, Congress acknowledged his military experience. Washington's committee work ably demonstrated his leadership. As the time to create the Continental Army approached, he was the obvious choice for commander in chief.[2] On Thursday, June 15, Congress unanimously appointed George Washington to command the Continental Army. He officially accepted the appointment the following day and arranged to have Charles Lee appointed a major general in the Continental Army.

The next Friday, June 23, Washington and Lee left Philadelphia on their way north to Cambridge, Massachusetts, accompanied by several other officers of the newly constituted army. They were escorted by both the light horse and the officers of the infantry on horseback. Will Lee, or Billy, as he was commonly called, also accompanied them. A devoted slave, Billy acted as Washington's manservant. "A square muscular figure, and capital horseman," according to a contemporary observer, Billy would serve General Washington throughout the war, establishing a reputation for hard work and kindheartedness and, in the process, earning the dubious distinction of the most famous slave in the United States.[3]

Many congressional delegates accompanied Washington for a few miles on his way out of Philadelphia. Letters from the delegates to their wives back home help reconstruct the event. Writing to his wife, Abigail, John Adams described Washington's departure. Adams noted the pomp surrounding the procession, all accompanied by the sound of fife and drum. His description shows that music has been an integral part of the American military since it began. Though Adams did not join Washington on the road from Philadelphia, Robert Treat Paine, a fellow delegate from Massachusetts, rode with him for three miles before returning to Philadelphia. Silas Deane rode with the commander in chief for six miles.[4]

Several hours after Washington left the city, a large crowd gathered at Christ Church to hear the Reverend Dr. William Smith, president of Philadelphia College, deliver an emotionally charged sermon. Writing from the vantage point of the late nineteenth century, Moses Coit Tyler characterized Smith's sermon as "the boldest words on the questions of the day, which had been spoken in America from an Anglican pulpit."[5] Those present that evening were greatly impressed. Having heard about Smith's oratorical abilities beforehand, Deane was not disappointed. He told his wife that he was "most agreeably entertained with a discourse of about Thirty Minutes," which "exceeded in Stile, and sentiment anything I ever heard on the Subject."[6] A cold front moved into Philadelphia that summer night, bringing with it some cool rain. Exiting Christ Church after Smith's sermon, the Revolutionary patriots could feel a change in the air.

Smith soon published *A Sermon on the Present Situation of American Affairs*, which he dedicated to the commander in chief. Though Washington had left Philadelphia before Smith's sermon, he received a copy of the printed version soon after its publication. Smith stopped short of advocating independence, but he did not stop far short. He expressed his confidence in colonial America. Whatever mistaken policies had set it back temporarily would not do so permanently:

> If we maintain our own virtue; if we cultivate the spirit of Liberty among our children; if we guard against the snares of luxury, venality and corruption; the Genius of America will still rise triumphant, and that with a power at last too mighty for opposition. This country will be free—nay, for ages to come, a chosen seat of Freedom, Arts, and heavenly Knowledge; which are now either drooping or dead in most countries of the old world.[7]

After leaving Philadelphia, Washington kept abreast of what was happening there, partly by acquiring additional pamphlets published during the time the Continental Congress remained in session. The pamphlets he added to his library include several other patriotic sermons. Congress proclaimed Thursday, July 20, 1775, a general day of fasting. Observed throughout the colonies of British North America, this fast day reinforced the growing sense of colonial unity.

In Philadelphia the Reverend Thomas Coombe delivered a fast day sermon, which Philadelphia printer John Dunlap issued as *A Sermon, Preached before the Congregations of Christ Church and St. Peter's, Philadelphia*. Washington added a copy of this sermon to his library. Coombe spoke for the rights of the American rebels, finding the defensive steps they had taken fully justified in the face of British colonial repression. Denying the colonists their rights, the British had violated the English constitution. So far, Coombe suggested, the American colonists had acted only as British precipitancy and violence had compelled them to act, "a precipitancy bordering upon frenzy, and a violence which Rome scarce ever exercised over her conquered provinces."[8]

Unwilling to sanction American independence, especially from the pulpit of the Church of England, Coombe resorted to the comfort of cliché, blaming the current strife on that eighteenth-century bugbear luxury. By reverting to simplicity, recapturing the austerity of the colonial past, and foregoing the "superfluities of commerce," those living in

America could achieve a sense of peace. Reluctant to consider the possibility of American independence, Coombe sought refuge in an idealized past.

Having reached Cambridge on Sunday, July 2, Washington and Lee had the pleasure to witness an army parade in their honor the next day. Lieutenant Joseph Hodgkins told his wife that a sense of grandeur surrounded the event. A huge military band—one and twenty drummers and an equal number of fifers—performed for the commander in chief.[9] Together Washington and Lee took up residence on Harvard Square at the home of the Reverend Dr. Samuel Langdon, president of Harvard College. The Massachusetts provincial congress gave them the run of the whole house, save for a single room reserved for Langdon's use. A staunch patriot, Langdon did not resent the intrusion. Willing to make the sacrifice in the cause of freedom, he welcomed Washington into his home.

Langdon was impressed. Years later he told Washington:

> As soon as I was honored with an acquaintance with you at Cambridge, upon your arrival at my house with your Suite, I was ready to look up to heaven, and say, "Blessed be God; who hath given us a General who will not rashly throw away the lives of his Soldiers, or hazard the fate of his Country unnecessarily upon a single Battle, but will proceed with all wisdom and caution!"

General Lee, on the other hand, did not impress Langdon, not one single bit. He saw Lee as vain and self-centered, "a man void of all principles, both religious and moral."[10]

Like William Smith and Thomas Coombe, Langdon used the pulpit to voice his opposition to tyranny. The month before Washington arrived, Langdon had delivered a sermon to the provincial congress of Massachusetts, which he published as *Government Corrupted by Vice and Recovered by Righteousness*. Langdon presented a copy of this sermon to Washington. In the coming years their relationship remained cordial. Langdon would continue to give him copies of his sermons as he published them. Washington saw similarities between Langdon's *Government Corrupted by Vice* and the sermons by Smith and Coombe. He had all three bound together under the collective title "Political Sermons."

Langdon understood that the American colonists faced a turning point in 1775. Though English law had long been a symbol of freedom—"the glory and strength of the English nation"—the oppressive behavior of the British government toward the American colonists marked the end of British liberty.[11] Conveying these political views in a sermon, Langdon had to reconcile them with his faith. The cruel oppression of the British legislators seemed like divine retribution. But why would God punish New England? The sinners, Langdon concluded, were the American Tories, those who supported the mother country. Their support of the British government undermined God's divine plan for New England. The Tories, paradoxically, were the true rebels, because they rebelled against God's laws.[12]

General Washington built up the fortifications along the siege lines surrounding Boston. Recognizing the military significance of Prospect Hill, he assigned General Lee command of the left wing division, which included the advantageous hill. Washington frequently visited to view the situation. Professor David Howell, who would later serve in the Continental Congress, first met Washington on Prospect Hill. The professor found the general deep in thought and greatly concerned about the military situation and the welfare of his men.[13]

Washington left Langdon's home on Harvard Square in mid-July and moved into the Cambridge mansion on Brattle Street that had belonged to John Vassal, a wealthy Tory who had fled the city for Boston to save himself from the Revolutionaries. Vassal's mansion would remain Washington's headquarters throughout his time in Cambridge. Henry Wadsworth Longfellow, who lived there in the nineteenth century and took Washington's study for his bedroom, called it "a great house, which looks like an Italian villa."[14]

Living in Cambridge, Washington had the opportunity to meet several community leaders. Langdon was not the only preacher he came to know. William Gordon, pastor of the Third Congregational Church in Roxbury and chaplain to the provincial congress of Massachusetts, also befriended him. Gordon's political sympathies had originally drawn him and his wife, Elizabeth, from England to America in 1770. By the time they met Washington, Gordon was absolutely fascinated by the Revolution.[15] On July 19, 1775, he delivered an election sermon to the provincial congress, published as *A Sermon Preached before the Honorable House of Representatives, on the Day Intended for the Choice of Counsellors, Agreeable to the Advice of the Continental Congress.* Apparently Gordon presented a copy to Washington.

Had he read all the political sermons he received, Washington could have discerned their similarities. Like Langdon, Gordon tried to reconcile an apparent contradiction. According to the traditional concept of the chain of being, the king occupied a position between man and God: he was God's chosen representative on earth. How could someone rebel against the king without going against God? Like many of the American

Washington's Headquarters in Cambridge, Massachusetts, wood engraving.
From Evert A. Duyckinck and George L. Duyckinck, *Cyclopaedia of
American Literature* (New York: Charles Scribner, 1856), 2:444. Kevin J.
Hayes Collection, Toledo Ohio.

Revolutionaries, Washington included, Gordon situated the rebellion as
one against the British ministry, not the king. Gordon argued, "We
should certainly rebel against the Sovereign of the universe in his prov-
idential dispensations, and reject the divine council communicated to us
by that medium, did we not resolve to persist in our present opposition
to the wicked designs of an arbitrary ministry." Gordon remained vague
about precisely what steps should be taken. He, too, took refuge in nostalgia. American legislators should try to restore the more virtuous past,
"to bring back the manners of the people to what they were originally,
so that our children may be as aforetime, virtuous, disinterested, patriotic and pious; and to extirpate those vices that have crept in unawares
among us."[16]

Gordon would continue to correspond with Washington. Before another year passed, he formulated a grand plan to write the history of the American Revolution. To that end Gordon met as many generals and legislators as he could. In addition he doggedly sought public documents and private correspondence as he researched what he hoped would be an impartial history. He would pursue his research throughout the war and continue gathering information once the war ended. His research would bring him and Washington together again.

As the commander of the Continental Army, General Washington had approximately fourteen thousand troops under his command, and he faced extraordinary challenges when it came to training and disciplining them. After several months of effort, he conveyed his frustrations to his brother Jack. Though hyperbolic, Washington's words are nonetheless heartfelt: "I believe I may, with great truth affirm, that no Man perhaps since the first Institution of Armys ever commanded one under more difficult Circumstances than I have done—to enumerate the particulars would fill a volume."[17] The books in George Washington's life, it seems, were not just literal ones. His use of this figurative expression illustrates how book culture could influence traditional lore. In this case the book had become a proverbial comparison useful for expressing the weightiness of a situation. Writing to his brother, George conveyed the extent of his difficulties as commander in chief by comparing them to the contents of a book.

Martha Washington's arrival on December 11 gave her husband much comfort. Throughout the war she would continue to join him at his winter quarters, wherever they happened to be. Once she reached Cambridge, George no longer needed to worry about her safety at Mount Vernon, which was vulnerable to amphibious assault. He still had other worries. Enlistments, which only lasted a year, would expire in December. Would the army simply disappear? To their credit, many soldiers re-enlisted, but many others did not. By the year's end the strength of the Continental Army fell to fewer than ten thousand troops.

Outside the Boston area the Revolution continued as a war of words. The previous year Thomas Paine had come to Philadelphia with little more than a letter of recommendation from Benjamin Franklin. Though Franklin called him an "ingenious, worthy young man," his letter reveals that Paine, thirty-seven when he arrived, remained unsure which career path to follow. Franklin thought he could find a position as a clerk, an assistant tutor, or an assistant surveyor.[18] Paine had a physical presence that impressed others. After meeting him, Charles Lee called Paine a man with "Genius in his Eyes."[19] Richard Bache—Franklin's son-in-law—introduced Paine to his

George Romney, *Thomas Paine* (1792), engraving. Library of Congress, Prints and Photographs Division, Washington, DC (reproduction number: LC-USZ61-388).

Philadelphia friends, who were similarly impressed. Robert Aitken, one of the city's most prominent booksellers and publishers during the Revolutionary era, offered to employ Paine as managing editor of the *Pennsylvania Magazine*, a monthly periodical he had just begun to publish.[20]

Paine accepted. Besides editing the *Pennsylvania Magazine*, he also contributed a number of poems and essays to its pages. Aitken wanted him to avoid religious and political controversy, but many of Paine's contributions to the magazine introduced ideas he would develop more fully in *Common Sense*. For example, contemporary European thinkers held that plants, animals, and even people from the Old World degenerated in the New. Paine refuted the notion, turning it on its head by suggesting that the only thing imported from Europe that degenerated in America was vice, which lost its vigor in America, where goodness thrived. Paine would reiterate the idea in *Common Sense*.[21]

The role as editor and contributor to the *Pennsylvania Magazine* let Paine recognize his keen ability to perceive the crucial issues of the day, distill them to their essence, and convey his views in a manner the public could readily understand and accept. Others encouraged him to articulate his thoughts on American freedom. Benjamin Rush, who privately advocated American independence, hesitated to publish his thoughts on the matter, afraid that political controversy would destroy his growing medical practice. With few ties to the community Paine could, in Rush's view, risk uttering his opinions publicly.[22]

In late 1775 Paine drafted *Common Sense*. He tested out his ideas by reading passages aloud to Rush and discussing them with him. At least that's what Rush claimed. Rush also said that Paine shared the draft with Samuel Adams, Benjamin Franklin, and David Rittenhouse.[23] Owen Aldridge doubts that he shared the manuscript with Franklin: Paine very much wanted to surprise the oldest revolutionary with the printed work.[24]

More forcefully and more convincingly than any author before him, Paine made the case for American independence. But he did more than that. He also advocated a republican form of national government—which was not necessarily a given.[25] And he did so in clear and beautifully cadenced prose. *Common Sense*, in Leo Lemay's words, displays "Paine's great genius for memorable phrases, incantatory rhythms, and emotion-packed language."[26] Summarizing the argument for Independence, Paine wrote, "Every thing that is right or natural pleads for separation. The blood of the slain, the weeping voice of Nature cries, 'TIS TIME TO PART."[27]

Independence was important not only as a way for Americans to escape from British tyranny but also to let them show the world that no one had to endure repression. Paine saw that the American situation had universal repercussions: "'Tis not the concern of a day, a year, or an age; posterity are virtually involved in the contest, and will be more or less affected, even to the end of time, by the proceedings now."[28]

Benjamin Rush introduced Paine to Robert Bell, who agreed to issue *Common Sense* as an anonymous pamphlet. The first edition appeared on or around January 10, 1776. The first printing of a thousand copies sold out in a week. Writing just three days after *Common Sense* appeared, Josiah Bartlett, a delegate from New Hampshire, said it was "greedily bought up and read by all ranks of people."[29] Dissatisfied with Bell's handling of the work, Paine arranged for another firm, William and Thomas Bradford, to issue the second edition. Undaunted, Bell released another edition of his own. He and Paine engaged in a newspaper controversy regarding these competing editions, which boosted sales, as the savvy Bell knew it would.

Printers throughout Revolutionary America issued their own editions. Paine himself estimated that *Common Sense* sold 120,000 copies. Aldridge more conservatively estimates that the pamphlet sold 100,000 copies. Avoiding precise numbers, William Gordon put it in simpler terms, saying that *Common Sense* was "read by almost every American."[30] By any account *Common Sense* deserves recognition as the biggest bestseller in Revolutionary America.

The date Washington received his copy is unknown. The earliest reference to *Common Sense* in his papers occurs in a letter from Charles Lee. The second week of January Washington had ordered Lee to New York to defend the city. At the request of the New York Committee of Safety, Lee paused at Stamford, Connecticut, where he read *Common Sense*. Lee did not know that Paine had written the work, at least not yet. (Both John Adams and Benjamin Franklin would independently inform Lee of Paine's authorship the following month.)[31] The title page of the second edition ascribes its authorship simply to "An Englishman."

Common Sense left Lee awestruck. He wrote Washington, wondering whether he had read the work and letting him know how much he enjoyed it: "I never saw such a masterly irresistible performance—it will if I mistake not, in concurrence with the transcendent folly and wickedness of the Ministry give the coup de grace to G. Britain—in short I own myself convinc'd by the arguments of the necessity of separation." Later recalling the impact *Common Sense* had on American readers, Lee said that Paine "burst forth upon the world like Jove in thunder."[32]

By the end of January Washington had read *Common Sense* for himself. Writing to Colonel Joseph Reed the last day of the month, he predicted that "the sound Doctrine, and unanswerable reasoning contain (in the pamphlet) *Common Sense*, will not leave numbers at a loss to decide upon the Propriety of a Separation."[33] Two months later he wrote a follow-up letter to Reed reiterating Paine's persuasiveness. Though Washington suspected Virginians would come to the side of independence reluctantly, he suggested that "time, and persecution, brings many wonderful things to pass; and by private Letters which I have lately received from Virginia, I find common sense is working a powerful change there in the Minds of many Men."[34]

Not all the letters Washington received from Virginia supported Thomas Paine's *Common Sense*. The third week of February Landon Carter wrote to Washington to attack Paine for publishing the work and to argue against independence.[35] As he was a long-standing advocate of colonial American rights, Carter's opposition to *Common Sense* seems unusual. Discussing the pamphlet with some Virginia neighbors, he elaborated his opinion. When one man pulled out a copy of *Common Sense* and called it "a most incomparable Performance," Carter vehemently disagreed, saying it was as "rascally and nonsensical as possible" and calling it "a sophisticated attempt to throw all men out of Principles."[36] Carter took the man's copy of the work and pointed out several passages to prove his point.

Though many contemporary readers, Thomas Jefferson included, praised Paine's literary style, Carter disliked it. Carter himself had exquisite literary tastes, but he could find nothing to admire in *Common Sense*. To him Paine's text was too overwrought. He bristled at Paine's rhetoric, which almost seemed to make readers ashamed to believe any other viewpoint than the one he espoused. Carter wanted to support the Revolutionary War, but he also wanted to make the decision for American independence on his own: he did not want the author of *Common Sense* to inveigle him into it.

Carter's opposition to *Common Sense* was a minority opinion, as Washington realized. Fielding Lewis's comments about the reception of *Common Sense* in Virginia provided a more representative viewpoint. Describing the Virginia situation to Washington, Lewis wrote: "The opinion for independentcy seems to be gaining ground. Indeed most of those who have read the Pamphlet Common Sence say it's unanswerable."[37] John Penn, a delegate to the Continental Congress from North Carolina, recorded similar impressions regarding the influence of Paine's pamphlet in the South. Traveling to Philadelphia for the spring session of Congress, Penn wrote that throughout his journey he heard nothing praised "but Common Sense and Independence. That was the cry throughout Virginia."[38]

Believing in American independence and achieving it were, needless to say, two different things. After months in Massachusetts, Washington had been unable to budge the British. Since his first firefight in 1754—the one in which he found something charming in the sound of whistling bullets—Washington had become more cautious. People still remembered what he had said on that occasion.[39] Speaking with him privately one day in Cambridge, the Reverend Thomas Davis asked Washington if he had really said that he knew of no music so pleasing as the whistling of bullets.

"If I said so," Washington replied, "it was when I was young."

While the Boston stalemate between the Continental troops and the British persisted, something was happening in the backwoods of New York that would change the situation. On May 10, 1775, the same day the Second Continental Congress convened in Philadelphia, Ethan Allen and his Green Mountain Boys captured Fort Ticonderoga from the British, seizing possession of both the fort and its precious arsenal. Since then, Colonel Henry Knox had been busy transporting dozens of artillery pieces from the fort to Boston. With Knox's arrival in early 1776, Washington now had sufficient firepower to threaten the British.

The finest account of the ensuing events may be the one Washington wrote himself. In a letter to Landon Carter he related his decision to take possession of Dorchester Heights, which had a commanding view of the British forces in Boston.[40] By positioning the Ticonderoga artillery to point downward at the enemy troops, Washington forced them to make a decision: fight or flee. The biggest challenge he faced beforehand was taking Dorchester Heights undetected. To that end he ordered his men to bombard Boston for three nights running to divert British attention from their true objective. On Monday, March 4, 1776, under the cloak of darkness, Washington took possession of Dorchester Heights "without the loss of a single Man," he told Carter.

The next morning the British officers discovered what had happened and made preparations to assault Washington's position. Before they could amass their troops, a sudden storm arose, forcing them to call off their attack. As Washington phrased it in his letter to Landon Carter, "The Weather getting very tempestuous much Blood was Saved, and a very important blow (to one Side or the other) prevented." Though the adverse weather conditions forestalled the British, Washington prepared for the worst and kept his men working throughout the storm. In other words the cold rain that stopped the British assault did nothing to prevent American troops from working to strengthen their defenses. Washington downplayed this detail in his letter, burying it in a parenthetical aside, but he created a vivid image nonetheless, an image of American troops working hard to help themselves despite the pelting of the pitiless storm.

On the evening of March 16 American troops moved their heavy artillery forward to Nook's Hill, menacingly close to Boston. Waking up to see American artillery pointed down on them, the British commanders saw that Boston was untenable and ordered an evacuation.[41] The British troops, in Washington's words, embarked in "as much hurry, and as much confusion as ever Troops did," leaving behind a vast amount of artillery and property. Concluding the episode in his letter to Carter, Washington wrote, "Boston has shared a much better Fate than could possibly have been expected considering the time it was close shut up—the damage being nothing equal to report—We are now in full possession of the Town and are fortifying the harbour to prevent a return if they should Incline to it."[42]

Upon receiving this letter, Landon Carter was thoroughly impressed, not only with Washington's ability as a military commander but also with his ability as a writer. Whereas Paine's writing was all flourishes and rhetoric, Washington wrote in a clean, spare, straightforward, manly style. After reading it, Carter inscribed the letter with the following note: "A magnum in Parvo. A mere history of his glorious Manoeuvres in a single sheet of Paper—so, he seems as good a Judge of arranging words to express his facts to advantage, as he is of his Army to effect Success." Carter enjoyed the letter so much he read it aloud with great pleasure to his friends.[43]

Boston celebrated the victory and hailed General Washington. Harvard awarded him an honorary doctorate of laws "in recognition of his civic and military virtue."[44] President Samuel Langdon and five fellows of the college signed Washington's diploma, dated April 3, 1776. Samuel Cooper, one of the fellows of the college, went to Cambridge the following afternoon to say goodbye only to discover that General Washington was already gone.

Washington appreciated the recognition Boston accorded him but knew that any celebrations now were premature. With Boston secure New York would be the next target for the British. Washington had left Boston to take measures for New York's security.[45] He reached Manhattan on April 13, 1776. In late June, the British fleet anchored off New York and, on July 3, began landing troops on Staten Island.

After the Continental Congress declared independence and officially created the United States of America, John Hancock informed Washington, sending him copies of the Declaration of Independence with instructions to have them read before the army. On Tuesday, the ninth, General Washington ordered the Declaration of Independence read before the entire army. At six o'clock that evening all the brigades in New York City formed themselves into hollow squares, and a man placed in the center of each square read the Declaration of Independence for everyone to hear. Zachariah Greene, seventeen at the time, belonged to the brigade encamped on the common. Washington himself was inside the square Greene's brigade formed, and one of Washington's aides read the declaration in a loud, clear voice. When the aide had finished reading, Greene's brigade gave three hearty cheers.[46]

Through considerable effort Washington had managed to swell his forces to nineteen thousand troops, but most were either raw hands or poorly trained militiamen. On the enemy side General William Howe had command of thirty-two thousand regular troops, at that time the largest expeditionary force in British history. Though inspired by the Declaration of Independence, the American troops could only go so far on inspiration. Systematically, the superior British forces defeated the Americans at one battle after another, taking Long Island, landing on Manhattan, and forcing Washington and his troops first to Harlem Heights and then to White Plains. Fort Washington, the remaining American stronghold on Manhattan, fell on November 16, with the British taking nearly three thousand prisoners of war.

And still the British persisted. From Fort Washington they crossed the Hudson River into New Jersey and forced the evacuation of Fort Lee. They pursued the Americans all the way across New Jersey until December 8, when Washington crossed the Delaware River into Pennsylvania. As he had the previous December, once more he feared the Continental Army would simply disappear after the volunteers' enlistments expired. With winter approaching, General Howe temporarily decided against continuing into Pennsylvania and attacking Philadelphia. Instead he dispersed his army into garrisons throughout New Jersey. The Hessian troops, a mercenary force enlisted to aid the British, were garrisoned in Trenton.

Thomas Paine had joined the army as a volunteer in July and subsequently served at Fort Lee, where he became an aide-de-camp to General Nathanael Greene. He also acted in the capacity of a war correspondent: Paine was the first embedded reporter in the history of American warfare. In his dispatches he made no pretense to objectivity. Reporting the battles in and around New York, Paine celebrated the bravery of American soldiers in the face of the British invaders. Once Fort Lee fell Paine stayed with the army during its trek across New Jersey, befriending officers and infantrymen alike. They enjoyed his company and appreciated his willingness to endure hardship with them. By this time Paine's authorship of

Common Sense was widely known, so, naturally enough, his army nick-name became "Common Sense."[47]

As he retreated with Washington's army, Paine began writing a new work, an essay series he would call *The American Crisis*. By the time he returned to Philadelphia in December, he had drafted its first number. The desolation of the city, abandoned by many of its citizens as British troops neared, increased Paine's anxiety and his sense of urgency. He revised his manuscript, quickly preparing a final draft for publication.[48] It initially appeared in the *Pennsylvania Journal* on December 19, 1776. William Ellery, a delegate to the Continental Congress from Rhode Island, sent a copy of the newspaper to a correspondent, calling Paine's essay "an animated useful Performance," which should be "reprinted every where in America."[49] Four days later, Philadelphia printers Melchior Styner and Charles Cist issued it separately as an eight-page pamphlet, *The American Crisis: Number I.*

The author of *Common Sense* went himself one better in his opening to this new pamphlet, which, more than two hundred years later, can still raise a reader's gooseflesh:

> These are the times that try men's souls. The summer soldier and the sunshine patriot will, in this crisis, shrink from the service of his country; but he that stands it now, deserves the thanks of man and woman. Tyranny, like hell, is not easily conquered; yet we have this consolation with us, that the harder the conflict, the more glorious the triumph. What we obtain too cheap, we esteem too lightly:—'Tis dearness only that gives every thing its value.[50]

Two days before *The American Crisis: Number I* appeared, Washington had written, "Our only dependence now, is upon the Speedy Inlistment of a New Army; if this fails us, I think the game will be pretty well up, as from disaffection, and want of spirit and fortitude, the Inhabitants instead of resistance, are offering Submission."[51] *The American Crisis* worked. Desertions stopped, and men re-enlisted. Of course, *The American Crisis* was not the only reason why desertions stopped. Washington's leadership, combined with a ready infusion of cash, also helped. Paine's inspired words nonetheless did their part to motivate the Continental troops and reinforce their commitment to the cause of freedom.

Copies of the pamphlet reached General Washington's camp by Christmas Day. Tradition has it that he ordered *The American Crisis* to be read to the assembled troops to encourage them before they crossed the Delaware River to attack the Hessian garrison in Trenton.[52] It is not unusual for devout soldiers to carry a pocket Bible into battle with them.

Emanuel Leutze, *Washington Crossing the Delaware* (1851?), Library of Congress, Prints and Photographs Division, Washington, DC (reproduction number: LC-DIG-det-4a26226).

Crossing the Delaware River on that cold, dangerous Christmas night, some soldiers had copies of a different book in their possession: *The American Crisis*. And when they had to face down the bayonet-wielding Hessians in Trenton, Paine's words stayed with them. The proof? The copy of *The American Crisis* that survives at the American Philosophical Society is badly stained with blood.

CHAPTER 12

A Green Baize Bookcase

Alexander always carried the Works of Homer with him; in which, he used to say, he found every military Expedient necessary to form his own Troops for Action.

Thomas Webb, *A Military Treatise*

Crossing the Delaware River and defeating the Hessian garrison at Trenton greatly boosted the morale of the American troops, but Washington did not stop his winter offensive there. The following week he ordered another attack on British forces and successfully routed the enemy troops garrisoned at Princeton. In the face of Washington's aggressive tactics, Lord Howe consolidated the British garrisons in New Jersey and established winter quarters in New York City. Washington's army, in turn, went into winter quarters at Morristown, New Jersey. The following summer brought a new series of challenges once Lord Howe decided to lead his army from New York through New Jersey toward Philadelphia. By the end of August Washington had repositioned the Continental Army to defend Philadelphia.

On Tuesday, September 2, 1777, General Anthony Wayne wrote Washington to propose a strategic plan designed to pre-empt an enemy attack, suggesting that three thousand of the best armed and disciplined Continental troops should "hold themselves in Readiness on the Approach of the Enemy to make a Regular and Vigorous Assault on their Right or Left flank."[1] This strategy, he argued, would be far better than waiting for the enemy to attack. Washington, who had much respect for General Wayne, seriously considered his suggestion.

The two men had come to know one another the previous year. Having established himself as a local leader in revolutionary Pennsylvania politics, Wayne became a colonel in the Continental Army the first week of January 1776, commanding the Fourth battalion of the Pennsylvania line. In mid-May he joined Washington at New York but quickly proceeded north to reinforce the Continental troops retreating from Canada. That winter Wayne became commander of Fort Ticonderoga, an arduous assignment given the harsh weather conditions and meager supplies. Promoted to brigadier general in February, Wayne soon rejoined the main army in New Jersey. Given command of two brigades, he took the initiative and began plotting his strategy.

After outlining his battle plan in the letter to Washington, Wayne described how his strategy would impact the British forces. Not only would a surprise attack startle the enemy troops, it would also prevent their advance and force them to retreat. Wayne was trying to impress Washington with his knowledge of military maneuvers. On several occasions already Washington had encouraged his officers to study the art of war, or, to use his words, "to devote some part of your leisure hours to the study of your profession, a knowledge in which can not be attained without application; nor any merit or applause to be achieved without a certain knowledge thereof."[2] Clearly aware of the emphasis Washington placed on the study of military history and strategy, Wayne attempted to prove the efficacy of his plan with reference to historical precedent, going as far back as Julius Caesar's Gallic War to make his point.

Besieged by the Gauls, Caesar, according to Wayne, "Sallied out with his Cohorts" and threw the Gauls into the "utmost Consternation and Obtained an easy Victory." Wayne did not stop with this example. Caesar had employed the same maneuver against the Gauls at Alesia with similar success. On both occasions Caesar's unexpected attack surprised and terrorized the Gauls. To reinforce his argument Wayne cited another leading authority: Marshal Saxe's *Reveries; or, Memoirs Concerning the Art of War*. While Saxe's work underwent a revaluation in the nineteenth century—Thomas Carlyle called it "a strange Military Farrago, dictated, I should think, under opium"[3]—it was well respected in the eighteenth. Analyzing the psychological motivations of soldiers in battle, Saxe had said that an enemy's confused and frightened behavior in the face of a surprise attack "proceeds from that Consternation which is the Unavoidable effect of Sudden and unexpected Events."[4]

Wayne's letter makes it seem as if he had a thorough understanding of the art and history of war, but his knowledge was more limited than it appears. Though he does not say so, the historical and theoretical basis for his planned attack came directly from Thomas Simes's *Military Guide for Young Officers*, a manual first published in London and republished in Philadelphia at the start of the Revolutionary War. Not only did Wayne take his general strategy from Simes, he also borrowed both his Caesar examples and his Marshall Saxe quotation from the same source.

Having already received a presentation copy of the Philadelphia edition of Simes's *Military Guide* from publisher Robert Aitken, perhaps Washington realized that Wayne was cribbing from the work. Wayne's practical application of Simes's manual reveals the book's power. Military historian J. A. Houlding calls Simes a "long-winded drudge" but admits that the *Military Guide* presents the fullest collection of basic material on regimental administration and daily military activity to appear in English during the eighteenth century.[5]

Wayne never had the opportunity to carry out the strategy he took from Simes, but when Lord Howe's forces successfully attacked the Americans at the Battle of the Brandywine on September 11, 1777, Wayne and his troops maintained their position long enough to cover Washington's retreat. A few days later Washington detached Wayne from the main army to harass the left flank of Lord Howe's forces as they advanced on Philadelphia.

Anthony Wayne's experience reveals much about the place of military books on the battlefield during the Revolutionary War. He obviously kept a copy of Simes's *Military Guide* with him, read it carefully, and reread it as he shaped his combat strategy. By no means was Wayne alone. Other American officers took to heart Washington's advice to read military books. Captain Johann Ewald, a Hessian officer who served on the British side with the Field Jäger Corps, recalled: "I was sometimes astonished when American baggage fell into our hands during that war to see how every wretched knapsack, in which were only a few shirts and a pair of torn breeches, would be filled up with military books."[6]

Seeing so many American knapsacks filled with so many military manuals, Captain Ewald made some general conclusions about the officers of the Continental Army, especially compared with their British counterparts. Ewald named the titles of a number of European military books he had found among the Americans, some of which turned up, by his estimate, a hundred times. Impressed with their desire for knowledge on the battlefield, Ewald concluded that the American soldiers "studied the art of war while in camp, which was not the case with the opponents of the Americans, whose portmanteaus were rather filled with bags of hair-powder, boxes of sweet-smelling pomatum, cards (instead of maps), and then often, on top of all, some novels or stage plays."[7]

Washington found out early the importance of military books for the field officer. While two classic works—Caesar's *Commentaries* and Quintus Curtius's *History of the Wars of Alexander the Great*—gave him a basic understanding of military tactics, biographies of more recent generals and commanders provided much additional information about the lives and decisions of famous officers. Historical works could only go so far. By the start of the Seven Years' War, Washington recognized serious gaps in his military knowledge and sought to deepen his knowledge of the art of war.

In late 1755, some months after General Braddock's disastrous campaign against the French, Washington ordered a copy of Humphrey Bland's *Treatise of Military Discipline*. Already familiar with the work, Washington most likely ordered it to share with his regiment.[8] An officer under the Duke of Marlborough, Bland later served as lieutenant colonel of the king's regiment of horse. He wrote his treatise during this service. From its initial publication in 1727 into the 1760s, it remained the standard manual of drill and discipline in the British army.[9]

Bland's *Treatise* was the bible of the British army. Major General James Wolfe, the renowned officer who had achieved victory over the French in Canada during the Seven Years' War, called it one of his favorite works.[10] So well known was Bland's treatise that its author's name became synonymous with the book itself. During the middle third of the eighteenth century, to read "Bland," or, as it was sometimes called, "Old Humphrey," was the duty of every young British officer.

Washington had encountered Bland before he ordered his own copy in 1755. He may have read his brother Lawrence's copy: young men with military ambitions often read Bland before they joined the army. In *The Plain Dealer*, to take an example from the stage, William Wycherley depicts a weedy youth named Jerry Blackacre, whose mother catches him reading a jestbook. She suggests *The Young Clerk's Guide* instead.[11] A grizzled veteran named Major Oldfox tells Jerry to read Bland, at which point the boy's mother exclaims, "Away with such trash! Do you want to send him to the devil headlong? I should have him teazing me to-morrow or next day, to buy him an ensign's commission. I would as lief he should read a play!" As Mrs. Blackacre's words suggest, Bland could fire boyish imaginations and help young men foresee all sorts of military glory.

The 1754 campaign against the French gave Washington another opportunity to encounter Bland's work. At Fort Necessity at least one officer in the Virginia Regiment had a copy of Old Humphrey with him. Left behind as a French hostage, Captain Robert Stobo kept the copy of Bland's *Treatise* he had purchased in Williamsburg and carried it with him to

Quebec City, where he was imprisoned. When he escaped from prison in 1757, he left the book behind.[12] Perhaps he did not want any excess baggage slowing him down, or perhaps he did not need it anymore. After reading it countless times during his imprisonment, he must have had the book by heart.

When Washington finally received the copy of Bland he had ordered in the spring of 1756, he was disappointed with it. A sixth edition of the work had appeared by this time, but the British merchant from whom Washington had ordered the book sent him the second edition, which was nearly thirty years old. This situation was not unprecedented or even unusual: London booksellers often foisted off copies of old editions onto colonial consumers, knowing full well that the width of the Atlantic effectively prevented them from returning unsatisfactory purchases. Sometimes British merchants had the audacity to overcharge for these out-of-date works. Well aware of this situation, Washington complained to his London agent: "'Tis a custom, I have some Reason to believe, with many Shop keepers, and Tradesmen in London when they know Goods are bespoke for Exportation to palm sometimes old, and sometimes very slight and indifferent Goods upon Us taking care at the same time to advance 10, 15 or perhaps 20 prCt. upon them."[13]

Washington's writings verify that he was familiar with Bland even before his personal copy arrived. He expressed confidence in the work and recommended it to others. As commander of the Virginia Regiment in January 1756, he prepared an address to his officers containing some practical advice regarding how they should carry out their duties. He reminded them, "It is the actions, and not the commission, that make the Officer." He also recommended they devote time to cultivating their military knowledge: "As we now have no opportunities to improve from example; let us read, for this desirable end. There is Blands and other Treatises which will give the wished-for information."[14]

Two years later Washington wrote to Major Andrew Lewis, an officer under his command, reiterating his conviction that the major and his fellow officers should keep up with the latest military literature. He strongly emphasized "the necessity of qualifying yourself (by reading) for discharging the Duty of Major; a post that requires a thorough knowledge of the Service; and on the due execution of which, your own, as well as the Credit of your Regiment, greatly depends."[15]

Serving under General John Forbes during the expedition against Fort Duquesne in late 1758, Washington received an object lesson in the practical value of books for military commanders. To cope with a French force much larger than his own, Forbes would establish a stockaded camp and blockhouse every forty miles along his route. Forbes's strategy safely protected his troops, though it was both costly and time-consuming. General Forbes did have a precedent for his actions. His strategic approach follows the one Count Turpin de Crisse recommended in *Essai sur l'Art de la Guerre*. Justifying his strategy to William Pitt, Forbes suggested that Pitt consult Turpin's essay on the art of war to understand the theoretical principles on which he proceeded.[16]

Though Washington and Forbes did not always see eye to eye, Washington did appreciate his commander's knowledge of military literature. First published in French in 1754, Turpin's treatise was initially unavailable in English translation. (So many excellent works of military theory and practice were written in the language that French became a required subject for first-year cadets once the military academy at West Point was established.) Washington's inability to read French limited, or at least delayed, the development of his knowledge. He did not read the French treatises until they were rendered into English. Once Captain Joseph Otway translated Turpin as *An Essay on the Art of War* in 1761, for instance, Washington acquired a copy for himself.

A practical work detailing the operations of an army in the field, Turpin's *Essay* is generally considered the best work on the art of war written in the eighteenth century. Turpin has a spirited yet intelligent and authoritative writing style. His tactical descriptions are marked by an extraordinary flexibility. He clearly understood that no two situations are the same; officers needed to adjust both their strategy and their tactics to suit the moment.[17]

Though Washington's surviving copy of Turpin's *Essay* has been rebacked, the rest of the original sprinkled calf binding survives, including its bookseller's label:

> Sold by David Hall
> at the New Printing-Office
> in Market-street
> Philadelphia

Hall imported the London edition of Turpin's *Essay* in 1763, at which time he advertised it for sale.[18] It seems unlikely that Washington bought the book this early. It does not appear in the 1764 catalogue of the Mount Vernon library. Besides, he purchased virtually no military books between 1763 and 1774, that is, between the end of the Seven Years' War and the start of the Revolutionary War. Either someone else bought it from David Hall and Washington acquired it secondhand, or the work remained a part of David Hall's inventory until his death, and Washington purchased it from Hall and Sellers, the new partnership that David's son William Hall formed with William Sellers. Washington could have obtained his copy of Turpin's *Essay* when he visited Philadelphia to attend the Continental Congress in 1775, the year he was appointed commander in chief of the Continental Army, but he may have obtained it the previous year when he was in the city for the First Continental Congress.

Other evidence shows Washington expanding his military library after returning home from the First Continental Congress. In October 1774 he wrote William Milnor, asking him to send a work he called "Treatise on Military Discipline." Unsure which book Washington meant, Milnor sent Thomas Webb's *Military Treatise on the Appointments of the Army*, a brief volume published in Philadelphia in 1759. Given the age of this work, in addition to the dissimilarity of its title, it seems unlikely that Webb's treatise was the one Washington intended, but, as he did with other books received by mistake, he added it to his library and learned what he could from it.

An officer in the British army, Webb had much to teach his readers. He had served with the Royal American forces during the Seven Years' War. Severely wounded at Quebec, Webb had learned from experience that North America presented formidable challenges for the European soldier. He wrote his treatise to describe how to fight a war in the face of the unique topographical conditions of North America. Like Washington, Webb understood that since war in America differs significantly from war in Europe, officers must adjust their strategy and use different techniques to succeed.

Webb also realized that the successful officer should be well read. To know the art of war, one must know the history of war. His common sense reinforces an attitude toward reading akin to the one Washington had already established for himself. Webb observed, "It oftentimes happens in reading, as it does in eating; he that eats the most is not always the most healthy, but he who eats sparingly of that which is good: So in reading, he who runs over the greatest Number of Books is not always the most sensible, but he who reads the best, with clearness and Perspicuity."[19]

Individual chapters of Webb's treatise discuss other topics—the importance of geography, the necessity of the army engineer, the role of the artificer, the regulation of artillery—but chapter 11, which specifically concerns forming a regiment for North America, is Webb's most original contribution to military strategy. He observed that North America largely consists of thick, woody country filled with mountains, swamps, and rivers, many of which were difficult or nearly impossible to cross.[20] In contrast to the British troops, the French and their Indian allies were both equipped for and accustomed to the woods. For military success in North America, Webb argued, British officers must appoint lightly armed troops and adjust their marching style to suit the local terrain.

The outbreak of the Revolutionary War at Lexington and Concord sparked a boom in the publication of military books. Everyone suddenly started reading them, including John Adams. The last week of May 1775, he wrote his wife from Philadelphia, "Oh that I were a soldier! I will be. I am reading military books. Everybody must, and will, and shall be a soldier."[21] Thomas Hanson's *Prussian Evolutions in Actual Engagements*, published by subscription that same year, was one work Adams read. So did Washington. Both men subscribed to its publication, as did many other American patriots: Benjamin Franklin, John Hancock, Richard Henry Lee, Peyton Randolph, and Anthony Wayne. Washington himself subscribed for eight copies, apparently intending to distribute them to several of his officers.[22]

Hanson identified himself on his title page as adjutant to the Second Battalion and a teacher to the American militia. Little else is known of him, but his book constitutes a lasting legacy. Hanson subdivided *Prussian Evolutions* into two parts, the first discussing the infantry, the second devoted to the subject of gunnery. As a physical artifact, the book reflects the best and worst of the colonial printing industry. Issued by J. Douglass M'Dougall, a printer just starting out on his own, *Prussian Evolutions* contains a huge number of typographical errors, but its handsome illustrations—thirty engraved plates altogether—make it a noteworthy contribution to the art of printing in America. Most of the plates were engraved by John Hutt, but the opening one was engraved by John Norman, who would subsequently distinguish himself as the first engraver to attempt a portrait of George Washington.[23]

A mixture of patriotism and opportunism motivated the republication of other military manuals in 1775. Roger Stevenson's *Military Instructions for Officers* reflects both impulses. Stevenson's precise identity remains a mystery. Encyclopedist Abraham Rees held that Stevenson's *Military Instructions* reflected its author's "military genius, and the evident result of extensive experience."[24]

Though the title of Stevenson's work can be shortened to *Military Instructions*, the long title indicates its contents more precisely: *Military Instructions for Officers Detached in the Field Containing, a Scheme for Forming a Corps of a Partisan: Illustrated with Plans of the Manoeuvres Necessary in Carrying on the Petite Guerre*. Whereas Bland gave contemporary readers information on drill and garrison duty, Stevenson offered practical instructions regarding an officer's duties in the field. Since detachments of regulars, or "partisan corps," could conduct small-scale operations beneficial to their larger armies, all officers, Stevenson argued, should be familiar with the tactics of the *petite guerre*. His military instructions describe ambushing the enemy, attacking posts, constructing redoubts, defending entrenchments, establishing camps, marching with stealth, mounting a guard, patrolling at night, and reconnoitering enemy positions. J. A. Houlding considers Stevenson's chapters on both attack and defense excellent, calling *Military Instructions* the single best work on the subject of the *petite guerre* to appear in the eighteenth century.[25]

The dedicatory epistle to the Philadelphia edition describes America as "a country where every gentleman is a soldier, and every soldier a student in the art of war." The editor recommends that officers in the Continental Army carry Stevenson's *Military Instructions* with them as a portable primer to the art of war. Its convenient size made the book "a pocket volume, to be consulted on any emergency."[26] The empirical evidence shows that American officers took his advice. Before 1775 ended, its publisher Robert Aitken sold nearly five hundred copies of the work. Two years after its initial publication he had sold over eight hundred copies total.[27]

Other evidence places Stevenson's *Military Instructions* in the hands of Washington's officers, according to Henry Wadsworth Longfellow. Trying to locate a book about partisan warfare for his brother, Longfellow learned that Mr. Simon Greenleaf—the father of his friend James—owned the copy of Stevenson's *Military Instructions* that had belonged to Lieutenant Moses Greenleaf—Simon's father—who had served under Washington during the siege of Boston. Sending the book to his brother, Longfellow cautioned him to treat it gently because the volume had gone "through the Revolution in the hands or pocket of Mr. Greenleaf's father. It is a precious relique, and must be treated accordingly. Mr. Greenleaf says it is as precious to him, as his father's sword would be."[28] Besides indicating the importance of Stevenson's *Military Instructions* during the Revolutionary War, Longfellow's anecdote demonstrates the book's ongoing symbolic value long after the war had ended.

Washington's financial accounts record that he purchased five military books on June 7, 1775. The fact that he bought these books the week *before* Congress appointed him commander in chief provides further evidence to demonstrate that Washington had a good idea Congress would make the appointment. Though he did not list any of the titles of these books in his financial accounts, a letter he wrote Colonel William Woodford of Virginia soon afterwards suggests what some of them were.

Colonel Woodford had written to ask General Washington if he could recommend some good military books. Washington initially suggested Bland's *Treatise of Military Discipline*, emphasizing that Woodford should obtain the latest edition of the work. Washington's words of advice show he still smarted from his experience with the British merchant who had palmed off an old edition of Bland on him years earlier. Washington also recommended Turpin's *Essay of the Art of War* and Stevenson's *Military Instructions*. In addition he recommended a book called *The Partisan* and another work he identified simply as "Young."

The Partisan; or, The Art of Making War in Detachment was a translation of a French work by Louis Michel De Jeney, a captain of Hungarian origin who served in the French army but about whom little else is known. De Jeney elaborated the concept of the *petite guerre*, detailing how to fight in small, lightly armed detachments and describing methods of secret reconnaissance and surprise attack. Outlining an early form of guerrilla warfare, De Jeney also related how to interdict enemy supply lines using light infantry.[29] De Jeney's work reinforced what Washington had learned during the Seven Years' War, especially during General Braddock's disastrous campaign against Fort Duquesne.

By no means was Washington the only officer of the Continental Army to read *The Partisan*. De Jeney's work was one of those titles Captain Ewald had turned up around a hundred times in the knapsacks of American troops. Ewald's hundred knapsacks may seem like an exaggeration, but he was an authority on partisan warfare. The fact that Ewald would write a treatise on the subject based on his experiences during the Revolutionary War adds credence to his statement.[30]

By "Young," Washington meant Major William Young's *Manoeuvres; or, Practical Observations on the Art of War*. Describing drill techniques, field tactics, and the fundamentals of the *petite guerre*, Young's *Manoeuvres* contains little Washington could not find elsewhere.[31] His copy of Young is historically significant because it survives with annotations in Washington's hand, which reveal how he read the work and what aspects of it he emphasized.

To call Young's *Manoeuvres* a separate work is somewhat misleading. It is actually a compilation of seven pamphlets published between 1766 and 1770, which Young collected and reissued with a common title page.[32] In the order they appear in the volume, these titles are: *The Manual Exercise*; *An Essay on the Command of Small Detachments*; *A New System of Fortification*; Young's edition of General Wolfe's *Instructions to Young Officers*, a collection of the regimental and general orders Wolfe issued in the decade before his death, which present the thoughts of a diligent and professional officer;[33]

Manoeuvres for a Battalion of Infantry, Upon Fixed Principles; *Manoeuvres for a Battalion of Infantry, Upon Fixed Principles*, which constitutes an expanded version of the previous title with nearly twice as many illustrations; and *The Practice of Manoeuvring a Battalion of Infantry*.

As he did with other books, Washington corrected the errata in Young's *Manoeuvres*, but his annotations in this volume go much further. Washington created a partial index for it, inscribing key topics and corresponding page numbers onto the blank leaves at the end of the volume. The first topic in Washington's manuscript index is "On the Command of a Small Detachment," which indexes specific passages from the second pamphlet. The pages Washington indexed stress the importance of having a guide on a march, the value of a sufficient supply of food and water for a detachment, the way to construct redoubts, and the utility of practical military experience.

Other entries in Washington's manuscript index refer to subjects covered in *General Wolfe's Instructions to Young Officers*: adjutants' duties, orders for the infantry in camp, orders for the infantry on the day of march, and quartermaster's orders. The passage on adjutants' duties that Washington indexed begins: "Adjutants are to see all detachments before they are sent to the parade; that their arms be clean, their ammunition, accoutrements, etc. in good order, and that a serjeant be sent with them to the parade."[34] The orders for behavior to follow in camp present rules for maintaining proper sanitary conditions. Wolfe's instructions for young officers advise that they should "make themselves perfect masters of the exercise of the firelock, that they may be able to assist in training the young soldiers in arms."[35]

Perhaps it should come as no surprise that the first pamphlet in Young's *Manoeuvres* to catch Washington's eye was the second pamphlet in the volume: *An Essay on the Command of Small Detachments*. An extraordinary continuity links together the works that formed Washington's field library. Most treat the subject the *petite guerre*. Webb emphasizes the importance of using lightly armed troops in the American wilderness, and both Stevenson and De Jeney are devoted to the subject of partisan warfare. The *petite guerre* held a vital place in Washington's success over the British in the Revolutionary War. Though his field library is seldom discussed in biographies of him or histories of the war, the collection of books he assembled and carried with him throughout its duration emphasizes the strategic value of partisan warfare, which would be crucial to American success on the battlefield.[36]

Take the winter of 1776–77, for example. The victories of the Continental Army at Trenton and Princeton threw the British troops off balance.

Though Howe consolidated his forces for greater security, he still faced the problem of getting sufficient forage for their horses. Whenever British regiments went into the field that winter, it seemed, Continental troops attacked them. The New Jersey militia was largely responsible for initiating this forage war, but Washington quickly understood that its success confirmed what he had read about the *petite guerre* in the books from his field library. He actively encouraged the militia to keep attacking small parties of British regulars. Though the size of the Continental Army dwindled significantly that winter, it remained large enough for it to use partisan warfare successfully.[37]

The comments of British officers who survived that New Jersey winter testify to the effectiveness of Washington's partisan warfare, which also served to embolden the Continental troops and reinforce their confidence. Writing to a correspondent the third week of February, Colonel Allan Maclean observed, "The Rebels have the whole winter gone upon a very prudent plan of constantly harassing our quarters with skirmishes and small parties, and always attacking our foraging parties. By this means they gradually accustom their men to look us in the face, and stand fire which they never dared to attempt in the field."[38] The last week of March Colonel Charles Stuart said that the *petite guerre* "kept the army the whole winter in perpetual harassment."[39] Captain Ewald found the partisan forces well-nigh unstoppable. He wondered:

> What can you do to those small bands who have learned to fight separate, who know how to use any molehill for their protection, and who, when attacked, run back as fast as they will approach you again, who continuously find space to hide. Never have I seen these maneuvres carried out better than by the American militia, especially by that of the province of Jersey.[40]

During the forage war in New Jersey, American troops repeatedly defeated well-trained British regulars under many different conditions. The American soldiers' ability to dodge infantry fire, reconnoiter enemy positions, confiscate British armament, capture enemy forces, overcome natural and man-made obstacles, fight in both rural and urban environments, and know when to advance and when to retreat demonstrated their mastery of the art of the *petite guerre*.[41]

The more he learned from his field library, the more books Washington acquired. His collection of military treatises grew so large that it became cumbersome to transport. Consequently, he ordered from Philadelphia joiner John Martin a special portable bookcase to hold his camp library.

To protect his books Washington instructed Martin to line the shelves of the bookcase with green baize.[42] A coarse woolen fabric with a long nap often used to cover card tables, baize would cushion the books and protect them from damage during travel. Beyond a manuscript voucher indicating its purchase, Washington's green baize bookcase is not mentioned anywhere else in his surviving papers, but it is not difficult to surmise the whereabouts of this portable bookcase during the rest of the war.

Once Washington received the bookcase from Martin, he filled it with his field library, which grew as the war continued. When Washington moved his military headquarters from one place to another, his green baize bookcase went with him. When the Continental Army went into winter quarters at Morristown, New Jersey, after the victory at Princeton, the bookcase was there. Despite the success of the *petite guerre* that winter, the Continental Army experienced crushing defeats, first at the Brandywine and then during the Battle of Germantown, which allowed the British to occupy Philadelphia.

Washington brought the Continental Army into winter quarters at Valley Forge in December 1777. As he and his officers plotted strategy in a stone farmhouse during that freezing cold Valley Forge winter, the green baize bookcase was there. When American troops battled the British to a standstill at Monmouth on June 28, 1778, the longest, hottest day of the war, his military library was nearby. When Washington returned to Morristown in 1779 to establish his winter quarters, he brought his camp library with him. Perhaps the corners of that cloth-covered bookcase were becoming as bumped and rubbed as the corners of the books they contained, but it sturdily performed the function for which it was built.

Not all the military books in Washington's field library were practical manuals. In 1780 David Humphreys, then serving as aide-de-camp to General Nathanael Greene, wrote a poem praising the American cause and celebrating its military heroes. Printed at New Haven, the sixteen-page work appeared under the title *A Poem, Addressed to the Armies of the United States of America*. Humphreys presented a copy to General Washington and sent one to Martha Washington too. Speaking of Washington in this poem, Humphreys wrote:

> His martial skill our rising armies form'd;
> His patriot zeal their gen'rous bosoms warm'd;
> His voice inspir'd, his godlike presence led.
> The Britons saw, and from his presence fled.[43]

The overblown rhetoric and highfalutin diction make the poem seem quite dated now, but Humphreys was working within the neoclassical poetic conventions of the eighteenth century, and General Washington was impressed. A month after Washington received the poem, Humphreys was transferred to his command. His service as Washington's aide-de-camp began a friendship that would last a lifetime.

After Comte de Rochambeau landed at Newport, Rhode Island, in 1780 in charge of a French expeditionary force of over five thousand

David Humphreys, wood engraving. From Evert A. Duyckinck and George L. Duyckinck, *Cyclopaedia of American Literature* (New York: Charles Scribner, 1856), 1:255. Kevin J. Hayes Collection, Toledo, Ohio.

troops, he presented Washington with a copy of Drummond de Melfort's *Traité sur la Cavalerie*, which also became a part of Washington's military library. Consisting of a large folio volume with an even larger volume of plates, it might have been too big to fit within his bookcase. Nevertheless Washington kept it with him instead of sending it back to Mount Vernon.[44]

Having established winter quarters at New Windsor, New York, in December 1780, Washington received a visit from the Marquis de Chastellux, a high-ranking French officer who took advantage of the season to travel through North America. Their dinner conversation turned to military literature, and Washington, according to Chastellux, expressed his appreciation of French writings on the subject:

> The dinner was excellent; tea succeeded dinner, and conversation succeeded tea, and lasted till supper. War was frequently the subject: on asking the General which of our professional books he read with most pleasure, he answered me that they were the King of Prussia's *Instruction to his Generals*, and the *Tactics* of M. de Guibert, from which I concluded that he knew as well how to select his authors as to profit by them.[45]

Though detailed, Chastellux's account is not necessarily accurate. Washington could have read the king of Prussia's *Military Instructions*, which had been translated into English in 1762. It, too, offered information about partisan warfare as it provided the king of Prussia's instructions for the use of lightly armed infantry. Washington would not have read Comte de Guibert's *Essai Général de Tactique* unless he had hired someone to translate it for him. An English translation of Guibert's essay on military tactics would not be published until the following year.

Instead of Guibert, Washington may have meant General de Grandmaison's *Treatise on the Military Service, of Light Horse, and Light Infantry*. Robert Bell had published Lewis Nicola's English translation of Grandmaison in 1777. Captain Ewald frequently found copies of both the king of Prussia's *Military Instructions* and Grandmaison's *Treatise on the Military Service* in the knapsacks of American officers.[46]

When Washington and Rochambeau traveled from Connecticut to Yorktown in 1781, Washington stopped at Mount Vernon on the way, the first time he had been home since leaving to attend the Second Continental Congress in 1775. Though he still carried his camp library with him, he did not leave any part of it at Mount Vernon. That green baize bookcase stood close at hand during the siege of Yorktown. After his brilliant victory there, which effectively ended any British hope of winning the war, Washington traveled to Philadelphia to confer with Congress. During the winter of 1781–82, General Washington established head-quarters at Newburgh, New York, on the Hudson River north of West Point, and his green baize bookcase came with him. He would keep it by his side until the end of the war.

CHAPTER 13

Planning for Retirement

Retirement without study is death.
Seneca, *Epistles*

The Revolutionary War, it could be said, ended with an act of reading. After hostilities between American and British forces concluded at Yorktown, George Washington had to cope with conflict of a different sort as he faced disgruntled Continental officers ready to mutiny. Their pay in arrears and their pensions in jeopardy, they would rebel if their demands were not met. Having petitioned Congress in late 1782, they learned the following March that the nation's legislators had rejected their petition, snubbing the very men who had fought to win the nation its freedom. On March 15, 1783, General Washington met with representative officers to deliver a speech and read the message from Congress. Standing before them, he looked at the men and then looked at the message, paused for a moment, removed his spectacles from his pocket, and placed them on his nose.

"Gentleman, you must pardon me," he said. "I have grown gray in your service and now find myself growing blind."

Washington then proceeded to read the message from Congress. He scarcely needed to utter another word. Having maintained a façade of invulnerability throughout the war, he briefly let his mask slip before this gathering of Continental officers. For a moment they realized that he, too, had suffered during the war. He, too, had given his all in the Revolutionary cause and grown old in the process. After finishing the message, he left the officers alone to debate what to do. Little debate was necessary. They adopted resolutions affirming their loyalty to Congress. Washington, in turn, wrote Congress to voice their grievances himself.[1]

With that fiery situation defused, Washington had several lesser tasks to accomplish as he brought the war to conclusion. He set April 19, the eighth anniversary of Lexington and Concord, as the official end of hostilities. Finally he could look forward to returning home. Eight months would pass before he reached Mount Vernon, but he did not need to wait until he was back in Virginia to start planning his retirement. From Newburgh he could tie up many loose ends. He also spent time imagining what life would be like after he resigned his commission as commander in chief. For one thing, he would catch up on his reading. Over the past eight years, he had read little other than military manuals and official communiqués, and now he longed for leisure, time enough to relax at Mount Vernon and enjoy his well-earned rest.

From early spring through the summer of 1783 Washington spent time perusing booksellers' catalogues and deciding which books to buy. It would be easier to stock up on reading material when he was near New York City than after he returned to Mount Vernon. To help him in this literary task he recruited the services of William Stephens Smith, an aide-de-camp stationed in the city. After receiving an excellent education at the College of New Jersey, Smith had joined the Continental Army and served as an officer throughout the war. He would later become secretary to the American legation in England under John Adams and Adams's son-in-law once he married his daughter Abigail.

The earliest books Smith bought for Washington were three recently published travel narratives, which he sent to him in March 1783: Arthur Young's *Tour in Ireland* and two by Dr. John Moore, *A View of Society and Manners in France, Switzerland, and Germany* and *A View of Society and Manners in Italy*.

Young had already established himself as one of Britain's leading agricultural experts. Washington had known about him since the mid-1760s, when Young contributed several articles to *Museum Rusticum*. His contributions to this serialized collection of agricultural and technical essays stress the importance of both practical experimentation and empirical observation. He subsequently toured Europe himself to observe different methods of farming. Young's travel writings detail the practice of husbandry in the lands through which he traveled. Many contemporary readers preferred his entertaining and informative travel books to Young's purely agricultural works.[2]

Tour in Ireland offered the kind of reading material Washington liked best: an amusing travel narrative interspersed with useful observations.

Currier and Ives, *Washington's Head-quarters 1780: at Newburgh, on the Hudson*, lithograph. Library of Congress, Prints and Photographs Division, Washington, DC (reproduction number: LC-USZ62-60399).

Admitting that Ireland was somewhat backwards in terms of its agricultural technology, Young argued that no place was so backwards that it could not have some good practices to copy. Young, who had great respect for General Washington, would initiate a correspondence with him a few years later, and the two men would correspond sporadically over the next decade and a half, exchanging their thoughts about agricultural theory and practice. As a mark of his respect Young would present Washington with several of his books.

Though Dr. John Moore separately published *A View of Society and Manners in France, Switzerland, and Germany* and *A View of Society and Manners in Italy*, the two works, totaling five volumes in the Dublin edition, were known collectively as "Moore's *Travels*." John Gillies, an eighteenth-century historian, enjoyed Moore's candor, discernment, and objectivity but appreciated most his narrative approach, which situated personal insights within a fast-paced tale of travel. "By presenting a continual scene of action to the eye," Gillies observed, Moore "enables the mind of his reader to anticipate his just and natural, though by no means obvious reflections."[3]

Moore's *Travels* proved to be enormously popular, going through several editions during the early 1780s. Washington's acquisition of both Young's

Tour in Ireland and Moore's *Travels* reflects his desire to catch up with the latest British literature now that the war was over. Though he was buying books to take back to Mount Vernon, the documentary evidence suggests that Washington did not wait until he got home to begin reading his new books: he started Moore's *Travels* at Newburgh. The work reminded him how pleasurable reading could be. He soon wrote a letter to Smith listing the titles of several books he wished to buy. Reading a newspaper advertisement from a New York bookseller, Washington wrote Smith a follow-up letter requesting many additional books.[4]

The most renowned part of Moore's *Travels* is his account of Voltaire, which combines anecdotes with its author's personal impressions of the great philosophe in his twilight. Moore observed, "The most piercing eyes I ever beheld are those of Voltaire, now in his eightieth year. His whole countenance is expressive of genius, observation, and extreme sensibility."[5] Reading Moore, Washington apparently grew eager to read Voltaire. Though he may have known *Candide* before the war, he now wished to broaden his knowledge of its author and asked Smith for three different Voltaire works, all available in English translation.

Letters from M. de Voltaire to Several of His Friends presents an English translation of selected correspondence. Eighteenth-century authors customarily published ideas on a variety of subjects under the guise of personal letters. Voltaire was no exception. His accomplishments in other literary genres have overshadowed his letter writing, but readers in his time recognized what Owen Aldridge has called Voltaire's "epistolary brilliance."[6] Brief as it is—fewer than two hundred pages—this edition forms a good introduction to the life and mind of Voltaire. Its text reveals Voltaire's playful style and particular interests as he treats such topics as books and booksellers, comedy and tragedy, dictionaries and encyclopedias, the Italian language, literary history, men of letters, philosophy, poetry, religious dogmatism, and science.[7]

Biography—a literary genre Voltaire attempted with uneven results—also appealed to Washington, whose curiosity about the lives of great men, especially great military men, extends back to his childhood. He asked Smith for two biographies by Voltaire: *The History of Charles XII King of Sweden* and *The Age of Louis XV*.[8]

Smith successfully obtained a copy of the first, which reveals Voltaire's strengths and weaknesses as a biographer. Voltaire lacked the scholarly rigor biography demands. He was more comfortable working in a colorful, imaginative, freewheeling style, supplying general impressions of his subject's life rather than digging deeply through biographical arcana to connect together factual tidbits and create a unified whole. Furthermore,

Voltaire was often willing to ignore biographical fact when it conflicted with his philosophy. Even when Voltaire is wrong, he remains entertaining and provocative.

Unable to acquire a copy of Voltaire's *Age of Louis XV*, Smith obtained for Washington a different book on the subject by Mouffle d'Angerville: *The Private Life of Lewis XV*. The title does not do the work justice: Mouffle d'Angerville elaborated both the private and the public life of Louis XV. Washington left no comments about the book, but it contains much to admire, being remarkably free from prejudice. British educator and essayist William Enfield said that its author speaks "not as a Frenchman, but as a philosopher and citizen of the world. Facts are related with minuteness of detail, yet without tedious prolixity: characters are drawn with striking features, and boldness of colouring; and the narrative is frequently enlivened with entertaining anecdotes."[9]

The same time Washington placed the order for the works by Voltaire, he also asked for some histories by another influential French author, the abbé Vertot: *History of the Revolutions that Happened in the Government of the Roman Republic* and *History of the Revolutions in Portugal*. Washington placed one condition on his request. He asked Smith to obtain them only "if they are esteemed." This condition reflects both Washington's innocence and his experience. Having spent years commanding the Continental Army, he understood how to delegate responsibility, an understanding he now applied to the acquisition of books. He respected Smith's intelligence and discrimination, placing confidence in his ability to decide whether these two books deserved a place at Mount Vernon. Yet this condition also reveals Washington's limited knowledge of literature. Gauging by their titles, Vertot's works sounded like they might interest him, but he apparently did not know much about either of the works or their author.

Washington's ignorance of the abbé Vertot—the historian of revolutions—represents a significant gap in his literary knowledge. Vertot's writings were known throughout colonial America decades before the American Revolution, and they have been recognized for their influence on the thought of the Founding Fathers. Adams, Franklin, Jefferson: all had copies of Vertot's writings in their libraries. In fact, a copy of Vertot's *History of the Revolutions in Sweden* had been among the Custis books shelved at Mount Vernon for many years. Perhaps Washington never read it. Whereas other Founding Fathers had read Vertot before the American Revolution, Washington would read him after the war. His curiosity about Vertot's works shows him trying to understand the revolutionary experience more fully, to see how the American Revolution fit into the worldwide history of revolutions.

Unable to obtain the three-volume edition of Vertot's *History of the Revolutions of the Roman Republic*, Smith did locate a different edition. He also acquired some books Washington had not specifically requested. Smith had a good enough sense of the general's literary tastes to obtain additional volumes for him. Encountering an edition of Robert Watson's *History of the Reign of Philip II, King of Spain*, Smith knew Washington would appreciate this biography, so he bought it for him. Watson's engaging style, intuitive judgment, and sense of drama kept contemporary readers riveted to his life of Philip II from beginning to end. Washington thanked Smith for having the foresight to send him a copy.[10]

Washington also asked Smith to forward other available booksellers' catalogues so he could select additional volumes for his Mount Vernon library. No New York booksellers published separate catalogues in 1783.[11] They did continue to advertise sale books in the newspapers. Smith sent Washington a copy of one New York newspaper containing a bookseller's advertisement listing many titles he thought Washington might like.[12]

The third week of June Washington ordered several works from the list Smith had sent. Some were similar to ones he had recently obtained— biographies of military leaders and heads of state—but others show Washington broadening his interests to encompass natural history, philosophy, and the sciences. One major anthology would let him return to a favorite genre: travel writing. Washington hesitated to purchase a fairly expensive twenty-volume collection of travels published under the title *The World Displayed*. He eventually let Smith determine its worth, placing the same condition on the purchase of *The World Displayed* he had placed on Vertot: "if it is an esteemed work."[13]

With these latest requests, Smith continued to acquire substitute works for ones he could not obtain. Vicomte de Turenne—one of the greatest men of the seventeenth century, Rousseau thought—was another historical figure Washington hoped to understand. Smith, who could not locate the specific work Washington requested, did find another book on the subject: Andrew Michael Ramsay's *History of Viscount de Turenne*. Washington knew Ramsay as the author of *Travels of Cyrus*, a work he had at Mount Vernon. Ramsay's life of Turenne, his second-best work, has some drawbacks. Rousseau criticized Ramsay's decorum and thought the biography needed more anecdotes to bring out Turenne's true nature.[14]

Smith decided *The World Displayed* was an esteemed work that belonged in the Mount Vernon library: he obtained the whole twenty-volume set for Washington. The set has since been broken up, though Washington's autographed copy of the twelfth volume survives.[15] This particular volume includes a selection from a work Washington already knew: Thévenot's *Travels into the Levant*. It also contains "Travels through Egypt," a long and handsomely illustrated excerpt from Bishop Richard Pococke's *Description of the East*. Since Pococke visited Egypt in the late 1730s, his detailed account presents vital information about ancient Egyptian culture, information that was obliterated with the plundering of Egypt that occurred late in the century.[16]

Washington asked Smith for another big, multivolume work from his headquarters at Newburgh: Oliver Goldsmith's *History of the Earth and Animated Nature*.[17] Goldsmith worked on this project off and on for the last fifteen years of his life. When Samuel Johnson heard about it, he said of Goldsmith: "He has the art of compiling, and of saying everything he has to say in a pleasing manner. He is now writing a Natural History, and will make it as entertaining as a Persian Tale."[18]

Dr. Johnson's comment encapsulates Goldsmith's essential method: to rewrite an existing work of nonfiction to make it as entertaining as possible. When Goldsmith started *Animated Nature*, as it became known, he originally planned an updated version of Pliny's *History*. Once he encountered the early volumes of the Comte de Buffon's *Histoire Naturelle*, he recognized that Buffon's vast collection of curious details ideally suited his method. Goldsmith combined Buffon with other works of natural history. He referred to John Ray's *Wisdom of God Manifested in the Works of Creation*, for instance, to reconcile natural history and religion. Goldsmith's engaging style and sensitivity to public taste helped his work remain popular for decades.

The most controversial yet influential aspect of *Animated Nature* is Goldsmith's human taxonomy. He created a hierarchy of human beings, putting each type in its place. Goldsmith situated the "Polar" type at the bottom, two categories of Asians next, followed by Africans and Native Americans, with Europeans at the top. He subdivided the European category, ranking the English at the very top. The English are the whitest, Goldsmith asserted, and "whiteness is the colour to which mankind naturally tends." Disturbing from a modern perspective, this racist and chauvinistic theory found many welcome readers, and *Animated Nature* helped perpetuate such racist notions in the English-speaking world.[19]

Washington was now buying books so extensively that he tried to get them at a bulk discount. He still hesitated to buy too many: he did not want to duplicate titles he already had at Mount Vernon. Consequently he wrote Lund Washington, asking him to catalogue the library there. Lund frankly admitted that he did not have much bibliographical skill but agreed to do what he could. The catalogue he created represents the first time the Mount Vernon library had been inventoried since John Parke

Custis had removed his books and brought them to Abingdon. When Custis left Mount Vernon after his marriage, he had taken some of his stepfather's books with him—and left a few of his own. *Loimologia*, Nathaniel Hodges's graphic account of the London plague, was one work he left at Mount Vernon. Some books Custis may have left behind intentionally. Given Washington's enjoyment of Alexander Pope, for instance, perhaps Custis gave his stepfather the broken set of Pope's *Poetical Works*.

Dated July 23, 1783, Lund's list, even with its errors and omissions, presents a good picture of the Mount Vernon library after John Custis had removed his books but before George Washington returned from the war. Altogether it lists sixty-three titles, totaling ninety-eight volumes. Washington, a little surprised by how short Lund's list was, wondered how many of his books Custis had taken to Abingdon. He asked Lund to check the library there to see if any of its books contained his autograph or his bookplate and prepare a list of their titles. Either Lund never made the list or it has since disappeared.[20]

As it stands, Lund's list somewhat misrepresents the size of the Mount Vernon library, which easily contained more than a hundred volumes. Lund was careless when it came to listing the number of volumes for each title: he listed several multivolume works as single-volume ones. Some books he did not bother to mention by title at all, as a note near the end of the list indicates: "Several old Sermon and Religious Books that probably may never be read again—I did not think worth Listg. Some Pamphlets, Plays etc. etc. of but little worth."[21]

When George Washington had catalogued the Mount Vernon library himself in 1764, he listed such books from his boyhood as Offspring Blackall's *Sufficiency of a Standing Revelation* and Matthew Hale's *Contemplations*. Unaware of the personal memories attached to these works, Lund Washington did not recognize their significance and did not list them separately, thinking they were just more stale old religious treatises. Counting the books at Mount Vernon, the handful of Washington books at Abingdon, and the war library in the green baize bookshelf Washington had with him at Newburgh, the total size of his personal library at the end of the Revolutionary War amounted to perhaps 150 volumes.

All in all it was a modest collection, especially compared with the libraries assembled by other Founding Fathers. This same year Thomas Jefferson prepared the first detailed catalogue of his library at Monticello, which contained approximately two thousand volumes; it would triple in size over the next three decades.[22] When Benjamin Franklin returned to the United States two years later, he combined his Paris library with his

Philadelphia library, creating a collection totaling more than four thousand volumes.[23]

Washington's personal collection of books was tiny compared with these great early American libraries. His library was smaller than those of Jefferson and Franklin partly because he was neither an intellectual nor a bookman, but also because the Revolutionary War had interfered with his book-buying plans. Prior to the war he had intended to expand his library significantly.

After George and Martha married, the Custis library largely fulfilled their pleasure-reading needs through the mid-1760s. By the end of the decade, George had begun adding to his collection of histories and travels. To that end he had started reading current catalogues from the London booksellers. Perusing the latest sales catalogue of Thomas Cadell, a bookseller located in the Strand in 1768, Washington found an item he absolutely had to have: Robert Beverley's *History of Virginia*. Beverley had published the first edition of his renowned history in London in 1705, with a revised edition in 1722. By 1768 copies of either were hard to find. Upon reading Cadell's catalogue, Washington wrote his London agent and asked him to obtain Beverley's *History* for him. Washington's letter is filled with detail. He specifically mentioned where the book could be located. His agent did what Washington asked and acquired Beverley's *History* for him, the 1722 edition.[24]

Washington's biographers typically date his revolutionary activities to 1769, the year he joined the growing colonial opposition to the Townshend Acts. His request for Robert Beverley's *History of Virginia* the year before constitutes an important precursor. Beverley synthesized the ideas of the English opposition writers of the seventeenth century with a uniquely American perspective. His attack on "Rapacious and Arbitrary Governours," for example, foreshadows similar attacks in the run-up to the Revolution. Leo Lemay has called Beverley's *History of Virginia* "the first sweeping, memorable, published indictment of a series of English governors."[25] Beverley celebrates his American identity, characterizing himself on the title page of his history as "a Native and Inhabitant of the Place." Acquiring a copy of Beverley, Washington revealed his growing love of the land where he was born. Beverley influenced some of the ideas Washington and his neighbor and fellow patriot George Mason incorporated in the *Fairfax County Resolves*.

It was 1771 when Washington had Stephen Valliscure, a London jeweler, engrave a handsome armorial bookplate, another indication of the pride he took in his library. Writing his agent to request the bookplate, he not only asked for the engraving, he also asked to have four or five

Cost Sterl £9 51   *G: Washington*

1763

THE
HISTORY
OF
VIRGINIA,
In Four PARTS.

I. The HISTORY of the First Settlement of *Virginia*, and the Government thereof, to the Year 1706.

II. The natural Productions and Conveniencies of the Country, suited to Trade and Improvement.

III. The Native *Indians*, their Religion, Laws, and Customs, in War and Peace.

IV. The present State of the Country, as to the Polity of the Government, and the Improvements of the Land, the 10th of *June* 1720.

By a Native *and* Inhabitant *of the* PLACE.

The SECOND EDITION revis'd and enlarg'd by the AUTHOR.

LONDON:
Printed for F. FAYRAM and J. CLARKE at the *Royal-Exchange*, and T. BICKERTON in *Pater-Noster-Row*, 1722

Washington's copy of Robert Beverley, *The History of Virginia* (1722). Boston Athenaeum.

hundred copies struck.[26] Since his personal collection of books amounted to fewer than a hundred volumes at the time, Washington obviously hoped to expand his library three- or fourfold. A large personal library and an armorial bookplate fulfilled similar social functions. Both would impress visitors to Mount Vernon with a sense of sophistication and help elevate Washington to a status shared by the wealthiest planters. The armorial bookplate was a sign that he had arrived, that he had reached Virginia society's upper echelon.

Lund's list reveals other books added to the Mount Vernon collection during the 1770s. George Washington obtained an English edition of Jean-Bernard Bossu's *Travels through Louisiana* in 1772. Combining adventure, anthropology, geography, and natural history, this work contained much to allure Washington. Captain Bossu traveled through French North America during the 1750s. His autobiographical account has much in common with *The Journal of Major Washington*. As authors both Washington and Bossu combined a military officer's sense of precision with a keen eye for detail.

Bossu's account of Native American folkways in *Travels through Louisiana* constitutes the work's most lasting contribution. It meticulously describes the Alabama, Arkansas, Choctaw, Fox, and Illinois Indians, detailing their marriage ceremonies and child-rearing customs, medical practices, and superstitions. Bossu's *Travels* evinces a genuine appreciation for the Indians, championing Native American simplicity above an overly refined, even decadent European society. *Travels through Louisiana* gave contemporary readers much food for thought. Classical scholar William Beloe, for one, found Bossu's depiction of the Native Americans similar to Herodotus's portrayal of the Scythians. Beloe used Bossu to annotate his edition of Herodotus, hypothesizing that North America was originally peopled from northern Europe.[27]

Like other travel authors of his day, Bossu embellished his work with examples of Native American oratory. So many American travelers included Indian speeches in their works that they had almost become cliché. Reviewing *Travels through Louisiana*, Jabez Hirons explained, "We generally read these Indian harangues with a degree of diffidence." John Reinhold Forster, Bossu's English translator, shared a similar opinion. At one point Bossu quotes an old Indian who tells his men, "Go, my comrades, as men of courage, and with the heart of a lion." Forster footnoted the closing prepositional phrase, calling it "an hyperbole no Indian in America would make use of, not knowing that creature, which is not to be met with in that country."[28] Though generally knowledgeable in the field of natural history, Forster ignores the possibility that Bossu's Indian meant another type of cat that inhabited the North American wilderness: the panther. Regardless, his skepticism toward Native American oratory is well founded.

The presence of Bossu's *Travels through Louisiana* at Mount Vernon reinforces Washington's interest in travel writing, but, like his copy of Beverley's *History of Virginia*, it also reveals his curiosity about the meaning of America. How are the different parts of North America interrelated? What would happen once British colonial settlements continued farther west and approached French North America? As his own personal holdings in the Ohio valley grew, Washington understood that the land Bossu described was not too far away from land he owned, making *Travels through Louisiana* not just a geographical curiosity but also a practical manual. In the 1760s Washington had invested in the Mississippi Land Company, which sought to secure a tract of more than two million acres east of the Mississippi River. Though he had written off his investment in what he called the "Mississippi Adventure" in January 1772, his acquisition of Bossu's *Travels* shows that he remained curious about the region and still sought to learn as much about it as he could.

Upon receiving Lund's list, George Washington could order additional books confident he would not be duplicating any he already had at Mount Vernon. With what he ordered through William Stephens Smith, Washington increased the size of his personal library by nearly a third, bringing its total to around two hundred volumes. His desire before the war to amass a library large enough to rival those of the wealthiest planters in Virginia may reflect his social ambitions; his book-buying spree after the war reflects his intellectual curiosity. He no longer needed to create a great library to verify his social status: George Washington was now the most widely revered man in America. He did not need to buy books as status symbols. The books he bought at the end of the war were ones he genuinely wanted to read during his retirement.

In August the Continental Congress summoned Washington to confer on the shape and size the American military should take in the postwar period. Congress was meeting at Princeton, New Jersey, temporarily, that is, after mutinous troops from Lancaster, Pennsylvania, had descended on Philadelphia to demand back pay. Washington delayed his trip to Princeton until Martha, who had fallen ill at Newburgh, was healthy enough to travel. After stopping in Princeton, they hoped to proceed directly to Mount Vernon, so they arrived with considerable baggage. Washington established his headquarters about four miles outside Princeton at Rocky Hill, the home of Mrs. Margaret Berrien.

Greetings from friends and well-wishers poured into Rocky Hill. One came in the form of a poem from Annis Boudinot Stockton, the sister of Elias Boudinot, current president of the Continental Congress. "To General Washington," as she titled the poem, places him foremost

> on the Sacred Scroll
> With patriots who had gain'd Eternal fame,
> By wonderous deeds that penetrate the soul.[29]

Flattered, Washington responded with a letter of thanks. His thank-you letters are usually matter-of-fact. Writing to a poet, he demonstrated his own literary skill, assuming the fictional pose of an unworthy subject and crafting a simile with an allusion to the book of Exodus:

> I must beg leave to say a word or two about these Fine things you have been telling in such harmonious and beautiful Numbers. Fiction is to be sure the very life and Soul of Poetry. All Poets and Poetesses have been indulged in the free and indisputable use of it, time out of Mind. And to oblige you to make such an excellent Poem, on such a subject, without any Materials but those of simple reality, would be as cruel as the Edict of Pharaoh which compelled the Children of Israel to Manufacture Bricks without the necessary Ingredients.[30]

On Friday, September 5, Washington hosted a dinner for the delegates to the Continental Congress. The Berrien home at Rocky Hill was not roomy enough to seat everyone, so Washington had his men erect a large tent they had confiscated from the British. Elias Boudinot sat to Washington's right, and the chevalier de La Luzerne, the French minister, sat to his left. David Howell, a delegate from Rhode Island, may have had the best seat at the dinner. He sat directly across the table from Washington and thus had the opportunity to hear everything he said. As Howell told a correspondent afterward, "The repast was elegant—but the General's Company crowned the whole."[31]

In his letter Howell did more than simply express his appreciation for Washington's personal company; he also described the General's physical appearance and quoted some snippets of conversation. Having first met Washington toward the start of the war eight years earlier, Howell could compare past and present. He wrote: "I observed with much pleasure that the General's front was uncommonly open and pleasant—the contracted, pensive Air betokening deep thought and much care, which I noticed on

Prospect Hill in 1775 is done away; and a pleasant smile sparkling vivacity of wit and humour succeeds."[32]

Finally, Washington could let down his guard and indulge his sense of humor. According to Howell, his conversation that afternoon was sprinkled with playful repartee. When Boudinot remarked that Robert Morris, US superintendent of finance, had his hands full, Washington quipped, "I wish he had his Pockets full, too."

As part of their elegant repast, Washington and his guests drank wine from some silver cups, which, though locally made, were somewhat deficient in their workmanship. Richard Peters, a delegate from Pennsylvania who sat nearby, informed Washington that the man who made the cups had since become a Quaker preacher.

"I wish he had been a Quaker preacher before he had made the cups," Washington replied.

"You t'ink de penitence wou'd have been good for de cups," La Luzerne added, catching General Washington's humorous spirit.

Learning that Thomas Paine was currently living in nearby Bordentown, General Washington invited him to stay at Rocky Hill, hoping to get Congress to acknowledge Paine's importance to the American Revolution and reward him for his literary contributions during the war. In his letter of invitation Washington told Paine, "Your presence may remind Congress of your past Services to this Country, and if it is in my power to impress them, command my best exertions with freedom, as they will be rendered chearfully by one who entertains a lively sense of the importance of your Works."[33]

Paine accepted Washington's invitation and soon came to visit. His reminiscences confirm David Howell's portrayal of Washington at Rocky Hill. Paine similarly depicted him letting down his guard, indulging his sense of fun, and devoting his intellect to something beyond the battlefield.[34]

Considering what some local residents said about the Millstone River, both Washington and Paine gave their scientific curiosity free reign. The locals had told them that the river could actually be set on fire. So many people mentioned this New Jersey Phlegethon that Washington decided to perform an experiment to test what they had told him. To make the experiment work, he and Paine learned they had to stir the mud on the river bottom and then hold a torch made from straw or paper slightly above the surface of the water.

Once everything was ready, they chose Wednesday evening, November 5, to attempt the experiment. They placed a scow on the river near the mill dam. General Benjamin Lincoln, David Cobb, and three or four soldiers joined Washington and Paine in the scow to help them perform the experiment.

Washington armed the soldiers with poles to stir up the mud, and he and Paine—one at the bow, the other at the stern—each had a roll of cartridge paper, which they lit and held two or three inches above the surface of the water. The soldiers stirred; gas bubbles surfaced, and, sure enough, the gas was ignited by the burning cartridge paper Washington held above the water. As darkness fell, flames covered the surface of the water, giving the Millstone River an eerie glow.

Though verifying their hypothesis, neither Washington nor Paine knew exactly what they had discovered. Paine theorized that the gas caused yellow fever. Its usefulness would remain unknown for decades to come, but George Washington was experimenting with natural gas, which would eventually be a vital source of energy for the nation.

George and Martha were unable to proceed directly from Princeton to Mount Vernon together as they had planned; he had to return to Newburgh to take care of some last-minute business. Before another month had passed, he was back on the road heading south again. On December 4 Washington formally parted from his officers at Fraunces Tavern in New York City. From there he continued farther south, being touted and celebrated wherever he went. The Continental Congress had appointed December 11 as a day of thanksgiving. By then General Washington had reached Philadelphia, where he attended a service conducted by the Reverend Dr. John Rodgers, who delivered a sermon lavishly praising him. Rodgers had this thanksgiving sermon printed as *The Divine Goodness Displayed, in the American Revolution* and sent Washington a copy for his library at Mount Vernon.

Washington lingered in Philadelphia a few more days, attending a magnificent dinner and a ball in his honor. Besides reacquainting himself with old friends, he took the opportunity to make some new ones. He was drawn to people who offered not flattery and accolades but practical advice he could put to use. One new friend he made was Samuel Vaughan, an English merchant and Jamaica planter. Earlier that year Vaughan and his family had left London to settle in Philadelphia. They were currently living with Richard Bache and his wife, Sarah, the daughter of Vaughan's good friend Benjamin Franklin.

In London Vaughan had moved in the same circles as Franklin, befriending the city's leading scientists and foremost dissenting ministers. Like Franklin, Vaughan was attuned to the latest developments in science and technology. As Washington spoke with him about some new building projects he planned for Mount Vernon, their conversation turned to the topic of cement. Vaughan recommended a book on the subject by Bryan Higgins, a British physician and scientist who had been part of his intellectual circle in London. Not only did Vaughan recommend *Experiments and Observations Made with the View of Improving the Art of Composing and Applying Calcareous Cements*, he lent Washington his personal copy of the work.[35]

Washington's interaction with Vaughan provides a good example of how the book borrowing and lending process worked in early America. Their conversation about building projects encouraged Vaughan to mention Higgins's *Experiments*. Vaughan's willingness to help Washington prompted him to loan the book. Accepting the gracious offer, Washington brought the volume with him to Mount Vernon.

Reading Higgins's *Experiments*, he took extensive notes from it or, in his words, "extracted such parts as I mean to carry into practice." Returning Higgins's *Experiments*, Washington thanked Vaughan but asked if he would clarify something about stucco: "And now my good sir, as I have touched upon the business of stuccoing, permit me to ask you if the rooms with which it is encrusted are painted, generally; or are they left of the natural colour which is given by the cement made according to Mr Higgins's mode of preparing it?"[36] Ultimately, the notes Washington took from Vaughan's copy of Higgins proved insufficient. He remembered many valuable ideas from the book that he had not written down and wanted a copy of his own. Washington soon added Higgins's *Experiments* to his Mount Vernon library.

His correspondence with Vaughan clarifies a bibliographical incongruity: why did Washington take extensive notes from books he had in his library? In this instance he made his notes before he acquired the book. Only after he realized that his notes were inadequate did he obtain a copy of the book for himself. Other books from which Washington took extensive notes may have a similar history. He borrowed friends' books and transcribed or summarized selected passages from them to obviate the need to acquire them himself. Only when he noticed his notes were inadequate—in other words, when he recognized discrepancies between the notes he took from a work and his memory of reading it—did he obtain a copy of the work for his personal library.

Their book exchange solidified the friendship between Vaughan and Washington. The two would keep in contact with one another as time went on. When business brought Vaughan to London in the early 1790s, he used the opportunity to send Washington some of the latest British books and pamphlets. These works covered such topics as the French Revolution; the thought of Edmund Burke; Russian politics; the voyages of Prince Madoc, the legendary Welsh explorer who supposedly discovered America three centuries before Columbus; and the life and death of one of America's greatest British supporters: Richard Price.[37]

Leaving Philadelphia on his way home from the war, Washington continued to Annapolis, where the Confederation Congress had temporarily relocated. On December 23 he formally submitted the resignation of his military commission as commander in chief, announcing to Congress: "Having now finished the work assigned me, I retire from the great theatre of Action; and bidding an Affectionate farewell to the August body under whose orders I have so long acted, I here offer my Commission and take my leave of all the employments of public life."[38]

After his announcement, Washington got back on the road. A hard day's ride brought him to the Potomac. The ferry soon brought him to the other side of the river. Now no more than a few miles separated him from his beloved home, which he had seen only once since the war began.

The joy of coming home was tinged with melancholy. The family had changed considerably since he had left Mount Vernon at the start of the war. At that time his stepson, Jack Custis, was entering his second year of marriage to Nelly Calvert. Jack had wanted to join the army, but his mother and stepfather opposed it. Jack and Nelly divided their time between Mount Airy and Mount Vernon. Nelly had since given birth to five children, four surviving beyond infancy. Nelly had been a positive influence on Jack, helping him achieve a seriousness and sense of purpose he had lacked before their marriage. As an adult Jack assumed new responsibilities, being elected to the Virginia House of Burgesses in 1778. Still he could not shake his desire to serve in the war and urged his stepfather to let him join the army. Returning to Virginia in 1781, Washington, with Martha's consent, finally relented, allowing her only son to join the campaign against the British in Virginia. Sadly, Jack contracted camp fever during the siege of Yorktown and died shortly after the British surrender.

Nelly, in poor health since her second-to-last pregnancy, had sent her youngest daughter, Eleanor Parke Custis, also nicknamed "Nelly," to Mount Vernon to be nursed. Similarly, her last child and only son, George Washington Parke Custis, or "Wash," as he became known in the family, had also come to Mount Vernon to be nursed. Since she had recently remarried, her two youngest children remained at Mount Vernon to be raised by their grandmother and her famous husband. Saddened by Jack's death, George and Martha Washington found solace in the joy the two little children gave them. In the coming years, the halls of Mount Vernon would ring with the sounds of the two Custis children.

Currier and Ives, *The Home of Washington, Mount Vernon, Virginia* (New York, ca. 1856), lithograph. Library of Congress, Prints and Photographs Division, Washington, DC (reproduction number: LC-USZ62-1462).

The sight of Mount Vernon in the distance quickly dispelled whatever Washington was contemplating as he neared home. Having returned home earlier, Martha anxiously awaited her husband. In a matter of minutes, the two were reunited. It was Christmas Eve.

CHAPTER 14

Haven of History

In Books lies the soul of the whole Past Time; the articulate audible voice of the Past, when the body and material substance of it has altogether vanished like a dream.

Thomas Carlyle, *The Hero as Man of Letters*

After George Washington returned home from the war a private citizen, Mount Vernon became a favorite destination for many travelers. Aware how tiresome visitors could be, Washington's best friends hesitated to write too many letters of introduction. Despite their caution countless tourists showed up at Mount Vernon without introduction. They proved to be a bother and a burden, but George and Martha Washington graciously extended their hospitality to those who reached their doorstep. The impulse of these visitors is understandable. They simply wanted to meet the most famous man in the nation, the man who had won the war for American freedom.

Thomas Mullett, a British merchant traveling through the United States after the war, proved to be an unexpectedly pleasant visitor when he appeared at the threshold of Mount Vernon. Mullett hailed from the Quaker stronghold of Bristol. Like many British Quakers he had sympathized with the American cause and opposed the conflict. Once the war ended, he crossed the ocean to establish a transatlantic mercantile trade. Before reaching Mount Vernon, Mullett had traversed much of the new nation. Curious to hear about his American travels, Washington invited him into his library for a one-on-one chat. A perceptive man noted for his judgment, Mullett had met many influential people and made numerous contacts throughout the new nation. Washington asked if he had met anyone qualified to write the history of the Revolutionary War.

"I know of one, and one only, competent to the task," Mullett replied.

"Who, Sir, can that individual be?" Washington asked.

"Caesar wrote his own Commentaries!" Mullett exclaimed, implying, of course, that Washington himself was the only one qualified to undertake the task of writing the war's history.

"But, Sir," Washington responded, "I know the atrocities committed on both sides have been so great and many, that they cannot be faithfully recorded, and had better be buried in oblivion!"

In the coming years Mullett entertained friends and relatives with this anecdote. He secured a promise from one of them to write it down and preserve Washington's words for posterity.[1] Though now a member of the Church of England, Mullett retained many of his Quaker beliefs and greatly enjoyed General Washington's antiwar message. It took someone who knew war from firsthand experience to understand the magnitude of its atrocities.

By no means was Mullett the only person who thought Washington would be the ideal historian of the Revolutionary War. Traveling through the nation after the war's end, David Humphreys met several "gentlemen of candor and information" who believed their commander in chief should be the one to write the history of the war.[2] Proud of what he had accomplished, Washington no longer wished to dwell on it. Instead he wanted to return to the life of the gentleman farmer, which he had left voluntarily to fight for his country. Though unwilling to write its history himself, he remained curious about how the Revolutionary War would be remembered. The books he read, the letters he wrote, and the people he met during his first two years home from the war all reflect Washington's curiosity about how the story of the American Revolution would be told.

His correspondence indicates Washington's mood the winter he came home. The first Sunday in February 1784 he wrote several letters to distant friends, announcing that he had resigned his commission and returned to Mount Vernon. Though these letters express similar sentiments, Washington, like any good letter writer, shaped his message to suit individual correspondents. To the Marquis de Chastellux, for example, he wrote: "I am at length become a private citizen of America, on the banks of the Potowmac; where under my own Vine and my own Fig tree—free from the bustle of a camp and the intrigues of a Court, I shall view the busy world, 'in the calm lights of mild philosophy'—and with that serenity of mind which the Soldier in his pursuit of glory, the Statesman of fame, have not time to enjoy."[3]

Washington's words present a rich mix of allusions. The dual image of the vine and the fig tree comes from the Old Testament, Micah 4:4. The preceding biblical verse provides its context: "And he shall judge among many people, and rebuke strong nations afar off; and they shall beat their swords into plowshares, and their spears into pruninghooks: nation shall not lift up a sword against nation, neither shall they learn war any more." In short, Washington's biblical allusion offers a shorthand way to describe a time of peace, plenty, and harmony once war has ended.

To enhance the complexity of his allusion, Washington added a literary reference. The phrase he put in quotation marks comes from the first scene of Joseph Addison's *Cato*. As Portius and Marcus—Cato's sons—discuss how Caesar has ravaged the land, the hot-headed Marcus admires the steady temper of his brother, who can look on "Guilt, Rebellion, Fraud and Caesar, / In the calm Lights of mild Philosophy."[4] Washington used this literary allusion to evoke an image in Chastellux's mind of an ideal personal space. As Washington foresaw his life, Mount Vernon would become a place of prosperity separated from the world of conflict and political strife, a place where he could enjoy the pleasures that come with being a gentleman farmer.

Anxious to make improvements to his plantation, he could do little outdoors this cold and snowy winter. With the river frozen and nearby roads impassable, few visitors and little mail reached Mount Vernon in early 1784.[5] Washington had to wait six weeks after returning home from the war before he could announce his retirement to Chastellux and other distant correspondents. The harsh winter weather prevented him from sending letters any sooner. As heavy snow blanketed Mount Vernon, he kept busy with indoor improvements, not least of which was organizing his library and finding room to shelve all the books he had bought in New York.

By no means was he finished buying books. One of the few pieces of mail he received that winter was a catalogue from a new bookshop in Philadelphia established by Daniel Boinod and Alexander Gaillard, who specialized in imported French books. Boinod and Gaillard also stocked some English books, which they listed in the back of their catalogue. To put their business on a firm footing, they used some aggressive marketing techniques. Seeking a distinguished American clientele, Boinod and Gaillard contacted some of the nation's foremost leaders and readers. Besides Washington, they also wrote to Thomas Jefferson and James Madison. The third week of February Washington acknowledged his receipt of the catalogue.

What begins as a letter of acknowledgment becomes an eloquent statement regarding the public's responsibility to literature. Washington wrote: "To encourage Literature and the Arts, is a duty which every good Citizen owes to his Country, and if I could be instrumental in promoting these, and in aiding your endeavours to do the like, it would give me pleasure."[6] By cultivating a love of literature, citizens could advance their nation's intellect and contribute to its greatness. Perhaps no one has expressed this idea better than George Washington. To repeat: "To encourage Literature and the Arts, is a duty which every good Citizen owes to his Country."

Since Washington could not read French, the catalogue listed few titles that appealed to him. Many of the English authors—Eliza Haywood, Tobias Smollett, Edward Young—he already had in his Mount Vernon library. He managed to find a handful of appealing titles and listed them in his letter to Boinod and Gaillard. He never received the books he ordered, but the list itself, read in conjunction with the catalogue, reveals much about his literary tastes. The order of the titles indicates precisely how he read the catalogue.

Some works in the English section piqued his curiosity. The titles he requested affirm his interests in biography, history, and travel writing. William Lothian's *History of the United Provinces of the Netherlands*, for one, shows Washington recognized that knowledge of the Dutch confederacy could aid the development of the United States.[7] Clearly he was eager to learn the history of other nations to understand his own.

After listing a handful of English titles, he read the catalogue a second time, scrutinizing the French section more closely. He did find two basic French works that might prove useful, a grammar and a pocket French-English dictionary. Often during the war he had wished that he could understand French. Even if he never used these books personally, Wash and Nelly might learn from them. Going through the English section of the catalogue a second time, Washington found John Williams's *On the Rise, Progress, and Present State of the North Governments*, a history of several northern European nations from the Netherlands to Russia. The presence of this title among the books Washington requested further reveals his desire to learn more about how other nations worked.

Some titles that caught Washington's eye also attracted Madison's attention. After reading the catalogue himself, Madison wrote Jefferson, telling him Boinod and Gaillard had for sale several items about Dutch, German, and Swiss governments. Madison explained why these books interested him so much: "The operation of our own must render all such lights of consequence."[8] Thinking deeply about the shape the United States government would take, Madison sought any and all available information concerning how other governments worked.

Eng⁴ by H.B Hall & Sons. New York

H. B. Hall, *James Madison*, engraving. From Lyon Gardiner Tyler,
Encyclopedia of Virginia Biography, vol. 2 (New York: Lewis Historical
Publishing, 1915), facing p. 23. Kevin J. Hayes Collection, Toledo, Ohio.

   Washington's attention to the historical accounts of European nations
seems differently motivated. Assuming his service to the nation had
ended with the war, he was not directly involved in the creation of its new
government, at least not yet. He was more interested in reading accounts
of other nations to compare their history with that of the United States.
How would the history of America be told?

   Before the story of the Revolutionary War had been written, the military officers who participated in it had found one way to commemorate
the conflict: they formed a veteran's organization for officers who had

fought in the war. In 1783 General Henry Knox had proposed the establishment of a military society whose membership would be open to all officers who had served in the Continental Army during the Revolutionary War for three years or were serving in the army at the end of the war. According to Knox's proposal, the organization would also be open to French officers of the rank of colonel and above.

Knox and the other founding members of the society chose to name it after Cincinnatus, the Roman general who left his farm to lead the war against the Aequi. Much like their Roman predecessor, many American officers had left their farms at considerable financial sacrifice to serve their country. Knox and the other founding members drafted the "institution," as they termed the society's constitution. Before securing Washington's approval, the organizers selected him to preside over the Society of the Cincinnati.

Initially Washington was unsure whether to support the organization. While the Cincinnati promised to benefit American veterans, it possessed potentially dangerous powers. According to the organizers, it would function as a benevolent society, helping former officers in times of need and giving veterans a strong political base, making sure Congress would not ignore them in the future. So far, so good. But the idea of a powerful and well-funded group of military officers fueled American fears of a standing army. Worst of all, a hereditary clause that allowed each member of the society to pass membership to his eldest son reeked of European aristocracy. With these controversial ideas circulating, the organizers of the Cincinnati scheduled its first national assembly for May 1784.[9]

In the months before the meeting Washington remained skeptical about the Cincinnati. Knox wrote from Boston in February to allay his concerns. He narrowed the objections down to one. "The cool dispassionately sensible men," Knox observed, "seem to approve of the institution generally, but dislike the hereditary descent." Knox identified a specific source for the opposition: "Burke's pamphlet has had its full operation."[10] By "Burke's pamphlet," Knox meant *Considerations on the Society or Order of Cincinnati*, a scathing attack by Aedanus Burke, a justice of the South Carolina Supreme Court. First published in Philadelphia, Burke's pamphlet was reprinted in Connecticut, Rhode Island, and South Carolina and excerpted in newspapers throughout the nation and across the Atlantic.[11] Washington himself added a copy of the pamphlet to his library at Mount Vernon.

Burke argued that the Society of the Cincinnati effectively created an American nobility, or what he called on his pamphlet's title page a class of "hereditary patricians." In other words, the organization threatened the very principles Americans had fought and died for during the war, potentially undermining the liberty and happiness of all American citizens. Burke told legislators to put a stop to the society and, for that matter, any organization that dared to establish a European-style social hierarchy. His arguments made Washington all the more skeptical about the Society of the Cincinnati.

Unwilling to base his decision solely on what Burke said in this inflammatory pamphlet, Washington sought the advice of Thomas Jefferson, then in Annapolis serving in the Confederation Congress. He sent Jefferson a copy of the institution and mentioned its adverse effects on popular opinion toward the Cincinnati. Jefferson himself was well aware of Burke's *Considerations*. He had been in Philadelphia when the pamphlet first came out, obtained a copy for himself, and heard firsthand the clamor it provoked. He recalled, "The epigraph of Burke's pamphlet was 'Blow ye the trumpet in Zion.' Its effect corresponded with its epigraph." Burke's clarion call led to heated discussions among lawmakers regarding the potential dangers of the Society of the Cincinnati.[12]

Upon receiving Washington's request, Jefferson gave the matter much further thought. While appreciating the officers' desire to maintain wartime friendships, Jefferson feared the Society of the Cincinnati was fraught with dangers that would threaten the fragile republic. Like Burke, Jefferson attacked the hereditary provision. He also thought foreign membership inappropriate. In his view the Cincinnati blurred the boundary between military and civilian. He feared the powerful organization could subvert the democratic process.[13]

Washington agreed to attend the national assembly of the Cincinnati in Philadelphia but planned to speak against the institution, urging members to alter it radically. Until they did, he would refuse to lend the society his support. On his way to Philadelphia Washington stopped by Annapolis, where the Confederation Congress was is session. Mainly he wanted to speak with Jefferson. They discussed the Society of the Cincinnati at great length. Jefferson suggested the institution could be modified to resolve the dangers it currently posed, but Washington disliked half measures.

"No!" he exclaimed. "Not a fibre of it must be retained—no half-way reformation will suffice. If this thing be bad, it must be totally abolished." Speaking with Jefferson, Washington seemed determined to end the institution altogether.[14] He reached Philadelphia by Tuesday, May 4, when the national assembly of the Cincinnati was scheduled to convene. He would address the assembly the following day.

Prior to his speech Washington prepared "Observations on the Institution of the Society," a document sternly warning the Cincinnati to mend its ways. Apparently he backed away from eliminating the institution. "Observations" reveals Washington's thoroughness. It synthesizes ideas gleaned from Burke's pamphlet, Jefferson's letter, and his conversation with Jefferson. Overall Washington recommended several changes. He urged the society to strike anything of a political nature in the institution, eliminate the hereditary provision, admit no more honorary members, refuse donations from people who were not US citizens, and abolish general meetings. Washington presented all these ideas in his speech, threatening to withdraw his support if the institution were not revised accordingly. Unless its founders accepted his advice, Washington told them they should put an end to the society altogether.

The French had already been informed of the Society of the Cincinnati, and they responded with great enthusiasm. By chance Pierre Charles L'Enfant reached Philadelphia during the organization's first national assembly. Coming directly from France, L'Enfant announced to his American friends that the French army officers who had served in the Revolutionary War had already formed their own branch of the Cincinnati and pledged a considerable donation to the American society.

L'Enfant pleased the founders of the society by his arrival, but his presence put Washington in a quandary. No longer could he threaten either to withdraw from the Society of the Cincinnati (and thus effectively abolishing it) without offending his French friends and allies, the men who had been instrumental in his victory over the British. Instead, Washington compromised, agreeing to work with an appointed committee to revise the institution. He now sought the middle ground. He did not realize how many years it would take to hammer out a solution.

While in Philadelphia for the national assembly of the Cincinnati, Washington also shopped for books. On May 15 he purchased a copy of Laurence Sterne's fictionalized travel narrative, *A Sentimental Journey through France and Italy*.[15] It is difficult to say precisely what motivated Washington to acquire a copy of this book for himself when he did, but it was a popular work in Revolutionary America. Charles Lee had subscribed to the first edition, which appeared in 1768, and Thomas Jefferson enjoyed it too. American editions appeared in Boston and Philadelphia. It became a favorite work of the Washingtons. George and Martha had two framed prints illustrating scenes from Sterne's *Sentimental Journey* in their bedchamber.[16]

A Sentimental Journey was not the only one of Sterne's works in Washington's library. He also owned a copy of *Yorick's Sermons* and *The Beauties of Sterne*, a collection of memorable quotations from Sterne's works published in London by George Kearsley, who issued other similar works, a series Washington quite liked. Besides the Sterne volume, he also owned copies of *The Beauties of the Late Rev. Dr. Isaac Watts* and *The Beauties of Swift*.[17]

Organized under several subject headings, *The Beauties of Sterne* presents quotations on such topics as charity, compassion, curiosity, forgiveness, generosity, happiness, justice, mercy, pride, sincerity, and wisdom. Washington read the book carefully and took Sterne's words to heart, including an excerpt from *Tristram Shandy* under the heading "Consolation": "Before an affliction is digested,—consolation ever comes too soon;—and after it is digested—it comes too late:—there is but a mark between these two, as fine almost as a hair, for a comforter to take aim at."[18] Writing a letter of condolence to a friend whose father had passed away, Washington made use of this quotation. After honoring the memory of his friend's father, Washington wrote:

> I can offer nothing which your own reason has not already suggested upon this occasion—and being of Sterne's opinion, that "Before an affliction is digested, consolation comes too soon—and after it is digested— it comes too late: there is but a mark between these two, as fine almost as a hair for a comforter to take aim at." I rarely attempt it, nor shall I add more on this subject to you, as it would only be a renewal of sorrow by recalling afresh to your remembrance things which had better be forgotten.[19]

During his spare moments in Philadelphia in 1784, Washington caught up his correspondence. He wrote the Reverend William Gordon, whom he had first met in Cambridge, Massachusetts, during the siege of Boston and who had continued researching the history of the Revolutionary War throughout its duration, collecting newspaper clippings, interviewing generals and legislators, studying public documents, and reading private papers. With the war's end, Gordon hoped to finalize his research and draft his manuscript. In 1784 he planned a fact-finding tour from his home in Massachusetts to Annapolis. Since Mount Vernon was not too far from Annapolis, Gordon thought he might also see Washington. Two months earlier he had written to ask if he could come to Mount Vernon and inspect the collection of papers Washington had amassed throughout the war.

The collection of manuscript material deserves consideration as a crucial part of Washington's library. Returning home from the war, he brought a vast amount of personal and professional writings. Some of these writings were already copied into letter books; others would be copied in the future by Washington's secretaries. Letter books would remain extremely important in the years Washington spent at home. They provided the first draft of outgoing correspondence from Washington to his correspondents. Washington would dictate these letters to his secretaries and then copy the letter (sometimes with a few alterations) and send that version to his correspondents. After he returned home at the end of 1783, Mount Vernon became the single most important archive in the United States outside the papers of the Continental Congress. He spent considerable time organizing this collection of correspondence and papers.

Washington understood that the letters he wrote and those he received during the war constituted the primary documents on which any responsible history would be based. He strongly believed that whoever wished to write an authoritative history of the American Revolution would have to read the primary documents thoroughly, as he explained to Gordon from Philadelphia: "No Historian can be possessed of sufficient materials to compile a perfect history of the revolution, who has not free access to the archives of Congress—to those of the respective States—to the papers of the commander in chief, and to those of the officers who have been employed in separate Departments."[20] While understanding the historic significance of his own papers, Washington also knew they contained much sensitive information, so he hesitated to share them. Not until Gordon secured Congressional approval would Washington grant him access to the documents in his collection.

Upon receiving Washington's letter, Gordon petitioned Congress to use both its manuscript holdings and Washington's papers. Congress agreed to open its archives for Gordon and permitted Washington to share his papers with him. Relieved at securing these permissions, Gordon made plans to visit Mount Vernon. When he arrived on Wednesday, June 2, 1784, he showed the written approval from Congress to Washington, who warmly welcomed him to his home and provided full access to his papers, letting him use his discretion in choosing which documents to quote. By securing permission from Congress to access Washington's papers, Gordon enabled other Mount Vernon visitors to enjoy them. When British historian Catherine Macaulay Graham came to Virginia, for example, Washington happily opened up his personal archive for her perusal and amusement.[21]

Gordon developed a routine at Mount Vernon. Each morning he rose with the sun and settled himself in the library once it was light enough to read. He continued reading every day until dark, taking time out for meals and occasional conversations with Washington. Gordon boasted that within three weeks he had finished his work, "having searched and extracted thirty and three volumes of copied letters of the General's, besides three volumes of private, seven volumes of general orders, and bundles upon bundles of letters to the General."[22]

Putting up a houseguest for several weeks was an inconvenience, of course, but Washington tolerated Gordon's presence because he understood the value of his historical research. Gordon's announcement that he had finished going through all the papers less than three weeks after his arrival astonished him. Privately Washington questioned Gordon's thoroughness. Three weeks seemed much too short a time for any researcher to have sifted through the documents that had taken the commander of the Continental Army eight years to assemble.[23]

With his research complete Gordon returned to Massachusetts to draft his manuscript. He kept writing through early 1786, when he was ready to send the book to press. Gordon had sympathized with the American cause throughout the war but chose to end his days in England. Gordon's acerbic personality created enemies within his Massachusetts congregation and among some of the state's prominent political leaders. He also decided to publish his history in London. Determined to make the work as objective as possible, he concluded that it would be impossible to publish an objective history in the United States. Apparently it did not occur to Gordon that publishing an impartial account of the Revolutionary War would be no more possible in England than in America.

Only after returning to England in 1786 did Gordon realize he could not publish his history as it stood. It was too favorable toward the Americans and too critical of the British. John Adams, then in London serving as American minister plenipotentiary to Great Britain, saw the manuscript Gordon originally completed and heard the rumors about how he had changed it. Adams recorded the situation in the margins of his copy of Gordon's history. His marginalia reveal the complexities of history writing and history reading.[24] Having asked some London friends their opinion, Gordon was crestfallen. Adams explained: "These Judges were of opinion that [the] Book would not sell if the Style was not made more fashionable, if the severity of Reflexions on the English were not softened, and if the Praises of Americans were not moderated. All this was done!"

Precisely how the manuscript underwent revision remains a mystery. The published version is not divided into chapters. Instead, it is structured as a series of letters written during the war. In the late eighteenth century the epistolary format was a fashionable way of presenting both historical information and philosophical ideas—think of Crèvecoeur's

Letters from an American Farmer. Gordon explains in his preface: "The form of letters, instead of chapters, is not altogether imaginary, as the author, from his arrival in America in 1770, maintained a correspondence with gentlemen in London, Rotterdam and Paris, answering in general to the prefixed dates."[25]

A chronological series of letters, according to Gordon, could create an impression "similar to what is felt when a well-executed historical painting is examined."[26] Gordon's remarks reinforce the close association between history writing and history painting in the late eighteenth century. According to John Adams, however, Gordon's letter format was an afterthought; he had not used it originally. Describing the circumstances of the book's revision, Adams noted: "The form of Letters too was the Effect of Booksellers Advice. The original Manuscript had it not."

Gordon's manuscript does not survive, so the extent of his revision remains conjectural. Adams said the Reverend Dr. Joseph Towers and his son Joseph Lomas Towers were largely responsible for the revisions. According to another theory, Gordon let a professional writer recast his manuscript but became so enraged that he rewrote it himself. The whole process resulted in three distinct manuscript versions of the history. Literary historian Moses Coit Tyler surmises that all the revisions badly mutilated Gordon's *History*. Besides recasting its form, Gordon toned down many expressions, modified numerous factual details, and cut out big chunks of narrative, amounting to perhaps a hundred pages.[27] Even with all its changes, Gordon's work remains a vital contribution to the history of the war, based as it is on personal interviews with all the major players in the drama of the American Revolution.

In addition to revising the work, Gordon spent much time recruiting subscribers. The four-volume London edition finally appeared in 1788 as *The History of the Rise, Progress, and Establishment of the Independence of the United States of America*. The first volume includes a list of subscribers. Gordon listed the British and European ones alphabetically, followed by a separate list of American subscribers. Prominent Americans then living in England or Europe appear in the first list.

Given its alphabetical arrangement, John Adams's name is the very first one listed, but the ever-vain Adams was still dissatisfied. The list identified him as "American Plenipotentiary." Thomas Jefferson, then serving as American minister plenipotentiary to the Court of France, is listed as "American Ambassador to Paris." Adams queried: "How happened it that Jefferson was an Ambassador and the first Subscriber only a Minister? Of History how accurate those art?"

The list of subscribers helps situate Gordon's *History* in the political and social contexts of the day. It lists many British men who had been sympathetic to the American cause during the war, including some Dissenting ministers who were close friends of Benjamin Franklin and members of his Club of Honest Whigs: Andrew Kippis, Richard Price, and Abraham Rees. Thomas Mullett, the Bristol merchant who had visited Mount Vernon, is also listed among the subscribers. Though Mullett personally knew that Washington would not write the history of the Revolutionary War, he still remained eager to read more on the subject.

Gordon listed American subscribers by state. Washington, whose name appears first among the Virginians, subscribed for two copies. Most American subscribers came from either Massachusetts or Virginia. The list of Virginia subscribers is fairly substantial, suggesting that Washington had helped Gordon recruit local subscribers. Their correspondence bears out this suggestion.[28] Gordon did not actively recruit subscribers from elsewhere, but a few men from other states did subscribe to the work.

Altogether Gordon had 1,250 copies of his four-volume history printed, 250 of them on extra-fine paper. Besides Washington's two subscription copies, Gordon sent him a set printed on the good paper and elegantly bound. Furthermore, Gordon sent Washington the copies for many of the American subscribers. When the books reached Mount Vernon, Washington found a total of forty-three sets, amounting to 172 volumes! These included the sets for all the Virginia subscribers, as well as those from New York, Pennsylvania, Rhode Island, Vermont, and Nova Scotia.[29] Gordon apparently expected Washington to distribute these sets to their subscribers, a considerable burden to place on anyone, let alone the man who would soon be president of the United States.

A three-volume American edition of Gordon's history appeared in 1789. The publisher—a victim of bad timing—asked Washington to subscribe to the American edition soon after those 172 volumes arrived from London. In his response to the American publisher, Washington was curt: "I received your letter of yesterday requesting permission to add my name to your list of subscribers for an American edition of Dr Gordon's history of the late revolution. As I have already several sets of that work I would wish to decline adding my name as a subscriber for more."[30]

From the time he returned home from the war until the end of his life, Washington received many requests to subscribe to new publications. In addition a steady stream of books flowed to Mount Vernon, not only books Washington ordered or subscribed to but also books their authors sent as presents. Many helped expand his collection of Americana significantly.

Atkinson Bush, a British admirer, presented Washington with *City Petitions, Addresses, and Remonstrances*. After a touching presentation inscription, Bush wrote a Latin motto meaning "This hand is hostile to tyrants."[31] A collection of city petitions from the 1770s may seem like an odd book to present to General Washington, but several petitions specifically involve the American Revolution. The petitioners express their concerns to the leaders of London. These documents offer a perspective on the American conflict that cannot be found elsewhere. "There can be no doubt," said one reviewer, "that some papers in this collection merit preservation."[32]

In September 1784 Washington traveled to Ohio and Kentucky to inspect his lands there and research a route for a possible canal to connect the Potomac with the Ohio.[33] Soon after returning from the trip, he received in the mail a strangely appropriate book, John Filson's *Discovery, Settlement and Present State of Kentucke*. The first published history of Kentucky, Filson's book also contains the first published account of the life and adventures of Daniel Boone. Part history, part biography, and part promotional tract, Filson's book sought to encourage settlement in Kentucky. Washington well understood the power Filson's promotional rhetoric could have. In the essay Washington wrote at the end of the journal of his trip to the Ohio valley, he beautifully summarized the attitude of local residents: "The Western Settlers—from my own observation—stand as it were on a pivot—the touch of a feather would almost incline them any way."[34]

Given Washington's great love of the land, his appreciation of history, and his enjoyment of wilderness adventure, he should have liked Filson's book, but it came with an impossible request that soured his pleasure. Aware of Washington's familiarity with Kentucky and the Ohio Valley and hoping to publish a second edition of his book to encourage both settlement and investment in Kentucky, Filson asked Washington to supply whatever information he could about the topography and the natural history of the region. Ideally, Filson suggested, Washington should send the requested information in the form of a detailed letter that could be inserted verbatim into a new edition of his history of Kentucky. Filson, it seems, wanted Washington to do his work for him.

Filson had published a map with his first edition, which he published separately as well. The map also functioned as a promotional work. Filson dedicated it to George Washington without his permission, making it look as if Washington had sanctioned the map, which he definitely had not. Washington had been hoping someone would publish a detailed, accurate map of the Ohio Valley, but Filson's map of Kentucky was littered with errors. While thanking him for the book, Washington made clear his attitude toward the map: "It has long been my wish to see an extensive and accurate map of the Western Territory set on foot, and amply encouraged: but I would have this work founded upon actual surveys and careful observations—any thing short of these is, in my opinion, not only defective and of little use, but serves as often to mislead as to direct the examiner."[35] Once Washington refused to endorse the work, Filson abandoned his plans for a second edition.

If Washington got over his disappointment with Filson's *Discovery, Settlement and Present State of Kentucke*, he could have found much to enjoy. Not only did Filson tell the story of Kentucky's past and present state, he looked toward to its future, foreseeing what Kentucky would become. And the appended story of Daniel Boone, written by Filson but told in the first-person voice of its hero and based on Filson's interviews with him, offered an exciting tale of backwoods adventure that would take hold of the American imagination and never let go.

Imagine George Washington, having recently returned from Kentucky, seated in his library at Mount Vernon reading the adventures of Daniel Boone. Mason Locke Weems—the bookselling biographer who invented the story of George Washington chopping down the cherry tree, among other legends—saw similarities between Filson's story of Daniel Boone and Washington's life. Weems borrowed the heroic pattern of Daniel Boone to create his mythic biography of George Washington.[36]

After coming home from the war, Washington waited a long time before he visited Belvoir. Even though he was aware it burned down, he hated to see destroyed a place that had meant so much to him in his youth. The last Thursday in January 1785—a clear, cold day—he finally brought himself to ride over to Belvoir to view the ruins of what had formerly been one of the grandest plantations on the Potomac. Washington told George William Fairfax, its former owner, that Belvoir was now little more than a heap of ruins. Despite how many pleasant hours he had spent here, Washington could scarcely recognize the place after fire destroyed it. Neither could he bear to look upon the ruins very long. He explained to Fairfax: "I was obliged to fly from them; and came home with painful sensations, and sorrowing for the contrast."[37] At a time when Washington was thinking deeply about the process of history, the disparity between his memories of Belvoir and its ruinous state reminded him how difficult it could be to make sense of the past in the face of the present.

Historians and biographers were not the only ones seeking to record the story of the American Revolution. Portraitists and history painters also recognized the importance of capturing images of Revolutionary heroes from life. On April 28, 1785, Robert Edge Pine, an English painter who had immigrated to Philadelphia, came to Mount Vernon. Pine was a tiny little fellow, but Washington makes no mention of his diminutive stature in his diary, describing him solely by his accomplishments. Washington said that Pine was "a pretty eminent Portrait, and Historian Painter."[38] Perhaps Washington had meant to write "history painter," not "Historian Painter," but his term reveals how closely he paralleled the roles of historian and painter.

Before he left England Pine had befriended George William Fairfax, who provided much help when Pine painted *America*, the most ambitious work he created in England. *America* was an allegorical piece, which depicted Heroic Virtue presenting Liberty to America. When Pine prepared to emigrate, he asked Fairfax for a letter of introduction to George Washington. Fairfax agreed, sending a mezzotint of *America* with his letter, in which he explained that the figure of Heroic Virtue was supposed to represent Washington, though it looked nothing like him.[39]

Upon settling in Philadelphia in 1784, Pine sought to establish himself as a history painter. Already he was well on his way. The story of his artistic

Joseph Strutt, after the painting by Robert Edgar Pine, *America* (Boston 1781), stipple engraving. Library of Congress, Prints and Photographs Division, Washington, DC (reproduction number: LC-DIG-pga-04178).

career is filled with superlatives. In October 1784 he had organized an exhibit of his work in Philadelphia, the first artist to give a one-man show in America. In conjunction Pine published his *Descriptive Catalogue of Pictures Painted by Robert Edge Pine*, the first exhibit catalogue published in America.[40]

On the recommendation of Francis Hopkinson, Pine came to Mount Vernon. He hoped to paint Washington's portrait from life, which he planned to make part of a projected set of eight paintings that would record the foremost events of the Revolutionary War. Pine stayed at Mount Vernon for nearly three weeks. During that time he painted Washington's portrait, Martha's, and those of her four grandchildren. His personal manner of painting was distinctive. Rembrandt Peale, who had an opportunity to watch him paint, observed, "He seemed to my young mind as a conjuror with his mahl-stick wand, and the rainbow tints of his palette."[41]

Pine was not the only distinguished artist to visit Mount Vernon in 1785. The foremost sculptor in Europe, Jean-Antoine Houdon, had agreed to visit the New World to sculpt Washington's head from life as part of his preliminary work for creating a life-size statue of George Washington to stand in the state capitol in Richmond. Thomas Jefferson worked hard to make Houdon's American visit possible, though he characteristically downplayed his own efforts, attributing Houdon's decision to visit the United States solely to the artist's personal motivation. In Jefferson's words, Houdon "was so anxious to be the person who should hand down the figure of the General to future ages, that without hesitating a moment he offered to abandon his business here [in Europe], to leave the statues of kings unfinished, and to go to America to take the true figure by actual inspection and measurement."[42]

Once Houdon was ready to leave Paris, David Humphreys wrote a letter introducing him to Washington. Humphreys was in Paris serving as secretary to the commission to negotiate treaties of amity and commerce. His letter of introduction expresses his confidence that Houdon would create an excellent likeness of Washington: "Not only the present but future generations will be curious to see your figure taken by such an Artist. And indeed, my dear General, it must be a pleasing reflection to you amid the tranquil walks of private life to find that history, poetry, painting, and sculpture will vye with each other in consigning your name to immortality."[43]

At Mount Vernon Houdon made a life mask of Washington, modeled a bust in terra cotta, and took his measurements to make the statue as accurate as possible. Houdon returned to his Paris studio to create the statue, which took him around three years—time well spent. Many consider the statue of Washington to be Houdon's masterpiece. In addition it has been recognized as the most accurate likeness of Washington ever created. Yet it is more than that. Describing Houdon's *Washington*, art historian Wayne Craven observes: "The details of the clothing are simplified so that they do not demand undue attention in themselves, and the eye of the spectator is continually drawn to the head, which portrays the nobility, the pensiveness, the gentleness, and the calm dignity of the man."[44] Important as a reflection of Houdon's art and Washington's character, the statue would also play a part in the development of American art. Once erected in the Virginia Capitol, Houdon's *Washington* rapidly encouraged the growth of monumental sculptural art in the United States.

When David Humphreys said that poetry was vying with sculpture to depict Washington, he had a specific work in mind. Along with the letter introducing Houdon to Washington, Humphreys included a copy of his latest work, *A Poem on the Happiness of America*, several pages of which do indeed commemorate Washington. Since Humphreys had been with the general when he resigned his commission in Annapolis, he had heard the eloquent speech Washington had delivered to Congress on that occasion. *A Poem on the Happiness of America* incorporates a lengthy versification of Washington's speech, rendered into regular heroic couplets.

Humphreys belonged to a group of American poets known as the Connecticut Wits, all of whom commemorated the Revolutionary War in their own way. The Reverend Timothy Dwight, another one of the Connecticut Wits, sought to honor Washington with his verse, though not in the way their mutual friend Colonel Henry Babcock had hoped. Babcock, having served as colonel of a regiment at Fort Ticonderoga in 1775, was dismissed as commander of the Rhode Island forces the following year because of what Washington called a "distempered mind."[45] In 1784 Babcock wrote his former commander in chief to suggest that Dwight could "do Justice to your matchless Achievements, perhaps equal to Alexander Pope, Swift or Dryden." If Dwight came to Mount Vernon, he could write an epic poem that would be better "than any History yet wrote, not excepting Mr Gordons history of the American Revolution; It would be read with Great Avidity, thro out the Globe."[46] Babcock's letter, which continues in the same vein at some length, shows he remained a little touched in the head.

Dwight's poem was neither historical nor biographical but biblical. He called it *The Conquest of Canaan* and dedicated it to Washington. Unlike Filson, Dwight secured Washington's permission before dedicating his work to him.[47] Beyond the dedication, *The Conquest of Canaan* makes no direct mention of Washington, but it is impossible to read the poem and not think of him. Dwight's biblical epic retells the story of Joshua, a powerful military hero who leads the chosen people to victory. Dwight's poem has numerous ties to American history. The portrayal of New England as the "New Canaan" had been an important part of Puritan literature since

Jean-Antoine Houdon, *George Washington* (1792), Virginia State Capitol, Richmond, Virginia. Library of Congress, Prints and Photographs Division, Washington, DC (reproduction number: HABS VA, 44-RICH, 9–41).

the early seventeenth century. Joshua resembles Washington in terms of both leadership and military prowess.

In his footnotes to *The Conquest of Canaan* Dwight made the analogy between the biblical story and American history explicit with reference to the heroes of the Revolution. Furthermore, the poem embodies some key

Wood engraving of Timothy Dwight. From Evert A. Duyckinck and George L. Duyckinck, *Cyclopaedia of American Literature* (New York: Charles Scribner, 1856), 1:357. Kevin J. Hayes Collection, Toledo, Ohio.

concepts that were already a part of early American historiography. Late in the poem, for example, Dwight presents his version of *translatio*: "In that dread hour, beneath auspicious skies, / To nobler bliss yon western world shall rise." Footnoting these lines, Dwight explains what he is talking about: "Freedom and glory of the North American States."[48]

When George Washington came back to Mount Vernon after the war, he was curious about how history would record the story of the American Revolution. His experience at home during the first two years after his return taught him that the situation was much more complex. With historians, biographers, painters, sculptors, and poets vying to capture his image and record his story, Washington could see that the process of telling the story of the American Revolution was not merely a matter of recording history. It was a process of making myth.

CHAPTER 15

The Slave, the Quaker,
and the Panopticon

Disguise thyself as thou wilt, still, Slavery! said I—still thou art a
bitter draught!
   Laurence Sterne, *A Sentimental Journey through France and Italy*

As Elkanah Watson neared Mount Vernon in 1785, he could scarcely
contain his excitement. He recalled, "I had feasted my imagination
for several days in the near prospect of a visit to Mount Vernon, the seat of
Washington. No pilgrim ever approached Mecca with deeper enthusiasm."[1]
A young merchant from Massachusetts, Watson was not disappointed. He
was impressed with the general's physical bearing as well as the expressive
quality of his face: "I observed a peculiarity in his smile, which seemed to illuminate his eye; his whole countenance beamed with intelligence, while it
commanded confidence and respect." Writing up the story of his visit to
Mount Vernon, Watson called the time he spent there "two of the richest
days of my life." In his reminiscence, Watson seems almost awestruck by his
host's presence. He found Washington "reaping the reward of his illustrious
deeds, in the quiet shade of his beloved retirement. He was at the matured
age of fifty-three. Alexander and Caesar both died before they reached that
period of life, and both had immortalized their names. How much stronger
and nobler the claims of Washington to immortality!"

   Watson did not come to Mount Vernon empty-handed. He had recently returned from a trip to England, where he had befriended Granville
Sharp, a prominent British philanthropist and vehement antislavery

advocate. Learning about Watson's plan to visit Mount Vernon, Sharp gave him some political pamphlets to present to Washington, whom he saw as the most influential man in America. Placing pamphlets in Washington's hands, Sharp hoped, would help spread his ideas for legal, political, and social reform across the United States.

The package consisted of two bundles of books embracing Sharp's thoughts on what Watson called "congenial topics."[2] Watson does not clarify what he meant by "congenial," but the surviving pamphlets discuss such diverse subjects as constitutional law, due process, ethics, parliamentary reform, public property, representative government, and slavery.

One, *The Law of Retribution*, presents a detailed indictment of slavery. It is an angry work. The title page sternly warns readers, threatening God's vengeance against all "tyrants, slave-holders, and oppressors." With *The Law of Retribution*, Sharp's hope that Washington would assimilate his ideas and spread his message fell flat. The pamphlet was so off-putting that Washington set it aside, seeing no reason to read beyond the title page. His copy of *The Law of Retribution* verifies that he never read it: the pages remain uncut.[3]

Perhaps Washington did not need to read the work. *The Law of Retribution* was largely obsolete by the time he received a copy from Watson. Sharp's antislavery message remained valid, of course, but his dire prediction that the practice of slavery would destroy the British Empire no longer applied. Sharp had written the pamphlet soon after Lexington and Concord. Now that the Revolutionary War was over, his prediction had come true: Great Britain had lost a big chunk of its empire. But the loss of the American colonies was not due to slavery.

Washington may not have read Sharp's *Appendix to the Representation*, either. Another pamphlet on slavery in the bundles of books Watson delivered, Sharp's *Appendix* supplements an earlier work, *A Representation of the Injustice and Dangerous Tendency of Tolerating Slavery*. At first glance Sharp's *Appendix* might seem incomprehensible to readers who did not know the work it appended. Actually, *Appendix to the Representation* marks a significant departure from *Representation of the Injustice*. It stands on its own as an impassioned plea for the abolition of slavery based on what one contemporary reader called arguments drawn from law, reason, and humanity.[4] In addition, Sharp added a religious component to his critique of slavery, something absent from *Representation of the Injustice*.[5]

Though Sharp's pamphlets on slavery did not appeal to Washington, the topic was entering the conversation more and more at Mount Vernon, a place that over a hundred slaves called home. Touring the grounds, visitors could hardly avoid thinking about slavery, given its place in

Washington's house and throughout his plantation. The presence of slaves often seemed incongruous at the home of the man who had fought, and won, American freedom. On either side of his bright and spacious greenhouse, Washington built two wings, which provided cramped, poorly lit quarters for many slaves. Shrewd visitors have noticed that the orange trees had it better than the slaves.

Wherever they went on the grounds of Mount Vernon, people could witness slaves at work. Watson was one of many visitors who saw fit to bring up the subject in conversation. In terms of the activities of its slaves, Mount Vernon was in a transitional period, at least compared with other plantations in the South. The shift from tobacco to wheat and other staple crops in the 1760s had made Washington less dependent on slave labor than many Virginia planters, giving his slaves the opportunity to undertake tasks that involved more skill and greater training.[6]

No slave was more visible than Billy Lee. The veterans who came to Mount Vernon remembered him well. And those who had never met Billy had heard about his wartime exploits in General Washington's service. After the war, Billy had suffered some debilitating injuries, breaking one knee in 1785, leaving him partly lame, and breaking the other knee three years later. To continue to be useful, Billy began cobbling shoes. No matter what he was doing when visitors arrived, Billy Lee typically offered a friendly greeting. G. W. P. Custis's pen portrait of Billy captures his affable spirit, but, written in the heyday of the plantation novel, it comes dangerously close to racial stereotype:

> Billy carefully reconnoitered the visiters as they arrived, and when a military title was announced, the old body-servant would send his compliments to the soldier, requesting an interview at his quarters. It was never denied, and Billy, after receiving a warm grasp of the hand, would say, "Ah, colonel, glad to see you; we of the army don't see one another often in these peaceful times. Glad to see your honor looking so well; remember you at headquarters. The new-time people don't know what we old soldiers did and suffered for the country in the old war. Was it not cold enough at Valley Forge? Yes, was it; and I am sure you remember it was hot enough at Monmouth. Ah, colonel, I am a poor cripple; can't ride now, so I make shoes and think of the old times; the gineral often stops his horse here to inquire if I want anything. I want for nothing, thank God, but the use of my limbs."[7]

Since returning from the war, Washington had been devoting much thought to the issue of slavery. The Reverend Francis Asbury, a Methodist minister who visited the same year as Elkanah Watson, found the master of Mount Vernon expressing "his opinion against slavery."[8] When William Gordon was at Mount Vernon researching the history of the Revolutionary War, he and Washington discussed the possibility of emancipating his slaves. Washington told Gordon that someday he hoped to eliminate slavery at Mount Vernon altogether.[9]

The other tracts on slavery in Washington's personal library—those that do show signs of reading—provide a rough guide to his attitude. The earliest tract at Mount Vernon that broached the theme of emancipation dates from 1774, but Washington did have one earlier pamphlet in his collection that took African American slavery as its subject: *A Letter to an American Planter from His Friend in London*. First printed in 1771, the work was reprinted ten years later to distribute in Antigua.[10] Several copies of the second edition survive, but Washington's is only one of two copies of the first edition to survive in the United States.[11]

Both editions of *A Letter to an American Planter from His Friend in London* appeared anonymously. John Van Horne has identified John Waring as its author.[12] Waring was secretary to the Associates of the Late Reverend Dr. Bray, an organization formed to continue Bray's vigorous philanthropic efforts. For this pamphlet, Waring assumed the persona of a London friend offering advice to an American planter regarding how to treat his slaves. In his letter the London friend suggests that the planter could mitigate the condition of his slaves by converting them to Christianity.

Waring's argument constitutes an impassioned plea for racial equality: regardless of the color of their skin, people's souls are equal in the eyes of God. Though well intentioned, Waring somewhat undermined his plea for equality when he denigrated the "idolatrous rites and practices" slaves had brought with them from Africa, finding those traditional customs ridiculous.[13] By accepting Christianity, Waring argued, slaves will assure themselves of more humane, benevolent treatment.

Upon its publication, Waring shipped forty copies of this pamphlet to a Virginia friend, Robert Carter Nicholas. More than two years later Waring sent Nicholas a follow-up letter, wondering whether the bundle of pamphlets had ever arrived. Since Waring had never received a letter from Nicholas acknowledging their receipt, he assumed they had been lost in transit.[14] The fact that Washington had a copy in his library at Mount Vernon confirms that the pamphlets did arrive. Other evidence reveals the whereabouts of an additional copy. The estate inventory of Dabney Carr—Thomas Jefferson's brother-in-law—lists a copy of *Letter to an American Planter*.[15] Upon receiving the bundle of forty copies,

Nicholas apparently distributed individual pamphlets to friends and fellow members of the Virginia House of Burgesses.

The beginning of Washington's interest in the antislavery cause has been dated between the late 1760s to the mid-1780s. Some place it around the time of the Declaration of Independence; others suggest he did not become deeply engaged in the issue of slavery until the time of the Constitutional Convention.[16] That he received this pamphlet around 1771 and kept his copy while other Virginians disposed of theirs supports the argument that his engagement with the antislavery issue began early during the Revolutionary period.

Other people in colonial Virginia also grew concerned about slavery during the early 1770s, wondering if there were any essential differences between Africans and Englishmen. Samuel Henley, for one, questioned whether people from Europe and Africa really differed at all. After settling in Williamsburg to take a professorship at the College of William and Mary, Henley had the chance to test the acuity of some African slaves. He asked one of them "how it happened that, as Adam and Eve were white, he, their descendant should be black."

"I don't know," the man replied, "but, prick your hand and prick mine, my blood is as red as yours."

Henley was delighted with this response. It reminded him of a scene in *The Merchant of Venice* in which the prince of Morocco, one of Portia's suitors, pleads with her, arguing that she should not be prejudiced against him solely because of the color of his skin. "Bring me the fairest creature northward born," he implores, "And let us make incision for your love, / To prove whose blood is reddest, his or mine."[17] The perceptive reply from this Virginia slave, echoing Shakespeare no less, prompted Henley to reconsider the essence of European and African, colonist and slave.

In the political discourse of the Revolutionary era American patriots likened their own oppression under British colonial rule to slavery. The pamphleteers and polemicists who made their case emphasized the natural rights of the American colonists by comparing them to slaves held in bondage. During the years leading to the Revolution, they clamored for freedom from the chains of British tyranny. All this talk of freedom emboldened those who spoke for the African slaves in America. In writing *Letter to an American Planter*, Waring had sought to ameliorate the condition of the slaves but stopped short of arguing for emancipation. The pamphleteers who came after him would make the case for freeing the slaves.

Washington himself may have begun talking about emancipation as early as 1774, when he went to Philadelphia as a delegate to the First

Continental Congress. Almost surely he met Anthony Benezet, the Quaker activist known throughout the city for his efforts to enlist others to various causes: peace, temperance, and emancipation. Benezet worked tirelessly toward the complete and total eradication of slavery.[18] Recalling his own experience in the City of Brotherly Love, the Marquis de Barbé-Marbois, the head of the French legation there, exclaimed, "Who could have lived a month in Philadelphia without knowing Anthony Benezet!"[19] The arrival of major political figures from throughout the colonies for the First Continental Congress gave Benezet an ideal platform for conveying his antislavery message to the most powerful men in America.

Benezet had a busy network of Quaker correspondents across the colonies. To facilitate his contact with the Virginia delegates to the First Continental Congress, Benezet's friend Robert Pleasants, a prominent Virginia Quaker, wrote a letter of introduction for the entire contingent. After naming them, Pleasants suggested that most, perhaps all of the Virginia delegates, were sympathetic to the Quakers and would appreciate his friendship. Benezet left a detailed account of his conversation with Patrick Henry. Presumably, he also spoke with other Virginia delegates.[20]

One volume in Washington's library provides crucial evidence to indicate that he and Benezet did meet in Philadelphia. Whereas most bound volumes of pamphlets at Mount Vernon consisted of ones Washington received separately and arranged to have bound, this particular volume contains two separately published pamphlets, which Benezet had combined into a single volume, subjoining them with a common title page: *The Potent Enemies of America Laid Open.*

Besides being a pioneer in the fight against slavery, Benezet was also a pioneer of what is now called custom publishing.[21] He would often have printed a general title page, which he used for different collections of pamphlets. Benezet thus customized the contents of each volume of tracts he presented, piggybacking one cause onto another. *The Potent Enemies of America* shows up in the libraries of other delegates to the First Continental Congress, including Robert Treat Paine and Roger Sherman.[22] Apparently Benezet presented copies to several congressional delegates.

The first pamphlet in Washington's copy of this custom-made collection has an imposing title: *The Mighty Destroyer Displayed: In Some Account of the Dreadful Havock Made by the Mistaken Use as Well as Abuse of Distilled Spirituous Liquors.* Benezet edited the text himself, using his own prose to connect pertinent quotations from several medical experts on the subject of alcohol abuse. The Philadelphia edition of John Wesley's *Thoughts upon Slavery* forms the second pamphlet in the volume. Wesley first published *Thoughts upon Slavery* in London in 1774; the ever-industrious Benezet prepared the Philadelphia edition himself and published it before the year's end. Editing the work for American readers, he added many explanatory notes to *Thoughts upon Slavery*, making Wesley's arguments as urgent and pertinent as possible.[23]

Serious Considerations on Several Important Subjects, another one of Anthony Benezet's works that could be found at Mount Vernon, came to Washington as a present from Warner Mifflin, a Delaware Quaker who, like Benezet, advocated peace and worked toward the abolition of slavery. A slave owner himself, Mifflin gradually understood that it was "a sin of a deep dye" to enslave his fellow man, so he freed his in 1774. Mifflin's emancipation of his slaves set an example, and other slaveholding Quakers followed suit and freed theirs.[24]

Washington may have met this Delaware Quaker during the Revolutionary War, when Mifflin developed a reputation for his antiwar activities. His story became well known in Europe, mainly because Crèvecoeur retold it at length in *Letters from an American Farmer*. English readers should not rush to their copies of Crèvecoeur: the Mifflin chapter appears only in the French text, which was widely disseminated across Europe. After reading the story in the French edition of *Letters from an American Farmer*, Brissot de Warville labeled Mifflin the "Angel of Peace." Once the German playwright August von Kotzebue read Crèvecoeur, he adapted Mifflin's war story as a one-act play, *The Quaker*.

According to Crèvecoeur, whose account of Warner Mifflin falls somewhere between an embellishment of facts and an outright fabrication, the Quaker Yearly Meeting chose Mifflin to fulfill a mission of peace. During the Battle of Germantown he supposedly braved the dangers of the battlefield and crossed the British lines to speak with General Howe, urging him to find a peaceful solution to the conflict between the United States and Great Britain. Mifflin subsequently returned to the American side and spoke with General Washington, delivering a similar message. Washington appreciated Mifflin's courage and candor but told him that both sides were long since past a peaceful solution.

With the war's end Mifflin resumed his antislavery efforts, presenting several petitions to the First Federal Congress and urging the legislators to take measures toward the abolition of slavery. During Washington's presidency, Mifflin visited him to see if he could exert any pressure on behalf of the antislavery cause. "After much general conversation," Washington wrote in his diary, Mifflin "used Arguments to shew the immorality—injustice and impolicy of keeping these people in a state of Slavery; with declarations, however, that he did not wish for more than a gradual abolition, or to see any infraction of the Constitution to effect it."[25] Though Washington privately looked forward to the abolition of slavery, he remained diplomatic in his reply to Mifflin, hesitating to commit himself one way or the other, since this matter could very well require him to make an official decision in the not-too-distant future.

Short Observations on Slavery, another one of Benezet's pamphlets at Mount Vernon, excerpts the Abbé Raynal's thoughts on the subject, which Benezet ties together with his own opinions. Benezet's remarks in this pamphlet are among his angriest and most unforgiving. He castigates the practice of compensating slave owners whose runaways are killed by slave hunters, suggesting that it is tantamount to government-sanctioned murder.[26] No one associated with slavery escapes Benezet's vitriol. Slave owners who placed the blame on slave traders rationalized their behavior: there could be no slave traders without slave owners. People who inherited slaves or acquired them through charitable means were as guilty for per-petuating slavery as those who bought them. The practice of slavery, Benezet continued, corrupted American youth and undermined the moral fiber of the nation.[27]

Washington's connections with the Quaker community acquainted him with other antislavery literature. In *A Serious Address to the Rulers of America, on the Inconsistency of Their Conduct Respecting Slavery*, David Cooper, a leading New Jersey Quaker, addressed the contradiction be-tween the freedom the American Revolution represented and the ongo-ing practice of slavery. Cooper published his pamphlet pseudonymously, signing himself simply "A Farmer."

Cooper spoke with so much passion and conviction that some readers thought Benezet had written *A Serious Address*. Cooper proclaimed: "Now is the time to demonstrate to Europe, to the whole world, that America was in earnest, and meant what she said, when, with particular energy, and unanswerable reasoning, she plead the cause of human nature, and with undaunted firmness insisted, that *all mankind* came from the hand of their Creator *equally free*."[28] Stressing that all men and women are gov-erned by natural law, Cooper stated, "With equal justice may negroes say, By the immutable laws of nature, we are equally entitled to life, liberty and property with our lordly masters."[29] He aggressively circulated his pamphlet, presenting copies to several members of the Continental Congress. Benezet was so impressed with the work that he helped Cooper distribute it.[30]

Writing in 1785, Robert Pleasants delivered a message similar to the one Cooper expressed in *A Serious Address*. Among the Virginia Quakers Pleasants was an exemplary figure. He, too, had freed his slaves, hiring them back as free men and women and paying them wages for their work. He also supported a school to educate free black children.[31] In a personal letter, Pleasants reminded Washington:

> Remember the cause for which thou wert call'd to the Command of the American Army, was the cause of Liberty and the Rights of Mankind: How strange then must it appear to impartial thinking men, to be informed, that many who were warm advocates for that noble cause during the War, are now sitting down in a state of ease, dissipation and extravagance on the labour of Slaves?[32]

Pleasants suggested that Washington could have as much impact on African American freedom as he had had on American freedom: "Thy example and influence at this time, towards a general emancipation, would be as productive of real happiness to mankind, as thy Sword may have been."[33]

Along with this letter Pleasants sent Washington a copy of a pamphlet by Robert Bell: *Illuminations for Legislators, and for Sentimentalists.* A grab bag full of essays, this collection contained extracts from many previously published works, including John Dickinson's *Letters from a Pennsylvania Farmer.* Bell titled the excerpt from Dickinson "Sentiments on What Is Freed, and What Is Slavery." Dickinson's text does not really have anything to do with the practice of slavery in America. The fact that Pleasants sent Bell's pamphlet with his antislavery letter does suggest a curious reversal in the political discourse. During the Revolutionary era, the plight of the American colonists under the yoke of British tyranny was compared to slavery. Now the plight of slaves in the United States was likened to the former situation of the American colonists: the slaves needed to follow the pattern established by the colonists to secure their freedom from tyranny.

In 1786 Washington took a census of his slaves at Mount Vernon and his outlying plantations. He counted a total of 216 slaves. About half belonged to him. The rest were dower slaves, meaning they were the property of his wife, which he held in trust for the Custis heirs. Around this same time, Washington wrote privately, "It [is] among my first wishes to see some plan adopted, by which slavery in this Country may be abolished by slow, sure, and imperceptible degrees."[34]

Washington continued to ponder the situation and add books on the subject to his library, including the Philadelphia edition of Thomas Clarkson's *Essay on the Impolicy of the African Slave Trade.* There's no telling how Washington acquired this work. It may have been another present from a Quaker correspondent. When Warner Mifflin and other Quakers petitioned the First Federal Congress to pass legislation against slavery—one of the first instances of organized political lobbying in Congress—they informed the lawmakers of their position partly by sending Congress a small library of antislavery literature, which included Clarkson's *Essay on the Impolicy of the African Slave Trade*.[35]

The Mount Vernon copy of Clarkson caught the attention of others. Once David Humphreys returned to America from Paris, he became a fixture at the Washington home, staying there for extended periods of time. Humphreys took advantage of Washington's library, something other guests did as well. During a visit to Mount Vernon, the Marquis de Lafayette spent time in his host's library reading books "written during [his] absence."[36]

Humphreys similarly found much to read in Washington's library. In a surviving notebook he summarized several works he read at Mount Vernon, including Clarkson's *Essay*. The notebook also reveals that Humphreys and Washington discussed Clarkson's work. Shortly after summarizing the book, Humphreys transcribed something Washington had said about slavery. Since Humphreys used direct discourse to record Washington's comments, they lend a sense of immediacy to the account in his notebook.

"The unfortunate condition of the persons, whose labour in part I employed," Washington admitted, "has been the only unavoidable subject of regret. To make the Adults among them as easy and as comfortable in their circumstances as their actual state of ignorance and improvidence would admit; and to lay a foundation to prepare the rising generation for a destiny different from that in which they were born; afforded some satisfaction to my mind, and could not I hoped be displeasing to the justice of the Creator."[37]

That he recorded these words in direct discourse does not necessarily mean Humphreys transcribed the precise words Washington had spoken. Don't forget he rendered Washington's resignation speech to the Confederation Congress in heroic couplets. But the comments Humphreys has his friend and mentor say on this occasion jibe with remarks Washington made on other occasions. More and more Washington understood that something had to be done about slavery. The optimistic, forward-thinking remarks Washington made in conversation with Humphreys indicate that he was already thinking about emancipation.[38]

Another book from Washington's library Humphreys read and summarized was Adam Smith's *Inquiry into the Nature and Causes of the Wealth of Nations*. Presumably this work entered his conversation with

Washington, who read the work thoroughly himself. Washington's surviving copy contains a characteristic correction that reveals him in the process of reading. On the subject of grain prices in both Scotland and England, Smith offered evidence to prove how expensive grain used to be. The price of grain in Scotland, Smith observed, is "supported by the evidence of the public fiars, annual valuations made upon oath, according to the actual state of the markets, of all the different sorts of grain in every different county of Scotland."[39]

In his copy of the work Washington corrected "fiars" to "fairs," but his zeal for perfection led him astray in this instance. Unique to Scotland, "fiars" is a real word meaning annually fixed prices of grain. Reading Smith's text with Washington's correction, Joseph Wharton, who later owned the book, noted at the bottom of the page: "The above alteration, from fiars to fairs, was perhaps made by Washington, but fiars is the word intended by the author. It means the price of grain as fixed in each Scotch county by the sheriff and a jury."

As the foremost economic treatise of the era, Adam Smith's *Wealth of Nations* surveys many different aspects of the economy, including slavery. Smith had spoken against slavery earlier. In his *Theory of Moral Sentiments*—one of the ethical treatises Washington had purchased for Jack Custis in 1773—Smith observes: "There is not a negro from the coast of Africa who does not . . . possess a degree of magnanimity which the soul of his sordid master is scarce capable of conceiving."[40]

Smith's comments on slavery in *The Wealth of Nations* take a different tack. Instead of expressing moral outrage, he now treats the issue of slavery with pragmatism. His remarks are so pragmatic, in fact, that they border on cynicism. He critiqued slavery's economic inefficiency with a simple fact: people want property. Property provides an incentive to work and thus forms a basis for economic efficiency.[41] By preventing slaves from owning property, the system of chattel slavery denied them the incentive to work. The system also made slaveholders reluctant to free their slaves: Who would willfully relinquish property they owned?

Having learned about some Pennsylvania Quakers who had resolved to free their slaves, Smith dared to question their magnanimity: "The late resolution of the Quakers in Pennsylvania to set at liberty all their negro slaves, may satisfy us that their number cannot be very great. Had they made any considerable part of their property, such a resolution could never have been agreed to."[42] To end slavery, Smith concluded, abolitionists must appeal to self-interest.

David Humphreys's presence contributed greatly to the talk about books and literature that occurred at Mount Vernon, but he was not the only friend who had become a part of Washington's household. Looking for someone to serve as both private secretary for himself and domestic tutor for Nelly and Wash Custis, George Washington welcomed Tobias Lear to Mount Vernon. A Harvard graduate with a proficiency in French, Lear had the skills to fill the dual position of secretary and teacher. The letters of recommendation Washington received on his behalf speak of Lear's excellent education, goodness of heart, honor, integrity, and modesty.[43] Lear arrived at Mount Vernon the last week of May 1786. Washington was impressed with him from the start, finding him "a genteel, well-behaved young man." He would remain an important part of Washington's life for years to come.[44]

As part of his effort to organize the library at Mount Vernon, Washington collected and arranged many of the loose pamphlets and sent them to his bookbinder. Handsomely bound in tree calf—a type of leather binding decorated to resemble wood grain—the resulting volumes made beautiful additions to his library shelves. Many of these volumes are miscellaneous, but a few contain additional works on slavery. One pamphlet volume that survives from Washington's library, for example, contains *Proceedings of the Hon. House of Assembly of Jamaica, on the Sugar and Slave-Trade*—one of the few works in Washington's library that spoke in defense of slavery—but none of the other pamphlets in the volume concern the subject. The binder's title simply designates the volume as "Miscellanies."[45]

Some of the pamphlet volumes from Mount Vernon do collect works treating the same subject. One surviving volume has the spine title "Tracts on Slavery." In addition to the works by Clarkson and Cooper it contains several other pamphlets, including one titled *Oration upon the Moral and Political Evil of Slavery*, which its author, George Buchanan, had delivered in Baltimore on the Fourth of July 1791 at a meeting of the Maryland Society for Promoting the Abolition of Slavery, and the Relief of Free Negroes, and Others Unlawfully Held in Bondage. When Jefferson Davis visited the Boston Athenaeum in 1858, he had the opportunity to examine this volume. Buchanan's *Oration* astonished him. The librarian vividly captured Davis's reaction: "Nothing so fixed his attention as this; he read it and expressed himself amazed. He had heard that such sentiments were expressed at the South, but had never seen them."[46]

Several additional antislavery pamphlets from Washington's library are bound together in another surviving volume. It contains John Waring's *Letter to an American Planter from His Friend in London* and three works by Anthony Benezet. Besides *Serious Considerations* and *Short Observations*, it also includes Benezet's *Notes on the Slave Trade*, an eight-page pamphlet repeating comments Benezet had made in *Serious Considerations*.[47] What makes this particular pamphlet volume stand out is its first work: Jeremy Bentham's *Panopticon*. Did the bookbinder choose to group all these titles together, or was Washington the one who chose which pamphlets belonged together? The subject of slavery links together the other pamphlets in the volume. Did Washington recognize a continuity between the tracts against slavery and Bentham's *Panopticon?*

In the broadest sense Bentham's *Panopticon* and the late eighteenth-century antislavery discourse concern power, specifically, how people in power maintain control over others. With his panopticon concept Bentham devised a way to keep inmates of any penal institution under continual surveillance. An observation tower would be located at the center of a prison, and the inmates' cells would radiate outward from it. Prisons constructed along the panopticon plan would let guards easily keep all the prisoners under their watchful gaze.

Though Jeremy Bentham's *Panopticon* largely concerns the organization of prisons and the observation of prisoners, the work was inspired by his brother Samuel's experience in Russia. A naval engineer, Samuel Bentham oversaw a large workforce at the shipyards consisting of skilled British shipbuilders and unskilled Russian serfs, or, in other words, free and forced labor.[48] Recent critical discussion has emphasized the panopticon's use for incarceration. Grouping Jeremy Bentham's *Panopticon* with several antislavery tracts, Washington's pamphlet volume returns the concept to its original context.

Jeremy Bentham adds something that is largely absent from the other works in the volume and the antislavery literature in general. Speaking for the slaves, that is, men and women subjected to the power of their owners, the antislavery advocates argued that they should be freed and, consequently, empowered. Though recognizing the injustice of slavery and the need to eliminate it, they remained somewhat vague in terms of practical solutions. Their idealism is inspiring, but the antislavery advocates are a little short on practical solutions. Bentham, whose name is synonymous with pragmatism, devised an ingenious way to supervise workers, which could be applied to many different forms of labor.

This particular pamphlet volume, which straddles the pragmatic and the idealistic, prompts some questions about where Washington stood. If he freed his slaves, what would happen to them? He would still need workers at Mount Vernon. Could he adopt a plan along the lines of the one Robert Pleasants used after freeing his slaves? Would former slaves, once freed, continue to work for him? If so, how could he supervise them? When Washington had designed his gardens at Mount Vernon, he had started with Batty Langley's elaborate plans and radically simplified them to suit the local conditions. Could he similarly adapt Bentham's panopticon for the purpose of plantation management?

Washington never answered these questions, but, after much reading, discussion, and contemplation, he decided to free his slaves in his will. He could do nothing about the dower slaves, which would descend in the Custis family, but he could free the slaves he owned outright. When he wrote his will, he made provisions for them. Billy Lee received special treatment. Washington gave him the choice of immediate freedom or a lasting home at Mount Vernon. Either way, he provided Billy with a substantial annuity "as a testimony," he wrote, "of my sense of his attachment to me, and for his faithful services during the Revolutionary War."[49] With his other slaves he devised a system for their gradual emancipation after his wife's death. When the details of Washington's will became public after his death, the Quaker community rejoiced.[50]

Not only did Washington's will free his slaves, it also provided for those who were too young or too elderly to work and for educating the young and giving welfare to the elderly. Indirectly, it could be said, Washington did adapt Bentham's panopticon to control the slaves he freed. The best way to assure that free men and women behave responsibly is not to keep them under constant surveillance but to educate them. Nothing can assure responsible behavior more than an educated citizenry.

CHAPTER 16

Politics and the Picaresque

If mankind were to resolve to agree in no institution of
government, until every part of it had been adjusted to the most
exact standard of perfection, society would soon become a general
scene of anarchy, and the world a desert.

Alexander Hamilton, *Federalist* no. 65

A most unusual book arrived at Mount Vernon in March 1787. It had
been published in Philadelphia. Nothing too unusual about that;
Philadelphia was the foremost publishing center in eighteenth-century
America. Titled *The Lyric Works of Horace*, it largely consisted of English
translations of Horace and other classical poets. That was not so unusual
either. American editions of classical texts had appeared sporadically since
the Philadelphia printer Samuel Keimer had issued an English translation of Epictetus in the 1720s. According to its title page, *The Lyric Works
of Horace* had been translated by "A Native of America." Again, not too
unusual: many contemporary works of poetry appeared anonymously or
pseudonymously, and pseudonyms expressing pride in America had
become increasingly common during the Revolutionary era. Besides, the
author, a Delaware poet named John Parke who had served as a lieutenant colonel in the Continental Army, identified himself in the cover letter
he sent with the book, so his authorship was no big secret. What does
make this work unusual is the original play Parke appended to his Latin
translations: "Virginia: A Pastoral Drama."

In Parke's verse drama rural swains and carefree shepherdesses sing
happy songs as they gambol along the shores of the Potomac, celebrating the

greatness of the man who lived there, a godlike war hero named Daphnis, which, of course, is a thinly veiled portrait of Washington. One character conveys the sentiments Washington felt since returning to Mount Vernon:

> Now war's alarms are haply o'er,
> Again we meet,—to part no more,
> Ne'er to forsake again Patowmac's shore.[1]

Besides writing a play about him, Parke had also dedicated *The Lyric Works of Horace* to Washington. Upon receiving the book, Washington wrote to thank this bard of the Brandywine, though he did wish Parke had asked permission before dedicating the work to him.[2] Since Parke had published the book by subscription, the list of subscribers printed with it includes the names of many of the most prominent men in the nation. Washington often subscribed to books by American authors to encourage the growth of American literature; he was disappointed Parke had not asked him to subscribe. His thank-you letter gives the impression that he would rather have been a subscriber to this book than the subject of a mawkish pastoral drama elevating him to godlike status.

Despite his shortcomings as a dramatist, Parke correctly inferred the feelings of contentment Washington experienced upon returning to the life of a gentleman farmer on the Potomac. Unlike Daphnis in the drama, Washington would forsake Potomac's shore to serve his country further. Increasingly divisive conflicts between the states convinced him that more had to be done to safeguard the new nation against internal strife. Though hesitant to get involved in politics again, Washington saw that the United States needed his leadership. Before March gave way to April, he would write to Edmund Randolph, effectively agreeing to attend the Constitutional Convention as a delegate from Virginia. Less than two months later he found himself on the road to Philadelphia.[3]

Sunday morning, May 13, 1787, Washington reached Chester, Pennsylvania, where he met up with some old friends, including one of his best, David Humphreys. They traveled together as a group to Philadelphia, arriving later that day. Once they entered the city, Washington went to Franklin Court on Market Street, where he renewed his friendship with Benjamin Franklin, whom he had not seen since 1775, when Franklin had visited the headquarters of the Continental Army in Cambridge, Massachusetts, on behalf of Congress.

Franklin had returned home from Paris on the same ship that brought Houdon to America in 1785, but so far Washington had not had the opportunity to see him. From the time Franklin left for Paris in 1776 until his return, he and Washington had exchanged letters sporadically. Their letters mainly concerned the business of the new nation, but both sides of their correspondence express warm personal feelings. In Philadelphia that May, Washington and Franklin were happy to see one another after a lapse of a dozen years.

Benjamin Franklin Bache had accompanied his grandfather when he went to Paris in 1776. Only seven years old then, Benny, as he was known in the family, received an excellent education in Europe, living part of the time at a boarding school in Geneva. He spent his last two years in Paris on the outskirts of the city at Passy, where his grandfather taught him the basics of the printing trade at the small press he operated as a hobby. Two years after they returned to Philadelphia, Franklin established a business for his grandson as printer, publisher, and newspaper editor.

Franklin scarcely realized the powerful forces he unleashed when he taught his grandson how to control the printed word and gave him the voice to express himself to the public. Washington scarcely realized that this young printer and newspaperman, this grandson of a dear friend, would become a thorn in his side over the next decade. During Washington's presidency, Bache's newspaper, the *Aurora*, would be the single most important opposition paper in the nation.

During the absence of her father and son, Sarah Bache and her husband Richard had been taking care of Franklin Court. When Benjamin Franklin returned from Paris, he found his house chock-full of little Baches. There was scarcely enough room for his ample girth or the thousands of books he brought from Paris. Consequently, he built a new addition to his home. After her father's return, Sarah Bache continued to function as the mistress of Franklin Court, but Benjamin Franklin enjoyed showing off the new wing and its library, which housed the books and curiosities he had spent a lifetime collecting.[4]

Franklin took an interest in all fields of science and technology. Displaying his library to visitors, he would choose books from it that suited their tastes and interests. Though he was not a farmer, he had a very good collection of agricultural books. When it came to agricultural libraries, few could surpass the one at Mount Vernon, so Franklin could hardly teach Washington anything new about farming. Still, his collection was impressive, not only for its agricultural books but also for its overall breadth and depth. With more than four thousand volumes, all easily locatable due to the ingenious catalogue he had devised, Franklin's personal library impressed everyone who visited.

Washington's correspondence records one work Franklin showed him. When he and Don Diego de Gardoqui, the Spanish envoy to the United

States, happened to visit Franklin Court together, they enjoyed seeing their host's library.[5] Franklin showed them the four-volume edition of *Don Quixote* published in Madrid by Joaquin Ibarra. Commissioned by the Real Academia de la Lengua, which oversaw its publication, the edition was absolutely gorgeous.

Printed on elegant paper using a new typeface specially designed for it and illustrated with handsome engravings, this edition established *Don Quixote* as a landmark of Spanish literature. Paradoxically, *Don Quixote* had been recognized as a great book among English readers before it was accepted as a classic in Spain. The Spanish formerly saw the work as little more than a burlesque of chivalric romance, but the Real Academia edition made *Don Quixote* a national treasure.[6]

Franklin enjoyed showing his copy of the edition to those who visited. When he showed his copy to Washington and Gardoqui, Washington was impressed, having never seen this beautifully printed and illustrated edition before.[7] A good diplomat, Gardoqui stored away this piece of information. In an effort to curry Washington's favor, he would subsequently present him with a copy of the Real Academia *Don Quixote* for his library at Mount Vernon.

The Constitutional Convention was scheduled to begin on Monday, May 14. Though the delegates from Pennsylvania and Virginia had reached Philadelphia in time, representatives from all the other states had not, thus preventing a quorum and delaying the start of the convention for over a week. Washington, who prided himself on being prompt, found such irresponsible delays frustrating.

Franklin, who took pride in his patience, accepted the delay with grace, choosing to host a party in the meantime. On Wednesday the delegates already in town gathered at Franklin Court for dinner. Having recently received a cask of porter from the London brewer Thomas Jordan, Franklin could think of no better time to broach it. Subsequently writing Jordan a letter of thanks, Franklin described how his guests received the cask: "Its contents met with the most cordial reception and universal approbation." A hearty dark beer, Jordan's porter was the best the delegates had ever tasted.[8]

His thank-you letter captures the conviviality of the moment but makes no mention of the conversation that occurred around the cask. Among well-educated and well-read Americans in the eighteenth century, literature often was a topic of polite conversation. When it came to literature, Joel Barlow's *Vision of Columbus* was the talk of the town that spring. Many convention delegates had subscribed to Barlow's epic of America and looked forward to its forthcoming publication. Franklin had subscribed for six copies. Several months earlier Washington had subscribed for twenty copies, but he did not pay for his subscription or receive his copies until he reached Philadelphia. He did not have time to read this 250-page poem right away, but he may have dipped into it long enough to notice how effusively Barlow praised him.

Washington subscribed for so many copies of Barlow's epic partly because he knew they would make great presents. He gave some away shortly after obtaining his subscriber copies. He presented others to friends near the end of the Constitutional Convention. During his time in Philadelphia, Washington frequently dined with George Clymer, a signer of the Declaration of Independence, and his wife, Elizabeth. As a show of gratitude for her hospitality, Washington presented a copy of Barlow's *Vision of Columbus* to Elizabeth Clymer.[9]

Similarly, Washington presented another copy to Sarah Bache. She did not really need a copy of Barlow's *Vision of Columbus*. Had she wanted to read it, she could have read one of her father's copies. Presenting the book to Sarah Bache, Washington expressed his gratitude for her hospitality during his many visits to Franklin Court while he was in town for the Constitutional Convention. Giving her a book instead of, say, a set of silver napkin rings, Washington subtly complimented Sarah Bache, acknowledging her intellectual ability as well as her capacity as a hostess.

Washington took advantage of his time in Philadelphia to renew some old acquaintances. Since visiting Mount Vernon, the painter Robert Edge Pine had finished construction on a combination home and gallery to display his paintings—the first building in the United States designed specifically to exhibit works of art. Located on the second floor, the exhibit hall was fifty feet wide and thirty-three feet deep, with a lofty ceiling. According to one contemporary description, it was "lighted from above in an elegant style."[10] Washington spoke with Pine and enjoyed the exhibit. *America*, the allegorical painting Washington had so far seen only in a mezzotint reproduction, was massive, nine and a half feet across and nearly seven feet tall. The figure of Heroic Virtue still looked nothing like him, though.

From May 25, the day his fellow delegates unanimously elected George Washington president of the Constitutional Convention, until it adjourned the third week of September, the business of founding a new government kept him quite busy. From his presidential chair, he attentively listened to all the debates, weighing the arguments on both sides of the question.

Washington remained fairly quiet during the day-to-day proceedings, but one surviving anecdote suggests that he kept his sense of humor in the midst of heated arguments regarding the nation's new government.

The issue of a standing army proved to be quite controversial. What form would it take? How large should it be? These are some of the questions the framers of the Constitution sought to answer. When one delegate moved that a standing army should be limited to five thousand troops at any given time, Washington whispered to another delegate that they should "amend the motion, by providing that no foreign enemy should invade the United States, at any one time, with more than three thousand troops."[11]

The business of establishing a government required intense study. Throughout the convention Washington read everything he could get his hands that pertained to the Constitution.[12] He benefitted from James Madison's extensive research on the subject. "An Abstract of the General Principles of Ancient and Modern Confederacies," a work which fills eighteen pages in Jared Sparks's edition of Washington's writings, shows how beholden he was to Madison. Having prepared a detailed set of notes on the history of confederacies from ancient times to the present, Madison shared his notes with Washington, who diligently transcribed them. Omitting Madison's erudite Latin quotations and his scholarly documentation, Washington created a reader-friendly version of Madison's notes, which he could consult himself and share with other delegates.[13]

Though the proceedings of the Constitutional Convention occupied much of Washington's time in Philadelphia, he did pursue other activities in his spare moments. As he always did when he was in Philadelphia, he spent time shopping for books. Some of the books he obtained that summer came as gifts; others he purchased. All would make handsome additions to his home library and give him many hours of reading pleasure.

Hector St. Jean de Crèvecoeur, then serving as French consul to New York, sent him a copy of the French edition of *Letters from an American Farmer*. Though unable to read the French text, he appreciated the gift and wrote Crèvecoeur to tell him so. Washington also acquired the English version, which he read thoroughly and recommended to others. He told one correspondent that *Letters from an American Farmer* "will afford a great deal of profitable and amusive Information, respecting *the private Life* of the Americans; as well as the progress of agriculture, manufactures and arts in their Country."[14]

If there were any faults to the book, in Washington's opinion, they involved Crèvecoeur's tendency to paint too rosy a picture: "Perhaps the picture he gives, though founded in fact, is in some instances embellished with rather too flattering circumstances."[15] Washington's interpretation of *Letters of American Farmer* reflects the book's contemporary reception. The dark ending of the work—from the disturbing image of the tortured and mutilated slave to Farmer James's desperate flight from his plantation— apparently did not faze Crèvecoeur's eighteenth-century readers.

The last week of July Washington purchased a copy of Samuel Butler's *Hudibras*, a small but attractive edition illustrated by William Hogarth. This purchase, combined with references to *Hudibras* in Washington's letters, reveals much about his literary knowledge. *Hudibras* is a rollicking, mock-heroic, quasi-picaresque satire of English Protestantism written in short rhyming couplets and filled with comic references. Since its initial publication in the mid-seventeenth century, it had become a popular work in England and the colonies, strongly influencing early American verse.

Hudibras also functioned as social capital. When Governor Alexander Spotswood came to Virginia, for example, he presented a copy of *Hudibras* to one of the colony's leading citizens, William Byrd II.[16] John Parke Custis, Byrd's brother-in-law, had a copy of *Hudibras* in his library, which came to Mount Vernon with the rest of the Custis collection. The Custis copy stood on the shelves of Washington's library for years, but he apparently never read it.

His correspondence confirms that he did not read *Hudibras* until after he obtained a copy of his own during the Constitutional Convention. In the poem Butler versified a proverb about things being worth only what they will fetch:

> For what is Worth in any Thing,
> But so much Money as 'twill bring?[17]

Butler paraphrases an age-old proverb that Washington had been using before he read *Hudibras*. Washington's earliest known usage of it occurs in a 1767 letter. Writing to a man who wished to pay off a considerable debt by giving him land instead of cash, Washington told him he had greatly overestimated the value of the land: "This at best is only worth what it will fetch and if it sells for half that Sum I will acknowledge myself extreamly mistaken."[18] In a place like colonial Virginia, where land was more plentiful than hard currency, this traditional saying was especially appropriate.

Though the proverb occurs elsewhere in Washington's correspondence, he does not attribute it to *Hudibras* until 1788, the year after he purchased his copy of the book. That year Washington wrote a correspondent, asking him to appraise another tract of land he had been offered as payment for a debt: "Butler says 'every thing is worth what it will fetch'—but in these times of scarcity every thing will not fetch what it is worth—and it is for that reason I have asked your opinion respecting the latter."[19] After reading *Hudibras*, in other words, Washington could reuse a favorite saying, but instead of attributing it solely to traditional wisdom, he could attribute it to a literary source, enhancing the sophistication of his correspondence and, in a subtle way, showing off his literary knowledge.

Another purchase Washington made when he was in Philadelphia for the Constitutional Convention seems similarly motivated: James Thomson's lengthy philosophical poem *The Seasons*. Like *Hudibras*, *The Seasons* found favor among many sophisticated early American readers. Benjamin Franklin, for one, told a friend: "I had read no Poetry for several years, and almost lost the Relish of it, till I met with his *Seasons*. That charming Poet has brought more Tears of Pleasure into my Eyes than all I ever read before. I wish it were in my Power to return him any Part of the Joy he has given me."[20]

Thomson originally published *The Seasons* in the 1720s. That it had so far escaped Washington's attention indicates another gap in his literary knowledge. That he purchased an edition of it now reflects his desire to fill that gap. Beyond his financial accounts Washington's papers make no further mention of *The Seasons*, but this acquisition parallels his acquisition of *Hudibras*.

Dropping references to renowned works of English literature, far from being pretentious, was merely a part of the everyday conversation among well-to-do gentlemen in early America. Washington's purchase of both *Hudibras* and *The Seasons* reveals a crucial aspect of his intellectual life. Despite his strength of character, his presence of mind, his ability to bend men to his will, Washington remained quite self-conscious about his spotty knowledge of literature. He apparently felt uncomfortable when others alluded to works he did not know. Reading *Hudibras* and *The Seasons*, he familiarized himself with two well-known and widely respected works.

Washington's behavior at the end of the Constitutional Convention is remarkably similar to his behavior at the end of the Revolutionary War: he imagined his retirement from public life and bought books to read at his leisure. On September 17, the last day of the convention, he ordered two books, both works of fiction: a four-volume English edition of *Don Quixote* and Thomas Amory's two-volume novel *The Life of John Buncle*.

The purchase of fiction was unusual for Washington. He had not added any novels to his library since he was a young man. His acquisition of *Don Quixote* parallels his purchase of *Hudibras* and *The Seasons*. It, too, was a work familiar to many convention delegates, a group that included some of the best-educated and well-read men in the nation. Franklin Court was not the only place in Philadelphia where *Don Quixote* entered the conversation. The work was so well known that friends and fellow delegates would toss off allusions to it in conversation. William Livingston, a delegate from New Jersey, was known as the "Don Quixote of the Jerseys."[21] Simply put, the imaginative world of Don Quixote and Sancho Panza was part of the everyday world of the eighteenth-century gentleman.

Whereas his acquisition of an English edition of *Don Quixote* reflects Washington's desire to catch up his literary knowledge and align it with that of his peers, his acquisition of *John Buncle* shows him deepening his literary knowledge with another pleasurable picaresque novel. Amory's *Life of John Buncle* was not nearly as well known as *Don Quixote*. Rarely did eighteenth-century readers toss off allusions to *John Buncle*. With this purchase Washington was not just catching up on his literary knowledge, he was going beyond the standard works to broaden his knowledge. *John Buncle* was ideal for that purpose. In the twentieth century George Saintsbury would remark, "It may be doubted whether anybody really understands the eighteenth century, as it was and as it might have been, until he has read *John Buncle*."[22]

More than any of the books Washington obtained in Philadelphia during the Constitutional Convention, *John Buncle* verifies his literary predilections. A modern editor calls this novel "an object of interest to the connoisseur, the explorer of curious by-paths of literature, and to all who have a liking for the eccentricities of human nature, when conjoined with strength and shrewdness, and with candour of expression."[23]

Narrated in the first person from its hero's point of view, *John Buncle* begins by describing his journey through northern England, where he encounters a series of beautiful, learned women, whom he marries, Bluebeard-like, one after another. The plot itself is less important than its digressions on a variety of literary, religious, and scientific topics. Like *Tristram Shandy*, *John Buncle* is a veritable celebration of digression. William Hazlitt said that the soul of Rabelais passed into Thomas Amory when he wrote *John Buncle*. Charles Lamb, another one of the book's admirers, found in it "an infinite fund of pleasantry," describing *John Buncle* as "an extraordinary compound of all manner of subjects, from the depth of the ludicrous to the heights of sublime religious truth."[24]

Washington's surviving copy of *John Buncle* is the two-volume 1766 edition.[25] This particular copy had originally been sold by Philadelphia bookseller John Sparhawk, whose label appears in the first volume. Both

volumes are handsomely bound in sprinkled calf. But Sparhawk, or whoever bound the set, was somewhat careless. Washington did not realize
the binding error until after he returned to Mount Vernon and started
reading *John Buncle*. He might have returned the book to Sparhawk with
a request to rebind it with all its parts in the proper order, but he did not.
Instead, Washington devised an original way to cope with the binding
error. Usually he wrote in his books only to correct typographical errors.
The binding mistake in his copy of *John Buncle* is an error on a greater
scale. Consequently Washington inscribed detailed instructions for himself or whoever else might read it.

In his misbound copy the first page of Part II occurs after the table of
contents in the first volume. At the bottom of that page and continuing
onto the bottom of the following one, Washington wrote:

> To read this work in the order it is written, the reader must begin with
> the first page of the 2d volume, and read to the 225th page; then proceed
> from the same page in this 1st volume, and continue to the end thereof—
> After which he or she is to return to the first page of the same and read
> to the 225th—and lastly begin at the 225th page of the 2d volume read
> to the end[,] a mistake in binding having occasioned these errors.

Elsewhere in his copy of this two-volume work, Washington elaborated
on his reading road map. At the bottom of page 1 in the second volume,
he wrote: "This, though called the 2d Volume, is the beginning of the first
Volume and continues to be part thereof to the 225th page." At the bottom
of page 224 in the second volume, he placed an asterisk next to the catchword with the instruction: "Turn to the 225th page of the 1st Volume for
the continuation of the Work in its due course." At the end of Vol. 1,
he wrote another note: "Return to the beginning of this Volume for the
regular continuation of the life of Jno. Buncle Esqr—occasioned by a mistake
in binding the work together." And at the bottom of page 224 of Vol. 1, he
placed an asterisk next to the catchword and a corresponding asterisk
with the direction: "Turn to the 225th page of the 2d Volume for the continuation of this work."

Washington's reading instructions make his copy of *John Buncle* one of
the most fascinating items to survive from his library. They show his
mind in action. Instead of returning the volume to his Philadelphia bookseller, he found a way to fix the problem himself. The reading instructions
Washington wrote inside the volume show him using his ingenuity and
his determination to overcome an obstacle. They display in miniature the
same skills he used on the battlefield and in politics.

These reading instructions also display Washington's courtesy. His conjoined pair of pronouns—"he or she"—shows that he wrote these instructions not only for himself but for anyone else who might read the book. Whoever might borrow it would not have to struggle with the out-of-order binding; the reader could simply follow Washington's directions. The instructions reveal Washington's awareness that his books would survive him. Whoever read his copy of *The Life of John Buncle* in the future would have George Washington as a guide.

He acquired another picaresque novel around the same time he obtained *Don Quixote* and *John Buncle*: Alain-René Lesage's *History of Gil Blas* in Tobias Smollett's four-volume translation. Precisely how he obtained this work is a mystery. Unlike *Don Quixote* and *John Buncle*, *Gil Blas* is not mentioned in Washington's financial accounts. It may have been a gift. Its similarity to the other two works, combined with the fact that Washington's copy was a recent London edition, makes it likely that he obtained *Gil Blas* when he was in Philadelphia for the Constitutional Convention.

Washington's desire to read *Gil Blas* parallels his desire to read *Don Quixote*: it, too, was a work friends and fellow patriots knew well. A few years earlier, Thomas Jefferson had linked *Gil Blas* and *Don Quixote*, calling them "the best books of their class as far as I am acquainted with them." The year before the Constitutional Convention New York bookseller Archibald M'Lean promoted the sale of *Gil Blas* by calling it "a favourite novel."[26]

Episodes from *Gil Blas* were part of the lingua franca of the eighteenth-century gentleman. Washington's friends often alluded to the novel in conversation and in writing. Elbridge Gerry, a delegate from Massachusetts who would serve as US vice president under James Madison, provides a good example. Once the Constitutional Convention ended, numerous essays for and against the Constitution appeared in the press. These essays sought to sway the opinions of those attending the state ratification conventions. One newspaper contributor who wrote under the pseudonym "Landholder" informed readers that it was their duty to follow the Constitution. Gerry had some misgivings about the Constitution and thought it deserved further scrutiny. He found Landholder's inflexibility wrongheaded and his overreliance on the printed word misguided. He compared Landholder to "Doctor Sangerado (in *Gil Blas*) who being advised to *alter his practice*, as it was founded on false principles and destructive to his patients, firmly determined to pursue it, *because he had written a book in support of it*."[27]

The episode Gerry remembered from *Gil Blas* is fairly typical of this picaresque novel, which presents a fictional autobiography of its title hero.

Gil Blas goes through a series of adventures, some exciting, others disappointing, all of which contribute to his knowledge of how the world works. Despite the book's episodic structure, it possesses a certain continuity. Time and again the characters who befriend Gil Blas and gain his confidence ultimately reveal their greed, hypocrisy, and capacity for underhanded double-dealing.

Elbridge Gerry used the character of Doctor Sangredo to critique Landholder's stubborn narrowmindedness. Other characters in *Gil Blas* could serve as examples to demonstrate the faults and foibles of modern man. Once he read *Gil Blas*, Washington himself started using characters as analogies for incidents in his own life.[28]

After the convention delegates hammered out the details of the Constitution and finished the final draft, they had copies printed to distribute throughout the nation to prepare citizens for the next phase: ratification by the individual states. Washington obtained several copies of the Constitution, one for himself and extras to pass along to friends and other influential figures. Catching up his correspondence before leaving Philadelphia, he wrote Thomas Jefferson in Paris, announcing the end of the convention and sending him a copy. Washington also sent one to Lafayette. In his cover letter to Lafayette, he called the Constitution "a Child of fortune, to be fostered by some and buffeted by others."[29]

Washington brought additional copies with him to Mount Vernon to distribute to Virginia friends. He sent one to Patrick Henry. He could have predicted how Henry would react to the Constitution before he sent him a copy. Henry felt it put far too much power in the hands of the federal government and not nearly enough in the states. As Washington suspected, Henry proved to be one of the strongest opponents of the Constitution in Virginia. The fierce opposition Henry expressed in his thank-you letter to Washington indicates the resistance the Constitution would face as it came before the state ratification conventions.

Cognizant of the objections opponents would make against the Constitution, three of its staunchest defenders—Alexander Hamilton, James Madison, and John Jay—took pre-emptive action. They began writing *The Federalist*, a newspaper essay series that contemporaries sometimes called the Publius essays after the pseudonym its authors chose, a pseudonym identifying them with the American public.

Though written as a partisan newspaper essay series, *The Federalist*, of course, remains a crucial document for interpreting the intentions of the framers. Time has given it the status of constitutional law. It explains how the US Constitution will work, what it will accomplish, and the pitfalls it will avoid. The Constitution, Publius assured readers, would guarantee the success of the democratic process and the American republic, giving a voice to the people and protecting their rights.

Both Hamilton and Madison sent Washington copies of some of the newspapers in which *The Federalist* appeared. Washington took the responsibility to disseminate *The Federalist* further. After Madison sent him the first seven numbers of the series, Washington forwarded them to Richmond printer John Dixon, who republished them in his weekly *Virginia Gazette and Independent Chronicle*. Washington continued to make sure the Publius essays reached as many readers in Virginia as possible, sending additional numbers to Dixon as he received them from Madison.

By the time the series reached its completion in 1788, eight states had ratified the Constitution. But it still faced serious opposition in both New York and Virginia, where delegations had yet to convene. To bolster support, the authors of *The Federalist* gathered the Publius essays together and issued a two-volume collected edition. The first volume appeared in March, the second in May.

Washington ultimately received two sets of *The Federalist*. Before the second volume appeared, he wrote a stirring appreciation of the work. Having read the entire series as the individual essays appeared, he did not need to wait for the second volume to be published before expressing his overall opinion. As the Virginia ratification convention approached, Washington predicted the fate of the Constitution in Virginia:

> Upon the whole I doubt whether the opposition to the Constitution will not ultimately be productive of more good than evil; it has called forth, in its defence, abilities (which would not perhaps have been otherwise exerted) that have thrown new lights upon the science of Government, they have given the rights of man a full and fair discussion, and have explained them in so clear and forcible a manner as cannot fail to make a lasting impression upon those who read the best publications on the subject, and particularly the pieces under the signature of Publius. There will be a greater weight of abilities opposed to the system in the convention of this State than there has been in any other, but notwithstanding the unwearied pains which have been taken, and the vigorous efforts which will be made in the Convention to prevent its adoption, I have not the smallest doubt but it will obtain here.[30]

As Washington predicted, Virginia did indeed ratify the Constitution, despite Patrick Henry's best efforts to thwart its approval. New York did

too. The ratification by these two powerful, populous, and geographi-
cally crucial states assured the acceptance of the Constitution across the
United States.

The visual culture reinforces the significance of *The Federalist* to
Washington's intellectual and political life. The Lansdowne portrait—
the full-length portrait of Washington that Gilbert Stuart painted during
his presidency—makes *The Federalist* a key text in Washington's life.
Stuart depicted several books in this painting, some with clearly legible
titles. These books do not necessarily replicate actual books from
Washington's library. Like other objects in the painting, they possess rich
symbolic power. Two volumes appear atop the table. The *Journal of
Congress* stands upright, with *The Federalist* propped against it. The image
suggests the ideas that *The Federalist* embodies provide the philosophical
and ideological support necessary for Congress to operate. Together the
two give President Washington the power and authority to rule the nation
with fairness and justice.

A corner of the tablecloth is turned up to reveal additional books beneath the table. Their appearance and position reinforce the importance
of books in Washington's life. Before taking the presidential oath of
office, Washington had read widely and learned much from his reading,
but he had no need to display his knowledge ostentatiously. He wears
his erudition lightly, keeping it hidden like a set of books beneath a
cloth-covered table. He does not need to show off his learning. He
knows it is there. He has synthesized his reading and can now use it to
govern the nation.

Reading the likes of *Don Quixote, Gil Blas*, and *John Buncle* at the same
time he was reading *The Federalist*, Washington would seem to have been
engaged in two very different literary activities. Perhaps the two types of
reading are not unrelated. The world of the picaresque novel is filled with
all types of people from the lowest blackguards to leaders of church and
state. Gil Blas starts his adventures in a cave full of robbers who force him
to live the life of a highway thief. After escaping their clutches, he encounters many other people, some of whom occupy positions of respect
and authority. Gil Blas learns that highwaymen and statesmen are not so
different after all. Leaders of church and state are no less liable to indulge
their desire for money and power than cave-dwelling robbers.

In its broadest perspective, the picaresque novel is a comment on
human nature, revealing the greed, thirst for power, and need for control that are inherent aspects of the human condition. Government itself
can be interpreted similarly. In *Federalist* no. 51, James Madison asks,
"But what is government itself but the greatest of all reflections on

human nature?" He followed this rhetorical question with a poignant observation: "If men were angels, no government would be necessary."[31] The picaresque novel portrays a world that is out of control, one where people grab all the money and power and control they can. The US Constitution, as *The Federalist* clarifies, provides a way to control human nature, to guard against the abuse of power and channel it to the common good.

CHAPTER 17

Presidential Patronage and the Development of American Literature

It is not so much in *buying* pictures, as in *being* pictures, that you can encourage a noble school.

John Ruskin, *Lectures on Architecture and Painting*

Great literary excitement swept across the country after the Revolutionary War. Though early American writers had expressed themselves in many ways throughout the colonial period, the birth of a new nation gave a new impetus to the literary culture. Authors grew anxious to create literature commensurate with the greatness of the United States, its ideals, values, landscape, and people. From the end of the war through his presidency, George Washington bore witness to the development of American literature. But he did more than watch it flourish. He actively encouraged authors to pursue their craft. Washington touched the lives of numerous writers during the final third of the eighteenth century. As president, he created an intellectual climate that fostered the development of American literature.

Few authors exemplified the new literary climate under Washington's leadership more than Jeremy Belknap, whose life as a writer presents a good way to structure the story of Washington's literary patronage before, during, and after his presidency. Born in Boston, Belknap attended Harvard, ultimately earning his master's degree. After college he became a Congregational minister in Dover, New Hampshire, where he remained throughout the Revolutionary War. While there he began writing a history of the state, the completion of which war, career, family, and a profound determination to base his historical work on original sources delayed for many years.

In 1784 Belknap finished the first volume of *The History of New-Hampshire* and arranged for Robert Aitken to publish it in Philadelphia. Since Belknap could not oversee publication himself, he asked his good friend and fellow historian Ebenezer Hazard to shepherd the work through the press. As its publication approached, Belknap wrote Hazard to see what he thought about sending a copy of the first volume of *The History of New-Hampshire* to George Washington. Hazard responded

Wood engraving of Jeremy Belknap. From Evert A. Duyckinck and George L. Duyckinck, *Cyclopaedia of American Literature* (New York: Charles Scribner, 1856), 1:255. Kevin J. Hayes Collection, Toledo, Ohio.

enthusiastically: "I think it will be quite polite to present General Washington with a copy of your History, and it will produce a letter from him in *his own handwriting*, which will be worth preserving. I have several, which I intend to hand down carefully to posterity as highly valuable."[1]

Belknap's desire to present a copy of his book to Washington seems altruistic: he apparently wished to give the former commander in chief the book as a token of respect for what he had accomplished during the war and what he meant to the nation. Hazard, on the other hand, seems quite mercenary. By presenting a book to General Washington, an author could receive in exchange a handwritten thank-you letter from the most famous man in America. Hazard's response raises the question: How many other authors sent Washington copies of their books primarily to receive autographed thank-you letters from him in return?

Giving Hazard the okay, Belknap told him to present a copy of the first volume of *The History of New-Hampshire* to Washington. Belknap also wrote a cover letter to accompany the book, explaining to Washington that the history related the "early struggles and sufferings of one of those states which now claim the honor of being defended by your sword." New Hampshire, he continued, "has bred an hardy race of men, whose merits as soldiers are well known to their beloved general, and who will always glory in having assisted to plant the laurel which adorns his brow."[2] Hazard had Robert Aitken handsomely bind the volume. Arguably the finest bookbinder in the nation, Aitken outdid himself this time, creating a sumptuous binding to touch the heart of any true bibliophile.

Washington did not receive the book with Belknap's cover letter until the end of 1784, but, as Hazard predicted, he responded with a letter of thanks. Though brief, Washington's message seems sincere. He appreciated Belknap's letter and the book it introduced: "For both, I pray you to accept my thanks—but my acknowledgments are more particularly due, for your favorable expression in the former, of my past endeavors to support the Cause of liberty."[3]

The thank-you letter seemed odd to Belknap. It sounded like Washington enjoyed the cover letter more than the three-hundred-page history that had taken Belknap a dozen years to write. Still, Belknap told Hazard he would keep the letter and "rank it among my valuables."[4] Washington's letter proved to be more than a keepsake. Belknap sometimes had difficulty motivating himself to write, but Washington's thank-you letter encouraged him to continue his literary efforts.

This presentation copy of *The History of New-Hampshire* made a handsome addition to Washington's library at Mount Vernon, which was

The lush gilt and tooled morocco binding of Washington's copy of David Humphreys's *Miscellaneous Works* (1790) demonstrates the elaborate lengths authors went to when they presented copies of their works to President Washington.

expanding rapidly during the mid- to late 1780s. Gradually, the collection was becoming just what he wanted: a library filled with informative works he could read for knowledge and pleasure. The Mount Vernon library symbolized the idyllic world Washington had often dreamt of when he was at war. Before the decade ended, however, his devotion to the United States would override his personal concerns, and he would part from his home to lead the United States, putting it on a solid foundation for the future.

On February 4, 1789, presidential electors from those states that had ratified the Constitution met to vote for president and vice president. The First Federal Congress, scheduled to convene in New York on March 4, would count the votes. Since Congress failed to achieve a quorum in March, the electoral votes would not be counted until the first week of April.

Before the votes were counted, rumors of Washington's election to the presidency circulated throughout the nation, and he reluctantly made plans to leave Mount Vernon for New York. On April 1, he conveyed his feelings in a letter to his good friend Henry Knox. The letter's congenial tone testifies to their friendship. Aware of Knox's literary bent, Washington took pains to make his letter entertaining. He observed that the extra month Congress required to count the electoral votes seemed like a reprieve to him. Developing his comparison to a condemned man, he told Knox:

> My movements to the chair of Government will be accompanied with feelings not unlike those of a culprit who is going to the place of his execution: so unwilling am I, in the evening of a life nearly consumed in public cares, to quit a peaceful abode for an Ocean of difficulties, without that competency of political skill—abilities and inclination which is necessary to manage the helm.[5]

Switching from simile to metaphor before this sentence ends, Washington evoked the ship-of-state theme, a figurative comparison that would appeal to numerous presidents after him. Regardless of which figures of speech he used, his letter to Knox embodies the self-effacing modesty Washington expressed in many of his statements concerning his role as a leader.

The day after counting the votes that officially elected George Washington president and John Adams vice president, Congress dispatched its secretary, Charles Thomson, to Mount Vernon. Having faithfully served as secretary to the Continental Congress and the Confederation Congress, Thomson fulfilled his new responsibility with diligence. Leaving New York on Tuesday, April 7, he endured bad roads, blustery weather, and rivers that overflowed their banks on his way from New York to Mount Vernon. After crossing the Potomac, he reached Washington's home the following Tuesday, when he informed him of his election to the office of the president of the United States of America.[6]

Since Washington had already heard rumors of his election, Thomson's arrival did not surprise him. By the time Thomson reached Mount Vernon, Washington was packed and almost ready to leave for New York. On April 16, about ten o'clock in the morning, Washington, Thomson, David Humphreys, and Billy Lee left together. Washington wrote a melancholy note in his diary: "I bade adieu to Mount Vernon, to private life, and to domestic felicity."[7]

They were greeted with pomp and pageantry throughout the journey. Billy, whose health had deteriorated in recent years, was forced to stay in Philadelphia for medical treatment as the others continued to New York. Overall they made good time on their northward trek, taking one day less from Mount Vernon to New York than it had taken Thomson to make the opposite journey. On April 30, 1789, George Washington took the oath of office at Federal Hall. There was no inaugural ball: that tradition would not start until James Madison became president, largely at the instigation of his wife, Dolley. After his inauguration President Washington simply got down to business.

Having proven himself in his capacity as Washington's personal secretary at Mount Vernon, Tobias Lear agreed to serve as presidential secretary and became the president's closest associate. Washington entrusted him with affairs of state; Lear carried out his responsibilities with diligence and dedication. In Washington's first year as president, Lear married Polly Long. When she gave birth to their first son, Benjamin, in 1791, the president became the boy's godfather. Washington grew fond of the little tyke, calling him "our little favorite."[8]

Washington was self-conscious about his behavior in office. He knew that everything he did would set a precedent for future presidents. Though the Constitution established the basic framework for the American government, the president and the legislators still had to flesh out the administration. This year Congress created three executive departments: state, war, and treasury. It was up to Washington to choose the men who would head each. He selected Alexander Hamilton for secretary of the treasury, Henry Knox as secretary of war, and Thomas Jefferson as secretary of state. Within the first few years of his administration, President Washington began meeting regularly with these department heads, who collectively became known as the president's cabinet.

A PRESIDENTIAL RECEPTION IN 1789.
BY GENERAL AND MRS. WASHINGTON

A Presidential Reception in 1789 by General and Mrs. Washington (New York: Currier & Ives, ca. 1876), lithograph. Library of Congress, Prints and Photographs Division, Washington, DC (reproduction number: LC-USZ62-2262).

Congress passed the Judiciary Act in September, creating the federal court system and the office of attorney general. By the end of the month Washington had selected John Jay to serve as chief justice of the United States Supreme Court and Edmund Randolph as attorney general. Even for someone who was as keen a judge of character as Washington, all this selecting and appointing was hard work. He would soon choose all the associate justices of the Supreme Court. Congress adjourned on September 29, 1789; Washington kept working.

His diary entry for Monday, October 5, provides a good indication of Washington's daily activities as the main business of establishing the government drew to a close that year. He dispatched commissions to the Supreme Court justices and the judges of the district courts. He also sent copies of the acts respecting the Department of Justice to others involved—marshals and attorneys and such. Between nine and eleven in the morning he exercised on horseback. He exercised a second time, taking a walk between five and six in the afternoon. Walking and riding helped clear his head and enabled him to concentrate on official business with greater intensity.[9]

At some point that day Washington enjoyed a conversation with his treasury secretary, who was quickly becoming his most trusted advisor. He asked Hamilton about the possibility of taking a tour of the New England states while Congress was in recess. Washington wanted to know the region a little better, to observe its products and its people, to get a feel for their attitude toward the federal government. Hamilton loved the idea and encouraged him to go. Washington began planning the journey.[10]

The diary does not list everything the president did on October 5, 1789. An additional document that has recently come to light reveals another activity. The ledgers of the New York Society Library show that Washington borrowed two books that Monday. Perhaps he stopped by the library on his morning horseback ride. Founded in 1754 and patterned on the Library Company of Philadelphia—the "Mother of all the North American Subscription Libraries," in Benjamin Franklin's words—the New York Society Library was a subscription library, meaning that members bought shares, which entitled them to borrow books from the collection and to help decide which books the library acquired. Usually members were the only ones who could borrow books from a subscription library. Understandably, the New York Society Library extended borrowing privileges to President Washington, and he was happy to patronize the place.

The library's holdings were quite similar to those of other contemporary subscription libraries. The collection contained biographies, histories, voyages, and works by many respected English authors, including Daniel Defoe and Alexander Pope.[11] In other words, it contained the same kinds of books that Washington enjoyed. Though he apparently hoped he might do a little reading before he left on his New England tour, Washington would not divert himself with belles-lettres during his few spare moments as president. Instead, he borrowed books that would help direct the policies of the new nation: Emmerich de Vattel's *Law of Nations* and the twelfth volume of *The Parliamentary Register; or, History of the Proceedings and Debates of the House of Commons*.

Law of Nations is a seminal work in the development of American foreign policy. Few subjects were more appropriate for Washington to read in his role as president than the law of nations. Philadelphia printer Thomas Bradford said as much in the edition of G. F. de Martens's *Summary of the Law of Nations* he issued in 1795, which he dedicated to Washington.[12] A Swiss diplomat and legal scholar, Vattel argued that since the European balance of power benefitted all nations, it must be defended at all costs. No single state should be allowed to dominate Europe. If one nation threatened to create an empire, the others should band together to prevent it.

Vattel's ideas shaped Alexander Hamilton's attitude toward national security and foreign policy. The following year Hamilton emphasized the importance of Vattel, whom he called "the most accurate and approved of the writers on the laws of Nations."[13] Hamilton concluded that Vattel's argument also applied to America. The national security of the United States, he believed, would depend on preserving the European balance of power. During Washington's administration, Vattel's *Law of Nations* would significantly shape US foreign policy. Washington's Neutrality Proclamation, which declared that the United States was neutral in the conflict between Great Britain and France, reflects ideas consistent with Vattel's theory.[14]

Whereas Vattel's work provided key concepts affecting national foreign policy, the *Parliamentary Register* gave American readers, especially those active with the establishment of the new government, an opportunity to see how another nation's legislature worked. Since the twelfth volume recorded legislative debates from 1779, it let Washington review what had happened in Parliament in a crucial year during the Revolutionary War. One section presents the debate over a motion for an enquiry into the conduct of the American war. Another records the debate over a motion that Lord Howe was not being properly supported or reinforced in America.

Reading the twelfth volume of the *Parliamentary Register*, Washington could have learned what had been happening in Parliament as he had confronted British troops on the battlefield. He obviously hoped to read both volumes he withdrew from the library, but he may not have had time to get through either. Though its borrowing ledgers indicate that the president checked the books out on October 5, nowhere do they show him returning them. When the borrowing ledgers recently resurfaced, they created a minor sensation by revealing that President Washington never returned these overdue library books.[15]

In mid-October Washington left New York for his tour of New England. The journey brought him through Connecticut, Massachusetts, and New Hampshire. He observed the progress of agriculture across the region and witnessed the start of some of the earliest factories in the United States. Everywhere he was honored and feted, and he had the opportunity to meet many of New England's leading citizens. In Boston, for example, he received the city's clergymen, a group that included the Reverend Jeremy Belknap.

Since publishing the first volume of his *History of New-Hampshire*, Belknap had grown dissatisfied with his position in Dover. He resigned from his pulpit in 1786 and accepted a new position with Long Lane

Church in Boston the following year. The position brought him back to his birthplace and closer to much of the primary research materials necessary for his historical research.

Though he could not talk with Washington very long, Belknap did speak with him long enough to remind the president of the ongoing New Hampshire history project and receive a message of encouragement. Recording the experience in the pages of his almanac, Belknap captured the words he received from the president.

"I am indebted to you, sir, for the *History of New Hampshire*," Washington told him. "It gave me great pleasure."

The president's acknowledgment encouraged Belknap to keep writing. Quoting the manuscript note from his almanac, Belknap's biographer commented, "This is the only instance that appears of his recording the approbation of others, and it shows how highly he valued these few and simple words of courtesy from the Father of his country."[16]

Leaving Boston the last week of October, Washington crossed the Charles River and proceeded to Cambridge, a place that held special significance as his first command post during the Revolutionary War. Harvard president Joseph Willard took him on a tour of the campus library. Then the greatest collection of books in the nation, the Harvard library contained thirteen thousand volumes, as Washington noted in his diary. Theological literature dominated the collection, but Harvard had expanded its holdings in recent years to include a substantial number of useful works on agriculture, architecture, astronomy, geography, history, law, mathematics, medicine, philology, and many other subjects.[17]

Once he returned from his journey through New England, Washington resumed the business of governing the nation. Earlier that year, he had emphasized to Congress the importance of creating a national militia, but so far the issue remained unsettled. Washington, who felt that the unresolved situation threatened national security, hoped to accelerate its creation. Once more he turned to books for help.

The third week of December 1789 he read Baron von Steuben's *Letter on the Subject of an Established Militia* as well as a recent government document on the same subject, *A Plan for the General Arrangement of the Militia of the United States*. After digesting both works, Washington spoke with Henry Knox, who agreed to prepare a report on the subject for Congress. Knox would write his report the following month, but it would take Congress two more years to pass an act providing for a national militia.

In December Washington also read Antoine Simon Le Page du Pratz's *History of Louisiana*, which may represent the closest he came to pleasure reading in his first year as president. Yet Le Page's personal history was not solely pleasure reading. Louisiana, a Spanish territory at the time, was becoming increasingly important to the settling of North America, as the extensive notes Washington took from Le Page's work indicate. His surviving manuscript notes fill twelve closely written pages and indicate Washington's desire to assimilate the essential facts about the region.[18]

Having come to Louisiana in 1718 and stayed for sixteen years, Le Page published an account of his experience in French in 1758, with an English translation five years later. Though more anecdotal than scientific, the book remains a pioneering work in the history of New Orleans and the Louisiana territory. As James Madison recognized, Le Page's information on the flora and fauna broadened the contemporary understanding of the region.[19] Le Page provided much original information regarding the lives and customs of the Natchez Indians as well. Furthermore, the detailed account of the land and its economic potential made the book a good guide for possible emigrants. In his review of the work, William Kenrick wrote that Le Page's *History of Louisiana* "contains many things that may be of use to those who shall hereafter visit, or settle, in those countries."[20]

Along with its useful information, Le Page's account also included moments of pure delight. The most charming personality to emerge from his story is the unnamed native he found to cook for him, a spunky woman who could handle herself in the face of all kinds of danger. One day an alligator approached their campfire. It stopped half a dozen feet away, apparently fixated by the light of the fire. Le Page ran into his cabin to retrieve his musket. In his absence the woman picked up a big stick and rapped the alligator on the snout, prompting it to make a hasty retreat. As Le Page returned with his gun, she just laughed, assuring him that a gun would be unnecessary to ward off the alligator.[21]

Viewed against his other literary activities as president, Washington's attention to Le Page's *History of Louisiana* in late 1789 is somewhat unusual. During his first year or so in office, his attention to the world of books largely involved the patronage of current American authors— historians, playwrights, poets, travel writers. His support usually took the form of subscriptions for forthcoming works, but sometimes he supplied authors with words of encouragement. In addition, he served as a figure of inspiration. Many contemporary authors put him into their works or based fictional characters on him.

In May 1790 Washington received two copies of *The Contrast*, the renowned comedy by the Vermont poet, playwright, and novelist Royall Tyler.[22] After its initial performance in 1787 Tyler had assigned copyright of the play to Thomas Wignell, the foremost comedian on the American stage. Not only had Wignell originally encouraged Tyler to write the work, he had also played the part of Jonathan in its first production. Tyler's writing and Wignell's performance combined to make Jonathan one of the most beloved characters on the early American stage. The character became the prototype for a classic American stereotype: Yankee Jonathan, the naive, rough-hewn, youthful hayseed who would come to represent the nation.

The character of Colonel Manly, the hero of *The Contrast*, was partly inspired by Washington. Making a direct comparison between himself and the commander in chief of the Continental Army, Manly states, "I have humbly imitated our illustrious Washington, in having exposed my health and life in the service of my country, without reaping any other reward than the glory of conquering in so arduous a contest."[23] Though the statement is ironic, it nonetheless pays homage to General Washington. When Wignell decided to publish *The Contrast*, he approached the president for help. Washington subscribed to the work, and his name appears prominently at the top of the list of subscribers.

Though Washington generally refused requests from authors who wished to dedicate their works to him, he made an exception in the case of Mercy Otis Warren. One of the finest poets and playwrights to emerge from the American Revolution, she was also the wife of James Warren, who had served as a general in the Continental Army during the Revolutionary War. Washington's personal association with her husband may explain his acceptance of Mercy Otis Warren's dedication, but Washington did not say so in his letter of acceptance, which he wrote the first week of June 1790. Instead, he explained, "Although I have ever wished to avoid being drawn into public view more than was essentially necessary for public purposes; yet, on the present occasion duly sensible of the merits of the respectable and amiable writer, I shall not hesitate to accept the intended honor."[24]

Mercy Otis Warren's book appeared later that year under the title *Poems, Dramatic and Miscellaneous*. It consists of two verse tragedies—"The Sack of Rome" and "The Ladies of Castile"—and eighteen poems, most written during the Revolutionary War. Besides being the subject of Warren's effusive dedicatory epistle, Washington received brief mention in two of the poems. In "To Honoria, on Her Journey to Dover, 1777," for example, the speaker of the poem looks forward to the end of the war:

> When Washington, conspicuous o'er the rest,
> By heroes, patriots, and by foes caress'd,
> May quit the field, and court the rural scene.[25]

The lines lack originality—Warren borrowed her language from Dryden's *Virgil*—but Washington appreciated them nonetheless. Once his copy arrived, he replied with a letter of thanks in which he predicted how the book would be received. He felt sure of "its gracious and distinguished reception by the friends of virtue and science."[26]

The week after accepting Mercy Otis Warren's dedication, Washington received a similar request from another author. Preparing to publish the story of his travels through southeastern North America in search of botanical specimens, William Bartram had his friend Robert Parrish visit New York to recruit additional subscribers. He also asked Parrish to meet with President Washington and obtain permission to dedicate the book to him. Washington's friend Samuel Powel wrote a letter of introduction for Parrish, praising Bartram's character, integrity, and intellect. Bartram's bashfulness, Powel hypothesized, prevented him from approaching the president himself.[27]

Equipped with Powel's letter of introduction, Parrish obtained an audience with the president. Washington was familiar with Bartram's botanical research, having visited his Philadelphia garden during the Constitutional Convention. He was happy to subscribe to Bartram's *Travels* but politely refused the dedication. Washington subsequently described his meeting with Parrish to Powel, telling him that he declined the dedication "not with a view to discourage a work of this kind, which I am persuaded, if executed by an able hand, may be very useful among us; but to avoid, with propriety, future applications of this nature, unless where some particular circumstances might induce a compliance."[28] Though refusing the dedication, Washington would become friends with Bartram. After the US government relocated its capital from New York to Philadelphia, Washington would patronize Bartram's garden, ordering many plant specimens from him, which he would cultivate at Mount Vernon.

Around the same time Washington subscribed to Bartram's masterwork, he received a request to subscribe to another book of travels, written by an obscure author who had recently come to New York from Massachusetts: Bartholomew Burges. Royall Tyler, Mercy Otis Warren, and William Bartram are all major figures in the field of early American literature and have received considerable attention from literary historians.[29] Bartholomew Burges, on the other hand, is a shadowy figure, someone who dwelt on the fringes of early American society during his lifetime and who has ever since been in danger of slipping through a rent in the fabric of history.

Having decided to publish a book of travels based on his experiences in India, Burges began soliciting subscribers for *A Series of Indostan Letters*.

The list of subscribers reveals Burges's boldness. He did not hesitate to approach leading figures in the nation. President Washington heads the list, followed by Vice President Adams. Other subscribers who lived in New York included Alexander Hamilton, Chief Justice John Jay, and Samuel Johnson, the president of Columbia University. Readers were impressed by Burges's capacity to elicit subscriptions. One reviewer of *Indostan Letters* commented: "Let not authors complain, that literary merit does not meet with encouragement in America—Bartholomew Burges has published a list of nearly *one thousand subscribers!*"[30]

Burges's name does not appear in Washington's correspondence, so it is unknown precisely how the president obtained his subscription copy of *Indostan Letters*. The work complemented many other books of faraway travel in Washington's library. Burges offers the kind of travel writing Washington had enjoyed since boyhood. He describes the customs, dress, folkways, and traditions in India. He also brings alive the street life: acrobats and actors, fakirs and falconers, mimes and musicians, puppeteers and snake charmers. A grand spectator sport native to India pitted one ornately decorated elephant against another. Burges found the battle of the elephants more engrossing than a Spanish bullfight.

Indostan Letters also contains some practical suggestions. Knowledge of the culture, Burges suggested, would help American merchants better understand how to do business in India. He argued that merchants from the United States should trade directly with India, providing a list of commodities suitable for American trade and discussing where to market which goods. He also included a glossary that would help American merchants understand key terms useful for commerce with India.

The month before Burges published *Indostan Letters*, George Washington received a letter from Jeremy Belknap, who had resumed his history of New Hampshire after an extended hiatus. Having learned that Washington had written to some Vermonters regarding a controversy with their neighboring state, Belknap hoped the president could supply him with copies, or at least abstracts, of them. Upon receiving Belknap's request, Washington asked Tobias Lear to look into the matter. Once Lear clarified the situation for him, Belknap could explain in his history how Washington had helped settle the boundary and smooth out the controversy between Vermont, New York, and New Hampshire.[31]

Belknap finished his second volume of *The History of New-Hampshire* by the end of 1790 and had the third and final volume close enough to completion that he could start soliciting subscribers. Washington subscribed for the three-volume set, expressing his pleasure with Belknap for finally bringing the work to completion.

When the United States relocated its national capital in November 1790, George and Martha Washington re-established the presidential residence in Philadelphia, leasing the home of wealthy financier Robert Morris as the new presidential mansion. The evidence suggests that President Washington used what little spare time he had to immerse himself in Philadelphia's rich literary culture. Among his surviving books is an autographed copy of *A Catalogue of the Books, Belonging to the Library Company of Philadelphia*. In January 1791 the Library Company extended borrowing privileges to the president.

Washington continued to support American writers during his time in Philadelphia, including Jeremy Belknap, who took a break from nonfiction to write *The Foresters*, a satirical allegory of events leading to the founding of the United States, which he published anonymously in 1792. A revised and expanded edition appeared in 1796. Though Washington read few novels, he did add a copy of *The Foresters* to his library. Since his copy does not survive, it is unknown whether it was the first or second edition. The work is not mentioned in his correspondence with Jeremy Belknap, who kept his authorship of *The Foresters* a closely guarded secret.

The first reference to Washington in *The Foresters* concerns his 1753 wilderness trek to present Governor Dinwiddie's message to the French commandant, an indication that the story of Washington's mission was already well established as part of his contemporary reputation. In this allegorical novel the "forest" represents the United States, and the "foresters" are the American people. Belknap personified the states and assigned each an allegorical name. Virginia, for example, is Walter Pipeweed, a name that reveals how closely Virginia was identified with Sir Walter Raleigh and tobacco culture. His grandson George Pipeweed represents George Washington. At one point in the story, Walter Pipeweed sends his grandson, "a smart, active, lively youth, across the hills, with his compliments to the intruders, desiring them to move off, and threatening them with a writ in case of non compliance."[32]

When Belknap revised and republished *The Foresters* in 1796, he brought the story up to date, incorporating several events from Washington's presidency. He especially emphasized the machinations of Edmond Genet, the French minister to the United States who sought to recruit Americans to fight against the British. Throughout his dealings with Teneg, to use Belknap's unimaginative name for Genet, George Pipeweed displays his sense of purpose, his strength of conviction, and his decisive action.[33]

Before he revised and republished *The Foresters*, Belknap began a new multivolume historical work, which would present a series of biographical essays of famous Americans. The first appeared in 1794 as *American Biography; or, An Historical Account of Those Persons Who Have Been Distinguished in America as Adventurers, Statesmen, Philosophers, Divines, Warriors, Authors, and Other Remarkable Characters*. Belknap published this work by subscription but presented a copy of the first volume to President Washington, who then subscribed for the second. Washington would subscribe for a total of four sets.

After Washington left office Belknap stayed in contact with him, providing progress reports and asking for additional help. The last week of May 1798 Belknap thanked him for his kind words about the first volume of *American Biography* and informed him that the second had gone to press and would soon be published.[34] In the meantime Belknap sent him a copy of a fast-day sermon he had delivered earlier that month.

Belknap projected several additional volumes of *American Biography* and asked for Washington's help with some particulars, concluding, "You will excuse, Sir, my importunity, when you consider the necessity of my having the best information and the most original and authentic materials. I never content myself with the streams when the fountain is accessible."[35]

Washington replied, writing one letter in June and a follow-up letter the next month. He promised to ask Samuel Chase, an associate justice of the US Supreme Court, for his help. Washington also agreed to solicit subscribers from Virginia for *American Biography*. His offer for help did not stop there. Washington continued: "If I can render you any service, in procuring materials for your valuable Biography, I shall feel pleasure in doing it. I hope both life and health will be dispensed to you by him, in whose hands all things are, until this and many others of your good works are completed."[36]

Sadly, Washington's best wishes for his life and health were in vain. The Reverend Jeremy Belknap passed away before either of Washington's letters reached him. His son Andrew informed Washington of the melancholy news but assured him that the second volume of *American Biography* was in press and would be published soon. With his letter Andrew Belknap sent another volume for Washington's library at Mount Vernon, a funeral sermon commemorating his father.

Before learning of Belknap's death, Washington did what he had promised. He wrote Justice Chase, asking him to help locate the information Belknap needed. His letter emphasizes the importance of encouraging such literary efforts: "As Mr Belknap is a man of character and abilities, writes well, and seems anxious to be correct in what he gives to the Public, he merits encouragement, and aid from those who have it in their power to afford it."[37] What Washington says about Belknap applies to the other American writers he admired. Throughout both his presidency and his retirement, George Washington recognized many American authors with character and ability. He worked hard to facilitate their literary pursuits.

CHAPTER 18

Official Letters to the Honorable American Congress

Here lived and labored the most felicitous letter writer in history.

J. M. Toner, *George Washington as an Inventor*

Besides encouraging numerous American authors, George Washington also assisted people engaged in other literary ventures. When Philadelphia publisher Mathew Carey launched the *American Museum* in 1787, for example, Washington subscribed to this monthly magazine. He enjoyed it very much, partly for Carey's sympathetic political stance, mainly for the magazine's eclectic contents. In large part Carey drew his articles from previously published works, reprinting such recent American authors as Timothy Dwight, Benjamin Franklin, Francis Hopkinson, David Humphreys, and John Trumbull.[1] Carey gave Washington and other subscribers the opportunity to reread important writings from the American Revolution. His choice of authors represents a groundbreaking effort in the formation of the canon of early American literature.

Searching for possible documents to republish in the *American Museum*, Carey encountered a previously published Washington letter, so he requested his permission to reprint it. An Irishman by birth, Carey had not immigrated to America until after the Revolutionary War, so he was unfamiliar with the background of some of the literature published during the conflict. Washington clued him in, letting Carey know he had not written the letter at all; it was a forgery.[2] By no means was it the only one. A pamphlet volume collecting several personal letters Washington had supposedly written had appeared in London in 1777 under the title *Letters from General Washington to Several of His Friends in the Year 1776*. These forgeries, now known as the "spurious letters," were republished in the United States after copies of the pamphlet crossed the Atlantic. One letter appeared as a separate broadside publication, and Loyalist printer James Rivington republished the rest of them in *Rivington's Gazette*. Editions of the complete volume also appeared in New York and Philadelphia.

The spurious letters were war propaganda of the spiteful kind. They were designed to undermine the trust the American people had placed in General Washington. Though their precise authorship remains a mystery, these letters were written by someone with significant knowledge of Washington's personal life. Specific references to actual events lend an aura of truth to these blatant lies. The letters make Washington seem haughty, indecisive, self-serving: a Loyalist in rebel's clothing. Years after the war he still resented that his personal word had been sullied. He appreciated that Carey had had the courtesy to ask permission before reprinting the letter in question. Carey's request gave Washington a welcome opportunity to explain the nature of these mean-spirited misrepresentations.

Even before he wrote him about the questionable letter, Carey had sought Washington's help with the *American Museum*. When he found it difficult to keep the magazine going, Carey had written him for assistance. Dismayed by the thought of the magazine's failure, Washington said its demise would be "an impeachment on the Understanding of this Country." So far he believed the *American Museum* had been edited with care, taste, and propriety and found it "eminently calculated to disseminate political, agricultural, philosophical and other valuable information."[3] Washington offered to do what he could to keep the *American Museum* afloat. His support helped sustain the magazine long enough to make it a landmark in Carey's career, a career that would establish him as the foremost publisher in Philadelphia during the late eighteenth and early nineteenth century.

As a journalist, Carey bore witness to the emergence of the uniquely American system of party politics. When Washington was president, two dominant political parties emerged. His cabinet members took sides against each other in this burgeoning political conflict. Alexander Hamilton represented the ideals of a central, national government with a strong fiscal policy that became known as Federalism; Thomas Jefferson stood for Republicanism, which recognized the rights and powers of individual states. Much might be said for both sides, Washington believed. Always a mediator, he tried to stay above such divisive politics. In this instance he could not mask his preference for a strong federal government. President Washington became increasingly identified with Federalism.

Though a Washingtonian Federalist at first, Carey would later change his stripes and begin advocating the political views of Jeffersonian Republicanism. Regardless, Carey never forgot Washington's assistance at a crucial moment in his career. In the coming years he would elevate Washington's reputation further. As the publisher of Mason Locke Weems's bestselling *Life of Washington*, Carey would disseminate a biography that captured the popular imagination and that continues to shape the historical perception of George Washington.

In light of Mathew Carey's success as an editor and publisher, his older brother John left their native Dublin for Philadelphia to see what he might accomplish in the bookselling line. Since John Carey had received an excellent classical education, he thought he might capitalize on his learning by buying and selling Greek and Latin classics. Like other attempts to turn knowledge into cash, John Carey's project was doomed from the start. Fewer and fewer people were learning the classics, which were slowly disappearing from the required curriculum of American colleges. In the early 1790s John Carey placed several notices in the Philadelphia papers advertising classical books for sale—with little success.[4] Around the same time another Philadelphia bookseller, the one who was trying to sell William Byrd's classics-laden library, sadly realized that the Byrd books "must remain on hand, or be sold very low and after they are picked the rest will sell no more than waste paper."[5]

Loath to abandon the world of bookselling and publishing, John Carey shifted his attention from the ancient past to recent history, taking on a large-scale editorial project: a documentary history of the Revolutionary War. His brother gave him the idea. Many of the documents that Mathew Carey had published in the *American Museum*, after all, chronicle dramatic moments from the Revolutionary War.

Mathew Carey's use of these documents in his periodical helped him see that they deserved more attention. Describing a key source for the material he reprinted in the *American Museum*, he told Washington: "For want of better resources, I am obliged at present frequently to recur to that corrupted publication, the *Remembrancer*."[6] Denigrating his source, Mathew Carey hoped Washington would select some documents from his own papers to publish in the *American Museum*. Though still willing to help, Washington was far too busy to oblige in this instance.

The specific work Mathew Carey mentioned was the *Remembrancer; or, Impartial Repository of Public Events*, a monthly report of American news that the London publisher John Almon had issued from 1775 to 1784. Though a major source for understanding the war, the *Remembrancer* was riddled with errors, as Mathew Carey recognized. He told his brother to create a new edition of the *Remembrancer*, freshly editing from manuscript the most important letters and state papers of the American Revolution.

John Carey took his brother's advice. In 1792 he solicited subscribers for this new work, placing advertisements in newspapers from Pennsylvania to South Carolina. According to his advertising copy, the *American Remembrancer* would include the proceedings of the Continental Congress, a collection of state papers from its files, letters written by leading figures during the Revolutionary War, and even some supposedly secret journals.[7]

Though Mathew Carey gave his brother the idea, the historical research of William Gordon really made John Carey's project possible. Having worked hard to obtain access to US government documents while researching the history of the American Revolution, Gordon paved the way for a documentary history of the war. John Carey's request for permission to Secretary of State Thomas Jefferson clarifies his debt to Gordon: "Encouraged by a Resolution of Congress, of May 25, 1784, allowing Mr. Gordon a free access to certain papers, now in your Office, I beg leave to request a similar indulgence, if you see no impropriety in granting it. If permitted to copy out such of those papers as no longer require Secresy, I would wish to incorporate them, in their proper places, in an abridgment of the Journals of the old Congress, which I mean to publish as soon as I shall have procured a Sufficient number of subscribers."[8]

Jefferson granted him the requisite permission, and together they settled upon a course of action. Despite all his other responsibilities as secretary of state, Jefferson would continue to assist John Carey with his research. As Carey worked his way through the material, he reconceived the project, narrowing its scope by limiting the number and type of documents he would include. He also jettisoned the title, *American Remembrancer*, which his brother would use for a different purpose.

Whereas John Almon's *Remembrancer* published contemporary documents about the conflict between the United States and Great Britain, that is, documents about the war published during the war, John Carey had conceived the *American Remembrancer* as a historical work, presenting documents about the war a dozen years after its end. Once John Carey abandoned the title, Mathew reconceived the *American Remembrancer*, making it into a set of documents about an ongoing conflict between the United States and Great Britain. He decided to publish serially a set of essays, resolves, and speeches pertaining to Jay's Treaty.

Since the end of the Revolutionary War, tension between Great Britain and the United States had re-escalated. The British were becoming more aggressive and belligerent in their dealings with the new nation. They refused to abandon their forts in the Great Lakes that were now on the American side of the border with Canada. After France declared war against Great Britain in 1793, the British had begun seizing American ships carrying goods to France. Washington commissioned John Jay to negotiate a settlement between the United States and Great Britain.

Jay's Treaty, as it became known, left many Americans, Federalist and Republican, north and south, dissatisfied with its results. While the treaty did provide for the evacuation of British garrisons stationed in the Great Lakes, it contained few British concessions regarding neutral maritime rights. Mathew Carey's *American Remembrancer* detailed the controversy over the treaty in great detail. Upon its completion, the work would fill three thick volumes. Washington would give the *American Remembrancer* a prominent place in his library at Mount Vernon.

Letting his brother have the title *American Remembrancer*, John Carey coined a new title for the collection of Revolutionary documents he planned: *American State Papers, Being a Collection of Original and Authentic Documents Relative to the War between the United States and Great Britain*. He also formulated a new scheme for this edition, which was really quite shrewd. Instead of publishing all the pertinent documents in chronological order, he settled upon a thematic organization, choosing to edit and publish George Washington's wartime correspondence first, exclusive of everything else. A collection of letters by the president of the United States and the most revered man in America, John Carey knew, would attract a much broader segment of the reading public than a collection of historical documents.

Once John Carey had copied numerous documents, he submitted them to Jefferson for his approval. Reading the material, Jefferson marked a few passages in the letters by Washington and his officers that he felt should be withheld from publication. He then submitted the letters with his edits to the president for his final approval. Washington read through them, approving Jefferson's suggestions and identifying a handful of other passages that should be withheld.[9]

Copying all these letters from the originals, Carey was not working alone. He hired two men from the state department to help transcribe the documents he needed. Having decided to publish the book in London, Carey wished to expedite the editorial process.[10] Since he planned to return to Great Britain before the men had finished copying all the documents he wanted, Carey arranged for Jefferson to have the manuscript copies sent to London. Hesitant to send the material directly to Carey, Jefferson mailed the manuscripts, which filled a dozen volumes, to Thomas Pinckney, US minister to Great Britain. Pinckney would hold on to them until Carey called for the manuscript volumes in person. Jefferson warned Pinckney not to share them with anyone else besides Carey: "Should any accident happen to him, be pleased to retain them till further orders as it is not meant to trust the publication to persons unknown."[11]

Carey's edition of Washington's letters came together with minimal input from the president. Beyond reading the edited letters that Jefferson submitted for his approval, Washington did nothing more to assist John Carey. He was too busy running the country to devote time to an edition of his letters. After war between France and Great Britain broke out, Washington held numerous cabinet meetings, which sometimes seemed like the war in microcosm. Fierce battles took place across the conference table with Hamilton supporting the British and Jefferson taking France's side. Edmund Randolph, the attorney general, was little help. Privately Jefferson called him "the poorest Cameleon I ever saw having no color of his own, and reflecting that nearest him. When he is with me he is a whig, when with H[amilton] he is a tory, when with the P[resident] he is what he thinks will please him."[12] As always, Washington was the man in the middle, listening to his cabinet ministers without taking sides, weighing the issues, and ultimately choosing a course of action that reconciled the differing points of view.

The Anglo-French war significantly shaped American foreign policy and, in this instance, resulted in the US Neutrality Proclamation. The international conflict put Washington in a precarious position: he wanted to remain neutral toward both warring nations while maintaining the treaties of alliance and amity established between the United States and France in 1778 as well as the treaty of commerce.

In addition, domestic conflicts were brewing to the west. Violence erupted in western Pennsylvania when revenuers attempted to serve papers on distillers who had not formally registered with the federal government. With fist and musket, the distillers resisted the imposition of federal excise taxes, which formed part of Alexander Hamilton's plan to fund the national debt. Washington denounced the violence and called for protesters to cease and desist. His proclamations fell on deaf ears. As this so-called Whiskey Rebellion continued, Washington himself led twelve thousand troops into the region in October 1794. The distillers did not stand a chance against such an overwhelming force. Besides, they quivered at the thought of taking a shot at President Washington. What citizen would want to go down in history as the man who shot George Washington? The rebellion collapsed without further bloodshed.

While Washington was preparing to face down a coterie of Pennsylvania distillers, the editor of his correspondence was busy bringing the book to completion. John Carey published his two-volume edition of Washington's wartime letters in April 1795. One title page identified the edition as part of *American State Papers*, but the Washington letters had a separate title page: *Official Letters to the Honorable American Congress, Written, During the War between the United Colonies and Great Britain, by His Excellency, George Washington, Commander in Chief of the Continental Forces, Now President of the United States.*

Carey sent Washington two copies, one a handsomely bound presentation copy, the other in boards (a kind of temporary cardboard binding). The binding of the two-volume presentation copy was absolutely sumptuous: tree calf with gilt backs, borders, and edges.[13] The copy in boards contained numerous marginal notes in which Carey explained his editorial decisions. In his cover letter to Washington, Carey described the marginalia in the volume as "some manuscript remarks expressive of the motives that influenced me on the occasion."[14]

Official Letters to the Honorable American Congress begins in June 1775 with the first letter Washington wrote as commander in chief and continues through 1778. John Carey had plenty more material edited and ready to publish, but a significant gap in General Washington's correspondence at the end of 1778 prompted him to stop his initial publication there. He was still planning to continue the edition as long as it remained profitable.[15]

The two-volume edition of Washington's *Official Letters* was well received. William Enfield began his review with the following observations:

> It may perhaps be hazarded as a general remark, that great men are commonly distinguished by a peculiar simplicity of style. Caesar wrote the history of his wars almost without a metaphor: Franklin, whether he wrote as a philosopher [i.e., scientist], as a moralist, or as a politician, always expressed himself with a luminous and dignified simplicity; and this is eminently the literary character of the official letters of Washington, here presented to the public. In this view, they afford an excellent specimen of the proper style for letters or papers on public transactions.[16]

Continuing his comments, Enfield observed that Washington's letters "exhibit a most interesting and wonderful example of the firm intrepidity with which a great and honest mind, engaged in a noble cause, can struggle with difficulties and at last overcome them; and at the same time they furnish an instructive lesson to the world, on the folly of attempting to crush the rising spirit of freedom."[17]

Enfield's remarks appeared in the *Monthly Review*, a Whig publication that had long expressed sympathy with the American cause. The *Critical Review*, a competing Tory publication, also reviewed *Official Letters* positively. Impressed with Washington's personality, the reviewer thought his letters would appeal to readers in many walks of life. Statesmen and soldiers would find in them "the profound observations of superior genius." Those wishing to understand history could read the work to witness the historical cause-and-effect process. All readers would find instruction and amusement sufficient to let them behold "such singular events, related with all the truth and feelings of the moment, and by the chief actor concerned in that surprising revolution."[18]

The *Critical Review* also praised the literary qualities of these letters:

The style of Washington is that of a superior character, clear and manly, expressing even great events, and profound ideas, with all the simplicity of genius. Firm, collected, pregnant in resources, while affairs are adverse; modest, severe, prepared for any change of fortune, while she smiles; an uniform vigour, an untainted patriotism, distinguish the illustrious writer, and pervade his whole correspondence.[19]

The *British Critic* was more tempered in its remarks. While suggesting that those interested in history would find little new information in this collection, it did praise Washington's literary style. In these letters, the *Critic* observed, he expresses himself with "great elegance and force of language; and with liberality of sentiment, as well as prudence, sagacity, and judgment."[20] The *Critic* was especially impressed by the circumstances of their composition. Though written during times of "imminent danger, difficulty, and distress," the letters are "remarkable for precision, force, and correctness; great accuracy of detail, and great perspicuity of arrangement."[21] As all these reviews suggest, *Official Letters* established George Washington's reputation as a major voice in the history of early American literature.

Besides highlighting Washington's literary skill, *Official Letters* also reveals Carey's editorial ability. Closing the first volume with the famous crossing of the Delaware, Carey effectively created a cliffhanger ending that would make readers eager to start the second volume. In the next-to-last letter of the first volume, that of December 27, 1776, Washington reports the army's success to the Continental Congress. Landon Carter's appreciative remarks about Washington's portrayal of the siege of Boston also apply to the letter about crossing the Delaware and attacking the Hessian troops quartered at Trenton. This letter, too, is a *magnum in parvo*, a brief account that captures the bravery, the danger, the grandeur of the experience.

Washington had already proven his ability to describe an icy river crossing in *The Journal of Major George Washington*. He did not play up the dramatic elements in his description of this new wintertime river crossing in the letter to the Continental Congress. He did mention the chunks of ice in the river early on, mainly to explain why it took him and his men so long to cross. It was three o'clock in the morning before they transported all the artillery across and four by the time the men began their march. Washington's depiction of the momentous events creates considerable tension. Would the delay stop the American troops from approaching Trenton under the cloak of darkness? Would it give the Hessians time to prepare for the American assault?

Returning to the icy, treacherous conditions toward the end of the letter, Washington did so mainly to praise the dedication of the men who served under him:

> In justice to the officers and men, I must add, that their behavior upon this occasion reflects the highest honor upon them. The difficulty of passing the river in a very severe night, and their march through a violent storm of snow and hail, did not in the least abate their ardor; but, when they came to the charge, each seemed to vie with the other in pressing forward; and were I to give a preference to any particular corps, I should do great injustice to the others.[22]

In the last letter of the first volume, that of December 29, Washington is on the verge of attempting a second crossing of the Delaware. Carey may have ended the volume here because he had reached the end of 1776, but this ending also contributes to the drama, leaving Washington after one victory about to attempt another, the outcome of which remains unknown as the first volume comes to a close.

Publishing Washington's letters in London, Carey edited them more heavily than he would have edited them had he published them in the United States. He omitted some passages from the letters he thought might offend British readers. Carey need not have worried. The editorial omissions actually had the opposite effect, as the response of one reader suggests. One day Carey happened to have coffee in London with a man who was quite knowledgeable when it came to American affairs. The man had read Washington's *Official Letters*, but, since Carey kept his editorship anonymous, the man was unaware of his role in their publication. He criticized the editor of the letters for having "suppressed a number of the most interesting passages, and presented the public with little better than the chaff."[23]

This irate reader recalled some passages the editor had purposely omitted. Carey was so flabbergasted that he cut short their conversation and never learned how this mystery man knew about passages from letters that Carey had read in manuscript yet excluded from his edition. The explanation may be simpler than Carey realized. William Gordon had used many of the same Washington letters in *The History of the Rise, Progress, and Establishment of the Independence of the United States of America*. Furthermore, Gordon had been bolder in his use of the documents, quoting the best parts of some letters without overthinking the propriety of his quotations. Carey's coffeehouse acquaintance obviously knew Gordon's history. He recognized passages Carey omitted because Gordon had already quoted them.

Though Carey sympathized with the American cause, his decision to publish Washington's *Official Letters* in London reflects an underlying British bias. An Irishman by birth, Carey considered London the center of the English-speaking world and the capital of English book publishing. Like William Gordon before him, Carey believed the best way to establish himself and his book would be to publish it in London. For all his shrewdness in publishing a collection of Washington's letters, he seems to have ignored the fact that the book would appeal much more to American readers than to British ones.

Carey apparently assumed that American booksellers would import his edition and sell it to their customers. He did not foresee that American publishers could reprint the work for less than it would cost to import his London edition. Furthermore, they would not have to pay him any royalties or permission fees for reprinting his edition. Since there was no international copyright, American publishers were free to reprint Washington's *Official Letters* without remunerating its editor. One Boston edition appeared before the end of 1795, with a second the following year. A New York edition appeared in 1796.

Sales of the London edition did not encourage Carey to continue either the collection of Washington letters or *American State Papers*. In the preface to the first volume of *Official Letters*, he looked forward to future volumes, explaining to readers that if the initial volumes met with a favorable reception, he would edit and publish additional ones, presenting "a variety of interesting pieces penned by the leaders and principal agents in the American Revolution."[24] Disappointed with the commercial failure of *Official Letters*, Carey discontinued *American State Papers* altogether.

The commercial success of the American reprints, on the other hand, encouraged publishers in the United States to issue other compilations of Washington letters. Unwittingly, John Carey contributed to these unauthorized sequels. His promise of further volumes gave American publishers the opportunity to promote alternate editions of Washington letters, making the new releases seem like the sequels Carey had promised.

In December 1795 a Philadelphia publisher issued *Letters from General Washington to Several of His Friends, in June and July 1776, in Which Is Set Forth, an Interesting View of American Politics, at that All-Important Period*. According to its title page, this pamphlet was "Republished at the Federal Press," but this imprint is a ruse. The work was printed by none other than Benjamin Franklin Bache, who had taken it upon himself to lead the attack on Washington's administration. Over time Bache's critiques of the president in the *Aurora* grew more and more radical and erratic. This pamphlet represents another salvo in Bache's incessant barrage. Its fictitious imprint gives the impression that the Federalists had approved and sanctioned the publication of these letters.

What Bache published was actually a reprint of the spurious letters originally issued as anti-American propaganda during the war. Identifying the volume as a republication of an out-of-print work in his preface, Bache deliberately linked this collection with Carey's, asserting that Washington's personal correspondence would furnish "an interesting appendix to the Official Letters of General Washington, which have lately made their appearance."[25]

Bache released *Letters from General Washington* in the aftermath of Jay's Treaty. He had been the one who first made the terms of Jay's Treaty public in early 1795. Incensed by the treaty, Bache sought to expose what he perceived as its inherent dangers.[26] He designed this edition to create further animosity, demonstrating the affection the president supposedly had for England, which Jay's Treaty seemed to validate.

Another edition of Washington letters appeared the following year under the title *Epistles Domestic, Confidential, and Official*. James Rivington issued this collection, though without his imprint. Like Bache, Rivington associated his edition with Carey's *Official Letters*. The main text reprinted the same spurious letters Bache had reprinted, and a lengthy appendix reprinted many of Washington's previously published letters.

Washington could not let this misleading collection pass without comment. Once *Epistles Domestic, Confidential, and Official* appeared, he denounced the fraudulent collection in a letter to Timothy Pickering, the current secretary of state. Pickering published Washington's letter in the *United States Gazette*. It was subsequently printed as a small broadside—the same size as an octavo page—and bound with some copies of the book.[27]

After a London edition of *Epistles Domestic, Confidential, and Official* appeared, John Carey could not ignore the collection either. Reviewing the book anonymously for the September 1796 issue of the *Critical Review*, he denounced the collection of domestic letters as a forgery. To be sure, he could recognize political propaganda when he saw it. These letters, Carey surmised, were assembled by Washington's opponents "to mislead the new generation that has sprung up since the war, and the numerous emigrants who have settled in America within the last twenty years."[28] Carey sent Washington a copy of the *Critical Review* containing his notice of *Epistles Domestic, Confidential, and Official.* Washington acknowledged Carey's gift, inscribing a note to that effect into the issue, which he added to his excellent collection of periodicals at Mount Vernon.

Though Carey never turned a profit with *Official Letters to the Honorable American Congress*, he deserves credit for assembling the letters that comprise the edition. The first published collection of Washington's correspondence, *Official Letters* looked forward to the numerous multivolume editions of Washington's letters and papers that have since appeared. When Jared Sparks outlined his plan for an extensive edition of Washington's writings in the nineteenth century, he acknowledged Carey's *Official Letters* as his predecessor. And the editors of the ongoing edition of *The Papers of George Washington* owe a debt to John Carey for his pioneering editorial work.[29]

Before Sparks published his edition of Washington's papers, *Official Letters* continued to be read and cited. The Reverend Dr. William Linn, for example, read the letters as a gauge of Washington's character. Though the letters chronicled Washington's wartime activities, Linn found that they reflected his statesmanship as well. *Official Letters* reminded a Maryland reader of an earlier battlefield commander, the prominent leader of the Wars of Scottish Independence. This reader observed that the letters Washington wrote from New York in September 1776 evoked the somber mood among the Continental troops: "Sir William Wallace, in the most gloomy era of his ill-fated country, never encountered greater difficulties than did Washington at this period, and no man can peruse his official letters to Congress of that date, without bowing in unspeakable reverence at the moral sublimity of his character."[30]

Others read the edition for different purposes. Historian John Adolphus used *Official Letters* to learn the background of the Revolutionary War as he wrote his *History of England.* Etymologist John Pickering scrutinized Carey's edition with an eye toward understanding Washington's use of language. Pickering recognized General Washington's willingness to add new words to the English language when current ones were inadequate. And Adjutant General Thomas H. Cushing read Washington's *Official Letters* to help conduct the War of 1812, to understand, for example, the proper proportion of army officers to enlisted men.[31]

For many book collectors of the time, *Official Letters to the Honorable American Congress* possessed the quality of a talisman. It gave them a little piece of Washington all their own. From medals to mezzotints, Washington memorabilia adorned American homes in the late eighteenth and early nineteenth centuries. In terms of both symbolic and practical value, a book of his writings could do more than any of these decorative keepsakes. It provided Washington's words, words he had written himself, words that expressed his personality, his belief in the new nation, his confidence in his men, and his strength of character. Washington's wartime letters demonstrate that he knew what he had to do as commander in chief, what Congress had to do to support the war, and what it took to win the war and establish the nation on a firm footing.

CHAPTER 19

Farewell Address

Farewell, and stand fast.
William Shakespeare,
Henry IV, Part I

Books form an essential part of the history of the US presidency. In the nineteenth century, the campaign biography emerged as a vital method of promoting presidential candidates. These idealized biographies purportedly showed the American people the manner of man they were electing president. Books authored by presidential candidates have occasionally aided their election as well. Think of such bestsellers as John F. Kennedy's *Profiles in Courage* or Barack Obama's *Audacity of Hope.* Before either the campaign biography or the candidate book emerged to promote the policies and personalities of those running for president, American readers sought whatever books they could to learn more about whom they were electing. Around the time of Thomas Jefferson's election to the presidency, for example, contemporary publishers issued new editions of *Notes on the State of Virginia.* Jefferson had written this book nearly two decades before his election to the presidency, but many Americans read it to learn more about the man who would be president.

Books played a part in Washington's presidency as well. In 1796, he could have run for a third term as president. The Twenty-Second Amendment to the Constitution, which limited a president to two terms, would not be ratified until 1951. Had he wanted to run for a third term, Washington could have found few better promotional tools than John Carey's edition of *Official Letters.* But he had no intention of running. To inform voters of his decision not to run for a third term, Washington decided to publish an address in the newspapers, which would also appear in book form. This work, now known as his *Farewell Address*, could be characterized as an anti-campaign book. In no uncertain terms, President Washington let the American people know he would not seek election to a third term.

Washington had considered retirement in 1792, the previous election year, but he realized the nation still needed his leadership. Before making his decision to stay for a second term, he asked James Madison to draft a farewell address for him. He liked what Madison had written so much that he held on to the address, thinking he might have the chance to use it in the future. Four years later Washington realized that Madison's text now required considerable revision, so he approached Alexander Hamilton for help. Though Hamilton had stepped down as secretary of the treasury, he remained the president's most trusted advisor. Washington sent Hamilton a copy of the address Madison had drafted, suggesting two possible courses of action. Hamilton could revise and update Madison's text, or he could draft a new address from scratch. Hamilton preferred the second course but decided it might be best to prepare the two versions Washington requested and let him choose which he preferred.[1]

By no means did Washington give Hamilton free reign to write whatever he wished. He provided him with a set of guidelines that not only stipulated the contents of the address but also suggested the tone and diction: "My wish is, that the whole may appear in a plain stile;—and be handed to the public in an honest;—unaffected;—simple garb."[2] With his emphasis on a plain style, Washington echoes words vital to American literature since early colonial days. In *A Description of New England*, Captain John Smith had asked his readers for pardon "if I chance to be too plaine, or tedious in relating my knowledge for plaine mens satisfaction." Similarly, William Bradford emphasizes in *Of Plymouth Plantation* that he had written his history "in a plain style, with singular regard unto the simple truth in all things."[3]

Having exerted such a powerful impact on the final version of the farewell address, Washington has sometimes been credited with its authorship. Washington conceived the work; Hamilton took the responsibility for putting the words on the page. Hamilton did not include everything the president wanted him to include. Washington's long list of suggestions contained some that seemed petty and spiteful to Hamilton. Understanding that the very first farewell address by a US president would be a work of lasting historical importance, he purged it of such pettiness.

Washington began planning his new farewell address in May 1796. He hoped to present it to the public in time to assure his name would not appear among the candidates for the next presidential election. Hamilton agreed to finish writing the address in a matter of months. While spending part of the summer at Mount Vernon, Washington eagerly awaited the arrival of Hamilton's draft. In early August he received two versions from his trusted advisor, the revised and expanded Madison text and Hamilton's newly written address. Washington quickly saw the superiority of Hamilton's version and chose it over the revised Madison text.

He did not accept Hamilton's version as it stood. Though chock-full of good stuff, it was much too long. It would not work without significant cutting. Washington explained to Hamilton: "All the columns of a large Gazette would scarcely, I conceive, contain the present draught."[4] Washington did not mention a large gazette solely as a means of illustrating the length of Hamilton's draft. Rather, he intended to publish the work as a newspaper article. Though it is usually called an address, Washington would not present the work orally. Wanting to direct his remarks to the general public, not their elected representatives in Congress, Washington designed the address, as he told Hamilton, "for the Yeomanry of this Country."[5] The printed word, he decided, would provide the best way to say goodbye to the American people. Hamilton trimmed the text to make it fit a single newspaper issue and sent the revised version to Washington.

On Friday, September 16, Washington dispatched Tobias Lear to pay a visit to printer and newspaper editor David Claypoole. Once Lear said that the president wished to see him, Claypoole left his print shop for the executive mansion, where he found the president alone. Washington let him know he was leaving office at the end of his second term and wished to publish a farewell address to the American people in his newspaper, *Claypoole's American Daily Advertiser*. Flattered that Washington had chosen his paper to announce the resignation, Claypoole assumed the president's choice was a sign that he appreciated the way he conducted his paper. Agreeing with Claypoole's assumption, Washington nodded and then asked how soon he could publish the address. Once the printer told the president that he could publish it whenever he wanted, they agreed to issue it on Monday, September 19.[6]

Lear brought the manuscript of the farewell address to Claypoole's print shop Saturday morning. Claypoole set the manuscript in type and struck some proof sheets, which he brought to Washington, who corrected the proofs himself. Once he was finished with the manuscript, Claypoole came to the executive mansion to return it. As he spoke with the president, he got up the gumption to ask him a favor. Could he keep the manuscript? Washington was happy to let him have it. Few printers have been so well rewarded for their work.[7]

After it appeared in *Claypoole's American Daily Advertiser* that Monday, Washington's farewell address was quickly reprinted in newspapers throughout the nation in the coming days and weeks. In Philadelphia, some newspapers reprinted the address the same day it appeared in *Claypoole's*. Andrew Brown, for example, included it in the September 19 issue of the *Philadelphia Gazette*. Jacob Hiltzheimer, whose diary provides a vital record of the period of Washington's presidency, read the farewell address in the *Philadelphia Gazette* and recorded his impressions: "The advice he gives to the nation I hope will be remembered by all good citizens to the end of time." William V. Murray, who read Washington's address in a Maryland paper later that week, said about it, "The effect of his piece has been immense. . . . The men, who can think at all, feel and acknowledge the force of his advice and maxims."[8]

Besides reprinting the address in their newspapers, printers from Lancaster, Pennsylvania, to Lansingburgh, New York, also issued it in pamphlet form.[9] Publishers of small-format newspapers often could not fit the entire address within the columns of a single paper. Some subdivided it into two installments, but many hesitated to destroy the work's strength and power by splitting it. Instead, they issued it in pamphlet form. When Benjamin Bache reprinted it in the *Aurora*, he avoided editorializing, but he did split the address into two parts, a reflection of his disrespect for Washington. Other publishers reprinted it in their papers first and then released the address as a pamphlet.

The printers faced a tricky problem as they attempted to issue the work separately. Neither Washington nor Hamilton had titled it *Farewell Address*. That title would not be coined until later. In *Claypoole's* the address appeared under the heading "To the People of the United States," but this heading would not do as the title of a pamphlet.

Printers were left to their own devices to devise titles for the work. Samuel Cushing, a printer in Amherst, New Hampshire, took the straightforward approach. Having published the address as "The President's Resignation" in the *Village Messenger*, he subsequently issued a pamphlet edition titled *The President's Address to the People of the United States, on His Declining Another Election*.[10] New York printer James Oram titled his edition *Resignation of His Excellency George Washington* but used a catchier phrase from the address as the pamphlet's running head: "The Disinterested Warnings of a Parting Friend."

In Newburyport, Massachusetts, William Barrett published the work under the title, *President Washington's Resignation, and Address to the Citizens of the United States*. Boston printer John Russell titled his edition *The Legacy of the Father of His Country*. This title emphasized the didactic nature of Washington's text. Besides announcing his resignation, the address provided advice for the nation and its people. As Barrett said in an advertisement for his edition: "This valuable legacy of good advice, which he has bequeathed on his departure from public life—the result of long experience, and expressed in the language of firmness and paternal affection, should, as we have no doubt it will, be engraven deeply on the minds of his fellow citizens, and transmitted with their sanction and approbation to their posterity."[11]

Many printers took pains to make their pamphlet editions examples of fine bookmanship. When he announced the publication of *The Legacy of the Father of His Country*, John Russell said it would be "elegantly printed, with a new type, on vellum paper." According to Russell's advertising copy, the pamphlet would be "a pretty specimen of American Arts—the type, paper, ink, and workmanship being wholly American—and which must if possible, enhance its value in the esteem of the friends to our country's progress in the Arts."[12]

As part of *The Legacy of the Father of His Country*, Russell included a preface justifying the reprint and characterizing the work. Since it had already appeared in newspapers across the nation, a pamphlet edition might not seem necessary, but, Russell assured his readers, it was: "Whoever contemplates, for a moment, the pure morality and political principles, the ardent patriotism, and useful information, contained in *all* the addresses of our endeared General in War, and President in Peace; and considers that this may be his valedictory, will readily see the propriety of its taking a form less perishable than the pages of a Gazette." Handsomely printed pamphlet editions, Russell explained, were more likely to preserve Washington's words from "the ruin of time."[13] Russell almost makes the purchase of the pamphlet a matter of civic duty. The more copies that are preserved, the more widely Washington's message will be disseminated and the more likely it will be preserved for future generations.

Though all these pamphlet reprints seem designed to capitalize on Washington's farewell address, their printers were not solely motivated by greed. Gauging by the comments in their prefaces and advertisements, they were also motivated by altruism. The printers wanted to produce handsome keepsakes to make sure Washington's farewell words would endure. The hyperbolic language they used to describe the work reinforces its lasting qualities. Speaking about Russell's edition, one extravagant reader said, "It is a valuable fund of truly republican and patriotic advice, and ought to be bound with the richest binding, covered with diamonds inlaid in gold, and grace the shelf of every library." An advertisement for another Boston edition said it was "Worthy a Page of Marble—and a Cover of Gold!"[14]

Washington's farewell address appeared in other forms as well. Some printers issued it as a broadside suitable for framing. An advertisement in the *Albany Gazette* announced: "The President's Address in gilt frames— Gentlemen who wish to be supplied with it, in this form, are requested to send their names, in the course of this week, to Webster's Bookstore."[15] Framed and hanging on the wall, Washington's address could be read time and again. And when it was not being read, its presence in the home still served as inspiration. Hanging on a wall inside the home, the farewell address took on the qualities of a talisman.

In both pamphlet and broadside form, Washington's farewell address was sold on city streets throughout the nation. While walking down Broadway in New York with his wife one day, Alexander Hamilton encountered an old soldier hawking copies of the address. Hamilton took pity on the tattered man and bought a copy, whereupon he said to his wife, "That man does not know he has asked me to purchase my own work."[16] Hamilton's old soldier recognized a hot commodity when he saw it. In short, Washington's farewell address was the bestseller of 1796.

Contemporary almanacs also reprinted Washington's address. Since it originally appeared in September, that is, shortly before the almanacs for the following year were printed, some almanac makers found it appropriate to include its text in their works. That way people could read and reread the address throughout the following year. For example, Hugh Gaine included Washington's farewell address in his almanac, *Gaine's New-York Pocket Almanack for the Year 1797*. With a copy of Gaine's almanac tucked inside a coat pocket, New Yorkers could reread Washington's address whenever they had a little spare time on their hands.

Whereas Russell argued that pamphlets were more lasting than newspapers, some of his contemporaries worried that newspapers, pamphlets, broadsides, and almanacs were all too ephemeral to assure the survival of Washington's address. They found yet another way to reprint it in a more lasting form. On November 5, 1796, the New York state senate resolved "That the said Address be inserted in the Journal of this Senate, as a perpetual testimony of our respect for the man, and our approbation of his sentiments." The New York Assembly followed suit, resolving "That the patriot Address of George Washington, President of the United States, to the People of the said States, be entered at length upon the Journals of this House, as a memorial, to future ages, of their unabated affection to that illustrious Citizen, and of the high sense of the eminent and disinterested services, which he has rendered his country."[17]

Legislators from several other states—Delaware, Maryland, Massachusetts, New Jersey—resolved to print Washington's address as part of their proceedings.[18] Aware that printed editions of legislative proceedings had a lasting quality that some other print genres lacked, the legislators from all these states could rest assured that they had preserved Washington's address for future generations by including it in their proceedings. Rhode Island legislators arranged to have Washington's address printed as part of the front matter of the 1798 edition of its state laws, along with the Declaration of Independence and the US Constitution. Washington's *Farewell Address* has been called "one of the great American documents." Its placement with the Declaration and the Constitution affirms its lofty status as a major national document.[19]

Readers obtained copies of the pamphlet not only to read, preserve, and perpetuate Washington's words but also to possess them. The experience of Allan Melvill (Herman's father) provides an example of what the farewell address meant to contemporary readers. Then a teenaged student at Amherst Academy, he obtained a copy of Samuel Cushing's edition, *The President's Address to the People*.[20] Melvill may have purchased this pamphlet, but he could have received it as a gift. All the students at another New Hampshire school, Phillips Exeter Academy, received free copies of the Exeter edition of Washington's *Farewell Address*.[21]

Allan Melvill's acquisition of the Amherst edition is consistent with his personality and taste. Not only did he venerate the heroes of the Revolutionary War, he also read numerous conduct books instructing him on proper behavior. Washington's inspiring words enhanced Allan Melvill's veneration for the Father of His Country and gave him advice regarding how future generations of American citizens should behave. Many contemporary readers of the *Farewell Address* characterized it as a conduct book. Senator George Cabot, for one, referred to the work as the "President's advice," and the editor of the *New-Jersey Journal* observed, "This address resembles the fond advice of a dying parent to his beloved children." Allan Melvill read the work often enough that he could repeat snippets of it by heart.[22]

Though Washington himself did not read the address aloud, it would be read aloud countless times in the coming years: it became a standard text in the American schoolboy's repertoire. At the end of each term, students would typically recite inspiring texts from their classroom readers. Almost as soon as Washington's address appeared in the newspapers, the textbook makers recognized its potential. Before the year was out, in fact, anthologists began including the work in their compilations. In Hudson, New York, the Reverend Bildad Barney included the complete text of

Washington's address in *An Introduction to the Art of Reading*, a textbook he published in late 1796.[23]

Washington's *Farewell Address* remains an inspiration. Instead of talking down to the American citizens, he addresses them eye to eye. Speaking in the persona of a departing friend, he demonstrates that he knows how they feel and shares their deepest convictions. Acknowledging their passion for political freedom, he says that he hardly needs to say anything. The love of liberty is already deeply ingrained within the American psyche. The US government symbolizes that liberty. Protecting government requires vigilance. National unity is his pre-eminent theme. People must cherish their national identity, which should take precedence over any local identity. We are Americans first and New Englanders, New Yorkers, Virginians, or Georgians second.

Continuing his argument, Washington stresses how the different parts of the nation are interdependent. The commerce of the North, for example, provides an outlet for the agricultural products of the South. Identifying North and South as two different parts of the nation, Washington reinforces an already well-established distinction. He proceeds to make a more forward-thinking geographical distinction: East and West. Kentucky and Tennessee had become states during his presidency, and Washington saw that the future of the West was the future of the nation. The further development of the East would depend upon the future development of the West, which would provide a "valuable vent" for the commodities the East imported from abroad or manufactured at home.

Washington's address also stresses the power of the US Constitution and the importance of following it. In addition, it emphasizes the value of maintaining peace and harmony with all nations. Americans should guard against foreign influence, sustaining their national identity as an example of "people always guided by an exalted justice and benevolence." Washington concludes by reinforcing his identity with his fellow citizens, telling them how much he has been looking forward to living as one of them: "I anticipate with pleasing expectation that retreat, in which I promise myself to realize, without alloy, the sweet enjoyment of partaking, in the midst of my fellow citizens, the benign influence of good Laws under a free government—the ever favourite object of my heart, and the happy reward, as I trust, of our mutual cares, labours and dangers."[24]

On September 19, the day David Claypoole first issued the farewell address in his newspaper, George and Martha Washington left Philadelphia to return to Mount Vernon for a brief visit. Throughout his presidency they had typically returned home around this time of year. By returning to Mount Vernon that fall, Washington escaped all the questions about his retirement—and all the pleas for him to remain president for a third term.

After returning to Philadelphia, one day Washington happened to have dinner with Robert and Henrietta Liston, the British minister to the United States and his wife. The Listons had only just arrived in the United States that May. Though Liston had not looked forward to the appointment beforehand, Washington had proven to be an unexpected delight. Both he and his wife were thoroughly impressed with the American president. Robert Liston wrote home, "I have read much about this great man; but no passage in his history prepared me to see such commanding dignity in person and behavior."[25] They, too, had been hoping Washington would serve a third term. When Henrietta Liston told him about their desire for him to stay in office, Washington smiled and asked if she remembered the story of the archbishop of Granada in *Gil Blas*.[26]

Fearing the debilitating effects of old age on his intellect, the archbishop asks Gil Blas, his servant, to let him know when the quality of his sermons begins to deteriorate, assuring him that his frankness would be rewarded. Once the archbishop suffers a stroke and his mind becomes impaired, his sermons appreciably decline. As gingerly as possible, Gil Blas informs his eminence that his sermons have deteriorated. Refusing to acknowledge his diminishing intellectual capacity, the archbishop flies into a rage and dismisses Gil Blas for insubordination.

"I feared," Washington told Henrietta Liston, "that the same might happen to me."

Washington need not have worried. The quality of his public speeches had in no way declined during the course of his presidency, as his last speech to Congress demonstrates. On Wednesday, December 7, 1796, President Washington delivered his final speech to Congress. The gallery was jam-packed with spectators, who met Washington's entrance into Congress Hall with awe. Adorned in a black velvet suit with his long sword at his side, Washington made an impressive sight—as he knew he would.[27] While sharing several points of contact with the farewell address, this speech took a somewhat different approach. Whereas his farewell address had offered many general guidelines for governing the nation to assure its survival, his last speech to Congress offered some practical suggestions.

In the farewell address, for example, Washington told people to promote "institutions for the general diffusion of knowledge."[28] He had wanted to develop this idea further in the farewell address, to emphasize the importance of establishing a national university "where the Youth from *all parts* of the United States might receive the polish of Erudition in the Arts, Sciences and Belle Letters."[29] Hamilton recommended that the speech to Congress, rather than the farewell address, would be a better place to express his educational scheme. After some thought Washington took Hamilton's advice.[30]

With his last speech to Congress the president stressed the importance of establishing both a military academy and a national university. A flourishing state of the arts and sciences, he explained, would contribute to the material prosperity and reputation of the United States. A national university could contribute to "the assimilation of the principles, opinions and manners of our countrymen, by the common education of a portion of our youth from every quarter." He continued: "The more homogeneous our citizens can be made in these particulars, the greater will be our prospect of permanent union; and a primary object of such a national institution should be the education of our youth in the science of government."[31]

Schools were not the only institutions President Washington recommended in his final speech to Congress. Emphasizing the importance of agriculture to the nation, he urged the establishment of a board of agriculture. Boards devoted to other fields of useful knowledge could also be established. Washington explained that "the establishment of Boards, composed of proper characters, charged with collecting and diffusing information, and enabled by premiums and small pecuniary aids" could "encourage and assist a spirit of discovery and improvement."[32]

Once he had presented his last speech to Congress, it, too, was published in pamphlet form. In no way did it achieve a level of status commensurate with his farewell address. Some readers did recognize that the two works complemented one another. The Philadelphia printing duo of Henry Sweitzer and John Ormond, for example, published the address and the speech together under the title *Columbia's Legacy*.

The 1796 election took place shortly after Washington delivered his last speech to Congress. The first contested presidential election in American history, this election pitted the Federalists against the Republicans. Though the American people had enjoyed the message of national unity Washington had conveyed in his *Farewell Address*, it did not seem to affect their behavior when it came to party politics. The 1796 election proved to be a heated contest. With seventy-one electoral votes, John Adams edged out Thomas Jefferson, who received sixty-eight electoral votes. As the government was then organized, the candidate who came in second place in the balloting would serve as vice president.

With John Adams's election to the presidency Washington could relax and enjoy his final few months in office before going home to Mount Vernon. Previously, at the end of both the Revolutionary War and the Constitutional Convention, Washington had stocked up on reading material, buying many new books before returning home. At the end of his presidency, he hardly needed to do so. During his two terms in office, he had accumulated far more books than he had had time to read as president. Some he had purchased himself. Others he had subscribed to as a way of encouraging the development of American literature. Many he had received as presentation copies from their authors. He looked forward to reading many of these unread books in his retirement.[33]

Some of the books Washington obtained as president indicate that as part of his future reading he would return to a literary genre that had been one of his favorites in the past: travel literature. Thomas Forrest, an explorer and navigator who had worked for the East India Company since the 1750s, sent Washington a copy of his *Voyage from Calcutta to the Mergui Archipelago*, which provided much detail about navigating the Bay of Bengal.[34] Washington received other works about the East Indies. He obtained a copy of Captain Matthew Jenour's *Route to India* and, best of all, William Bligh's *Narrative of the Mutiny, on Board his Britannic Majesty's Ship Bounty*.

Though Bligh is best remembered as a captain whose supposed cruelty had led to one of the most famous mutinies in the history of the British navy, his navigational skill and powers of endurance were extraordinary. After Fletcher Christian and his fellow mutineers left him and his few loyal crew members in an open boat in the middle of the Pacific, Bligh safely navigated the craft to Timor, a distance of some 3,500 miles. In *Narrative of the Mutiny*, Bligh relates his personal story in vivid detail.

Filled with technical details about navigation, the works of Forrest and Jenour lack the excitement of Bligh's narrative, but they do contain a few memorable moments. One contemporary reviewer suggested Captain Jenour provided just the kind of reading material someone might enjoy in retirement. Shortly after he retired, Washington informed a correspondent that he would no longer travel beyond a twenty-mile radius of his home.[35] His library would let him travel the world without leaving his home. Jenour's *Route to India*, the reviewer suggested, could "afford some amusement to those who are content to travel to India *by the fire-side*."[36]

Washington's last few weeks in office seemed like little more than a series of celebrations. February 22, of course, was Washington's birthday. Throughout his administration, the local clergymen, first in New York and then in Philadelphia, had made a point of visiting President

Washington en masse to wish him a happy birthday. This year he celebrated his sixty-fifth birthday, meaning that he was now entering his sixty-sixth year. The Reverend Ashbel Green, the Presbyterian minister who served as chaplain to the US Congress, recorded the event for posterity. Green found that on this occasion the president spoke with "singular vivacity."[37]

"Gentlemen, I feel the weight of years," Washington said to the clergymen. "I take a pair of sixes on my shoulders this day."

Though Green recorded the president's words, he didn't get his joke. The Reverend Green understood that the pair of sixes referred to Washington's age, but he did not know what the president meant by the word "sixes." Washington was referring to six-pounder guns. To a spiritual man like Green, the idea of a man carrying a couple of cannon around on his shoulders was unimaginable—but not to Washington.

On Friday, March 3, the day before John Adams was inaugurated, Washington hosted his last dinner party as president. It was a gala affair attended by many of the leading citizens in the nation. President-Elect Adams and his wife, Abigail, attended. So did Vice President–Elect Jefferson. The cabinet members were there, and so were several foreign ministers and their wives, including Robert and Henrietta Liston. Bishop William White left the fullest account of the occasion.[38] Hilarity prevailed during dinner. Afterward, the dinner guests suddenly grew quiet as Washington, having filled his glass, stood up and lifted it to toast his company. He spoke with a smile on his face.

"Ladies and gentlemen," he began, "this is the last time I shall drink your health as a public man. I do it with sincerity, and wishing you all possible happiness."

Bishop White looked around at the company. Washington's guests were visibly moved by his words. Henrietta Liston had tears running down her cheeks. She was not the only one.

CHAPTER 20

Home at Last

> Home is the resort
> Of love, of joy, of peace and plenty, where
> Supporting, and supported, polish'd friends,
> And dear relations mingle into bliss.
> James Thomson, *The Seasons*

Winter was slow to leave Philadelphia in 1797, much to the chagrin of George and Martha Washington. After John Adams's inauguration, they waited a few more days for the weather to clear before starting back to Mount Vernon. Washington used the spare time to catch up on his correspondence. On Monday, March 6, he wrote Sir John Sinclair, informing him that he was leaving Philadelphia "for a more tranquil theatre, and for the indulgence of rural pursuits." The purpose of this particular letter was to send Sinclair a copy of Richard Peters's *Agricultural Enquiries on Plaister of Paris* and some related pamphlets. In Washington's words, Peters was "one of the most intelligent, and best practical, as well as theoretical farmers we have." This pamphlet formed the fullest discussion of gypsum as a fertilizer Washington had ever read. Without naming the titles of the other enclosed pamphlets, he said that the agricultural writers in "this infant country" were finally providing essays that could contribute to the advancement of agricultural science.[1] Since Sinclair had been sending him numerous British books and pamphlets on the subject for the past five years, Washington was pleased to respond in kind.

Like Washington, Sinclair was dedicated to the advancement of useful knowledge, a goal he had been actively pursuing since a lengthy tour of

Europe in the mid-1780s. On his trip Sinclair had developed a passion for discovering and disseminating practical information in many fields of knowledge, including and especially agriculture. Returning to his native Scotland in 1790, he initiated extensive surveys of the economy, geography, history, and social conditions of every Scottish parish, collectively designed to serve as a guide for future development. A massive undertaking, his *Statistical Account of Scotland* would eventually fill twenty-one volumes. Huge as it was, this project could not exhaust Sinclair's almost limitless energies. In the coming years he founded organizations and initiated projects for the public good. In 1791, for example, he launched the British Wool Society, an organization founded to develop the quality of sheep throughout Great Britain.[2]

In 1793 Sinclair established the British Board of Agriculture. He served as its president but refused a salary, magnanimously devoting what he would have been paid to useful projects instead. Arthur Young, another prominent agricultural writer who corresponded with Washington, served as secretary. The Board of Agriculture conducted experiments, disseminated pertinent information, and sponsored legislation to benefit agricultural development. Under its auspices Sinclair initiated the General Views series, a set of county surveys throughout Great Britain. To spread his ideas beyond the British Isles, he corresponded with influential figures he met on his European tour and boldly contacted many world leaders, including George Washington.

Sinclair first wrote President Washington in May 1792, introducing himself, asking about wool production in the United States, and sending some of his latest publications. Washington was grateful for the books. Precisely which titles Sinclair sent that year are uncertain, but when he edited and published his correspondence toward the end of his life, he provided some context. Upon starting his *Statistical Account of Scotland*, Sinclair had resolved to send copies of the first volumes to "several distinguished characters in foreign countries."[3]

The initial exchange of letters between Sinclair and Washington marked the start of a rich and full correspondence. The following year Sinclair sent a copy of *Specimens of Statistical Reports: Exhibiting the Progress of Political Society from the Pastoral State, to that of Luxury and Refinement*, which essentially formed a how-to guide for collecting the kind of local statistics Sinclair considered the first step toward improving the national infrastructure.

Washington agreed with Sinclair's approach. Thanking him for the book, he approved of his plan to gather useful statistics for the betterment of society. Washington observed: "When enlightened men will take the trouble to examine so minutely into the state of society as your enquiries seem to go, it must result in greatly ameliorating the condition of the people—promoting the interests of civil society—and the happiness of Mankind at large."[4]

His appreciative remarks encouraged Sinclair. After founding the Board of Agriculture, he sent Washington copies of its publications, accompanied by letters urging him to do whatever he could to establish a similar board in the United States. Washington's efforts to create a US board of agriculture during his presidency were largely inspired by Sinclair, who kept a steady stream of books and pamphlets flowing from London to Philadelphia. Washington had little leisure time when he was president, but he did read some of the works Sinclair sent. He especially enjoyed the plan for the General Views series.[5] Sinclair would send Washington additional titles in the series as they were published. From James Anderson's *General View of the Agriculture and Rural Economy of the County of Aberdeen* to Arthur Young's *General View of the Agriculture of the County of Suffolk*, dozens of volumes reached Washington's hands. And, in 1795, Sinclair made Washington an honorary member of the Board of Agriculture.

The letters they exchanged are not only the letters of two public-minded men discussing plans for the improvement of society; they also strike a personal note. Writing to Sinclair in mid-December 1796, Washington looked forward to his retirement from the presidency, a time when he would be able to read the books Sinclair had sent, to peruse, he said, "with pleasure and edification, the fruits of your meritorious labours for the improvement of agriculture." He would also begin experimenting with some of Sinclair's innovative agricultural methods.[6] In short, Washington looked forward to retirement, when he could read about and experiment with new ideas, the kind of practical ideas Sinclair advocated.

The message Washington sent Sinclair from Philadelphia while waiting for the weather to clear in early March 1797 anticipates the literary and agricultural pursuits he intended for retirement. Thursday, the ninth, was as cold as Valley Forge, but the Washingtons could wait no longer. George and Martha Washington left Philadelphia accompanied by Nelly Custis, George Washington Lafayette—the Marquis de Lafayette's son, who had been living with his namesake at the presidential mansion—and Felix Frestel, young Lafayette's tutor. Nelly's brother Wash was currently attending the College of New Jersey (Princeton). Before leaving town, George Washington arranged for Tobias Lear to come to Philadelphia and supervise the packing and shipping of their belongings.

Having left President Washington's service after the death of his wife in 1793, Lear had organized a company to speculate in land near the new federal city, which would become known as Washington, DC. He later served as president of the Potomac Canal Company. Lear was happy to take a break from his business activities to help his old friend and mentor. Washington's instructions to Lear reveal that he did not want to withdraw himself fully from the political scene in his retirement. Hoping to stay informed, he instructed Lear to purchase any new pamphlets and bring them to him.[7]

Given the cold, wet winter, the Washingtons dreaded the road conditions between Philadelphia and Mount Vernon. Though some roads were quite bad, overall they proved better than expected. Regardless, the journey was, in Nelly Custis's words, "tedious and fatiguing." The unruly crowds may have slowed them down more than the muddy roads. Every town and city they entered welcomed the Washingtons with fanfare and falderal. They paused in the federal district to observe the construction of the US Capitol and the White House. Both seemed to be taking longer and costing more than expected. In addition, private housing was almost nonexistent. When a foreign visitor wondered where all the lawmakers and politicians would live, Washington came back with a witty reply:[8] "Oh well," he joked, "they can camp out. The Representatives in the first line, the Senate in the second, the President with all his suite in the middle."

Leaving the federal district, they crossed the Potomac and soon reached Mount Vernon, arriving seven days after they had left Philadelphia. Writing to a friend to inform her of their safe arrival, Nelly Custis expressed George Washington's feelings upon returning home the best: "Grandpapa is very well and much pleased with being once more Farmer Washington."[9]

Letter writing made less of a demand on Washington during retirement than it had when he was president, but he would correspond regularly with many intellectuals in the United States and Great Britain. Besides John Sinclair, Washington would maintain a correspondence with other prominent British agricultural writers, including James Anderson and Arthur Young. All would send him additional books inspiring new agricultural projects at Mount Vernon.

Sinclair looked toward ideas that could contribute to large-scale agricultural innovation: he sent books that could help get things done. Though Washington had been unable to establish a US board of agriculture during his administration, he had not abandoned the idea. Neither had Sinclair, who sent him several copies of his *Account of the Origin of the Board of Agriculture, and Its Progress for Three Years after Its Establishment*, one to keep and others to distribute to those who might help influence the establishment of a similar American board.[10]

Nathaniel Currier, *Washington at Mount Vernon 1797* (New York, 1852), lithograph. Library of Congress, Prints and Photographs Division, Washington, DC (reproduction number: LC-USZ62-27).

Washington was so busy during his first spring and summer back home that he did not have time to read the English and Scottish county surveys Sinclair had sent or, for that matter, any of the other books he had planned to read during his retirement. Before leaving Philadelphia, he told James McHenry, his secretary of war, how much he looked forward to reading in retirement, but when he wrote to describe his daily routine, he initially made no mention of books. Realizing that McHenry would think the omission strange, Washington added:

> Having given you the history of a day, it will serve for a year; and I am persuaded you will not require a second edition of it: but it may strike you, that in this detail no mention is made of any portion of time allotted for reading; the remark would be just, for I have not looked into a book since I came home, nor shall be able to do it until I have discharged my workmen; probably not before the nights grow longer; when, possibly, I may be looking in doomsday book.[11]

Though Washington could not find much time for reading early in his retirement, he did start reorganizing his books. His correspondence indicates that he devoted a fair amount of time to putting his personal library in order. Gathering the individual volumes of multivolume sets, he noticed some gaps and sought to fill them. Though he had received many books in Sinclair's General Views series, for example, he was unsure whether he had received all of them. He wrote Sinclair, hoping to complete his collection: "It is my intention to have them classed, and bound neatly."[12]

Washington also grew curious about the status of another major multivolume work published over a period of several years. He wondered whether Thomas Dobson had ever completed his *Encyclopaedia*.[13] Dobson had not, at least not yet. That the *Encyclopaedia* remained a work in progress is understandable: it was far and away the most ambitious project Dobson had undertaken since emigrating from Scotland, settling in Philadelphia and establishing himself as one of the city's leading publishers and booksellers. Washington had often patronized Dobson's shop during his presidency, using him as both a stationer and a bookbinder. Dobson became best known for publishing American editions of the most important books coming out of Great Britain. In 1789 Dobson published a three-volume American edition of Adam Smith's *Wealth of Nations*, the edition Washington owned. Also that same year Dobson advertised his proposal for an American edition of the *Encyclopaedia Britannica*.[14]

Not only would Dobson's *Encyclopaedia* be his most ambitious undertaking, it was also the most ambitious work ever undertaken in the United States by any publisher to that time. Unlike his edition of *The Wealth of Nations*, it would not be a verbatim reprint of the British text. Dobson planned to make the encyclopedia uniquely American, with hundreds of original copperplate illustrations engraved by American artists and many new articles on American themes. In addition, several of the articles from the London edition would be rewritten with an American slant.[15]

Emphasizing his encyclopedia as an American venture in the proposals he circulated, Dobson sought to attract subscribers from throughout the nation. Though many book buyers were interested in the project, Dobson still faced a considerable challenge. Upon learning about Dobson's plan for publishing an encyclopedia, Washington called him "a bold man" but nevertheless gave the project "every encouragement."[16] To help encourage Dobson's *Encyclopaedia*, he subscribed for two sets—another example of his literary patronage while president. The first volume appeared in 1790, but it would take nearly a decade for its publisher to complete the work, which ran to a total of eighteen volumes, not counting the supplements. Washington gave one set to Tobias Lear: a handsome reward for all the work Lear had done for him. Washington finally received his copy of Dobson's *Encyclopaedia* in 1798.[17]

Presentation copies continued to reach Philadelphia even after Washington had left. One day Timothy Pickering, who remained secretary of state under John Adams, received a visit from Joseph Nancrede. A Boston printer and publisher, Nancrede brought with him a copy of Bernardin de Saint-Pierre's *Studies of Nature*, which he had recently issued in an English translation. Nancrede dedicated this first American edition of Bernardin's work to Washington, though without his permission. To enhance the gift Nancrede had this presentation copy handsomely bound in red morocco and elegantly gilt.[18]

Washington received far more books than he had the time or the inclination to read. He was less likely to read a work like Bernardin's than those he received from Sinclair, Anderson, and Young, that is, works providing practical information he could put to use on his farms. The subject of Bernardin's *Studies of Nature* had appealed to Washington in his youth, but it contained little to interest him in old age. Bernardin studied natural history in an effort to demonstrate the existence of God. In terms of general content and philosophical outlook, Bernardin's *Studies of Nature* was reactionary. It contained nothing Washington had not read decades earlier in John Ray's *Wisdom of God*. No doubt the three volumes of gilt morocco looked good in the library at Mount Vernon, but once Washington put them on the shelf, one suspects, he never took them off.

Another book Pickering sent to Mount Vernon Washington did read carefully: James Monroe's *View of the Conduct of the Executive of the United States*. When Washington asked Pickering to send him a copy of this controversial book in January, he also asked his opinion of it. In his cover letter Pickering said that Monroe's book "is considered by every one whom I have heard speak of it, as his own condemnation, or as some have expressed themselves, his death warrant."[19]

This book, largely a collection of documents, represents Monroe's attempt to vindicate his public conduct as US minister to France during Washington's administration. Washington had appointed him to the post in May 1794. A protégé of Thomas Jefferson, Monroe was opposed to Federalist policies, but Washington made the appointment as a conciliatory gesture to France: by appointing a Republican partisan, he hoped to reassure the French of continuing friendship with the United States. Monroe was responsible for defending Jay's Treaty to the French government, a difficult task for any ambassador, let alone one who disagreed with the treaty. Two years into Monroe's appointment, Washington recalled him. Monroe did not return to Philadelphia until June 1797, after which he prepared a detailed defense of his official actions as ambassador.

Benjamin Franklin Bache, who had continued to attack Washington even after he left office, was happy to publish Monroe's screed.

His copy of Monroe's *View* is unique among Washington's books for the vast amount of marginalia it contains. Formerly he had written in his books to correct errors, mainly typographical ones. His marginalia in Monroe's *View* can also be seen as corrections, but they go far beyond correcting factual errors. None of Washington's other marginalia reveal his emotions as he read, but what he wrote in the margins of Monroe's *View* clearly indicates his anger. He was genuinely hurt by Monroe's comments, but, ever concerned with the good of the nation, he also saw them as threats to the American government. As his editors observe, Washington's marginal comments in Monroe's *View* comprise "the most extended, unremitting, and pointed use of taunts and jibes, sarcasm, and scathing criticism in all of his writings."[20]

Washington's marginal comments in the volume are largely restricted to Monroe's introduction. The documents section of his copy contains comparatively little marginalia. Washington's belligerence is clear from the start. Monroe's introduction begins with the following sentence: "In the month of May, 1794, I was invited by the President of the United States, through the Secretary of State, to accept the office of Minister Plenipotentiary to the French republic." Washington's marginalia begin with a sarcastic phrase modifying Monroe's opening sentence: "After several attempts had failed to obtain a more eligible character." Monroe continued: "It had been too my fortune, in the course of my service [as a US senator], to differ from the administration, upon many of our most important public measures." Washington responded with a rhetorical question: "Is this adduced as conclusive evidence that the Administration was in an error?"[21]

When President Washington had sent David Humphreys across the Atlantic to negotiate a treaty between the United States and Algiers, Humphreys stopped in Paris to speak with Monroe and see if France, which was at peace with Algiers, could help negotiate the treaty. Understanding the tensions between the United States and France, Monroe hesitated to approach the French government on Humphreys's behalf, especially since Humphreys had brought no letters from the Washington administration authorizing him to make an arrangement with the French regarding Algiers.

Monroe explained his attitude toward this issue in his introduction, but Washington did not buy it. Monroe seemed to think that every decision he made was the right one. Reading the introduction, Washington found Monroe obsessed with his own opinions and reluctant to consider other viewpoints. As he read Monroe's self-righteous explanation of the Algiers situation, Washington inscribed from memory the following snippet of verse:

> And he wrote to his father, ending with this line,
> I am my lovely Nevia ever thine.[22]

These lines come from an epigram by Martial that Washington had first read in *The Spectator* in his youth.[23] Using this couplet to characterize Monroe's behavior, Washington cast him as someone whose obsessions had led him into inadvertent error.

Reading Monroe's *View* in February or early March 1798, Washington read about issues that still affected the United States. During John Adams's administration, tensions with France continued to escalate. In May 1798 Adams approved the formation of a provisional army to be activated in case of French invasion. The first week of July the president commissioned Washington as lieutenant general and commander of the army. He had not told Washington about the commission beforehand. Washington was shocked to learn about the appointment in the papers. Suddenly all his well-earned rest, all his hard-fought leisure seemed to disappear before his eyes.

Once the news sank in, remarkably, Washington accepted the position. He informed John Trumbull, using a favorite metaphor: "When I bid adieu last to the Theatre of public life I thought it was hardly possible that any event would arise in my day that could induce me to tread that stage again. But this is an age of Wonders, and I have once more consented to become an Actor in the great Drama."[24] Washington had one proviso: he would only accept the position if he could choose his officers and staff. He selected Alexander Hamilton as second in command and Tobias Lear as his military secretary with the rank of colonel. Adams, who had long butted heads with Hamilton, had difficulty accepting him as Washington's second in command, but he eventually acquiesced, knowing full well that he could only have Washington if he took Hamilton with him.[25]

In November Washington left Mount Vernon for Philadelphia to consult with Hamilton and direct the planning of a new army. They devoted much time and effort considering possible officers for the provisional army, but Washington returned to Mount Vernon by Christmas. All the work and personal conflict involved with selecting officers for the new army proved unnecessary. In February 1799 Adams announced his decision to send a peace commission to France. The prospect of war with France dissipated, and the possibility of Washington continuing to serve as commander in chief disappeared. The happiest outcome of the experience for Washington may have been his reunion with Tobias Lear. Though no longer needing a military secretary, Washington did need a personal secretary. He offered the position to Lear, who accepted it and moved to Mount Vernon.

February 22, 1799, marked Washington's sixty-seventh birthday. The event was minor compared with the celebration that took place at Mount Vernon that same day: Nelly Custis married Washington's nephew Lawrence Lewis. At twenty Nelly had already accepted that she would be "a prim starched Spinster," but Lewis captured her heart. Though Nelly's life was going well, her brother Wash seemed destined to follow the same pattern of behavior as their father, Jack Custis—much to George Washington's chagrin. After being unable to give his lackadaisical stepson the ideal education he envisioned, Washington now found that his step-grandson similarly disdained a proper education. Expelled from Princeton for repeated misconduct, Wash transferred to Saint John's College in Annapolis but dropped out before finishing his studies. At the time of his sister's wedding, Wash's future remained uncertain.[26]

After the excitement of the wedding George Washington, his wife Martha, and Tobias Lear settled into a regular routine at Mount Vernon. Every day Washington rode around his farms to keep an eye on his crops, livestock, and agricultural experiments. He took these daily rounds regardless of the weather. On Thursday, December 12, for example, he set off on the daily tour of his plantations, though the thick cloud cover had an ominous look. Rain began to fall and gradually changed to snow, but Washington continued his ride. He returned home covered with snow but, seeing he had guests for dinner, did not bother to change clothes.[27]

The next day, Friday the thirteenth, it snowed another three inches. This time Washington skipped his daily tour of the farms, but he did brave the snow to mark some trees he wanted cut down. That evening George and Martha Washington, along with Tobias Lear, settled themselves in the parlor to catch up on the news, the latest papers having arrived from the post office. Newspaper reading had long been a regular activity at Mount Vernon. Washington subscribed to several papers, some of which he had bound into volumes to form a permanent part of his collection. His library catalogue lists the *Gazette of the United States*, the *Pennsylvania Gazette*, and the *Pennsylvania Packet*.

That Friday, as usual, Lear and the Washingtons read silently, but whenever George met with an article that caught his attention or captured his fancy, he would read it to the others. As he read aloud that evening, his voice sounded a little hoarse. With all the recent snow, he was apparently coming down with a cold.

Gilbert Stuart, *Mrs. Lawrence Lewis (Eleanor Custis)*. From Rufus Wilmot Griswold, *The Republican Court; or, American Society in the Days of Washington* (1854; New York: Appleton, 1867), facing p. 369. Kevin J. Hayes Collection, Toledo, Ohio.

His sore throat prevented Washington from reading aloud as much as he wished, so he asked Lear to read the debates of the Virginia Assembly regarding the nomination of James Monroe to the office of Virginia governor. Monroe's *View*, it turned out, was not the death warrant Pickering had predicted. Virginians had mixed feelings about Monroe. Some state legislators believed that his mission to France had hurt the reputation of the United States abroad. Electing him governor, they argued, would send the message that Washington had been wrong to recall him. James Madison, on the other hand, spoke eloquently in Monroe's defense. At Mount Vernon that evening Lear read aloud what Madison had to say in the legislature.

Madison saw no reason to delay Monroe's gubernatorial nomination. The matter had already been investigated thoroughly. Any further delay would reduce Monroe to "a singular and disturbing dilemma." Ambassadors could be recalled for reasons unconnected to their diplomatic character. Sometimes they had been remanded without being censured. Was Monroe to be banned from serving the nation on vague suspicions? Madison found Monroe's private character pure and his public character unimpeachable.[28] His argument carried the day, and Monroe was elected governor of Virginia. Once Lear finished reading, Washington "appeared much affected and spoke with some degree of asperity on the subject."

As Washington spoke, his voice sounded worse. When Lear commented on his hoarseness, Washington admitted his throat was sore but made light of the situation.

"You know I never take anything for a cold," he said. "Let it go as it came." He seemed cheerful enough. Shortly after nine o'clock that evening Washington went to bed, apparently in good health except for the cold.

Around two o'clock that morning he woke Martha, telling her he was quite sick. He feared he had an ague. A vague term that has since fallen from medical usage, ague referred to something much more serious than a cold. It involved such symptoms as fever, shivering, and shaking. Washington had escaped injury on the battlefield so often that it seems shocking to learn he was not ague-proof. He could hardly speak now and breathed with difficulty.

Caroline, a house servant, entered their bedroom at daybreak to light a fire. By this time Washington realized his condition was urgent; he might not be able to wait until a doctor arrived. He asked Caroline to fetch George Rawlins, an overseer who had often doctored the slaves when they were sick. On her way out Caroline stopped by Lear's room and apprised him of the situation. Lear dressed quickly and went to the Washingtons' bedroom. Washington tried to explain his condition, but he was short of breath and, it seemed, could hardly utter a word. Lear dashed off a note to Dr. Craik, dispatching a messenger to ride to Alexandria and bring the doctor back as quickly as he could.

Lear returned to the Washingtons' chamber, where someone prepared a folk remedy to soothe his sore throat. Washington could not swallow this mixture of butter, molasses, and vinegar, which made him gag. Rawlins arrived soon after sunrise. Washington asked Rawlins to bleed him. This long-standing therapy was based on the antiquated notion that illness stemmed from an imbalance of the four humors. Bloodletting supposedly cured illness by rebalancing the humors. Rawlins had bled sick slaves before, but bleeding the most respected man in America made him nervous. Washington could tell.

"Don't be afraid," Washington whispered. After Rawlins made the incision, the blood flowed slowly. "The orifice is not large enough," his distinguished patient told him.

It seemed plenty large to Martha Washington, who sensibly worried whether bloodletting was the right therapy in her husband's case. She begged Lear to halt the procedure. Lear tried to stop it, but Washington insisted Rawlins continue until he had taken a pint of blood. Needless to say, the loss of blood did not help Washington's condition. He still could not swallow. Lear proposed bathing the throat externally with salve, but that only irritated it further. Instead, they covered his neck with a piece of flannel. Next, for some odd reason, they soaked his feet in warm water.

Growing anxious as they waited for Dr. Craik, Martha asked Lear to send for Dr. Gustavus Brown, who lived across the river at Port Tobacco, Maryland. Craik arrived around nine o'clock. After examining Washington, he applied a paste made from cantharides to his throat and then bled him again. The prescription seems positively medieval: cantharides was a powder made from dried beetles. In addition, Craik had some vinegar and hot water put into a tea kettle to serve as a vaporizer. Craik also had some sage tea and vinegar mixed for a gargle. Washington tried to use it, but the gargle almost suffocated him. As the solution came out of his mouth, it brought up some phlegm: a good sign. Craik encouraged Washington to keep coughing to bring up some more phlegm, but to no avail.

After two hours Craik sent for more help, dispatching a servant to fetch Dr. Elisha Dick, another Alexandria physician. While waiting, Craik bled Washington again (the third time), but his throat did not improve. Craik next administered a glyster. Another attempt to rebalance the humors, the glyster produced an evacuation but did nothing to im-prove the throat infection.

Dr. Dick arrived around three o'clock Saturday afternoon. After Craik consulted with Dick, they bled Washington for a fourth time. By now they had removed over a third of the volume of blood in his body. When Dr. Brown arrived, he entered Washington's chamber and took his pulse. The three physicians left the room together to discuss the case. The situa-tion recalls a comment by Thomas Jefferson, who disagreed with blood-letting and who put much less stock in physicians than Washington. Jefferson joked that "whenever he saw three physicians together he looked up to discover whether there was not a turkey buzzard in the neighborhood."[29]

By four o'clock Washington could swallow a little, but he could tell his situation was dire. He asked his wife to retrieve the two wills from his desk and bring them to him. He told her to burn the old one and save the new one, the one he had drafted earlier that year, which would free his slaves upon her death. She followed his instructions, placing the old will into the fire.

"I find I am going, my breath cannot last long," Washington said to Lear late that afternoon. "I believed, from the first that the disorder would prove fatal." Maintaining his equanimity, he gave Lear some instructions regarding his letters, papers, and financial accounts.

During the afternoon, Lear could tell that Washington was in great pain, partly because of his difficulty breathing but also because of his dif-ficulty adjusting his position on the bed. Occasionally Lear would lie on the bed next to him, using his own body to lift Washington's and turn him as gently as possible. Lear performed these movements easily, willingly, simply, and with a goodness of heart that touched Washington.

"I am afraid I shall fatigue you too much," Washington said.

Lear assured him he felt nothing but a wish to comfort him.

"Well! it is a debt we must pay to each other, and I hope when you want aid of this kind you will find it," Washington replied.

After five o'clock, the three physicians returned. Craik asked Washing-ton if he could sit up in bed. Lear took his hand and helped raise him to a sitting position. Washington seemed resigned to his fate. He lay back down. Dick and Brown left the room, but Craik and Lear stayed by his bedside.

"Doctor, I die hard, but I am not afraid to go," Washington said. "I believed from my first attack that I should not survive it, my breath cannot last long."

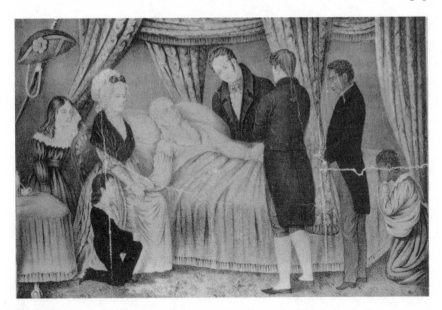

Death of Washington (New York: N. Currier, ca. 1840), lithograph. Library of Congress, Prints and Photographs Division, Washington, DC (reproduction number: LC-USZC2-2623).

Craik pressed his hand but could not utter a word. He left the bedside and took a seat by the fire, absorbed in grief. The other two physicians returned around eight that evening but left the room, as Lear said, "without a ray of hope."

About ten o'clock Washington attempted to speak. It took several tries, but he was finally able to say something.

"I am just going," he said. Premature burial was a common fear of the time, so Washington gave instructions to prevent being buried alive. "Have me decently buried, and do not let my body be put into the Vault in less than two days after I am dead."

Lear nodded his head.

"Do you understand me?" Washington asked.

"Yes, sir," Lear said.

"'Tis well," he said.

Lear continued to hold his hand. Toward eleven Washington's breathing became easier. He withdrew his hand from Lear's to reach across his body and feel his own pulse. Lear called Craik, still seated by the fire, to come to the bedside. As Washington was taking his own pulse, his arm went limp. Lear grabbed hold of his hand as it started to fall and placed it upon his breast. Washington expired without a sigh or a struggle. Craik reached out and closed his eyelids.

"Is he gone?" Martha asked.

Choked with sobs, Lear could not speak, but he held up his hand to indicate her husband was gone.

" 'Tis well," she replied with resignation. " 'Tis all now over. I have no more trials to pass through. I shall soon follow him."

George Washington's death, like everyone's, required some basic clerical tasks. For one thing, his estate had to be inventoried. As was common in the eighteenth century, the books were inventoried volume by volume. His library contained more than a thousand volumes, encompassing perhaps a third as many more titles with all the pamphlets taken into account. A man's library, it has been said, is a window to his soul. Because so many of the books Washington acquired during the last decade and a half of his life were presentation copies, his library may reveal less about the inner man than, say, the libraries of Thomas Jefferson or Benjamin Franklin. Yet the inventory of Washington's library that was taken upon his death does permit some conclusions.

Washington's library reflects his practical bent. Most of the books he acquired late in life were highly useful works. Dictionaries and encyclopedias provided references he could dip into whenever he needed specific information. His collection of military books, perhaps the finest in Revolutionary America, seems remarkably purposeful. He did not read military books as a hobby. He expanded his military library during times of war but added few volumes to it in times of peace. His collection of law books, tiny compared with the typical library of the eighteenth-century Virginia gentleman, consisted mainly of practical works too. When Washington wrote the landmark will that freed his slaves, he did so without consulting an attorney: his law books alone gave him guidance. The few theoretical works in his legal collection treated the laws of nature and nations, which contained the fundamental theories that formed the basis of the US government.

History and travel, two of the largest subject areas in Washington's library at Mount Vernon, proved ideal for recreational reading. Washington accepted the long-standing notion that literature must both delight and instruct. Travels offered exciting, action-packed narratives that nonetheless informed readers about geography and customs from around the world. Histories presented narratives of the past that could be used to shape the future. They let pragmatic readers like Washington know what to emulate and what to avoid. Biographies, in turn, presented patterns of behavior readers could use to shape their own.

The narrative aspect of travels and histories enhanced their readability, but another type of narrative, the novel, was largely absent from the library shelves at Mount Vernon. Washington did own such classics and *Don Quixote*, *Gil Blas*, and the picaresque English novels they inspired, but otherwise his library contained few novels. Washington had trouble reading fiction, that is, narratives lacking useful information. Agricultural treatises like those John Sinclair sent to him never seemed to tire Washington.

Viewed as literature, the novel and the agricultural treatise are polar opposites. The novel presents a narrative but lacks practical information; the agricultural treatise contains practical information but has no narrative. Or does it? Though agricultural treatises may lack any explicit narratives, they do have implicit ones. Forward-thinking readers like Washington could read an agricultural treatise with an eye toward what would happen once its schemes were put into practice. Instead of telling what has already happened, it foreshadows what will happen. The best agricultural treatises, like many of the other books in George Washington's life, project a vision for the future.

NOTES

Chapter 1: Meditations and Contemplations

Epigraph from Isaac Watts, *The Improvement of the Mind; or, A Supplement to the Art of Logick*, 2d ed. (London: for J. Blackstone, 1743), 45.

1. Griffin, *Catalogue*, 25; Sarah L. Wallace, "Editor's Note," *Quarterly Journal of the Library of Congress* 22 (1963): 2.

2. Adrienne M. Harrison, *A Powerful Mind: The Self-Education of George Washington* (Lincoln, NE: Potomac, 2015), 65, groups Blackall with several other religious authors in GW's library and asserts that they were all "standard reading." Though copies of other devotional works GW owned could be located in colonial Virginia, I have found no other references to Blackall's *Sufficiency of a Standing Revelation. VMHB* and *WMQ* published dozens of colonial Virginia library inventories in the early decades of the twentieth century, but none of those indexed in E. G. Swem, *Virginia Historical Index*, 2 vols. (1934; Baltimore: Genealogical Publishing, 2003), 1:645, list Blackall's *Sermons*.

3. *Benjamin Franklin's Autobiography: A Norton Critical Edition*, ed. J. A. Leo Lemay and P. M. Zall (New York: Norton, 1986), 45.

4. Robert Wickliff has previously escaped identity. On the front pastedown of GW's copy of Blackall's *Sufficiency of a Standing Revelation in General, and of the Scripture Revelation in Particular* (London: for Jer. Batley and T. Warner, 1717), he signed his name "Robert Wickloff." On the verso of the title page, however, he wrote "Robt Wickliff Junr, was born the 14th of febry 1728." Onto page one, he wrote "Robt Wickliff / 1740" (MBAt, no. Wa.70).

5. Blackall, *Sufficiency of a Standing Revelation*, 5.

6. Wallace, "Editor's Note," 2.

7. Blackall, *Sufficiency of a Standing Revelation*, 30.

8. E. Hinchcliffe, "The Washingtons at Whitehaven and Appleby," *Transactions of the Cumberland and Westmorland Antiquarian and Archaeological Society*, n.s., 71 (1971): 153, 170–71.

9. GW to Henry Knox, April 27, 1787, *Papers, Confederation Series*, 5:157.

10. Stephen Brumwell, *George Washington: Gentleman Warrior* (New York: Quercus, 2012), 24.

11. Henry Crouch, *A Complete View of the British Customs*, 2d ed. (London: for John Osborn and Thomas Longman, 1731) (MBAt, no. Wa.123).

12. James Hosmer Penniman, *George Washington at Mount Vernon on the Potomac* (Mount Vernon, VA: Mount Vernon Ladies Association of the Union, 1921), 13–14.

13. For this and other examples of traditional flyleaf rhymes, see Kevin J. Hayes, *Folklore and Book Culture* (1997; Eugene, OR: Wipf & Stock, 2016), 89–102.

14. "Inventory of Colonel Augustine Washington Dec'd," *Tyler's Quarterly Historical and Genealogical Magazine* 8 (1926–1927): 90–92.

15. John Gascoigne, "Clarke, Samuel," *ODNB*.

16. Douglas Southall Freeman, *George Washington: A Biography*, 7 vols. (New York: Scribner, 1948–1957), 1:71–72.

17. *David Humphreys' "Life of General Washington" with George Washington's "Remarks,"* ed. Rosemarie Zagarri (Athens, GA: University of Georgia Press, 1991), 6.

18. Amanda C. Isaac, *Take Note!: George Washington the Reader* (Mount Vernon, VA: George Washington's Mount Vernon, 2013), 3.

19. Quoted in Kevin J. Hayes, *The Library of William Byrd of Westover* (Madison, WI: Madison House, 1997), 90.

20. GW to the Citizens of Fredericksburg, ca. February 14, 1784, *Papers, Confederation Series*, 1:123.

21. James Kirke Paulding, *A Life of Washington*, 2 vols. (New York: Harper & Brothers, 1835), 1:22.

22. For a good perspective on the portrayal of Mary Ball Washington in biographies of her son, see Don Higginbotham, *Revolution in America: Considerations and Comparisons* (Charlottesville: University of Virginia Press, 2005), 57–59.

23. Ron Chernow, *Washington: A Life* (New York: Penguin, 2010), 11.

24. A. L. Bassett, "Reminiscences of Washington," *Scribner's Monthly*, May 1877, 78; Mary V. Thompson, "Religion: George Washington, Anglican Gentleman," in *A Companion to George Washington*, ed. Edward G. Lengel (Malden, MA: Wiley-Blackwell, 2012), 563.

25. Sharon E. Knapp and John L. Sharpe III, *An Exhibition of a Selection of Books and Manuscripts from the Library of Mary and Harry L. Dalton* (Durham, NC: William R. Perkins Library, Duke University, 1977), unpaginated; Mary V. Thompson, *In the Hands of a Good Providence: Religion in the Life of George Washington* (Charlottesville: University of Virginia Press, 2008), 20–21.

26. Stan V. Henkels, *This Valuable and Extraordinary Collection of the Effects of General George Washington* (Philadelphia: Thos. Birch's Sons, 1890), lot 144.

27. C. Malcolm Watkins, *The Cultural History of Marlborough, Virginia: An Archeological and Historical Investigation of the Port Town for Stafford County and the Plantation of John Mercer* (Washington, DC: Smithsonian Institution Press, 1968), 207; advertisement, *Virginia Gazette* (Hunter), July 30, 1752; Kevin J. Hayes, *A Colonial Woman's Bookshelf* (1996; Eugene, OR: Wipf & Stock, 2016), 13, 53–54; Hayes, *Library of William Byrd of Westover*, no. 1307; "Donald Robertson's School, King and Queen County, Va., 1758–1769," *VMHB* 33 (1925): 195; advertisement, *Virginia Gazette* (Purdie and Dixon), September 6, 1770; N. N., "On Reading Mr. Hervey's *Meditations* in the West Indies," *London Magazine* 23 (1754): 40.

28. Hayes, *Colonial Woman's Bookshelf*, 53–54.

29. James Hervey, *Meditations and Contemplations*, 7th ed., 2 vols. (London: for John and James Rivington, 1750), 1:xxx.

30. George Washington Parke Custis, *Recollections and Private Memoirs of Washington*, ed. Benson J. Lossing (Philadelphia: J. W. Bradley, 1861), 141, 148.

31. Hayes, *Colonial Woman's Bookshelf*, 39–40.

32. Robert Boyle, *Occasional Reflections upon Several Subjects* (Oxford: Alex. Ambrose Masson, 1848), 48.

33. Gregory Lynall, *Swift and Science: The Satire, Politics, and Theology of Natural Knowledge 1690–1730* (New York: Palgrave Macmillan, 2012), 23–27; Kevin J. Hayes, "Benjamin Franklin," in *The Oxford Handbook to Early American Literature*, ed. Kevin J. Hayes (New York: Oxford University Press, 2008), 436–37.

34. [John Cole], *Herveina; or, Graphic and Literary Sketches, Illustrative of the Life and Writings of the Rev. James Hervey, A.M.* (Scarborough: for John Cole, 1822), 6.

35. Scott Mandelbrote, "Ray, John," *ODNB*.

36. John Ray, *The Wisdom of God Manifested in the Works of Creation*, 11th ed. (London: W. Innys, 1743), 179–80.

37. John Foster, *Fosteriana: Consisting of Thoughts, Reflections, and Criticisms*, ed. Henry G. Bohn (London: Henry G. Bohn, 1858), 169.

38. Henkels, *This Valuable and Extraordinary Collection*, lots 145–47; "Libraries in Colonial Virginia," *1WMQ* 8 (1900): 147; Hayes, *Colonial Woman's Bookshelf*, 69.

39. Hayes, *Colonial Woman's Bookshelf*, 69.

40. [Eliza Haywood], *The Female Spectator*, 3d ed., 4 vols. (London: T. Gardner, 1750), 2:39–40.

41. Griffin, *Catalogue*, 485.

42. E. C. McGuire, *The Religious Opinions and Character of Washington* (New York: Harper, 1836), 48.

43. McGuire, *Religious Opinions*, 48.

44. Worthington Chauncey Ford, *The Boston Book Market, 1679–1700* (Boston: Club of Odd Volumes, 1917), 14–15; Horatio Rogers, ed. *The Early Records of the Town of Providence*, 21 vols. (Providence, RI: Snow and Farnam, 1892–1915), 6:79; "Libraries in Colonial Virginia," *1WMQ* 3 (1894): 134; "Carter Papers," *VMHB* 6 (1898): 147.

45. Paulding, *Life of Washington*, 19.

46. [William H. Bogart], *Who Goes There?; or, Men and Events* (New York: Carleton, 1866), 31.

47. Alexander Chalmers, *The General Biographical Dictionary: Containing an Historical and Critical Account of the Lives and Writings of the Most Eminent Persons in Every Nation*, vol. 10 (London: for J. Nichols, 1813), 107–8.

48. Edward Pearson, *An Admonition against Lay-Preaching* (Nottingham: Samuel Tupman, 1800), 49.

49. Jeffrey H. Morrison, *The Political Philosophy of George Washington* (Baltimore: John Hopkins University Press, 2009), 100–104; John E. Ferling, *The Ascent of George Washington: The Hidden Political Genius of an American Icon* (New York: Bloomsbury, 2009), 11–12.

50. *Seneca's Morals by Way of Abstract*, ed. and trans. Roger L'Estrange, 15th ed. (London: for G. Strahan, 1746), sigs. A2v, A3v.

51. Merton M. Sealts, Jr., *Melville's Reading*, rev. ed. (Columbia: University of South Carolina, 1988), no. 458; Herman Melville, *Mardi; and, A Voyage Thither*, ed. Nathalia Wright (Putney, VT: Hendricks House, 1990), 338.

52. "Library of Col. William Fleming," *1WMQ* 6 (1898): 161.

53. *Seneca's Morals*, 298, 299.

54. Richard Allestree, *The Causes of the Decay of Christian Piety* (London: F. H. for E. and R. Pawlet, 1704), 45.

55. GW, *Diaries*, 5:185.

Chapter 2: Every Boy His Own Teacher

Epigraph from Edward Young, *The Works of Edward Young*, 3 vols. (London: for J. Dodsley, 1798), 3:60.

1. David Humphreys, *Life of General Washington, with George Washington's Remarks*, ed. Rosemarie Zagarri (Athens, GA: University of Georgia Press, 1991), 6.

2. Humphreys, *Life of General Washington*, 6.

3. "School Exercises," *Papers, Colonial Series*, 1:4. GW's exercise books are available in the George Washington Papers (DLC), as Series 1: Exercise Books, Diaries, and Surveys 1741–99, the source of all manuscript quotations in this chapter, which will not be documented separately.

4. George Mason to GW, June 12, 1756, *Papers, Colonial Series*, 3:202; E. Polk Johnson, *A History of Kentucky and Kentuckians: The Leaders and Representative Men in Commerce, Industry and Modern Activities*, 3 vols. (Chicago: Lewis, 1912), 2:838.

5. Moncure D. Conway, "Poems in George Washington's Copy-Book," *Athenaeum*, December 20, 1890, 854.

6. [Elizabeth Teft], "On Christmas-Day," *Gentleman's Magazine* 13 (1743): 96; Isobel Grundy, "Teft, Elizabeth," *ODNB*.

7. "True Happiness," *Gentleman's Magazine* 4 (1734): 102.

8. "Inventory of Colonel Augustine Washington Dec'd," *Tyler's Quarterly Historical and Genealogical Magazine* 8 (1926–27): 90–92.

9. Anthony David Barker, "Cave, Edward," *ODNB*.

10. At Westover, William Byrd II had a near-complete set of the magazine. When he decided to have all the back issues he had accumulated bound, Byrd asked his bookbinder to locate the missing numbers before binding up the lot. See Kevin J. Hayes, *The Library of William Byrd of Westover* (Madison, WI: Madison House, 1997), nos. 1869, 2167.

11. Hayes, *Road to Monticello*, 579.

12. Recommending an article about Benjamin Franklin from the *Gentleman's Magazine* to the Reverend Thomas Dawson, president of William and Mary College, Williamsburg printer William Hunter assumed Dawson had held on to his back issues for ready reference. "William Hunter to Thomas Dawson," 2*WMQ* 1 (1921): 54. See also "Books in Colonial Virginia," *VMHB* 10 (1903): 404; C. Malcolm Watkins, *The Cultural History of Marlborough, Virginia: An Archeological and Historical Investigation of the Port Town for Stafford County and the Plantation of John Mercer* (Washington, DC: Smithsonian Institution Press, 1968), 201.

13. Barker, "Cave, Edward," *ODNB*.

14. Several talented American poets published in the *Gentleman's Magazine*, including Thomas Dale, Nathaniel Evans, Richard Lewis, and Charles Woodmason. See J. A. Leo Lemay, *A Calendar of American Poetry in the Colonial Newspapers and Magazines and in the Major English Magazines through 1765* (Worcester, MA: American Antiquarian Society, 1972), nos. 215, 257, 259, 408, 1135–37, 1144, 1178–79, 1204, 1929.

15. Barker, "Cave, Edward," *ODNB*.

16. Griffin, *Catalogue*, 493.

17. A. Franklin Parks, "The Establishment of the Printing Press," *A History of Virginia Literature*, ed. Kevin J. Hayes (New York: Cambridge University Press, 2015), 77–79.

18. Tom Killegrew [pseud.], *The Merry Quack Doctor; or, The Fun Box Broke Open* (London: for S. Smith, [1775?]), 119–20.

19. Unaware of the poem's British origins, Moncure Daniel Conway suggested in *Barons of the Potomack and the Rappahannock* (New York: Grolier Club, 1892), 87, that Augustine Washington could have written "True Happiness."

20. *George Washington's Rules of Civility and Decent Behaviour in Company and Conversation*, ed. Charles Moore (Boston: Houghton Mifflin, 1926), x–xiii.

21. Robert Middlekauff, *Washington's Revolution: The Making of America's First Leader* (New York: Knopf, 2015), 9, says GW consulted a book titled *Rules of Civility and Decent Behaviour in Company and Conversation*, confusing the title of GW's manuscript with the title of his source. Though a recent book, *Washington's Revolution* represents a traditional approach to GW's life, that is, one that neglects his literary and intellectual interests. Adrienne M. Harrison, *A Powerful Mind: The*

Self-Education of George Washington (Lincoln, NE: Potomac, 2015), though purportedly devoted to a study of GW's self-education, shows little more interest in the source of his "Rules." Like Middlekauff, Harrison, 19, also confuses the title of GW's source with the title of his manuscript.

22. Leland E. Warren, "Turning Reality Round Together: Guides to Conversation in Eighteenth-Century England," *Eighteenth-Century Life* 8 (1983): 71.

23. *ESTC*, no. W17982.

24. Francis Hawkins, *Youths Behaviour; or, Decency in Conversation amongst Men*, 5th ed. (London: W. Wilson for W. Lee, 1651), sig. A4r.

25. W. W. [William Winstanley], *The New Help to Discourse; or, Wit and Mirth, Intermix'd with More Serious Matters*, 8th ed. (London: T. Norris, 1721), 136.

26. *George Washington's Rules*, 3.

27. *George Washington's Rules*, 11, 13, 15.

28. *George Washington's Rules*, 5.

29. *George Washington's Rules*, 17.

30. Louis Chambaud, *Nouveau dictionnaire françois-anglois, et anglois-françois*, ed. Jean Perrin (London: W. Strahan, T. Cadell, & P. Elmsly, 1778) (PPL, no. *Am 1778 Cham AqW3 C45); Monique C. Cormier, "Fragments of History Prior to Two Editions of the Dictionary by Lewis Chambaud, a Rival of Abel Boyer," *International Journal of Lexicography* 23 (2010): 179–80.

31. [John Bell], "A Short Sketch of General Washington's Life and Character," in *A Poetical Epistle to His Excellency George Washington, Esq.* (1779; New York: J. Munsell, 1865), 15. The story Royall Tyler tells in *The Algerine Captive; or, The Life and Adventures of Doctor Updike Underhill, Six Years a Prisoner among the Algerines*, ed. Caleb Crain (New York: Modern Library, 2002), 26, that GW must have read Greek because his attack on the Hessians at Trenton was inspired by Ulysses' seizure of the horses of Rhesus in Homer's *Iliad*, is apocryphal.

32. GW to George Washington Parke Custis, July 23, 1797, *Papers, Retirement Series*, 1:267.

33. Robert Ainsworth, *Thesaurus Linguae Latinae Compendarius; or, A Compendious Dictionary of the Latin Tongue*, ed. Samuel Patrick (London: for W. Mount, 1746), sig. C2r.

34. Joseph Davidson, ed. and trans., *A New Translation of Ovid's Metamorphoses into English Prose* (Dublin: for John Exshaw, 1750), 10.

35. Rolfe Humphries, "Introduction," in Ovid, *Metamorphoses*, trans. Rolfe Humphries (Bloomington: Indiana University Press, 1955), viii.

36. "General Orders [October 3, 1778]," *Papers, Revolutionary War Series*, 17:233.

37. GW to Lafayette, April 28[–May 1], 1788, and GW to Henry Lee, Jr., September 22, 1788, *Papers, Confederation Series*, 6:245, 531.

38. Roger L'Estrange, ed. and trans., *Fables of Aesop and Other Eminent Mythologists, with Morals and Reflections*, 8th ed. (London: for A. Bettesworth, 1738), 145–47.

39. Henry Dixon, *The English Instructor; or, The Art of Spelling Improved*, 23d ed. (London: for C. Hitch, 1760), 143.

40. James Greenwood, *The Royal English Grammar, Containing What Is Necessary to the Knowledge of the English Tongue*, 3d ed. (London: for J. Nourse, 1747) (MBAt copy, no. Wa.204).

41. Greenwood, *Royal English Grammar*, vii.

42. GW to John, ca. 1749–1750, *Papers, Colonial Series*, 1:42.

43. Greenwood, *Royal English Grammar*, 143.

44. Greenwood, *Royal English Grammar*, 157.

45. Rollo Laverne Lyman, *English Grammar in American Schools before 1850* (Chicago: University of Chicago Libraries, 1922), 112–18.

46. *Benjamin Franklin's Autobiography: A Norton Critical Edition*, ed. J. A. Leo Lemay and P. M. Zall (New York: Norton, 1986), 13.

47. Worthington Chauncey Ford, *The Boston Book Market, 1679–1700* (Boston: Club of Odd Volumes, 1917), 94, 133, 166; *The Journals of Hugh Gaine, Printer*, ed. Paul Leicester Ford, 2 vols. (New York: Dodd, Mead, 1902), 195; Edwin Wolf 2nd, *The Book Culture of a Colonial American City: Philadelphia Books, Bookmen, and Booksellers* (Oxford: Clarendon Press, 1988), 71–73.

48. *Benjamin Franklin's Autobiography*, 13.

49. Nathaniel Friend [pseud.], "On the Practical Navigation of My Very Good Friend the Author," in John Seller, *Practical Navigation; or, An Introduction to the Whole Art*, ed. John Colson (London: for R. and W. Mount and T. Page, 1711).

50. Seller, *Practical Navigation*, 1.

51. Seller, *Practical Navigation*, 191; James D. Drake, "Appropriating a Continent: Geographical Categories, Scientific Metaphors, and the Construction of Nationalism in British North America and Mexico," *Journal of World History* 15 (2004): 326–27.

52. Stanley Ellis Cushing, *The George Washington Library Collection* (Boston: Boston Athenaeum, 1997), no. A-2.

53. Thomas Prince, *A Chronological History of New-England in the Form of Annals* (Boston: Kneeland and Green for S. Gerrish, 1736) (MBAt, no. Wa.241).

54. "A Valuable Relic: Washington's Text Book, His Autograph Copy of the *Young Man's Companion*," *New York Daily Tribune*, January 19, 1866, 8; "Washington's Text Book: His Autograph Copy of *The Young Man's Companion*," *Historical Magazine* 10 (1866), 47–48. George Emery Littlefield, *Early Schools and School-Books of New England* (Boston: Club of Odd Volumes, 1904), 189, presents a facsimile of the title page with the dated autograph and acknowledges the permission to reprint from the book's current owner, "Abner C. Goodale," misspelling Goodell's last name. After Goodell's death, the book went up for auction with the rest of Goodell's collection. See *Catalogue of the Private Library of the Late Abner C. Goodell, Salem, Mass., Editor of the Massachusetts Province Laws* (Boston: C. F. Libbie, 1918), lot 1627. The book sold on March 12, 1918, for $52.50.

American Book-Prices Current (New York: E. P. Dutton, 1918), 483. Its current whereabouts is unknown.

55. John C. Fitzpatrick, *George Washington Himself: A Common-Sense Biography Written from His Manuscripts* (Indianapolis, IN: Bobbs-Merrill, 1933), 24; "School Exercises," *Papers, Colonial Series*, 1:4.

56. George Fisher, *The Instructor; or, Young Man's Best Companion*, 5th ed. (London: for James Hodges, 1740), iii.

57. "David Black's Library," *VMHB* 4 (1897): 291; J. Bryan Grimes, *North Carolina Wills and Inventories* (1912; Baltimore: Genealogical Publishing, 1967), 491.

58. Buckner Stith to GW, March 22, 1787, *Papers, Confederation Series*, 5:100.

59. G. W. P. Custis, *Recollections and Private Memoirs of Washington* (Washington, DC: William H. Moore, 1859), 40–41.

60. J. A. Bennett, "Geometry and Surveying in Early-Seventeenth-Century England," *Annals of Science* 48 (1991): 352; Elizabeth Tebeaux, "Pillaging the Tombs of Noncanonical Texts: Technical Writing and the Evolution of English Style," *Journal of Business and Technical Communication* 18 (2004): 190.

61. Landon Carter's copy survives at the University of Virginia (Special Collections, no. F229.C28Z9.L49C6 1653).

62. Landon Carter to GW, May 9, 1776, *Papers, Revolutionary War Series*, 4:234–35.

63. Landon Carter to GW, October 7, 1755, *Papers, Colonial Series*, 2:82.

64. Fitzpatrick, *George Washington Himself*, 25.

65. John Clarke, *An Essay upon Study: Wherein Directions Are Given for the Due Conduct Thereof, and the Collection of a Library, Proper for the Purpose, Consisting of the Choicest Books in All the Several Parts of Learning*, 2d ed. (London: for A. Bettesworth, 1737), 151.

Chapter 3: Exemplars

Epigraph from *Terence's Comedies*, trans. Thomas Cooke, 2 vols. (London: for R. Ware, 1755), 2:323.

1. GW to John Sinclair, December 11, 1796, in *The Correspondence of the Right Honourable Sir John Sinclair, Bart. with Reminiscences of the Most Distinguished Characters Who Have Appeared in Great Britain, and in Foreign Countries, During the Last Fifty Years*, ed. John Sinclair, 2 vols. (London: Henry Colburn and Richard Bentley, 1831), 2:14.

2. GW to George William Fairfax, February 27, 1785, *Papers, Confederation Series*, 2:387–88.

3. W. H. Snowden, *Some Old Historic Landmarks of Virginia and Maryland* (Alexandria, VA: G. H. Ramey, 1904), 96.

4. Andrew Burnaby, *Travels through North America*, ed. Rufus Rockwell Wilson (New York: A. Wessels, 1904), 207.

5. Herbert A. Johnson, *Imported Eighteenth-Century Law Treatises in American Libraries, 1700–1799* (Knoxville: University of Tennessee Press, 1978), no. 112; William Hamilton Bryson, *Census of Law Books in Colonial Virginia* (Charlottesville: University Press of Virginia, 1978), no. 414.

6. *Henry Willoughby: A Novel*, 2 vols. (London: G. Kearsley, 1798), 1:59.

7. Anne McDermott, "Johnson's Definitions of Technical Terms and the Absence of Illustrations," *International Journal of Lexicography* 18 (2005): 125–26.

8. Larry Stewart, "Harris, John," *ODNB*; Griffin, *Catalogue*, 497.

9. GW, "List of Books at Mount Vernon," *Papers, Colonial Series*, 7:344.

10. Burnaby, *Travels*, 208.

11. GW to John Augustine Washington, May 28, 1755, *Papers, Colonial Series*, 1:289–90.

12. Edmund Berkeley, Jr., "Carter, Robert," *DVB*, 3:85.

13. Stuart E. Brown, Jr., *Virginia Baron: The Story of Thomas, 6th Lord Fairfax* (Berryville, VA: Chesapeake, 1965), 119.

14. Burnaby, *Travels*, 197–98.

15. *The Acts of Assembly, Now in Force, in the Colony of Virginia* (Williamsburg, VA: William Hunter, 1752), the only other book Lord Fairfax is known to have subscribed to in Virginia, may be one of the two volumes of "Virginia Laws" listed in his estate inventory.

16. Stan V. Henkels, *Rare American History from the Library of William Fisher Lewis, Esq.* (Philadelphia: Henkels, 1910), lot 48.

17. George Saintsbury, *The Peace of the Augustans: A Survey of Eighteenth Century Literature as a Place of Rest and Refreshment* (1916; New York: Oxford University Press, 1946), 269.

18. GW, *Journal of My Journey over the Mountains*, ed. J. M. Toner (Albany, NY: Joel Munsell's Sons, 1892), 66–67.

19. Isaac Watts, *The Improvement of the Mind* (London: Logographic Press, 1785), 93.

20. GW to John Armstrong, May 18, 1779, *Papers, Revolutionary War Series*, 20:518.

21. GW, "Comments on Monroe's *A View of the Conduct of the Executive of the United States*," *Papers, Retirement Series*, 2:181.

22. *The Guardian*, 7th ed., 2 vols. (Dublin: for G. Risk, G. and A. Ewing, and W. Smith, 1744), (MBAt, no. Wa.43).

23. *Guardian*, 2:297.

24. Many colonial Virginians had Baker's *Chronicle* in their libraries, including William Fairfax. See Louis B. Wright, "The 'Gentleman's Library' in Early Virginia: The Literary Interests of the First Carters," *Huntington Library Quarterly* 1 (1937): 52; Hugh Blair Grigsby, "The Founders of Washington College," *Historical Papers* (Washington and Lee University) no. 2 (1890): 79; Fairfax Harrison, *The Devon Carys*, 2 vols. (New York: DeVinne, 1920), 1:141. For other copies in colonial Virginia, see "Books in Colonial Virginia," *VMHB* 10 (1903): 399; "Libraries in Colonial Virginia," *1WMQ* (1899): 77.

25. Henry Fielding, *The Covent-Garden Journal; and, A Plan of the Universal Register-Office*, ed. Bertrand A. Goldgar (Middletown, CT: Wesleyan University Press, 1988), 87–88.

26. Kevin J. Hayes, *The Library of William Byrd of Westover* (Madison, WI: Madison House, 1997), no. 6. Baker's *Chronicle* has escaped the attention of Byrd's editors, but it significantly influenced his *History of the Dividing Line*. Narrating the history of Virginia in his preface as a story of dismemberment, Byrd demonstrated how several American colonies were lopped off Virginia. In terms of its structure, diction, and historical import, Byrd's narrative echoes Baker's story of the early division of England into separate kingdoms.

27. Richard Baker, *A Chronicle of the Kings of England, from the Time of the Romans Government to the Death of King James the First* (London: for Samuel Ballard, 1730), 1.

28. Baker, *Chronicle*, 4.

29. Baker, *Chronicle*, 8–9.

30. Baker, *Chronicle*, 21, 27.

31. John C. Fitzpatrick, *George Washington Himself: A Common-Sense Biography Written from His Manuscripts* (Indianapolis, IN: Bobbs-Merrill, 1933), 34.

32. Hippolyte du Chastelet de Luzancy, *Panegyrick to the Memory of His Grace Frederick, Late Duke of Schonberg* (London: for R. Bentley, 1690), 10, 12; Adrienne M. Harrison, *A Powerful Mind: The Self-Education of George Washington* (Lincoln, NE: Potomac, 2015), 68–69.

33. De Luzancy, *Panegyrick to the Memory*, 29.

34. GW to Sally, ca. 1749–50, *Papers, Colonial Series*, 1:43.

35. GW, "Poetry," (1749–50), *Papers, Colonial Series*, 1:46.

36. GW, "General Orders [August 31, 1778]" and "General Orders [November 18, 1778]," *Papers, Revolutionary War Series*, 16:433, and 18:187; GW, *Diaries*, 4:237.

Chapter 4: Travel Writing

Epigraph from Philip Dormer Stanhope, *Letters . . . to His Son*, ed. Eugenia Stanhope, 4th ed., 2 vols. (London: for J. Dodsley, 1774), 2:230.

1. GW, *Diaries*, 1:10.

2. Kathleen M. Brown, *Foul Bodies: Cleanliness in Early America* (New Haven, CT: Yale University Press, 2008), 139–40.

3. Ted Olson, "Virginia Folklore," in *A History of Virginia Literature*, ed. Kevin J. Hayes (New York: Cambridge University Press, 2015), 272–73.

4. GW, *Diaries*, 1:13.

5. Daniel Defoe, *A Tour thro' the Whole Island of Great Britain*, 4th ed., 4 vols. (London: for S. Birt, 1748), 4:44 (MBAt, no. Wa.91).

6. Defoe, *Tour*, 2:83.

7. [Benjamin Franklin], *A Catalogue of Books Belonging to the Library Company of Philadelphia* (Philadelphia: B. Franklin, 1741), 22. Robert B.

Winans, *A Descriptive Checklist of Book Catalogues Separately Printed in America, 1693–1800* (Worcester, MA: American Antiquarian Society, 1981), no. 15, describes Franklin's bibliographical entries as "full title entries," but in many cases Franklin substituted his own commentaries in the place of subtitles. Consequently this catalogue provides a rich and virtually untapped resource for understanding early American book culture.

8. Defoe, *Tour*, 2:167.

9. Jack P. Greene, *The Intellectual Heritage of the Constitutional Era* (Philadelphia: Library Company of Philadelphia, 1986), 28–29.

10. Virginia Woolf, *The Letters of Virginia Woolf*, ed. Nigel Nicolson and Joanne Trautmann Banks, 6 vols. (New York: Harcourt Brace Jovanovich, 1975–1980), 4:269.

11. Robert Beverley, *The History and Present State of Virginia*, ed. Louis B. Wright (Chapel Hill: University of North Carolina Press, 1947), 8.

12. Defoe, *Tour*, 1:212.

13. Defoe, *Tour*, 2:9.

14. W. H. Venable, *Beginnings of Literary Culture in the Ohio Valley: Historical and Biographical Sketches* (Cincinnati, OH: Robert Clarke, 1891), 6, finds *The Journal of Major George Washington* reminiscent of *Robinson Crusoe*.

15. Defoe, *Tour*, 3:146.

16. Defoe, *Tour*, 4:127.

17. GW to Richard Washington, August 10, 1760, *Papers, Colonial Series*, 6:453.

18. *A Compleat History of the Piratical States of Barbary* (London: for R. Griffiths, 1750), iii.

19. *Compleat History of the Piratical States*, vi.

20. *Compleat History of the Piratical States*, viii.

21. Kevin J. Hayes, *A Colonial Woman's Bookshelf* (1996; Eugene, OR: Wipf & Stock, 2016), 116.

22. Johann Wolfgang von Goethe, *The Autobiography of Goethe: Truth and Poetry from My Own Life*, trans. John Oxenford, 2 vols. (London: George Bell, 1891), 1:23.

23. Glyn Williams, "George Anson's *Voyage Round the World*," *Princeton University Library Chronicle* 64 (2003): 303–4.

24. *A Voyage Round the World, in the Years MDCCXL, I, II, III, IV. by George Anson, Esq.*, 6th ed. (London: for John and Paul Knapton, 1749), sig. A2v.

25. *Voyage Round the World*, 413.

26. *Voyage Round the World*, 110.

27. Laurence Echard, *The Gazetteer; or, News-man's Interpreter* (London: for S. and E. Ballard, 1751), sig. A2r.

28. Patrick Gordon, *Geography Anatomiz'd; or, The Geographical Grammar, Being a Short and Exact Analysis of the Whole Body of Modern Geography, after a New and Curious Method* (London: for J. and P. Knapton, 1749), 36–41.

29. Gordon, *Geography Anatomiz'd*, 41.

30. Con Coronneos, *Space, Conrad, and Modernity* (New York: Oxford University Press, 2002), 27.

31. Dennis Reinhartz, "Moll, Henry," *ODNB*.

32. Joseph Towne Wheeler, "Reading and Other Recreations of Marylanders, 1700–1776," *Maryland Historical Magazine* 38 (1943): 169–70; "Libraries in Colonial Virginia," *1WMQ* 8 (1900): 146, 149; Kevin J. Hayes, *The Library of William Byrd of Westover* (Madison, WI: Madison House, 1997), no. A4; "Library of Charles Dick," *1WMQ* 18 (1909): 112–13.

33. [Franklin], *Catalogue of Books*, 26.

34. Mark Carey, "Inventing Caribbean Climates: How Science, Medicine, and Tourism Changed Tropical Weather from Deadly to Healthy," *Osiris* 26 (2011): 136.

35. GW, *Diaries*, 1:24, 87.

36. Griffith Hughes, *Natural History of Barbados* (London, 1750), iii.

37. Raymond Phineas Stearns, *Science in the British Colonies of America* (Urbana: University of Illinois Press, 1970), 359.

38. GW, *Diaries*, 1:69.

39. *The Aviary; or, Magazine of British Melody, Consisting of a Collection of One Thousand Three Hundred and Forty Four Songs* (London: J. Mechell, [1745]), 385.

40. Jack D. Warren, Jr., "The Significance of George Washington's Journey to Barbados," *Journal of the Barbados Museum and Historical Society* 47 (2001): 6.

41. GW, *Diaries*, 1:73.

42. GW, *Diaries*, 1:78, 87; Kim D. Bowman and Frederick G. Gmitter, Jr., "Forbidden Fruit (*Citrus* sp., Rutaceae) Rediscovered in Saint Lucia," *Economic Botany* 44 (1990): 165–73.

43. GW, *Diaries*, 1:87.

44. Warren, "Significance," 20.

45. GW, *Diaries*, 1:93.

46. Tobias Smollett, *The Adventures of Peregrine Pickle*, ed. James L. Clifford (New York: Oxford University Press, 1969), 148.

47. GW, *Diaries*, 1:93.

48. No complete inventory of Dinwiddie's library survives. These generalizations are based on books in which his name is listed as a subscriber: Archibald Bower, *The History of the Popes, from the Foundation of the See of Rome, to the Present Times*, vol. 2 (London: for the author, 1750); Robert Boyle, *Works*, 5 vols. (London: for A. Millar, 1744); Gilbert Burnet, *History of His Own Time*, ed. Thomas Burnet, vol. 2 (London: for the editor, 1734); James Foster, *Discourses on All the Principal Branches of Natural Religion and Social Virtue*, 2 vols. (London: for the author, 1752); Henry Grove, *A System of Moral Philosophy*, 2 vols. (London: J. Waugh, 1749); and Mary Leapor, *Poems upon Several Occasions*, ed. Isaac Hawkins Browne (London: J. Roberts, 1748).

Chapter 5: *The Journal of Major George Washington*

Epigraph from William Cowper, *The Task, Table Talk, and Other Poems*, ed. James Robert Boyd (New York: A. S. Barnes, 1856), 220.

1. *French Policy Defeated: Being, An Account of All the Hostile Proceedings of the French, against the Inhabitants of the British Colonies in North America, for the Last Seven Years* (London: for M. Cooper, 1755), 51.

2. GW, *The Journal of Major George Washington* (London: for T. Jeffreys, 1754), 3.

3. "Major George Washington's Journal to the River Ohio," *Boston Gazette*, April 16, 1754.

4. J. B. Harley, "The Bankruptcy of Thomas Jeffreys: An Episode in the Economic History of Eighteenth Century Map-Making," *Imago Mundi* 20 (1966): 37; *Public Advertiser* (London), July 4, 1754.

5. "Major George Washington's Journal," *Massachusetts Magazine* 1 (1789): 346.

6. Richard Beale Davis, *Intellectual Life in the Colonial South, 1585–1763*, 3 vols. (Knoxville: University of Tennessee Press, 1978), 3:1438. William M. Ferraro similarly appreciates the "crisp pace" of the narrative as well as its cast of exotic characters. See his "George Washington's Mind," in *A Companion to George Washington*, ed. Edward G. Lengel (Malden, MA: Wiley-Blackwell, 2012), 553.

7. GW to John Robinson, May 30, 1757, *Papers, Colonial Series*, 4:174–75.

8. GW, *Journal*, 6.

9. W. H. Venable, *Beginnings of Literary Culture in the Ohio Valley: Historical and Biographical Sketches* (Cincinnati: Robert Clarke, 1891), 7.

10. W. H. Snowden, *Some Old Historical Landmarks of Virginia and Maryland, Described in a Hand-book for the Tourist* (Alexandria, VA: G. H. Ramey & Son, 1902), 96; Suetonius, *The Twelve Caesars*, trans. Robert Graves, ed. J. B. Rives (New York: Penguin, 2007), 16, 349; GW to William Woodford, March 3, 1777, *Papers, Revolutionary War Series*, 8:508.

11. William Fairfax to GW, May 13–14, 1756, *Papers, Colonial Series*, 3:125. Peter C. Luebke, "A Provincial Goes to War: George Washington and the Virginia Regiment, August 1755–January 1759," in Lengel, *Companion to George Washington*, 57, agrees that Washington owned a copy of Quintus Curtius's life of Alexander the Great.

12. GW, "Enclosure: Invoice to Robert Cary and Company," September 20, 1759, *Papers, Colonial Series*, 6:355; Amanda C. Isaac, *Take Note! George Washington the Reader* (Mount Vernon, VA: George Washington's Mount Vernon, 2013), 26.

13. John Seelye, "Cincinnatus," *Virginia Quarterly Review* 53 (1977): 546.

14. GW, *Journal*, 7.

15. GW, *Journal*, 9.

16. GW, *Journal*, 10.

17. GW, *Journal*, 11.

18. Lawrence C. Wroth, "The Indian Treaty as Literature," *Yale Review* 17 (1928): 766.

19. C. William Miller, *Benjamin Franklin's Philadelphia Printing, 1728–1766: A Descriptive Bibliography* (Philadelphia: American Philosophical

Society, 1974), no. 364; Lawrence C. Wroth, "A Maryland Merchant and His Friends in 1750," *Maryland Historical Magazine* 6 (1911): 223.

20. GW, *Journal*, 12.
21. GW, *Journal*, 14.
22. GW, *Journal*, 15.
23. GW, *Journal*, 17.
24. GW, *Journal*, 17.
25. Quoted in *Diaries*, 1:134.
26. GW, *Journal*, 20.
27. GW, *Journal*, 20.
28. Quoted in *Diaries*, 1:151.
29. GW, *Journal*, 23.
30. GW, *Diaries*, 1:151.
31. GW, *Journal*, 24.
32. Quoted in *Diaries*, 1:154.
33. GW, *Journal*, 25.
34. GW, *Journal*, 26.

35. Marshall Joseph Becker, "Matchcoats: Cultural Conservatism and Change in One Aspect of Native American Clothing," *Ethnohistory* 52 (2005): 754.

36. Quoted in *Diaries*, 1:157.
37. GW, *Journal*, 26–27.
38. GW, *Journal*, 27.

Chapter 6: *A Memorial Containing a Summary View of Facts*

Epigraph from Samuel Butler, *Hudibras*, ed. Treadway Russel Nash, 2 vols. (London: John Murray, 1835), canto 3, lines 1–2.

1. [William Smith], *A Review of the Military Operations in North-America, from the Commencement of the French Hostilities on the Frontiers of Virginia in 1753, to the Surrender of Oswego, on the 14th of August, 1756* (London: for R. and J. Dodsley, 1757), 6. Lawrence C. Wroth, *An American Bookshelf, 1755* (Philadelphia: University of Pennsylvania Press, 1934), 167–69, attributes this anonymous work to William Livingston. For the more recent attribution to Smith, see Beverly McAnear, "American Imprints Concerning King's College," *Papers of the Bibliographical Society of America* 44 (1950): 335.

2. GW to John Augustine Washington, May 31, 1754, *Papers, Colonial Series*, 1:118.

3. GW, "Copy of a Letter from Major-General Washington to His Brother, Dated at the Camp in Great Meadows in Virginia, May 31, 1754," *London Magazine* 23 (1754): 371; Horace Walpole, *Memoirs of the Reign of King George the Second*, ed. Henry Richard Vassall, 2d ed., 3 vols. (London: Henry Colburn, 1847), 1:400.

4. *French Policy Defeated: Being, An Account of All the Hostile Proceedings of the French, against the Inhabitants of the British Colonies in North America, for the Last Seven Years* (London: for M. Cooper, 1755), 67.

5. Voltaire, *The Works of M. de Voltaire*, trans. Tobias Smollett, 35 vols. (London: J. Newberry, 1761–1765), 22:256–57.

6. GW, "Comments on David Humphreys' Biography," *Papers, Confederation Series*, 5:517.

7. Thomas Jefferson to Walter Jones, January 2, 1814, *The Papers of Thomas Jefferson: Retirement Series*, ed. J. Jefferson Looney et al., 11 vols. to date (Princeton, NJ: Princeton University Press, 2004–), 7:101; François Jean, marquis de Chastellux, *Travels in North America in the Years 1780, 1781, and 1782*, ed. and trans. Howard C. Rice, 2 vols. (Chapel Hill: University of North Carolina Press, 1963), 1:111.

8. [Smith], *Review of Military Operations*, 10–11.

9. [John Huske], *The Present State of North America* (London: R. and J. Dodsley, 1755), 66. ESTC attributes this work to Ellis Huske, but Wroth, *An American Bookshelf*, 35–37, demonstrates convincingly that his son John wrote the work, which was written in London and not completed until after Ellis Huske's death.

10. Donald H. Kent, "Contrecoeur's Copy of George Washington's Journal for 1754," *Pennsylvania History* 19 (1952): 8.

11. Duquesne to Contrecoeur, September 8, 1754, in Kent, "Contrecoeur's Copy," 5.

12. Duquesne to Contrecoeur, September 8, 1754, in Kent, "Contrecoeur's Copy," 6.

13. Duquesne to Contrecoeur, March 5, 1755, in Kent, "Contrecoeur's Copy," 7.

14. Alexander Hamilton to Baillie Hamilton, August 1755, in Elaine G. Breslaw, "A Dismal Tragedy: Drs. Alexander and John Hamilton Comment on Braddock's Defeat," *Maryland Historical Magazine* 75 (1980): 131, 132–33.

15. GW, "Comments on David Humphreys' Biography of George Washington," *Papers, Confederation Series*, 5:520.

16. Oliver Goldsmith, *The Martial Review; or, A General History of the Late Wars; Together with the Definitive Treaty, and Some Reflections on the Probable Consequences of the Peace* (London: J. Newbery, 1763), 6.

17. Brent Tarter, "Craik, James," *DVB*, 3:531–32.

18. Hamilton, in Breslaw, "Dismal Tragedy," 136. Other contemporary accounts confirm what happened to GW in this battle. See John Bolling to Robert Bolling, August 13, 1755, in John A. Schutz, "A Private Report of General Braddock's Defeat," *Pennsylvania Magazine of History and Biography* 79 (1955): 377; GW to Robert Dinwiddie, July 18, 1755, *Papers, Colonial Series*, 1:340.

19. GW to John Augustine Washington, July 18, 1755, *Papers, Colonial Series*, 1:343.

20. For an excellent discussion of Smith's humor and its impact on American literary history, see Robert D. Arner, "John Smith, the 'Starving Time,' and the Genesis of Southern Humor: Variations on a Theme," *Louisiana Studies* 12 (1973): 383–90.

21. GW, "Comments on David Humphreys' Biography of George Washington," *Papers, Confederation Series*, 5:522.

22. GW to Robert Dinwiddie, July 18, 1755, *Papers, Colonial Series*, 1:339–40.

23. Samuel Davies, *Religion and Patriotism: The Constituents of a Good Soldier: A Sermon Preached to Captain Overton's Independent Company of Volunteers, Raised in Hanover County, Virginia, August 17, 1755* (Glasgow: William Duncan, 1756), 10.

24. Keith Michael Baker, *Inventing the French Revolution: Essays on French Political Culture in the Eighteenth Century* (New York: Cambridge University Press, 1990), 59–60.

25. David A. Bell, *The Cult of the Nation in France: Inventing Nationalism, 1680–1800* (Cambridge, MA: Harvard University Press, 2001), 88.

26. GW, *Diaries*, 1:173.

27. Jacob Nicolas Moreau, *Mémoire Contenant le Précis des Faits avec Leurs Pieces Justificatives* (Paris: de l'Imprimerie Royale, 1756), 117.

28. GW, "Comments on David Humphreys' Biography," *Papers, Confederation Series*, vol. 5, 516.

29. James Thomas Flexner, *George Washington: The Forge of Experience, 1732–1775* (Boston: Little, Brown, 1965), 72.

30. Moreau, *Mémoire*, 119; Moreau, *The Conduct of the Late Ministry; or, A Memorial; Containing a Summary of Facts with Their Vouchers, in Answer to The Observations, Sent by the English Ministry, to the Courts of Europe* (London: W. Bizet, 1757), 128.

31. Jacob Nicolas Moreau, *A Memorial, Containing a Summary View of Facts with Their Authorities, in Answer to the Observations Sent by the English Ministry to the Courts of Europe* (Philadelphia: James Chattin, 1757), 150.

32. James Chattin, *Proposals for Printing by Subscription* (Philadelphia: James Chattin, 1757). Hugh Gaine's proposal shows that he and Chattin were soliciting subscribers together. Gaine assured readers that the book would definitely be printed, "there being already Subscribers enough for that Purpose in the City of Philadelphia only." *The Journals of Hugh Gaine, Printer*, ed. Paul Leicester Ford, 2 vols. (New York: Dodd, Mead, 1902), 1:26.

33. Christopher Gist to GW, October 15, 1755, *Papers, Colonial Series*, 2:115.

34. Paul Leicester Ford, "Hildeburn: Printers and Printing," *American Historical Review* 1 (1896): 548. GW's copy of the work does not survive, and his accounts do not indicate which edition he acquired, but the date of his subscription clarifies that it was indeed Chattin's edition. The New York publishers would not start soliciting subscribers until February 28, 1757, when Gaine placed an advertisement in the *New York Mercury* (Gaine, *Journals*, 1:24–26).

35. Benjamin Franklin, *The Autobiography of Benjamin Franklin: A Genetic Text*, ed. J. A. Leo Lemay and P. M. Zall (Knoxville: University of Tennessee Press, 1981), 160.

36. Ford, "Hildeburn," 548.

37. GW to William Smith, ca. March-April 1757, *Papers, Colonial Series*, 1:169.

38. Isaiah Thomas, *The History of Printing in America, with a Biography of Printers, and an Account of Newspapers*, 2 vols. (Albany: J. Munsell, 1874), 1:246–47.

39. Gaine, *Journals*, 1:26.

40. "Monthly Catalogue," *Monthly Review* 16 (1757), 468.

41. "Monthly Catalogue," *Critical Review* 3 (1757), 383.

42. C. A. M. Fennell, *The Stanford Dictionary of Anglicised Words and Phrases* (Cambridge, U.K.: Cambridge University Press, 1892), 554.

43. "Monthly Catalogue," *Monthly Review* 20 (1759), 379.

Chapter 7: Home and Garden

Epigraph from *The Works of William Cowper: His Life, Letters, and Poems*, ed. T. S. Grimshawe, 3d ed. (London: William Tegg, 1851), 578.

1. Abigail Adams to Mary Cranch, June 18, 1789, *New Letters of Abigail Adams, 1788–1801*, ed. Stewart Mitchell (Boston: Houghton Mifflin, 1947), 13.

2. John Forbes to William Pitt, September 6, 1758, *Writings of General John Forbes Relating to His Service in North America*, ed. Alfred Procter James (Menasha, WI: Collegiate Press, 1938), 205.

3. John Forbes to Henry Bouquet, June 27, 1758, *Writings*, 125; E. M. Lloyd and Michael A. McDonnell, "Forbes, John," *ODNB*.

4. GW to Robert Cary and Co., May 1, 1759, *Papers, Colonial Series*, 6:316.

5. GW to Robert Cary and Co., May 1, 1759, *Papers, Colonial Series*, 6:315.

6. Alan Fusonie and Donna Jean Fusonie, *George Washington: Pioneer Farmer* (Mount Vernon, VA: Mount Vernon Ladies' Association, 1998), 8.

7. GW, "Enclosure: Invoice to Robert Cary and Co.," May 1, 1759, *Papers, Colonial Series*, 6:317–18.

8. "Invoice from Robert Cary and Co.," August 6, 1759, *Papers, Colonial Series*, 6:333.

9. "A New System of Agriculture," *Monthly Review* 12 (1755): 59.

10. Charles Carroll of Carrollton to GW, March 3, 1775, *Papers, Colonial Series*, 10:287.

11. W. H. Snowden, *Some Old Historic Landmarks of Virginia and Maryland, Described in a Hand-Book for the Tourist of the Washington, Alexandria and Mount Vernon Electric Railway* (Alexandria, VA: G. H. Ramey, 1904), 96.

12. Mac Griswold, *Washington's Gardens at Mount Vernon: Landscape of the Inner Man* (Boston: Houghton Mifflin, 1999), 35, 48, 64; George Colman and David Garrick, *The Clandestine Marriage, A Comedy* (London: W. Simpkin, 1818), 27.

13. Batty Langley, *New Principles of Gardening; or, The Laying and Planting Parterres, Groves, Wildernesses, Labyrinths, Avenues, Parks &c.* (London: for A. Bettesworth and J. Batley, 1728), xi.

14. Blanche Henrey, *British Botanical and Horticultural Literature before 1800: Comprising a History and Bibliography of Botanical and Horticultural Books Printed in England, Scotland and Ireland from the Earliest Times until 1800*, 3 vols. (1975; reprinted, New York: Oxford University Press, 1999), 2:499.

15. Langley, *New Principles*, xii.

16. William M. S. Rasmussen and Robert S. Tilton, *George Washington: The Man behind the Myths* (Charlottesville: University Press of Virginia, 1999), 185.

17. Julian Ursyn Niemcewicz, "Acute Observations: From Domestic Pursuits to Concern for the Nation," in *Experiencing Mount Vernon: Eyewitness Accounts, 1785–1865*, ed. Jean B. Lee (Charlottesville: University of Virginia Press, 2006), 72.

18. Rasmussen and Tilton, *George Washington*, 186.

19. Martha Washington, *Martha Washington's Booke of Cookery and Booke of Sweetmeats*, ed. Karen Hess (1981; New York: Columbia University Press, 1995); Kevin J. Hayes, *A Colonial Woman's Bookshelf* (1996; Eugene, OR: Wipf & Stock, 2016), 80–88.

20. "And Still It Grinds," *Collector* 4 (1893), 153; John Quincy Adams, *Diary of John Quincy Adams*, ed. David Grayson Allen, 2 vols. (Cambridge, MA: Belknap Press of Harvard University Press, 1981), 2:145.

21. In "List of Books at Mount Vernon [1764]," *Papers, Colonial Series*, 7:344, GW inventories the book as "Markhams Fary." The editors of *Papers, Colonial Series*, 6:300, identify the work as Gervase Markham's *Complete Farriar* (1639), but *Markham's Master-piece*, which first appeared in 1615 and went through numerous editions through 1734, seems a much likelier possibility, especially in light of the reference to Markham GW makes in *Diaries*, 1:245, discussed below.

22. GW, "Enclosure: Invoice to Robert Cary and Co.," May 1, 1759, *Papers, Colonial Series*, 6:318.

23. GW, *Diaries*, 1:243–44.

24. Gervase Markham, *Markham's Master-piece: Containing All Knowledge Belonging to the Smith, Farrier, or Horse-Leach, Touching the Curing All Diseases in Horses* (London: for G. Conyers and J. Clarke, 1734), 274.

25. Alan Fusonie and Donna Jean Fusonie, *A Selected Bibliography on George Washington's Interest in Agriculture* (Davis, CA: Agricultural History Center, 1976), 24.

26. Alexander Home, *Georgical Essays* (York: A. Ward, for J. Dodsley, 1777), 489.

27. Archibald Cochrane, earl of Dundonald, *A Treatise, Shewing the Intimate Connection that Subsists between Agriculture and Chemistry Addressed to the Cultivators of the Soil, to the Proprietors of Fens and Mosses, in Great Britain and Ireland, and to the Proprietors of West India Estates* (London: for the author, 1795).

28. Edmund Burke, "Original Letters of Burke," *New Monthly Magazine* 16 (1826): 157.

29. GW to Robert Cary and Co., June 12, 1759, *Papers, Colonial Series,* 6:327.

30. G. E. Fussell, "Who Was the 'Celebrated Thomas Hale'?" *Notes and Queries* 192 (1947): 366–67; Henrey, *British Botanical and Horticultural Literature,* 2:95.

31. Joseph Towne Wheeler, "Reading Interests of Maryland Planters and Merchants, 1700–1776," *Maryland Historical Magazine* 37 (1942): 296.

32. GW, "List of Books at Mount Vernon [1764]," *Papers, Colonial Series,* 7:344.

33. Paul P. Hoffman, ed., *Virginia Gazette Daybooks, 1750–1752 and 1764–1766* (Charlottesville: University of Virginia Library, 1967), fol. 73. Gregory A. Stiverson and Cynthia Z. Stiverson, *Books Both Useful and Entertaining: A Study of Book Purchasing by Virginians in the Mid-Eighteenth Century* (1976; Williamsburg, VA: Colonial Williamsburg Foundation, 1984), 106, 128, note that Buckner Stith paid for printing the work and advertising it in the *Virginia Gazette* during the summer of 1764. The *Virginia Gazette* for the period does not survive. Stith's treatise was reprinted in the nineteenth century, but no copies of the reprint survive either. In *Early History of Agriculture in Virginia* (Washington, DC: Lemuel Towers, n.d.), N. F. Cabell reports that he had seen a copy of the reprint but could no longer locate any copies. He dates the reprint between 1820 and 1824 and provides a good overview of its contents, comparing it to an article on tobacco cultivation in Virginia and Maryland in J. C. Loudon, *An Encyclopaedia of Agriculture* (London: Longmans, Green, 1883), 938.

34. Buckner Stith to GW, March 22, 1787, *Papers, Confederation Series,* 5:99–100.

35. [Tanfield Leman], "Immoderate Use of Snuff," *Monthly Review* 25 (1761): 127–28.

36. Walter Karcher, *Dibenzanthracenes and Environmental Carcinogenesis* (New York: Cambridge University Press, 1992), 193.

37. Fusonie and Fusonie, *George Washington,* 8–9.

38. Hayes, *Road to Monticello,* 424.

39. George Washington to Clement Biddle, February 10, 1786, *Papers: Confederation Series,* 3:553.

40. GW, *Diaries,* 1:293–98.

41. GW, *Diaries,* 1:298.

42. "Invoice from Robert Cary and Co.," April 10, 1762, *Papers, Colonial Series,* 7:127.

43. GW, *Diaries,* 1:299.

44. John Seelye, "Cincinnatus," *Virginia Quarterly Review* 53 (1977): 542–43.

45. "Invoice from Robert Cary and Co.," August 6, 1759, *Papers, Colonial Series,* 6:334.

46. Jonathan Swift, *The Works of Jonathan Swift*, ed. Walter Scott, 19 vols. (London: Bickers & Son, 1883), 14:49.

47. GW, "Enclosure: Invoice to Robert Cary and Co.," September 20, 1759, *Papers, Colonial Series*, 6:332.

48. Quoted in J. A. Leo Lemay, "The Rev. Samuel Davies' Essay Series: The Virginia Centinel, 1756–1757," in *Essays in Early Virginia Literature Honoring Richard Beale Davis*, ed. J. A. Leo Lemay (New York: B. Franklin, 1977), 124.

49. William Byrd had a copy of John Bancks's *History of John, Duke of Marlborough* at Westover. Kevin J. Hayes, *The Library of William Byrd of Westover* (Madison, WI: Madison House, 1997), no. 1904. Patrick Henry owned Bancks's *History of Francis-Eugene, Prince of Savoy*. Kevin J. Hayes, *The Mind of a Patriot: Patrick Henry and the World of Ideas* (Charlottesville: University of Virginia Press, 2008), 111.

50. J. A. Leo Lemay, *A Calendar of American Poetry in the Colonial Newspapers and Magazines and in the Major English Magazines through 1765* (Worcester, MA: American Antiquarian Society, 1972), nos. 1420, 1423, 1425, 1447, 1472, 1519.

51. [James Sterling], "The Royal Comet," *American Magazine and Monthly Chronicle* 1 (1758): 552.

52. "Invoice from Robert Cary and Company," March 15, 1760, *Papers, Colonial Series*, 6:400.

53. Rasmussen and Tilton, *George Washington*, 27.

54. Invoice from Robert Cary and Co., March 15, 1760, *Papers, Colonial Series*, 6:399.

55. George Berkeley, "Verses by the Author, on the Prospect of Planting Arts and Learning in America," in *A Miscellany, Containing Several Tracts on Various Subjects* (Dublin: George Faulkner, 1752), 186.

56. GW, "List of Books at Mount Vernon [1764]," *Papers, Colonial Series*, 7:344; GW to George William Fairfax, June 30, 1785, *Papers, Confederation Series*, 3:90.

57. Wheeler, "Reading Interests of Maryland Planters," 296–97.

58. Pehr Kalm, *Kalm's Account of His Visit to England on His Way to America in 1748*, trans. Joseph Lucas (New York: Macmillan, 1892), 111.

59. GW to George Augustine Washington, January 6, 1785; GW to George Clinton, December 8, 1784; and GW to George Clinton, April 20, 1785, *Papers, Confederation Series*, 2:258–59, 511, 174.

60. Duhamel du Monceau, *A Practical Treatise of Husbandry: Wherein Are Contained, Many Useful and Valuable Experiments and Observations*, ed. and trans. John Mills, 2d ed. (London: for C. Hitch and L. Hawes, 1762) (Virginia Historical Society copy, no. S 515 D87 1762).

61. Fusonie and Fusonie, *Selected Bibliography*, 8–9.

62. Rasmussen and Tilton, *George Washington*, 107.

63. Cowper, *Works*, 563.

64. GW to Tench Tilghman, August 11, 1784, and Tench Tilghman to GW, August 18, 1784, *Papers, Confederation Series*, 2:30–31, 42.

65. Sarudy, *Gardens and Gardening*, 48; GW to Margaret Tilghman Carroll, September 16, 1789, and Otho Holland Williams to GW, October 19, 1789, *Papers, Presidential Series*, 4:43, 159.

66. Griffin, *Catalogue*, 1–2.

Chapter 8: George Washington, Bibliographer

1. GW, "Inventory of the Books in the Estate [1759]," *Papers, Colonial Series*, 6:283.

2. GW to Bartholomew Dandridge, April 20, 1782, *Writings*, 9:478.

3. Kevin J. Hayes, *The Library of William Byrd of Westover* (Madison, WI: Madison House, 1997), 90–92.

4. GW, "Inventory," *Papers, Colonial Series*, 6:293.

5. G. F. Sensabaugh, *Milton in Early America* (Princeton, NJ: Princeton University Press, 1964), 62; Moses Coit Tyler, *The Literary History of the American Revolution, 1763–1783*, 2 vols. (New York: G. P. Putnam's Sons, 1897), 1:136.

6. GW, "Inventory," *Papers, Colonial Series*, 6:291, 289, 287, 294, 296.

7. Hayes, *Library of William Byrd*, 89.

8. Kevin J. Hayes, review of *Empire's Nature: Mark Catesby's New World Vision*, ed. Amy R. W. Meyers and Margaret Beck Pritchard, *VMHB* 108 (2000), 181.

9. G. W. P. Custis inherited the volume and, in 1833, donated it to Georgetown University, where it survives today (Special Collections, no. 77VB1); Artemis G. Kirk, and George M. Barringer, "Georgetown University Libraries," in *Encyclopedia of Library and Information Science*, ed. Miriam A. Drake, 2d ed., 4 vols. (New York: Marcel Dekker, 2003), 2:1142.

10. Hayes, *Library of William Byrd*, no. 100; Arthur Foley, *The Early English Colonies*, ed. Sadler Phillips (London: Elliot Stock, 1908), 39; Samuel Henley, "Notes," in William Beckford, *The History of the Caliph Vathek*, ed. and trans. Samuel Henley (London: Sampson, Low, Son, & Marston, 1868), 163.

11. Henley, "Notes," 163.

12. Thomas Jefferson to Walter Jones, January 2, 1814, *The Papers of Thomas Jefferson: Retirement Series*, ed. J. Jefferson Looney et al., 11 vols. to date. (Princeton, NJ: Princeton University Press, 2004–), 7:102.

13. GW, "List of Books at Mount Vernon [1764]," *Papers, Colonial Series*, 7:345.

14. Caroline Robbins, *The Eighteenth-Century Commonwealthman: Studies in the Transmission, Development and Circumstances of English Liberal Thought from the Restoration of Charles II Until the War with the Thirteen Colonies* (1959; New York: Athenaeum, 1968), 115–25.

15. GW, "List of Books," *Papers, Colonial Series*, 7:347; GW, "General Orders [October 24, 1778]," "General Orders [December 15, 1778]," "General Orders [December 29, 1778]," "General Orders [May 24, 1778]," *Papers, Revolutionary War Series*, 17:549 and 18:413, 524, 15: 207; *Plutarch's*

Lives, ed. and trans. John Langhorne and William Langhorne (New York: Harper & Brothers, 1872), 537.

16. Albert Furtwangler, "Cato at Valley Forge," *Modern Language Quarterly* 41 (1980): 38–53; Randall Fuller, "Theaters of the American Revolution: The Valley Forge *Cato* and the Meschianza in Their Transcultural Contexts," *Early American Literature* 34 (1999): 126–46; Mark Evans Bryan, "Slideing into Monarchical extravagance": *Cato* at Valley Forge and the Testimony of William Bradford, Jr." *3WMQ* 67 (2010): 123–44.

17. H. Trevor Colbourn, *The Lamp of Experience: Whig History and the Intellectual Origins of the American Revolution* (1965; New York: Norton, 1974), 24; Bernard Bailyn, *The Ideological Origins of the American Revolution* (Cambridge, MA: Belknap Press of Harvard University Press, 1967), 44; Gordon S. Wood, "The Legacy of Rome in the American Revolution," in *Thomas Jefferson, the Classical World, and Early America*, ed. Peter S. Onuf and Nicholas P. Cole (Charlottesville: University of Virginia Press, 2011), 19.

18. John Trenchard and Thomas Gordon, *The English Libertarian Heritage: From the Writings of John Trenchard and Thomas Gordon in the Independent Whig and Cato's Letters*, ed. David L. Jacobson (Indianapolis, IN: Bobbs-Merrill, 1965), 38.

19. Paul K. Longmore, *The Invention of George Washington* (1988; Charlottesville: University Press of Virginia, 1999), 120.

20. Byron Gassman, "Tobias Smollett," in *British Prose Writers, 1660–1800: Second Series*, ed. Donald T. Siebert (Detroit: Gale, 1991), 289; Kenneth Simpson, "Smollett, Tobias," *ODNB*.

21. GW, "List of Books," *Papers, Colonial Series*, 7:343.

22. *Virginia Gazette Daybooks, 1750–1752 and 1764–1766*, ed. Paul P. Hoffman (Charlottesville: University of Virginia Library, 1967).

23. Hayes, *Library of William Byrd*, 66; Edwin Wolf 2nd, and Kevin J. Hayes, *The Library of Benjamin Franklin* (Philadelphia: American Philosophical Society and Library Company of Philadelphia, 2006), 18–20; Hayes, *Road to Monticello*, 560–63.

24. Percy G. Adams, "Introduction to the Dover Edition," in Alexandre Olivier Exquemelin, *The Buccaneers of America* (New York: Dover, 1967), v; Edwin Wolf 2nd, *The Book Culture of a Colonial American City: Philadelphia Books, Bookmen, and Booksellers* (Oxford: Clarendon, 1988), 127.

25. Adams, "Introduction," xiv; Joel H. Baer, "Dampier, William," *ODNB*.

26. Griffin, *Catalogue*, 489.

27. [Jonathan Swift], *Travels into Several Remote Nations of the World: In Four Parts by Lemuel Gulliver, First a Surgeon, and Then a Captain of Several Ships*, 2d ed. (London: for Benj. Motte, 1727), 2:45 (NjP copy, no. 3950.391.12).

28. "Washington and the Pope," *American Catholic Historical Researches* 1 (1905): 399.

29. Tipped into the copy of Alexander Pope's five-volume translation *The Odyssey of Homer* (London: for Henry Lintot, 1758) that survives at the Huntington Library is a statement, signed Lawrence Washington, that this set was in GW's library (no. 124650).

30. Richard Beale Davis, *Intellectual Life in the Colonial South, 1585–1763*, 3 vols. (Knoxville: University of Tennessee Press, 1978), 3:1408; Henry Babcock to GW, February 25, 1784, *Papers, Confederation Series*, 1:156.

31. John Kirkpatrick to GW, September 22, 1756, *Papers, Colonial Series*, 3:410.

32. GW to Joseph Reed, February 26–March 9, 1776, *Papers, Revolutionary War Series*, 3:373.

33. Theophilus Lucas, *Memoirs of the Lives, Intrigues, and Comical Adventures of the Most Famous Gamesters and Celebrated Sharpers in the Reigns of Charles II. James II. William III. and Queen Anne* (London: for Jonas Brown and Ferdinando Burleigh, 1714), sig. A2r.

34. Richard Seymour, *The Compleat Gamester: In Three Parts*, 5th ed. (London: for E. Curll, 1734), v.

35. GW, "Enclosure: Invoice to Robert Cary and Company," June 23, 1766, *Papers, Colonial Series*, 7:448.

36. Henry Knox, *A Catalogue of Books, Imported and to Be Sold* (Boston: Henry Knox, 1773), 39.

37. GW ordered a mahogany card table in 1758. See GW to Thomas Knox, January 1758, *Papers, Colonial Series*, 5:88.

38. Jane Carson, *Colonial Virginians at Play* (Williamsburg. VA: Colonial Williamsburg Foundation, 1989), 27; Lucas, *Memoirs*, 126.

39. P. M. Zall, ed., *George Washington Laughing: Humorous Anecdotes by and about Our First President from Original Sources* (Hamden, CT: Archon, 1989), 31–32.

40. GW to Thomas Knox, January 1758, *Papers, Colonial Series*, 5:88.

41. Jonathan Swift, *Miscellanies* (London: for B. Motte and C. Bathhurst, 1736), 247.

42. [William Bewley], "The Handmaid to the Arts," *Monthly Review* 19 (1758): 277.

43. Rembrandt Peale, "Charles Wilson Peale," *Littell's Living Age* 44 (1855): 649; William Dunlap, *History of the Rise and Progress of the Arts of Design in the United States*, 2 vols. (New York: George P. Scott, 1834), 1:342.

44. GW, "Enclosure," *Papers, Colonial Series*, 7:448.

45. Arthur Lee to Richard Henry Lee, November 15, 1769, *Memoir of the Life of Richard Henry Lee and His Correspondence*, ed. Richard H. Lee, 2 vols. (Philadelphia: H. C. Carey and I. Lea, 1825), 1:261; "Invoice from Robert Cary and Company," November 17, 1766, *Papers, Colonial Series*, 7:473.

46. [William Kenrick], "Select Papers on Agriculture, etc.," *Monthly Review* 31 (1764): 322.

47. GW, "Enclosure: Invoice to Robert Cary and Company [July 20, 1767]," *Papers, Colonial Series*, 8:13.

48. Konstantin Dierks, *In My Power: Letter Writing and Communications in Early America* (Philadelphia: University of Pennsylvania Press, 2009), 184–85.

Chapter 9: The Education of John Parke Custis

1. GW, "Cash Accounts [January and November 1760]," *Papers, Colonial Series*, 6:379, 474.

2. Quoted in *Papers, Colonial Series*, 8:167.

3. Frederick Lewis Weis, *The Colonial Clergy of Maryland, Delaware, and Georgia* (Lancaster, MA: Society of the Descendants of the Colonial Clergy, 1950), 55.

4. GW to Jonathan Boucher, July 9, 1771, *Papers, Colonial Series*, 8:494.

5. GW to Robert Cary and Co., November 15, 1762, *Papers, Colonial Series*, 7:168.

6. Paul P. Hoffman, ed., *Virginia Gazette Daybooks, 1750–1752 and 1764–1766* (Charlottesville: University of Virginia Library, 1967), fol. 40.

7. John Clarke, "The Preface," in Erasmus, *Colloquia Selecta; or, The Select Colloquies of Erasmus*, ed. and trans. John Clarke (London: for W. Clarke, 1759), sig. A3r.

8. GW, "Cash Accounts [December 1766]," and GW to Jonathan Boucher, May 30, 1768, *Papers, Colonial Series*, 7:478 and 8:89.

9. GW to Jonathan Boucher, May 30, 1768, *Papers, Colonial Series*, 8:90.

10. GW to Jonathan Boucher, May 30, 1768, *Papers, Colonial Series*, 8:89–90.

11. GW to Jonathan Boucher, May 30, 1768, *Papers, Colonial Series*, 8:90.

12. Quoted in Jonathan Boucher, *Reminiscences of an American Loyalist, 1738–1789: Being the Autobiography of the Revd. Jonathan Boucher, Rector of Annapolis in Maryland and Afterwards Vicar of Epsom, Surrey, England*, ed. Jonathan Bouchier (Boston: Houghton, Mifflin, 1925), 80.

13. Hayes, *Road to Monticello*, 35.

14. Jonathan Boucher to GW, July 15, 1768, *Papers, Colonial Series*, 8:116.

15. GW to Jonathan Boucher, July 31, 1768, *Papers, Colonial Series*, 8:120.

16. Jonathan Boucher to GW, August 2, 1768, *Papers, Colonial Series*, 8:123.

17. GW to Jonathan Boucher, October 20, 1768, *Papers, Colonial Series*, 8:138.

18. GW to Jonathan Boucher, January 26, 1769, *Papers, Colonial Series*, 8:166.

19. GW, *Diaries*, 2:128.

20. GW to Robert Cary and Co., March 10, 1768, *Papers, Colonial Series*, 8:72.

21. GW to Jonathan Boucher, April 24, 1769, *Papers, Colonial Series*, 8:185.

22. GW to Jonathan Boucher, January 26, 1769, *Papers, Colonial Series*, 8:166.

23. "Catalogue of Books for Master Custis [July 25, 1769]," in *The Writings of George Washington from the Original Manuscript Sources, 1745–1799*, ed. John C. Fitzpatrick, 39 vols. (Washington, DC: GPO, 1931–1944), 2:515–17.

24. Marcus Tullius Cicero, *Opera Quae Supersunt omnia*, ed. P. J. Olivet, 20 vols. (Glasgow: Robert and Andrew Foulis, 1748–1749), vol. 20 (Virginia Historical Society, no. PA 6278 A2 1748).

25. Jonathan Boucher to GW, May 9, 1770, *Papers, Colonial Series*, 8:332.

26. GW to Jonathan Boucher, May 13, 1770, *Papers, Colonial Series*, 8:335.

27. Jonathan Boucher to GW, May 21, 1770, *Papers, Colonial Series*, 8:337–38.

28. Kevin J. Hayes, *The Mind of a Patriot: Patrick Henry and the World of Ideas* (Charlottesville: University of Virginia Press, 2008), no. 178; "Library of Col. William Fleming," *1WMQ* 6 (1898): 161.

29. GW to Jonathan Boucher, December 16, 1770, *Papers, Colonial Series*, 8:411.

30. Jonathan Boucher to GW, December 18, 1770, *Papers, Colonial Series*, 8:413–14.

31. GW to Jonathan Boucher, January 2, 1771, *Papers, Colonial Series*, 8:425–26.

32. GW to Jonathan Boucher, July 9, 1771, *Papers, Colonial Series*, 8:495.

33. GW to Jonathan Boucher, July 9, 1771, *Papers, Colonial Series*, 8:495.

34. G. W. P. Custis recorded two slightly different versions of the following anecdote, both based on reminiscences of Charles Willson Peale: *Recollections and Private Memoirs of Washington* (Washington, DC: William H. Moore, 1859), 41; "Bits of Biography," *Home Circle* 2 (1856): 238. The Walter Scott quotation comes from *The Lady of the Lake*, canto 5, stanza 23.

35. GW to Jonathan Boucher, January 7, 1773, *Papers, Colonial Series*, 9:154.

36. GW to Jonathan Boucher, January 7, 1773, *Papers, Colonial Series*, 9:154.

37. John Parke Custis to Martha Washington, July 5, 1773, *Papers, Colonial Series*, 9:266.

38. GW, "General Orders [April 6, 1778]," *Papers, Revolutionary War Series*, 14:410; *Henry V*, 4.3.60–62.

39. GW to Francis Hopkinson, May 16, 1785, *Papers, Confederation Series*, 2:561–62; *Twelfth Night*, 2.4.112–15.

40. GW to Henry Laurens, October 3, 1778, *Papers, Revolutionary War Series*, 17:238; *The Tempest*, 4.1.151.

41. GW, *Diaries*, 5:176; GW to Elizabeth Willing Powel, April 23, 1792, *Papers, Presidential Series*, 10:314.

42. GW to Burwell Bassett, June 20, 1773, *Papers, Colonial Series*, 9:243.

43. Michael J. Doherty, "The Sudden Death of Patsy Custis, or George Washington on Sudden Unexplained Death in Epilepsy," *Epilepsy and Behavior* 5 (2004): 598–600.

44. Jonathan Boucher to GW, April 8, 1773, *Papers, Colonial Series*, 9:212.

45. Jonathan Boucher, *A View of the Causes and Consequences of the American Revolution; in Thirteen Discourses, Preached in North America between the Years 1763 and 1775: With an Historical Preface* (London: for G. G. and J. Robinson, 1797), 197.

46. Richard Beale Davis, *Intellectual Life in the Colonial South, 1585–1763*, 3 vols. (Knoxville: University of Tennessee Press, 1978), 1:384.

Chapter 10: Revolutionary Pamphlets

Epigraph from Isaac D'Israeli, *Amenities of Literature, Consisting of Sketches and Characters of English Literature*, 2d ed., 2 vols. (New York: J. and H. G. Langley, 1841), 2:375.

1. GW, "Cash Accounts [August 1774]," *Papers, Colonial Series*, 10:139.

2. Hayes, *Road to Monticello*, 159–60.

3. GW recorded dining at Peyton Randolph's home on August 3, 1774 (*Diaries*, 3:268).

4. Edmund Randolph, *History of Virginia*, ed. Arthur H. Shaffer (Charlottesville: University Press of Virginia, 1970), 205.

5. Tobias Smollett, *A Complete History of England, from the Descent of Julius Caesar, to the Treaty of Aix La Chapelle, 1748*, 11 vols. (London: for James Rivington and James Fletcher, 1758–1760), 8:282–85.

6. Taylor Stoermer, "'What Manner of Man I Am': The Political Career of George Washington before the Revolution," in *A Companion to George Washington*, ed. Edward G. Lengel (Malden, MA: Wiley-Blackwell, 2012), 128.

7. GW to George William Fairfax, June 10–15, 1774, *Papers, Colonial Series*, 10:96.

8. GW to George William Fairfax, June 10–15, 1774, *Papers, Colonial Series*, 10:96.

9. GW, "Cash Accounts [June 1774]" and "Cash Accounts [November 1773]," *Papers, Colonial Series*, 10:76 and 9:355; Thomas Jefferson, *Jefferson's Memorandum Books: Accounts, with Legal Record and Miscellany, 1767–1826*, ed. James A. Bear, Jr., and Lucia C. Stanton, 2 vols. (Princeton, NJ: Princeton University Press, 1997), 1:375; *Virginia Gazette* (Purdie and Dixon), June 16, 1774.

10. "Yesterday the Society for the Advancement," *Virginia Gazette* (Purdie and Dixon), June 16, 1774.

11. Robert Polk Thomson, "The Reform of the College of William and Mary, 1763–1780," *Proceedings of the American Philosophical Society* 115 (1971): 199.

12. Samuel Henley, *A Candid Refutation of the Heresy Imputed by Ro. C. Nicholas, Esquire, to the Reverend S. Henley* (Williamsburg, VA: for B. White in London, D. Prince in Oxford, and J. Woodyer in Cambridge, 1774) (MBAt, no. Wa.216).

13. GW, *Diaries*, 3:271–73.

14. Edmund Pendleton to————, September, 1774?, *The Letters and Papers of Edmund Pendleton*, ed. David John Mays, 2 vols. (Charlottesville: for the Virginia Historical Society by the University Press of Virginia, 1967), 1:98. Mays cites Anna Hollingsworth Wharton, *Martha Washington* (New York: C. Scribner's Sons, 1897), 82, as his source for this letter but admits that Wharton did not indicate her source. In fact, she took it from Benson J. Lossing, *Mary and Martha: The Mother and the Wife of George Washington* (New York: Harper, 1886), 129, the earliest known instance of this anecdote.

15. Silas Deane to Elizabeth Deane, September 10–11, 1774, *LDC*, 1:61.

16. William Wirt Henry, *Patrick Henry: Life, Correspondence and Speeches*, 3 vols. (New York: Scribner's, 1891), 1:247.

17. Clifford K. Shipton and James E. Mooney, *National Index of American Imprints through 1800: The Short Title Evans*, 2 vols. (Worcester, MA: American Antiquarian Society, 1969), nos. 13703–4, 42724–25.

18. Colin Wells, "Revolutionary Verse," in *The Oxford Handbook of Early American Literature*, ed. Kevin J. Hayes (New York: Oxford University Press, 2008), 508.

19. Kevin J. Hayes, "Poetry in the Time of Revolution," in *The Cambridge History of American Poetry*, ed. Alfred Bendixen and Stephen Burt (New York: Cambridge University Press, 2014), 141.

20. Bob Jingle [pseud.], *The Association, &c. of the Delegates of the Colonies, at the Grand Congress, Held at Philadelphia, Sept. 1, 1774* ([New York?: James Rivington?], 1774), 8.

21. Jingle, *Association*, 11.

22. Gordon S. Wood, "Prologue: The Legacy of Rome in the American Revolution," *Thomas Jefferson, the Classical World, and Early America*, ed. Peter S. Onuf and Nicholas P. Cole (Charlottesville: University of Virginia Press, 2011), 24.

23. "To the Printer," *New-York Journal*, November 24, 1774.

24. [Samuel Seabury], *Free Thoughts, on the Proceedings of the Continental Congress, Held at Philadelphia Sept. 5, 1774* ([New York?: James Rivington?], 1774), 18.

25. Benjamin Rush to Thomas Ruston, October 29, 1775, *Letters of Benjamin Rush*, ed. Lyman H. Butterfield, 2 vols. (Princeton, NJ: Princeton University Press, 1951), 1:92.

26. Benjamin Rush, *The Autobiography of Benjamin Rush: His "Travels through Life" Together with his Commonplace Book for 1789–1813*, ed. George W. Corner (Princeton, NJ: Princeton University Press for the American Philosophical Society, 1948), 111.

27. Virginia Delegates to GW, October 24, 1774, *LDC*, 1:245.

28. Rush, *Autobiography*, 111–12.

29. William Milnor to GW, November 29, 1774, *Papers, Colonial Series*, 10:189.

30. William Hooper to James Duane, November 22, 1774, *LDC*, 1:263.

31. William Hooper to James Duane, November 22, 1774, *LDC*, 1:263.

32. "Remarks on the Friendly Address to All Reasonable Americans," *New-York Journal*, December 1, 1774.

33. Paul David Nelson, "Lee, Charles," *ODNB*.

34. Charles Carroll of Carrollton to GW, March 3, 1775, *Papers, Colonial Series*, 10:287; A Farmer [pseud.], *An Essay on the Culture and Management of Hemp, More Particularly for the Purpose of Making Coarse Linens* (Annapolis, MD: Anne Catherine Green & Son, 1775), 3.

Chapter 11: *Common Sense* and Independence

Epigraph from Thomas Paine, *Collected Writings*, ed. Eric Foner (New York: Library of America, 1995), 52.

1. William M. S. Rasmussen and Robert S. Tilton, *George Washington: The Man behind the Myths* (Charlottesville: University Press of Virginia, 1999), 294.

2. Paul K. Longmore, *The Invention of George Washington* (1988; Charlottesville: University Press of Virginia, 1999), 161–62.

3. G. W. P. Custis, *Recollections and Private Memoirs of Washington* (Washington, DC: William H. Moore, 1859), 28–29.

4. John Adams to Abigail Adams, June 23, 1775; "Robert Treat Paine's Diary [June 23, 1775]"; Silas Deane to Elizabeth Deane, June 23, 1775; all in *LDC*, 1:537–39.

5. Moses Coit Tyler, *The Literary History of the American Revolution, 1763–1783*, 2 vols. (New York: G. P. Putnam's Sons, 1897), 2:318.

6. Silas Deane to Elizabeth Deane, June 23, 1775, *LDC*, 1:537.

7. William Smith, *A Sermon on the Present State of American Affairs: Preached in Christ-Church, June 23, 1775* (Philadelphia; James Humphreys, 1775), 28.

8. Thomas Coombe, *A Sermon, Preached before the Congregations of Christ Church and St. Peter's, Philadelphia, on Tuesday, July 20, 1775* (Philadelphia: John Dunlap, 1775), 5.

9. Joseph Hodgkins to Sarah Perkins Hodgkins, July 3, 1775, in Herbert T. Wade and Robert A. Lively, *This Glorious Cause: The Adventures of Two Company Officers in Washington's Army* (Princeton, NJ: Princeton University Press, 1958), 171.

10. Samuel Langdon to GW, July 8, 1789, *Papers, Presidential Series*, 3:150.

11. Samuel Langdon, *Government Corrupted by Vice, and Recovered by Righteousness: A Sermon Preached before the Honorable Congress of the Colony of the Massachusetts-Bay in New England* (Watertown, MA: Benjamin Edes, 1775), 6.

12. Judith N. Shklar, *Redeeming American Political Thought*, ed. Stanley Hoffman and Dennis F. Thompson (Chicago: University of Chicago Press, 1998), 132–33.

13. David Howell to William Greene, September 9?, 1783, *LDC*, 20:646.

14. Henry Wadsworth Longfellow to George W. Greene, August 6, 1838, *The Letters of Henry Wadsworth Longfellow*, ed. Andrew R. Hilen, 6 vols. (Cambridge, MA: Belknap Press of Harvard University Press, 1967–82), 2:94.

15. William Gordon to GW, December 19, 1776, *Papers, Revolutionary War Series*, 7:376.

16. William Gordon, *A Sermon Preached before the Honorable House of Representatives, on the Day Intended for the Choice of Counsellors, Agreeable to the Advice of the Continental Congress* (Watertown, MA: Benjamin Edes, 1775), 26.

17. GW to John Augustine Washington, March 31, 1776, *Papers, Revolutionary War Series*, 3:569.

18. Benjamin Franklin to Richard Bache, September 30, 1774, *The Papers of Benjamin Franklin*, ed. Leonard W. Labaree et al., 41 vols. to date (New Haven, CT: Yale University Press, 1959–), 21:325.

19. John Adams to Abigail Adams, April 28, 1776, *LDC*, 3:594.

20. A. Owen Aldridge, *Thomas Paine's American Ideology* (Newark: University of Delaware Press, 1984), 28.

21. Aldridge, *Thomas Paine's American Ideology*, 29.

22. Aldridge, *Thomas Paine's American Ideology*, 37.

23. Benjamin Rush, *The Autobiography of Benjamin Rush: His "Travels through Life" Together with his Commonplace Book for 1789–1813*, ed. George W. Corner (Princeton, NJ: Princeton University Press, 1948), 113–14.

24. Aldridge, *Thomas Paine's American Ideology*, 38.

25. Aldridge, *Thomas Paine's American Ideology*, 24.

26. J. A. Leo Lemay, ed., *An Early American Reader* (Washington, DC: United States Information Agency, 1988), 692.

27. Paine, *Collected Writings*, 25.

28. Paine, *Collected Writings*, 21.

29. Josiah Bartlett to John Langdon, *LDC*, 3:88.

30. Aldridge, *Thomas Paine's American Ideology*, 45; William Gordon, *The History of the Rise, Progress, and Establishment, of the Independence of the United States of America: Including an Account of the Late War, and of the Thirteen Colonies, from Their Origin to That Period*, 4 vols. (London: for the author, 1788), 2:275.

31. John Adams to Charles Lee and Benjamin Franklin to Charles Lee, February 19, 1776, *LDC*, 3:277, 281. The earliest letter identifying Paine as the author of *Common Sense* is John Hancock to Thomas Cushing, January 17, 1776, *LDC*, 3:105.

32. Charles Lee to GW, January 24, 1776, *Papers, Revolutionary War Series*, 3:183; Edward Langworthy, *Memoirs of the Life of the Late Charles Lee, Esq.* (London: J. S. Jordan, 1792), vi–vii.

33. GW to Joseph Reed, January 31, 1776, *Papers, Revolutionary War Series*, 3:228.

34. GW to Joseph Reed, April 1, 1776, *Papers, Revolutionary War Series*, 4:11.

35. Landon Carter to GW, February 20, 1776, *Papers, Revolutionary War Series*, 3:348.

36. Landon Carter, *The Diary of Colonel Landon Carter of Sabine Hall, 1752–1778*, ed. Jack P. Greene, 2 vols. (1965; Richmond: Virginia Historical Society, 1987), 2:986–87.

37. Fielding Lewis to GW, March 6, 1776, *Papers, Revolutionary War Series*, 3:418.

38. John Penn, quoted in John Adams to James Warren, April 20, 1776, *Warren-Adams Letters: Being Chiefly a Correspondence among John Adams, Samuel Adams, and James Warren*, 2 vols. (Boston: Massachusetts Historical Society, 1917–1925), 1:230.

39. William Gordon, *History of the Rise*, 2:203.

40. GW to Landon Carter, March 27, 1776, *Papers, Revolutionary War Series*, 3:545.

41. David Hackett Fischer, *Washington's Crossing* (New York: Oxford University Press, 2004), 9.

42. GW to Landon Carter, March 27, 1776, *Papers, Revolutionary War Series*, 3:546.

43. Landon Carter to GW, May 9, 1776, *Papers, Revolutionary War Series*, 4:239, 234.

44. "Honorary Degree from Harvard College," *Papers, Revolutionary War Series*, 4:23.

45. GW to Landon Carter, March 27, 1776, *Papers, Revolutionary War Series*, 3:544–46.

46. Benson J. Lossing, *The Pictorial Field-book of the Revolution; or, Illustrations, by Pen and Pencil, of the History, Biography, Scenery, Relics, and Traditions of the War for Independence*, 2 vols. (New York: Harper & Brothers, 1852), 2:801; "Obituary," *Historical Magazine* 2 (1858): 250.

47. Fischer, *Washington's Crossing*, 138–39.

48. Fischer, *Washington's Crossing*, 140.

49. William Ellery to Nicholas Cooke, December 31, 1776, *LDC*, 5:711.

50. Paine, *Collected Writings*, 91.

51. GW to Lund Washington, December 10–17, 1776, *Papers, Revolutionary War Series*, 7:291.

52. Edwin Wolf 2nd, *Legacies of Genius: A Celebration of Philadelphia Libraries; A Selection of Books, Manuscripts, and Works of Art* (Philadelphia: Philadelphia Area Consortium of Special Collections Libraries, 1988), no. 198.

Chapter 12: A Green Baize Bookcase

Epigraph from Thomas Webb, *A Military Treatise on the Appointments of the Army* (Philadelphia: W. Dunlap, 1759), 20.

1. Anthony Wayne to GW, September 2, 1777, *Papers, Revolutionary War Series*, 11:131.

2. GW, "Instructions to Company Captains," July 29, 1757, *Papers, Colonial Series*, 4:344.

3. Thomas Carlyle, *History of Friedrich II. of Russia, Called Frederick the Great*, 8 vols. (London: Chapman & Hall, 1898), 8:87.

4. Anthony Wayne to GW, September 2, 1777, *Papers, Revolutionary War Series*, 11:131.

5. J. A. Houlding, *Fit for Service: The Training of the British Army, 1715–1795* (Oxford: Clarendon, 1981), 218.

6. Quoted in Edward J. Lowell, *The Hessians and Other German Auxiliaries of Great Britain in the Revolutionary War* (New York: Harper & Brothers, 1884), 226–27.

7. Quoted in Lowell, *Hessians*, 227.

8. Peter C. Luebke, "A Provincial Goes to War: George Washington and the Virginia Regiment, August 1755–January 1759," in *A Companion to George Washington*, ed. Edward G. Lengel (Malden, MA: Wiley-Blackwell, 2012), 57–58.

9. Stephen Brumwell, *George Washington: Gentleman Warrior* (New York: Quercus, 2013), 219–20.

10. Stanley Pargellis, "Braddock's Defeat," *American Historical Review* 41 (1936): 264.

11. William Wycherley, *The Plain Dealer: A Comedy* (London: George Cawthorn, 1796), 43.

12. Robert C. Alberts, *The Most Extraordinary Adventures of Major Robert Stobo* (Boston: Houghton Mifflin, 1965), 178–79.

13. GW to Robert Cary and Company, September 28, 1760, *Papers, Colonial Series*, 6:460.

14. "Address," *Papers, Colonial Series*, 2:257.

15. GW to Andrew Lewis, May 21, 1758, *Papers, Colonial Series*, 5:189.

16. John Forbes to William Pitt, October 20, 1758, *Writings of General John Forbes Relating to His Service in North America*, ed. Alfred Procter James (Menasha, WI: Collegiate Press, 1938), 240.

17. Houlding, *Fit for Service*, 201.

18. *Imported in the Last Vessel from Europe, and Sold by David Hall, at the New Printing-Office, in Market-Street, Philadelphia, the Following Books, &c.* (Philadelphia: David Hall, [1763]).

19. Webb, *Military Treatise*, 19.

20. Webb, *Military Treatise*, 59.

21. John Adams to Abigail Adams, May 29, 1775, *LDC*, 1:417.

22. GW, "Cash Accounts [May 1775]," *Papers, Colonial Series*, 10:357.

23. Barbara E. Lacey, *From Sacred to Secular: Visual Images in Early American Publications* (Newark: University of Delaware Press, 2007), 188.

24. [Abraham Rees], "Military Instructions for Officers Detached in the Field," *Monthly Review* 44 (1771): 354–60.

25. Houlding, *Fit for Service*, 222–23.

26. Roger Stevenson, *Military Instructions for Officers Detached in the Field: Containing a Scheme for Forming a Corps of a Partisan*, ed. Hugh Henry Ferguson (Philadelphia: R. Aitken, 1775), vii.

27. Joseph R. Riling, *The Art and Science of War in America: A Bibliography of American Military Imprints, 1690–1800* (Alexandria Bay, NY: Museum Restoration Service, 1990), 12–13.

28. Henry Wadsworth Longfellow to Stephen Longfellow, March 18, 1839, *The Letters of Henry Wadsworth Longfellow*, ed. Andrew R. Hilen, 6 vols. (Cambridge, MA: Belknap Press of Harvard University Press, 1967–1982), 2:137.

29. Sandra L. Powers, "Studying the Art of War: Military Books Known to American Officers and Their French Counterparts During the Second Half of the Eighteenth Century," *Journal of Military History* 70 (2006): 805; Louis Michel De Jeney, *The Partisan; or, The Art of Making War in Detachment* (London: for R. Griffiths, 1760), xii–xiii; Edward G. Lengel, *General George Washington: A Military Life* (New York: Random House, 2005), 79.

30. Don Higginbotham, "Military Education before West Point," in *Thomas Jefferson's Military Academy: Founding West Point*, ed. Robert M. S. McDonald (Charlottesville: University of Virginia Press, 2004), 34; Lowell, *Hessians*, 227; Johann Ewald, *Treatise on Partisan Warfare*, ed. and trans. Robert A. Selig and David Curtis Skaggs (Westport, CT: Greenwood, 1991).

31. Houlding, *Fit for Service*, 225.

32. Thomas M. Spaulding and Louis C. Karpinski, *Early Military Books in the University of Michigan Libraries* (Ann Arbor: University of Michigan Press, 1941), no. 291.

33. Brumwell, *George Washington, Gentleman Warrior*, 220.

34. James Wolfe, *General Wolfe's Instructions to Young Officers* (London: for J. Millan, 1768), v.

35. Wolfe, *General Wolfe's Instructions*, 1.

36. Mark V. Kwansy, *Washington's Partisan War, 1775–1783* (Kent, OH: Kent State University Press, 1996), 342, provides the most extreme example. In this four-hundred-page book devoted to the subject, Kwansy makes only one mention of GW's field library, which he buries in an endnote. Similarly, John W. Hall, "Washington's Irregulars," in *A Companion to George Washington*, ed. Edward G. Lengel (Malden, MA: Blackwell, 2012), 333–34, recognizes that several of GW's military books treated the *petite guerre* but downplays their influence.

37. David Hackett Fischer, *Washington's Crossing* (New York: Oxford University Press, 2004), 366.

38. Allan Maclean to Alexander Cummings, February 19, 1777, *A Prime Minister and His Son, from the Correspondence of the 3rd Earl of Bute and of Lt.-General the Hon. Sir Charles Stuart, K.B.*, ed. Violet Hunter Guthrie Montagu-Stuart-Wortley (London: J. Murray, 1925), 104.

39. Charles Stuart to Lord Bute, March 29, 1777, *A Prime Minister and His Son*, 101.

40. Ewald, *Treatise on Partisan Warfare*, 115.

41. Fischer, *Washington's Crossing*, 367.

42. John C. Fitzpatrick, ed., *George Washington's Accounts of Expenses While Commander-in-Chief of the Continental Army, 1775–1783* (Boston: Houghton Mifflin, 1917), 31; *General Washington's Swords and Campaign Equipment: An Illustrated Catalogue of Military Memorabilia in the Mount Vernon Collection* (Mount Vernon, VA: Mount Vernon Ladies' Association, 1944), 10.

43. [David Humphreys], *A Poem, Addressed to the Armies of the United States of America* (New Haven, CT: T. and S. Green, 1780), 9.

44. A list of books compiled by Lund Washington in 1783 before George Washington returned from the war indicates the makeup of the Mount Vernon library during Washington's wartime absence. It lists no military books (*Papers, Colonial Series*, 7:348–49).

45. François Jean, marquis de Chastellux, *Travels in North America in the Years 1780, 1781 and 1782*, ed. Howard C. Rice, Jr., 2 vols. (Chapel Hill: University of North Carolina Press, 1963), 1:190.

46. Lowell, *Hessians*, 227.

Chapter 13: Planning for Retirement

Epigraph from *The Epistles of Lucius Annaeus Seneca*, ed. and trans. Thomas Morrell, 2 vols. (London: T. Woodfall, 1786), 2:42.

1. The source of this anecdote, which has appeared in nearly every Washington biography since the mid-nineteenth century, is an April 1783 letter by Major Samuel Shaw, one of the officers present. The letter is quoted in *The Journals of Major Samuel Shaw: The First American Consul at Canton* (Boston: William Crosby & H. P. Nichols, 1847), 104. Whereas Shaw gives Washington's words in indirect discourse, I have followed biographical tradition in converting them to direct discourse.

2. [Edmund Cartwright], "Young's Tour in Ireland," *Monthly Review* 63 (1780): 39.

3. [John Gillies], "Moore's *View of Society and Manners in France*, etc.," *Monthly Review* 60 (1779): 463–64.

4. GW to William S. Smith, May 21, 1783, *The Writings of George Washington from the Original Manuscript Sources, 1745–1799*, ed. John C. Fitzpatrick and David M. Matteson, 39 vols. (Washington, DC: GPO, 1931–44), 26:435.

5. John Moore, *A View of Society and Manners in France, Switzerland, and Germany*, 2 vols. (Dublin: for W. Wilson, 1780), 1:180.

6. A. Owen Aldridge, "Reviews," *Eighteenth-Century Studies* 8 (1975): 360.

7. Voltaire, *Letters, from M. de Voltaire. To Several of His Friends*, trans. Thomas Francklin (Dublin: for H. Saunders, 1770), with GW's autograph and bookplate (New York Public Library, no. *KGW 1770).

8. GW's May 21 letter to Smith requesting these two books does not specify their authors, but the titles and descriptions clarify that both are Voltaire's.

9. [William Enfield], "Justamond's Translation of the Life of Lewis XV," *Monthly Review* 65 (1781): 183.

10. GW to William S. Smith, June 20, 1783, *Writings*, 27:24–25.

11. Robert B. Winans, *A Descriptive Checklist of Book Catalogues Separately Printed in America, 1693–1800* (Worcester, MA: American Antiquarian Society, 1981), lists no separate New York catalogues for 1783.

12. GW to William S. Smith, June 20, 1783, *Writings*, 27:24–25.

13. GW to William S. Smith, June 20, 1783, *Writings*, 27:24–25.

14. Jean-Jacques Rousseau, *Emile; or, On Education*, ed. and trans. Allan Bloom (New York: Basic Books, 1979), 241.

15. *The World Displayed; or, A Curious Collection of Voyages and Travels*, 3d ed., 20 vols. (London: for J. Carnan and J. Newbery, 1765–74), vol. 12 (NjP, no. EXKA Americana 1774 World).

16. A. Rosalie David, *The Experience of Ancient Egypt* (New York: Routledge, 2000), 68.

17. GW to William S. Smith, June 20, 1783, *Writings*, 27:24–25; *The Library of a Distinguished American Book Collector* (New York: Sotheby's, 2013), lot 180.

18. Quoted in James Boswell, *Boswell's Life of Johnson*, ed. George Birkbeck Hill, 6 vols. (Oxford: Clarendon, 1887), 2:237.

19. Oliver Goldsmith, *An History of the Earth, and Animated Nature*, 8 vols. (London: for J. Nourse, 1779), 2:240; Michael R. Hutcheson, "Oliver Goldsmith," *Eighteenth-Century British Historians*, ed. Ellen J. Jenkins (Detroit: Gale, 2007), 150–51.

20. Amanda C. Isaac, *Take Note! George Washington the Reader* (Mount Vernon, VA: George Washington's Mount Vernon, 2013), 33.

21. Lund's list is reprinted in *Papers, Colonial Series*, 7:348–49.

22. Hayes, *Road to Monticello*, 257–59.

23. Edwin Wolf 2nd and Kevin J. Hayes, *The Library of Benjamin Franklin* (Philadelphia: American Philosophical Society and Library Company of Philadelphia, 2006), 19.

24. Thomas Cadell, *A Select Catalogue of the Most Approved English Books, in the Several Branches of Useful and Ornamental Literature* (London: T. Cadell, 1768), 5; GW, "Enclosure: Invoice to Robert Cary and Co., June 20, 1768," and "Invoice from Robert Cary and Co., September 28, 1768," *Papers, Colonial Series*, 8:102, 132.

25. J. A. Leo Lemay, "Robert Beverley's History and Present State of Virginia and the Emerging American Political Ideology," in *American Letters and the Historical Consciousness: Essays in Honor of Lewis P. Simpson*, ed. J. Gerald Kennedy and Daniel Mark Fogel (Baton Rouge: Louisiana State University Press, 1987), 74.

26. Isaac, *Take Note!*, 33; GW to Robert Adam, November 22, 1771, *Papers, Colonial Series*, 8:552.

27. William Beloe, ed. and trans., *Herodotus, Translated from the Greek, with Notes*, 2d ed., 4 vols. (London: Leigh and S. Sotheby, 1806), 2:419.

28. [Jabez Hirons], "Bossu's Travels through Louisiana," *Monthly Review* 46 (1772), 57; M. Bossu, *Travels though that Part of North America Formerly Called Louisiana*, trans. John Reinhold Forster, 2 vols. (London: for T. Davies, 1771), 1:201.

29. Annis Boudinot Stockton, *Only for the Eyes of a Friend: The Poems of Annis Boudinot Stockton*, ed. Carla Mulford (Charlottesville: University Press of Virginia, 1995), 118.

30. GW to Annis Boudinot Stockton, September 2, 1783, *Writings*, 27:127–28.

31. David Howell to William Greene, September 9?, 1783, *LDC*, 20:646.

32. David Howell to William Greene, September 9?, 1783, *LDC*, 20:646–47. Howell's letter is also the source for the ensuing dialogue. For clarity, I have converted his indirect discourse to direct discourse.

33. GW to Thomas Paine, September 10, 1783, *Writings*, 27:146.

34. Thomas Paine, *The Writings of Thomas Paine*, ed. Moncure Daniel Conway, 4 vols. (New York: G. P. Putnam's, 1896), 4:470–72.

35. GW to Samuel Vaughan, January 14, 1784, *Papers, Confederation Series*, 1:45.

36. GW to Samuel Vaughan, January 14, 1784, *Papers, Confederation Series*, 1:45.

37. GW to Samuel Vaughan, August 25, 1791, *Papers, Presidential Series*, 8:454–55.

38. George Washington, "Address to Congress on Resigning Commission," *Writings*, ed. John Rhodehamel (New York: Library of America, 1997), 548.

Chapter 14: Haven of History

Epigraph from Thomas Carlyle, *Works*, 30 vols. (London: Chapman & Hall, 1897), 5:160.

1. John Evans, "Memoirs of Mr. Thomas Mullett," *Gentleman's Magazine* 85 (1815): 33–34.

2. David Humphreys to GW, July 15, 1784, *Papers, Confederation Series*, 1:527.

3. GW to Lafayette, February 1, 1784, *Papers, Confederation Series*, 1:87–88.

4. Joseph Addison, *Cato: A Tragedy*, 13th ed. (London: J. Tonson, 1733), 1.1.14–15.

5. GW to Samuel Vaughan, January 14, 1784, *Papers, Confederation Series*, 1:45.

6. GW to Boinod and Gaillard, February 18, 1784, *Papers, Confederation Series*, 1:126.

7. William H. Riker, "Dutch and American Federalism," *Journal of the History of Ideas* 18 (1957): 498.

8. James Madison to Thomas Jefferson, March 16, 1784, *The Writings of James Madison Comprising His Public Papers and His Private Correspondence,*

Including Numerous Letters and Documents Now for the First Time Printed,
vol. 2, *1783–1787*, ed. Gaillard Hunt (New York: G. P. Putnam's, 1901), 43.

9. Frank E. Grizzard, Jr., *George Washington: A Biographical Companion*
(Santa Barbara, CA: ABC-Clio, 2002), 286–90.

10. Henry Knox to GW, February 21, 1784, *Papers, Confederation Series*,
1:143.

11. Edwin Wolf 2nd and Kevin J. Hayes, *The Library of Benjamin
Franklin* (Philadelphia: American Philosophical Society and Library
Company of Philadelphia, 2006), no. 468.

12. Quoted in E. Millicent Sowerby, *Catalogue of the Library of Thomas
Jefferson*, 5 vols. (Washington, DC: Library of Congress, 1952–59), no. 3025.

13. Thomas Jefferson to GW, April 16, 1784, *Papers, Confederation Series*,
1:287–91.

14. Thomas Jefferson, "Notes on Fifth Volume of Marshall's *Life of
Washington*," *The Writings of Thomas Jefferson*, ed. H. A. Washington, 9 vols.
(Washington, DC: Taylor & Maury, 1854), 9:479.

15. GW, entry for May 16, 1784, Cash Memorandum Book, 1775–76,
1783–84 (DLC).

16. [Laurence Sterne], *A Sentimental Journey through France and Italy*,
2 vols. (London: for T. Becket and P. A. DeHondt, 1768), 1:xiii; Hayes, *Road
to Monticello*, 324–25; Amanda C. Isaac, *Take Note! George Washington
the Reader* (Mount Vernon, VA: George Washington's Mount Vernon,
2013), 55.

17. Griffin, *Catalogue*, 192, 488; *The Library of a Distinguished American
Book Collector* (New York: Sotheby's, 2013), lot 180.

18. Laurence Sterne, *The Beauties of Sterne: Including All His Pathetic
Tales, and Most Distinguished Observations on Life* (London: for T. Davies,
1782), 144.

19. GW to Jonathan Trumbull, Jr., October 1, 1785, *Papers, Confederation
Series*, 3:289–90.

20. GW to William Gordon, May 8, 1784, *Papers, Confederation Series*,
1:376.

21. *Diaries*, 4:149.

22. William Gordon to Horatio Gates, August 31, 1784, quoted in *Papers,
Confederation Series*, 1:178.

23. Julian Ursyn Niemcewicz, "Acute Observations: From Domestic
Pursuits to Concern for the Nation," in *Experiencing Mount Vernon:
Eyewitness Accounts, 1784–1865*, ed. Jean B. Lee (Charlottesville: University
of Virginia Press, 2006), 84.

24. Adams's copy of Gordon's *History* survives at the Boston Public
Library (no. Adams 251.3 E208.G66).

25. William Gordon, *The History of the Rise, Progress, and Establishment,
of the Independence of the United State of America: Including an Account of the
Late War; and of the Thirteen Colonies, from Their Origin to That Period*,
4 vols. (London: Charles Dilly, 1788), vol. 1, sig. A3r.

26. Gordon, *History*, vol. 1, sig. A3r.

27. Moses Coit Tyler, *The Literary History of the American Revolution, 1763–1783*, 2 vols. (New York: G. P. Putnam's, 1897), 2:427.

28. See, for example, GW to James Mercer, January 20, 1786, *Papers, Confederation Series*, 3:515.

29. William Gordon to GW, February 16, 1789, *Papers, Presidential Series*, 1:31, mentions the forty-two sets of subscriber copies he was sending. William Gordon to GW, February 20, 1790, *Papers, Presidential Series*, 5:160–61, clarifies sending "a case marked GW No. I. Mount Vernon, containing forty two sets of the History for the several subscribers." Minus the Massachusetts subscribers, the list of American subscribers plus the Nova Scotia subscribers equals exactly forty-two, including the two sets to which GW subscribed.

30. GW to Hodge, Allen, and Campbell, July 17, 1789, *Papers, Presidential Series*, 3:225.

31. *City Petitions, Addresses, and Remonstrances . . . Commencing in the Year M.DCC.LXIX* (London: for David Steel, 1778), (Indiana University, Lilly Library DA510.L84).

32. "Monthly Catalogue, Political," *Monthly Review* 59 (1778), 389.

33. Stuart Leibiger, *Founding Friendship: George Washington, James Madison, and the Creation of the American Republic* (1999; Charlottesville: University Press of Virginia, 2001), 38–39.

34. GW, *Diaries*, 4:66.

35. GW to John Filson, January 16, 1785, *Papers, Confederation Series*, 2:269.

36. Richard Slotkin, *Regeneration through Violence: The Mythology of the American Frontier, 1600–1860* (Middletown, CT: Wesleyan University Press, 1973), 330.

37. GW to George William Fairfax, February 27, 1785, *Papers, Confederation Series*, 2:387–88.

38. GW, *Diaries*, 4:129–30.

39. George William Fairfax to GW, August 23, 1784, *Papers, Confederation Series*, 2:52–53.

40. Robert G. Stewart, *Robert Edge Pine: A British Portrait Painter in America, 1784–1788* (Washington, DC: Smithsonian Institution Press, 1979), 13.

41. Rembrandt Peale, "Reminiscences," *Crayon* 3 (1856): 5.

42. Thomas Jefferson to Benjamin Harrison, January 12, 1785, *The Papers of Thomas Jefferson*, ed. Julian P. Boyd, et al., 42 vols. to date (Princeton, NJ: Princeton University Press, 1950–), 7:600.

43. David Humphreys to GW, July 17, 1785, *Papers, Confederation Series*, 3:131.

44. Wayne Craven, *Sculpture in America* (New York: Thomas Y. Crowell, 1968), 52.

45. GW to Nicholas Cooke, April 28, 1776, *Papers, Revolutionary War Series*, 4:158.

46. Henry Babcock to GW, February 25, 1784, *Papers, Confederation Series*, 1:156.

47. Timothy Dwight to GW, October 1785, *Papers, Confederation Series*, 3:331.

48. Timothy Dwight, *The Conquest of Canaan* (Hartford, CT: Elisha Babcock, 1785), 254.

Chapter 15: The Slave, the Quaker, and the Panopticon

Epigraph from Laurence Sterne, *A Sentimental Journey through France and Italy*, 2 vols. (London, 1768), 2:27.

1. Elkanah Watson, *Men and Times of the Revolution; or, Memoirs of Elkanah Watson, Including Journals of Travels in Europe and America, from 1777 to 1842, with His Correspondence with Public Men and Reminiscences and Incidents of the Revolution*, ed. Winslow C. Watson (New York: Dana, 1856), 243.

2. Watson, *Men and Times*, 233.

3. François Furstenberg, "Atlantic Slavery, Atlantic Freedom: George Washington, Slavery, and Transatlantic Abolitionist Networks," *3WMQ* 68 (2011): 260.

4. "Monthly Catalogue," *Critical Review* 33 (1772): 261.

5. Christopher Leslie Brown, *Moral Capital: Foundations of British Abolitionism* (Chapel Hill: University of North Carolina Press, 2006), 174.

6. Philip D. Morgan, " 'To Get Quit of Negroes': George Washington and Slavery," *Journal of American Studies* 39 (2005): 413.

7. G. W. P. Custis, *Recollections and Private Memoirs of Washington* (Washington, DC: William H. Moore, 1859), 76.

8. Francis Asbury, *The Journal of the Rev. Francis Asbury, Bishop of the Methodist Episcopal Church, from August 7, 1771, to December 7, 1815*, 3 vols. (New York: N. Bangs & T. Mason, 1821), 1:385.

9. William Gordon to GW, August 30, 1784, *Papers, Confederation Series*, 2:63.

10. Brown, *Moral Capital*, 359.

11. *National Union Catalog: Pre-1956 Imprints*, 754 vols. (London: Mansell, 1968–1981), no. L0292987, locates nine copies of the 1781 edition, but no copies of the 1771 edition. *ESTC*, no. T493575, lists only one copy of the 1771 edition, located at the British Library. In addition to the British Library copy, Worldcat, no. 20040317, lists Washington's copy at MBAt and another copy at the South Carolina Historical Library.

12. John C. Van Horne, ed., *Religious Philanthropy and Colonial Slavery: The American Correspondence of the Associates of Dr. Bray, 1717–1777* (Urbana: University of Illinois Press, 1985), 301.

13. [John Waring], *A Letter to an American Planter, from His Friends in London* (London: H. Reynell, 1781), 5.

14. John Waring to Robert Carter Nicholas, March 25, 1773, in Van Horne, *Religious Philanthropy*, 312.

15. "Dabney Carr's Library," *VMHB* 2 (1894): 226.

16. It has become something of a scholarly game to identify when Washington's attitude toward slavery changed. Henry Wiebcek, *An Imperfect God: George Washington, His Slaves, and the Creation of America* (New York: Farrar, Straus & Giroux, 2003), 188, chooses 1769 as the turning point. Alternatively, Kenneth Morgan, "George Washington and the Problem of Slavery," *Journal of American Studies* 34 (2000): 291, selects 1783 as the turning point. Furstenberg, "Atlantic Slavery," 260, dates the turning point to after 1785. Philip D. Morgan, "To Get Quit," 425, contends that there was no single turning point and instead argues for a series of stages across which Washington's attitude toward slavery changed.

17. *The Merchant of Venice*, 2.2.4–7, in *The Dramatick Writings of Will. Shakspere: With the Notes of All the Various Commentators; Printed Complete from the Best Editions of Sam. Johnson and Geo. Steevens*, 20 vols. (London: John Bell, 1788), 7:16.

18. A. R. Riggs, "Anthony Benezet (1713–1784)," in *American Writers before 1800: A Biographical and Critical Dictionary*, ed. James A. Levernier and Douglas R. Wilmes, 3 vols. (Westport, CT: Greenwood, 1983), 1:135; Peter A. Dorsey, *Common Bondage: Slavery as Metaphor in Revolutionary America* (Knoxville: University of Tennessee Press. 2010).

19. Quoted in Riggs, "Anthony Benezet," 135.

20. Anthony Benezet to Samuel Allinson, October 23, 1774, in George S. Brookes, *Friend Anthony Benezet* (Philadelphia: University of Pennsylvania Press, 1937), 321–22.

21. Kevin J. Hayes, *The Mind of a Patriot: Patrick Henry and the World of Ideas* (Charlottesville: University of Virginia Press, 2008), 67.

22. Two manuscript catalogues of Paine's library survive among the Robert Treat Paine Papers, Massachusetts Historical Society. Herbert A. Johnson, *Imported Eighteenth-Century Law Treatises in American Libraries, 1700–1799* (Knoxville: University of Tennessee Press, 1978), has identified the law treatises Paine owned, but little work has been done on Paine's library otherwise. George Brinley obtained Sherman's copy in the nineteenth century. See *Catalogue of the American Library of the Late Mr. George Brinley of Hartford, Conn.: Part IV* (Hartford: Case Lockwood & Brainard, 1886), lot 7314.

23. Henry J. Cadbury, "Quaker Bibliographical Notes," *Bulletin of the Friends' Historical Association* 26 (1937): 50.

24. *Biographical and Genealogical History of the State of Delaware, Containing Biographical and Genealogical Sketches of Prominent and Representative Citizens, and Many of the Early Settlers*, 2 vols. (Chambersburg, PA: J. M. Runk, 1899), 1:101.

25. *Diaries*, 6:47.

26. Maurice Jackson, "The Social and Intellectual Origins of Anthony Benezet's Radicalism," *Pennsylvania History* 66 (1999): 103.

27. Jackson, "Social and Intellectual Origins," 103.

28. [David Cooper], *A Serious Address to the Rulers of America, on the Inconsistency of Their Conduct Respecting Slavery: Forming a Contrast between*

the Encroachments of England on American Liberty, and, American Injustice in Tolerating Slavery* (Trenton, NJ: Isaac Collins, 1783), 4.

29. [Cooper], *Serious Address*, 9.

30. "Notices of David Cooper: No. XVII," *Friends' Review* 15 (1862): 722–24.

31. Kenneth L. Carroll, "Robert Pleasants on Quakerism: 'Some Account of the First Settlement of Friends in Virginia,'" *VMHB* 86 (1978): 4; Hayes, *Mind of a Patriot*, 65–67.

32. Robert Pleasants to GW, December 11, 1785, *Papers, Confederation Series*, 3:449.

33. Robert Pleasants to GW, December 11, 1785, *Papers, Confederation Series*, 3:450.

34. GW to John Francis Mercer, September 9, 1786, *Papers, Confederation Series*, 4:243.

35. William C. diGiacomantonio, "'For the Gratification of a Volunteering Society': Antislavery and Pressure Group Politics in the First Federal Congress," *Journal of the Early Republic* 15 (1995): 169, 180. DiGiacomantonio lists the other books in the antislavery library the Quakers sent to Congress but leaves two unidentified. These were [Stephen Fuller], *Notes on the Two Reports from the Committee of the Honourable House of Assembly of Jamaica, Appointed to Examine . . . the Subject of the Slave Trade* (London: James Phillips, 1789), and James Ramsay, *An Address on the Proposed Bill for the Abolition of the Slave Trade* (London: James Phillips, 1788).

36. Quoted in *Papers, Confederation Series*, 2:29.

37. David Humphreys, *Life of General Washington with George Washington's Remarks*, ed. Rosemarie Zagarri (Athens: University of Georgia Press, 1991), 78.

38. Morgan, "To Get Quit," 423.

39. Adam Smith, *An Inquiry into the Nature and Causes of the Wealth of Nations*, 3 vols. (Philadelphia: Thomas Dobson, 1789), 1:101.

40. Adam Smith, *The Theory of Moral Sentiments* (London: for A. Millar, 1761), 316.

41. Paul J. McNulty, "Adam Smith's Concept of Labor," *Journal of the History of Ideas* 34 (1973): 365.

42. Smith, *Wealth of Nations*, 2:78.

43. Tobias Lear and George Washington, May 7, 1786, *Papers, Confederation Series*, 4:34–35.

44. George Washington to Benjamin Franklin, June 7, 1786, *Papers, Confederation Series*, 4:103.

45. *Proceedings of the Hon. House of Assembly of Jamaica, on the Sugar and Slave-Trade: In a Session which Began the 23d of October, 1792* (St. Jago de la Vega: Alexander Aikman, 1792), Morgan Library copy (no. PML125675.2).

46. William Frederick Poole, *Anti-Slavery Opinions before the Year 1800* (Cincinnati, OH: Robert Clarke, 1873), 74.

47. Furstenberg, "Atlantic Slavery," 285–86, lists all four of these titles as "unbound pamphlets," but Griffin, *Catalogue*, 22, lists them as being bound together. When I examined them at MBAt in 2009, they were still bound together.

48. Alessandro Stanziani, "The Traveling Panopticon: Labor Institutions and Labor Practices in Russia and Britain in the Eighteenth and Nineteenth Centuries," *Comparative Studies in Society and History* 51 (2009): 715–41.

49. "George Washington's Last Will and Testament," *Papers, Retirement Series*, 4:480–81.

50. Paul F. Boller, Jr., "Washington, the Quakers, and Slavery," *Journal of Negro History* 46 (1961): 88.

Chapter 16: Politics and the Picaresque

Epigraph from Jacob E. Cooke, *The Federalist* (Middletown, CT: Wesleyan University Press, 1961), 444.

1. [John Parke], "Virginia: A Pastoral Drama, on the Birth-Day of an Illustrious Personage and the Return of Peace, February 11th, 1784," in *The Lyric Works of Horace*, ed. John Parke (Philadelphia: Eleazer Oswald, 1786), 331.

2. GW to John Parke, March 23, 1787, *Papers, Confederation Series*, 5:102.

3. GW to Edmund Randolph, March 28, 1787, *Papers, Confederation Series*, 5:112–14.

4. Edwin Wolf 2nd and Kevin J. Hayes, *The Library of Benjamin Franklin* (Philadelphia: American Philosophical Society and the Library Company of Philadelphia, 2006), 19.

5. Gardoqui to GW, November 9, 1787, *Papers, Confederation Series*, 5:419.

6. Rachel Schmidt, *Critical Images: The Canonization of Don Quixote through Illustrated Editions of the Eighteenth Century* (Montreal: McGill-Queen's University Press, 1999), 138–40.

7. Gardoqui to GW, November 9, 1787, *Papers, Confederation Series*, 5:419.

8. Benjamin Franklin to Thomas Jordan, May 18, 1787, *The Writings of Benjamin Franklin*, ed. Albert Henry Smyth, 10 vols. (New York: Macmillan, 1905–7), 10:304.

9. Sharon E. Knapp and John L. Sharpe III, *An Exhibition of a Selection of Books and Manuscripts from the Library of Mary and Harry L. Dalton* (Durham, NC: William R. Perkins Library, Duke University, 1977), unpaginated.

10. Robert G. Stewart, *Robert Edge Pine, A British Portrait Painter in America, 1784–1788* (Washington, DC: for the National Portrait Gallery by the Smithsonian Institution Press, 1979), 25.

11. "Anecdote of Washington," *Port Folio*, 4th ser., 3 (1817): 354.

12. GW to Alexander Hamilton, August 28, 1788, *Papers, Confederation Series*, 6:481.

13. "An Abstract of the General Principles of Ancient and Modern Confederacies," *The Writings of George Washington*, ed. Jared Sparks, 12 vols. (Boston: American Stationers' Company, 1834–37), 9:521–38; James Madison, "Notes of Ancient and Modern Confederacies, Preparatory to the Federal Convention of 1787," *Letters and Other Writings of James Madison*, 4 vols. (Philadelphia: J. B. Lippincott, 1865), 1:293–315.

14. GW to Richard Henderson, June 19, 1788, *Papers, Confederation Series*, 6:341.

15. GW to Richard Henderson, June 19, 1788, *Papers, Confederation Series*, 6:341.

16. Kevin J. Hayes, *The Library of William Byrd of Westover* (Madison, WI: Madison House, 1997), no. 843.

17. Samuel Butler, *Hudibras, in Three Parts: Written in the Time of the Late Wars* (London: for C. Bathurst, 1775), part 2, canto 1, lines 465–66.

18. GW to John Posey, September 24, 1767, *Papers, Colonial Series*, 8:34.

19. GW to Warner Lewis, December 19, 1788, *Papers, Presidential Series*, 1:192.

20. Benjamin Franklin to William Strahan, February 12, 1745, *Papers of Benjamin Franklin*, ed. Leonard W. Labaree et al., 41 vols. to date (New Haven, CT: Yale University Press, 1959–), 3:13–14.

21. Moses Coit Tyler, *The Literary History of the American Revolution, 1763–1783*, 2 vols. (New York: Putnam's, 1897), 2:20.

22. George Saintsbury, *The Peace of the Augustans: A Survey of Eighteenth Century Literature as a Place of Rest and Refreshment* (1916; New York: Oxford University Press, 1946), 153.

23. Ernest A. Baker, introduction to *The Life and Opinions of John Buncle*, by Thomas Amory (London: George Routledge, 1904), v.

24. Charles Lamb to S. T. Coleridge, June 24, 1797, *The Works of Charles and Mary Lamb*, ed. E. V. Lucas, 7 vols. (New York: Putnam's, 1905), 6:106.

25. Thomas Amory, *The Life of John Buncle, Esq.: Containing Various Observations and Reflections, Made in Several Parts of the World, and Many Extraordinary Relations*, 2 vols. (London: for J. Johnson & B. Davenport, 1766) (MBAt, no. Wa.29).

26. Thomas Jefferson to Marbois, December 5, 1783, *The Papers of Thomas Jefferson*, ed. Julian P. Boyd et al., 42 vols. to date (Princeton, NJ: Princeton University Press, 1950–), 6:374.

27. "Elbridge Gerry Responds to the Maryland 'Landholder' X Boston American Herald, 18 April [1788]," in *The Documentary History of the Ratification of the Constitution*, ed. Merrill Jensen et al., 24 vols. to date (Madison: Wisconsin Historical Society Press, 1976–), 17:173.

28. James C. Nicholls, "Lady Henrietta Liston's Journal of Washington's 'Resignation,' Retirement, and Death," *Pennsylvania Magazine of History and Biography* 95 (1971): 515–16. The general statement is based on a specific

example of Washington's use of *Gil Blas* in conversation recorded by Lady Liston, which will be discussed in detail in chapter 20.

29. GW to Lafayette, September 18, 1787, *Papers, Confederation Series*, 5:334.

30. GW to John Armstrong, April 25, 1788, *Papers, Confederation Series*, 6:226.

31. Cooke, *Federalist*, 349.

Chapter 17: Presidential Patronage and the Development of American Literature

Epigraph from John Ruskin, *Lectures on Architecture and Painting, Delivered at Edinburgh, in November 1853* (New York: John Wiley, 1884), 183.

1. Ebenezer Hazard to Jeremy Belknap, June 14, 1784, "Correspondence between Jeremy Belknap and Ebenezer Hazard," *Collections of the Massachusetts Historical Society* 2, 5th ser. (1877): 355. John P. Kaminski discusses this letter in "A Life Revealed: George Washington's Library," *Friends of the Libraries Magazine* 48 (2008): 16.

2. Jeremy Belknap to GW, July 19, 1784, *Papers, Confederation Series*, 2:3.

3. GW to Jeremy Belknap, January 5, 1785, *Papers, Confederation Series*, 2:251.

4. Jeremy Belknap to Ebenezer Hazard, February 11, 1785, "Correspondence," 412.

5. GW to Henry Knox, April 1, 1789, *Papers, Presidential Series*, 2:2.

6. *Diaries*, 5:445–47.

7. *Diaries*, 5:445.

8. Tobias Lear to GW, March 27, 1791, *Papers, Presidential Series*, 8:20.

9. *Diaries*, 5:452–53.

10. For an account of the trip, see T. H. Breen, *George Washington's Journey: The President Forges a New Nation* (New York: Simon & Schuster, 2016).

11. Kevin J. Hayes, "Libraries and Learned Societies," in *Encyclopedia of the North American Colonies*, ed. Jacob Ernest Cooke, 3 vols. (New York: Scribner's, 1993), 3:129–30.

12. G. F. de Martens, *Summary of the Law of Nations, Founded on the Treaties and Customs of the Modern Nations of Europe*, trans. William Cobbett (Philadelphia: Thomas Bradford, 1795), iii.

13. Alexander Hamilton, "Answers to Questions Proposed by the President of the United States to the Secretary of the Treasury," *Papers, Presidential Series*, 6:443.

14. Daniel G. Lang, *Foreign Policy in the Early Republic: The Law of Nations and the Balance of Power* (Baton Rouge: Louisiana State University Press, 1985).

15. Rich Shapiro, "Read It and Weep, by George: Prez Racks Up 300G Late Fee for Two Books," *New York Daily News*, April 17, 2010, 10.

16. Jane Belknap Marcou, *Life of Jeremy Belknap, D.D.: The Historian of New Hampshire* (New York: Harper, 1847), 171.

17. GW, *Diaries*, 5:483; Robert B. Winans, *A Descriptive Checklist of Book Catalogues Separately Printed in America, 1693–1800* (Worcester, MA: American Antiquarian Society, 1981), no. 138.

18. George Washington Papers, Series 8: Miscellaneous Papers ca. 1775–99, Subseries D: Extracts, Abstracts, and Notes, 1760–1799 (DLC).

19. James Madison, "Notes on Buffon's Histoire naturelle," *Papers*, 17 vols. to date (Chicago: University of Chicago Press, 1962–), 9:38.

20. [William Kenrick], "Du Pratz's History of Louisiana," *Monthly Review* 28 (1763): 449.

21. Antoine Simon Le Page Du Pratz, *The History of Louisiana, or of the Western Parts of Virginia and Carolina: Containing a Description of the Countries that Lie on Both Sides of the River Mississippi* (New Orleans: Pelican, 1947), 19.

22. Thomas Wignell to GW, May 22, 1790, *Papers, Presidential Series*, 5:416.

23. Royall Tyler, *The Contrast: Manners, Morals, and Authority in the Early American Republic*, ed. Cynthia A. Kierner (New York: New York University Press, 2007), 56.

24. GW to Mercy Otis Warren, June 4, 1790, *Papers, Presidential Series*, 5:404.

25. Mercy Otis Warren, *Poems, Dramatic and Miscellaneous* (Boston: I. Thomas & E. T. Andrews, 1790), 218.

26. GW to Mercy Otis Warren, November 4, 1790, *Papers, Presidential Series*, 5:404.

27. Samuel Powel to GW, June 11, 1790, *Papers, Presidential Series*, 5:513.

28. GW to Samuel Powel, June 20, 1790, *Papers, Presidential Series*, 5:513.

29. See, for example, Kevin J. Hayes, ed., *The Oxford Handbook to Early American Literature* (New York: Oxford University Press, 2008), 464–67, 473–75, 600–610.

30. "Impartial Review," *Universal Asylum and Columbian Magazine* 5 (1790): 406.

31. Jeremy Belknap to GW, October 25, 1790, *Papers, Presidential Series*, 6:579–80.

32. [Jeremy Belknap], *The Foresters, An American Tale: Being a Sequel to the History of John Bull the Clothier* (Boston: I. Thomas & E. T. Andrews, 1792), 104.

33. Pete Kyle McCarter, "Mother Carey's Jacobin Chickens," *Early American Literature* 14 (1979): 168–69.

34. Jeremy Belknap to GW, May 29, 1798, *Papers, Retirement Series*, 2:302–4.

35. Jeremy Belknap to GW, May 29, 1798, *Papers, Retirement Series*, 2:302–4.

36. GW to Jeremy Belknap, June 15, 1798, *Papers, Retirement Series*, 2:331.

37. GW to Samuel Chase, June 17, 1798, *Papers, Retirement Series*, 2:332.

Chapter 18: *Official Letters to the Honorable American Congress*

Epigraph from J. M. Toner, *George Washington as an Inventor and Promoter of the Useful Arts: An Address Delivered at Mount Vernon, April 10, 1891* (Washington, DC: Gedney & Roberts, 1892), 69.

1. Frank Luther Mott, *A History of American Magazines, 1741–1850* (1930; Cambridge, MA: Belknap Press of Harvard University Press, 1966), 102–3.

2. GW to Mathew Carey, October 27, 1788, *Papers, Presidential Series*, 1:74.

3. GW to Mathew Carey, June 25, 1788, *Papers, Confederation Series*, 6:354–55.

4. "To Be Sold," *Gazette of the United States,* November 2, 5, 9, 26, 30, 1791; December 7, 14, 24, 31, 1791; January 11 and 21, 1792; "To Be Sold," *National Gazette*, November 3, 1791; "To Be Sold," *Federal Gazette*, January 23, 1792. John Carey continued to place advertisements for rare classical books in the newspapers into May 1792.

5. Quoted in Kevin J. Hayes, *The Library of William Byrd of Westover* (Madison, WI: Madison House, 1997), 102.

6. Mathew Carey to GW, April 21, 1789, *Papers, Presidential Series*, 2:99.

7. "To Be Published by Subscription, *The American Remembrancer*," *National Gazette*, July 14, 1792; "To Be Published by Subscription, *The American Remembrancer*," *General Advertiser*, July 16, 1792; "To Be Published by Subscription, *The American Remembrancer*," *The Mail; or, Claypoole's Daily Advertiser*, July 19, 1792; "To Be Published by Subscription, *The American Remembrancer*," *Federal Gazette*, July 26, 1792. The advertisements appeared in many subsequent issues of these four papers into January 1793. John Carey also placed advertisements in distant papers. See "To Be Published by Subscription, *The American Remembrancer*," *City Gazette* (Charleston, South Carolina), August 29, 1792.

8. John Carey to Thomas Jefferson, June 30, 1792, *The Papers of Thomas Jefferson*, ed. Julian P. Boyd et al., 42 vols. to date (Princeton, NJ: Princeton University Press, 1950–), 24:140.

9. GW to Thomas Jefferson, November 19, 1792, *Papers, Presidential Series*, 11:410.

10. John Carey to Thomas Jefferson, April 23, 1793, *Papers of Thomas Jefferson*, 25:581–82.

11. Thomas Jefferson to Thomas Pinckney, April 27, 1793, *Papers of Thomas Jefferson*, 25:595.

12. Thomas Jefferson to James Madison, August 11, 1793, *Papers of Thomas Jefferson*, 26:652.

13. Stan V. Henkels, *Catalogue of Autograph Letters, Historical Documents and Rare Engraved Portraits, Being the Collection of J. Henry Rogers, of Newcastle, Del.* (Philadelphia: Stan V. Henkels, 1895), lot 1175.

14. John Carey to George Washington, March 31, 1795, *The Spurious Letters Attributed to Washington*, ed. Worthington Chauncey Ford

(Brooklyn, NY: privately printed, 1889), 127; *Catalogue of the Library of the Late Bishop John Fletcher Hurst* (New York: Anderson Auction Company, 1904), lot 28.

15. John Carey to Thomas Jefferson, April 6, 1795, *Papers of Thomas Jefferson*, 28:324.

16. [William Enfield], "Washington's Letters to the American Congress," *Monthly Review* 18 (1795): 389.

17. [Enfield], "Washington's Letters to the American Congress," 389.

18. "General Washington's Official Letters," *Critical Review* 13 (1795): 428.

19. "General Washington's Official Letters," 430.

20. "General Washington's Letters," *British Critic* 6 (1795): 235.

21. "General Washington's Letters," 237.

22. GW to John Hancock, December 27, 1776, *Official Letters to the Honorable American Congress: Written during the War between the United Colonies and Great Britain*, ed. John Carey, 2 vols. (London: for Cadell Junior & Davies, 1795), 1:362.

23. John Carey to Thomas Jefferson, September 1, 1796, *Papers of Thomas Jefferson*, 29:180.

24. John Carey, "Advertisement," in *Official Letters to the Honorable American Congress*, 1:vi.

25. [Benjamin Franklin Bache], "Preface to This Edition," *Letters from General Washington to Several of His Friends, in June and July, 1776; in Which Is Set Forth, An Interesting View of American Politics, at That All-Important Period* (Philadelphia: Republished at the Federal Press, 1795).

26. James Tagg, *Benjamin Franklin Bache and the Philadelphia Aurora* (Philadelphia: University of Pennsylvania Press, 1991), 239–63.

27. Worthington Chauncey Ford, "Preface," *Spurious Letters*, 28–29.

28. [John Carey], "Epistles from General Washington," *Critical Review* 18 (1796): 83.

29. Jared Sparks, "Washington's Papers," *Niles' Register* 32 (1827): 222.

30. William Linn, "A Funeral Eulogy on General Washington, Delivered February 22, 1800, before the New-York State Society of the Cincinnati," in *Eulogies and Orations on the Life and Death of General George Washington, First President of the United States of America* (Boston: W. P. and L. Blake, 1800), 167; Citizen of Frederick County, Maryland [pseud.], "Biographical Sketch of Colonel Richard Anderson," *Military and Naval Magazine* 6 (1835): 157.

31. John Adolphus, *The History of England, from the Accession of King George the Third, to the Conclusion of Peace*, 3d ed., 3 vols. (London: for T. Cadell & W. Davies, 1810), 2:229–30, 245; John Pickering, *A Vocabulary, or, Collection of Words and Phrases Which Have Been Supposed to be Peculiar to the United States of America* (Boston: Cummings & Hilliard, 1816), 74–75, 78–79, 88; Thomas H. Cushing, "Official Paper," *Weekly Register* 3 (1813): 309.

Chapter 19: *Farewell Address*

1. Victor Hugo Paltsits, ed., *Washington's Farewell Address in Facsimile, with Transliterations of All the Drafts of Washington, Madison, and Hamilton, Together with Their Correspondence and Other Supporting Documents* (New York: New York Public Library, 1935), 32–36.

2. GW to Alexander Hamilton, May 15, 1796, in Paltsits, *Washington's Farewell Address*, 241.

3. Captain John Smith, *The Complete Works of Captain John Smith, 1580–1631*, ed. Philip L. Barbour, 3 vols. (Chapel Hill: University of North Carolina Press, 1986), 1:325; William Bradford, *Of Plymouth Plantation, 1620–1647*, ed. Francis Murphy (New York: Modern Library, 1981), 1. Michael J. Hostetler, "Washington's Farewell Address: Distance as Bane and Blessing," *Rhetoric and Public Affairs* 5 (2002): 393–407, argues alternatively that Washington's address possesses a highly complex style.

4. GW to Alexander Hamilton, August 10, 1796, in Paltsits, *Washington's Farewell Address*, 250.

5. GW to Alexander Hamilton, August 25, 1796, in Paltsits, *Washington's Farewell Address*, 252.

6. William Rawle, "Conversation with David C. Claypoole," in Samuel M. Schmucker, *The Life and Times of George Washington* (Philadelphia: Keystone, 1890), 396–97.

7. Rawle, "Conversation," 397.

8. Jacob Hiltzheimer, *Extracts from the Diary of Jacob Hiltzheimer, of Philadelphia, 1765–1798*, ed. Jacob Cox Parsons (Philadelphia: William F. Fell, 1893), 234; William Vanns Murray to James McHenry, September 24, 1796, *The Life and Correspondence of James McHenry, Secretary of War under Washington and Adams*, ed. Bernard C. Steiner (Cleveland, OH: Burrows, 1907), 197–98.

9. These two places of publication have not been chosen solely for their mellifluous qualities. Paltsits, *Washington's Farewell Address*, 311–26, provides a detailed bibliography of separately published editions of the *Farewell Address*, but other imprints have surfaced since Paltsits, including *The President's Address, to the People of the United States* (Lancaster, PA: William Hamilton, [1796?]); and *The Address, and Resignation of His Excellency Geo. Washington* (Lansingburgh, NY: Luther Pratt, 1796).

10. Paltsits, *Washington's Farewell Address*, 338.

11. Paltsits, *Washington's Farewell Address*, 314.

12. Paltsits, *Washington's Farewell Address*, 313.

13. Paltsits, *Washington's Farewell Address*, 312.

14. Paltsits, *Washington's Farewell Address*, 331, 313.

15. Paltsits, *Washington's Farewell Address*, 317.

16. Elizabeth Hamilton, "Elizabeth Hamilton's Statement as to Washington's Farewell Address," in Allan McLane Hamilton, *The Intimate Life of Alexander Hamilton Based Chiefly upon Original Family Letters and*

Other Documents, Many of which Have Never Been Published (London: Duckworth, 1910), 111.

17. Paltsits, *Washington's Farewell Address*, 317.

18. *Journal of the House of Representatives of the State of Delaware* (New Castle, DE: Samuel and John Adams, 1797); *Votes and Proceedings of the House of Delegates of the State of Maryland, November Session, 1796* ([Annapolis, MD: Frederick Green, 1797]); *Resolves of the General Court of the Commonwealth of Massachusetts* (Boston: Young & Minns, 1796); *Journal of the Proceedings of the Legislative Council of the State of New-Jersey* (Trenton, NJ: Matthias Day, 1797).

19. *The Public Laws of the State of Rhode Island and Providence Plantations, as Revised by a Committee, and Finally Enacted by the Honourable General Assembly, at Their Session in January, 1798* (Providence, RI: Carter & Wilkinson, 1798), 55–74; John C. Fitzpatrick, *George Washington Himself: A Common-Sense Biography Written from His Manuscripts* (Indianapolis, IN: Bobbs-Merrill, 1993), 498.

20. Merton M. Sealts, Jr., *Melville's Reading*, rev. ed. (Columbia: University of South Carolina Press, 1988), no. 549.

21. Paltsits, *Washington's Farewell Address*, 315.

22. George Cabot to Oliver Wolcott, October 11, 1796, *Life and Letters of George Cabot*, ed. Henry Cabot Lodge (Boston: Little, Brown, 1878), 111; Paltsits, *Washington's Farewell Address*, 340; Hershel Parker, "Melville and Politics: A Scrutiny of the Political Milieux of Herman Melville's Life and Works" (PhD diss., Northwestern University, 1963), 21.

23. George Washington, "America's Legacy: Being the Address of George Washington, on His Declining a Re-election to the Presidency," in *An Introduction to the Art of Reading: Being a Collection of Pieces Suited to the Capacity of Children and Designed for the Use of Schools* (Hudson, NY: Ashbel Stoddard, 1796), 160–76.

24. Paltsits, *Washington's Farewell Address*, 159.

25. Quoted in William Spohn Baker, *Washington after the Revolution, 1784–1799* (Philadelphia, 1897), 225.

26. James C. Nicholls, "Lady Henrietta Liston's Journal of Washington's 'Resignation,' Retirement, and Death," *Pennsylvania Magazine of History and Biography* 95 (1971): 515–16.

27. Ron Chernow, *Washington: A Life* (New York: Penguin, 2010), 766.

28. GW, *Speech of the President of the United States to Both Houses of Congress, on Wednesday, December 7, 1796* (Philadelphia, 1796), 6.

29. GW to Alexander Hamilton, September 1, 1796, in Paltsits, *Washington's Farewell Address*, 254.

30. Alexander Hamilton to GW, September 4, 1796, in Paltsits, *Washington's Farewell Address*, 256.

31. GW, *Speech of the President*, 6.

32. GW, *Speech of the President*, 5–6.

33. John P. Kaminski, "A Life Revealed: George Washington's Library," *Friends of the Libraries Magazine* 48 (2008): 16; GW to John Sinclair,

December 10, 1796, in *The Correspondence of the Right Honourable Sir John Sinclair*, 2 vols. (London: Henry Colburn & Richard Bentley, 1831), 2:25.

34. GW to Thomas Forrest, June 20, 1792, *Papers of George Washington, Presidential Series*, 10:474–75.

35. GW to Oliver Wolcott, Jr., May 15, 1797, *Papers, Retirement Series*, 1:143.

36. "Monthly Catalogue, East Indies," *Monthly Review* 7 (1792): 227.

37. Ashbel Green, *The Life of Ashbel Green, V.D.M.*, ed. Joseph H. Jones (New York: Robert Carter & Brothers, 1849), 157.

38. Bird Wilson, *Memoir of the Life of the Right Reverend William White, D.D., Bishop of the Protestant Episcopal Church in the State of Pennsylvania* (Philadelphia: James Kay, Jun., 1839), 191–92.

Chapter 20: Home at Last

Epigraph from James Thomson, *The Poetical Works of James Thomson*, ed. Charles Cowden Clarke (Edinburgh: William P. Nimmo, 1868), 94.

1. GW to John Sinclair, March 6, 1797, *Papers, Retirement Series*, 1:14; GW to John Sinclair, June 12, 1796, *The Correspondence of the Right Honourable Sir John Sinclair, Bart. with Reminiscences of the Most Distinguished Characters Who Have Appeared in Great Britain, and in Foreign Countries, During the Last Fifty Years*, ed. John Sinclair, 2 vols. (London: Henry Colburn & Richard Bentley, 1831), 2:23.

2. Rosalind Mitchison, "Sinclair, Sir John," *ODNB*.

3. GW to John Sinclair, October 20, 1792, *Papers, Presidential Series*, 11:247–48; Sinclair, *Correspondence*, 2:5.

4. GW to John Sinclair, March 15, 1793, *Papers, Presidential Series*, 12:323.

5. GW to John Sinclair, July 20, 1793, *Papers, Presidential Series*, 16:394.

6. GW to John Sinclair, December 10, 1796, *Correspondence*, 2:25.

7. GW to Tobias Lear, March 9, 1797, *Papers, Retirement Series*, 1:24.

8. Julian Ursyn Niemcewicz, *Under Their Vine and Fig Tree: Travels through America in 1797–1799, 1805, with Some Further Account of Life in New Jersey*, ed. and trans. Metchie J. E. Budka (Elizabeth, NJ: Grassmann, 1965), 86.

9. Nelly Custis to Elizabeth Wolcott, March 19, 1797, *An Extraordinary Collection of Washington's Letters, Washington Relics, Revolutionary Documents*, ed. Stan V. Henkels (Philadelphia: Thos. Birch's Sons, 1891), lot 25.

10. John Sinclair to GW, March 29, 1797, and GW to John Sinclair, July 15, 1797, *Papers, Retirement Series*, 1:55, 251.

11. GW to James McHenry, May 29, 1797, *Papers, Retirement Series*, 1:160.

12. GW to John Sinclair, November 6, 1797, *Papers, Retirement Series*, 1:463.

13. GW to Clement Biddle, August 14, 1797, *Papers, Retirement Series*, 1:298.

14. Robert D. Arner, *Dobson's Encyclopaedia: The Publisher, Text, and Publication of America's First Britannica, 1789–1803* (Philadelphia: University of Pennsylvania Press, 1991), 29–30.

15. Arner, *Dobson's Encyclopaedia*, 31–32.

16. William Dunlap, *History of the Rise and Progress of the Arts of Design in the United States*, 2 vols. (New York: George P. Scott, 1834), 2:69.

17. GW to Clement Biddle, August 14, 1797, *Papers, Retirement Series*, 1:298.

18. Timothy Pickering to GW, January 27, 1798, *Papers, Retirement Series*, 2:51.

19. Timothy Pickering to GW, January 20, 1798, *Papers, Retirement Series*, 2:31.

20. GW, "Comments on Monroe's *A View of the Conduct of the Executive of the United States*," *Papers, Retirement Series*, 2:170.

21. GW, "Comments on Monroe's *A View*," *Papers, Retirement Series*, 2:170–71.

22. GW, "Comments on Monroe's *A View*," *Papers, Retirement Series*, 2:181.

23. Amanda C. Isaac, *Take Note! George Washington the Reader* (Mount Vernon, VA: George Washington's Mount Vernon, 2013), 115.

24. GW to John Trumbull, July 25, 1798, *Papers, Retirement Series*, 2:457.

25. Ron Chernow, *Washington: A Life* (New York: Penguin, 2010), 785–89.

26. Frank E. Grizzard, Jr., *George Washington: A Biographical Companion* (Santa Barbara, CA: ABC-Clio, 2002), 192–95; Sara B. Bearss, "Custis, George Washington Parke," *DVB*, 3:630–33.

27. Tobias Lear, "Narrative Accounts of the Death of George Washington," *Papers, Retirement Series*, 4:542–55, provides the detailed information about Washington's death, forming the basis of the ensuing story, and will not be cited additionally.

28. James Madison, "Election of James Monroe," *The Papers of James Madison: Congressional Series*, William T. Hutchinson et al., 17 vols. (Charlottesville: University of Virginia Press, 1962–1991), 17:286–87.

29. Samuel X. Radbill, ed., "The Autobiographical Ana of Robley Dunglison," *Transactions of the American Philosophical Society*, n.s., 53 (1963): 26.

SOURCES

By no means does the present work exhaust the subject of the books in George Washington's life. The starting point for further research is Appleton P. C. Griffin's *Catalogue of the Washington Collection in the Boston Athenaeum*. Though over a hundred years old, this bibliography remains a treasure trove of information. The first half presents a finely annotated catalogue of the books from Washington's library that survive at the Boston Athenaeum, the single largest collection of Washington's books that have stayed together. The second half contains much supplemental information, including an appendix by William Coolidge Lane identifying and classifying books listed in Washington's estate, including those that have not survived, or at least that have survived beyond Beacon Street. Lane's analytical catalogue represents the first attempt to create a comprehensive list of Washington's library since it started being dispersed after his death.

For the story of how so many Washington books ended up at the Boston Athenaeum, see Stanley Ellis Cushing, *The George Washington Library Collection*, an accompanying catalogue published for an exhibition held at the Boston Athenaeum Gallery in 1997. Michael Wentworth's opening essay, "George Washington's Library," provides an excellent overview of what happened to Washington's books after his death. The rest of the volume consists of a highly selective catalogue of books from the Washington collection at the Boston Athenaeum, annotated with many useful tidbits of historical, biographical, and bibliographical information. Amanda C. Isaac's *Take Note! George Washington the Reader*, a catalogue published to celebrate the opening of the Fred W. Smith National Library for the Study of George Washington at Mount Vernon in 2013, provides a wealth of information on the books in Washington's life.

Abbreviations

ANB	John A. Garraty and Mark C. Carnes, eds., *American National Biography*, 24 vols. (New York: Oxford University Press, 1999)
Diaries	Donald Jackson and Dorothy Twohig, eds., *The Diaries of George Washington*, 6 vols. (Charlottesville: University Press of Virginia, 1976–79)
DLC	Library of Congress
DVB	John T. Kneebone, J. Jefferson Looney, Brent Tarter, and Sandra Gioia Treadway, eds., *Dictionary of Virginia Biography*, 3 vols. to date (Richmond: Library of Virginia, 1998–)
ESTC	*English Short Title Catalogue* (London: British Library, 2012)
Griffin, *Catalogue*	Appleton P. C. Griffin, *A Catalogue of the Washington Collection in the Boston Athenæum* (Boston: Boston Athenaeum, 1897)
GW	George Washington
Hayes, *Road to Monticello*	Kevin J. Hayes, *The Road to Monticello: The Life and Mind of Thomas Jefferson* (New York: Oxford University Press, 2008)
LDC	Paul Hubert Smith and Ronald M. Gephart, eds., *Letters of Delegates to Congress, 1774–1789*, 26 vols. (Washington, DC: Library of Congress, 1976–2000)
MBAt	Boston Athenaeum
NjP	Princeton University Library
ODNB	H. C. G. Matthew and Brian Harrison, eds., *Oxford Dictionary of National Biography*, 60 vols. (New York: Oxford University Press, 2004)
Papers, Colonial Series	W. W. Abbot, Dorothy Twohig, and Philander D. Chase, eds., *The Papers of George Washington, Colonial Series*, 10 vols. (Charlottesville: University Press of Virginia, 1983–95)

Papers, Confederation Series	W. W. Abbott and Dorothy Twohig, eds., *The Papers of George Washington, Confederation Series*, 6 vols. (Charlottesville: University Press of Virginia, 1992–97)
Papers, Presidential Series	Dorothy Twohig and W. W. Abbott, eds., *The Papers of George Washington, Presidential Series*, 18 vols. to date (Charlottesville: University Press of Virginia, 1987–)
Papers, Retirement Series	Dorothy Twohig, ed., *The Papers of George Washington, Retirement Series*, 4 vols. (Charlottesville: University Press of Virginia, 1998)
Papers, Revolutionary War Series	Philander D. Chase et al., eds., *The Papers of George Washington, Revolutionary War Series*, 24 vols. to date (Charlottesville: University Press of Virginia, 1985–)
PPL	Library Company of Philadelphia
VMHB	*Virginia Magazine of History and Biography*
WMQ	*William and Mary Quarterly*; Arabic numerals preceding the abbreviation denote the series

INDEX